THE WAR

STORIES OF LIFE AND DEATH FROM WORLD WAR II

THE WAR

STORIES OF LIFE AND DEATH FROM WORLD WAR II

EDITED BY CLINT WILLIS

adrenaline

Thunder's Mouth Press/
Balliett & Fitzgerald Inc.

New York

An Adrenaline Book

Published by
Thunder's Mouth Press
841 Broadway, 4th Floor
New York, NY 10003

and

Balliett & Fitzgerald Inc.
66 West Broadway, Suite 602
New York, NY 10007

Book design: Sue Canavan

frontispiece photo: U. S. soldiers in Algeria, courtesy of Corbis

Manufactured in the United States of America

ISBN: 1-56025-231-6

Library of Congress Catalog Card Number: 98-83231

To
Jennifer Evin Schwamm Willis

Isn't an artist a person who can produce riches from the depths of himself and put them before people so that their lives will in turn be enriched by his art?

—Kim Malthe-Bruun (1923-1945)

contents

1 photographs

2 introduction

7 from *Goodbye, Darkness*
by William Manchester

13 from *Doing Battle: The Making of a Skeptic*
by Paul Fussell

51 from *The Longest Day*
by Cornelius Ryan

63 from *The Long Walk*
by Slavomir Rawicz as told to Ronald Downing

97 from *Heroic Heart: The Diary and Letters of*
Kim Malthe-Bruun 1941-1945
edited by Vibeke Malthe-Bruun

111 from *Pacific War Diary 1942-1945*
by James J. Fahey

129 *Mollie*
by A. J. Liebling

159   from *The Thin Red Line*
by James Jones

181   *The Escape of Mrs. Jeffries*
by Janet Flanner

219   from *Parachute Infantry*
by David Kenyon Webster

237   from *The Normandy Diary of
Marie-Louise Osmont: 1940-1944*
by Marie-Louise Osmont

263   from *The Bloody Battle for Suribachi*
by Richard Wheeler

285   from *We Were Each Other's Prisoners*
by Lewis H. Carlson

289   *Bond Rally*
by E. B. White

297   from *With the Old Breed at Peleliu and Okinawa*
by E. B. Sledge

323   from *Citizen Soldiers*
by Stephen E. Ambrose

329   from *Letters from the End of the World:*
A Firsthand Account of the Bombing of Hiroshima
by Toyofumi Ogura

345   from *Flights of Passage*
by Samuel Hynes

370   **acknowledgments**

374   **bibliography**

p h o t o g r a p h s

7   U. S. Marines at Okinawa
courtesy of Double Delta Industries

13   U. S. soldiers in Belgium
courtesy of Double Delta Ind.

51   U. S. soldiers on D-Day
courtesy of Double Delta Ind.

63   Polish cavalrymen
courtesy of UPI/Corbis-Bettmann

97   The Danish resistance
courtesy of UPI/Corbis-Bettmann

111   A kamikaze plane
courtesy of AP/Wide World Photos

129   Stateside revelers and waiter
courtesy of Corbis/Bettmann

159   U. S. Marines and Japanese dead at
Guadalcanal
courtesy of AP/Wide World Photos

181

French refugees
courtesy of AP/Wide World Photos

219   U. S. paratroopers during
the invasion of France
courtesy of UPI/Corbis-Bettmann

237   Bomb in French field
courtesy of Double Delta Industries

263   U. S. Marines at Iwo Jima
courtesy of UPI/Corbis-Bettmann

285   U. S. soldier searches
German sniper
courtesy of UPI/Corbis-Bettmann

289   Dorothy Lamour on her
War Bonds tour
courtesy of AP/Wide World Photos

297   U. S. soldiers in the Pacific
courtesy of Corbis

323   Veterans back home
courtesy of UPI/Corbis-Bettmann

329   Hiroshima
courtesy of UPI/Corbis-Bettmann

345   U. S. Dive Bomber
over the Pacific
courtesy of Corbis

369   U. S. Soldier
courtesy of Double Delta Industries

introduction

N o one knew it was going to be that bad. World War II killed some 60 million people—about 20 million of them soldiers. It inflicted wounds, bereavement, poverty and other suffering on countless others. But such destruction was as impossible to imagine in advance as it was for young pilots-in-training to imagine their coming fiery deaths; or for Jews to foresee their last moments in the gas chambers; or for parents to imagine their children killed by the mortars and bullets and other munitions that factories churned out in such enormous quantities. As impossible, perhaps, as it is for us to imagine a disaster of similar scale in our future.

Literary historian and critic Paul Fussell, in one of his books about the war *(Wartime: Understanding and Behavior in the Second World War)*, cites an American woman who was married to a B-26 tailgunner for 18 months before he was killed: "I was naive about pain and suffering," she says.

This anthology wasn't assembled to remind readers that war is awful, nor is this introduction meant to accomplish that daunting task. Only war itself, it seems, can do that job. But good, honest writing about the war— and there is a lot of it—can connect us to the people who waged and endured the century's greatest conflict. Once that connection is made, we begin to understand at least some of the things war taught them.

In reading for this collection, I searched mainly among memoirs and fiction; world history doesn't interest me as much as the history of an individual or a small group. I scanned scores of books, relying upon past reading as well as friends, family and literary scholars such as Fussell and Samuel Hynes *(The Soldiers' Tale: Bearing Witness to Modern War)* to guide me to the best work.

Some war memoirs—especially those of some soldiers—have a hollow, pseudohappy, sentimental ring to them: Something is missing. I suspect that what is missing is the truth of how much the writers suffered, how guilty they felt, and how angry they remain. These are memoirs by people who at bottom don't want to remember. That makes for bad writing, but I admire them for trying to do something so difficult.

Others succeed: They remember. William Manchester in *Goodbye, Darkness* remembers the killing he did as a marine sergeant in the Pacific War, and the animal lust death excited in him; he is ashamed. Hynes, who flew dive-bombers for the navy at Okinawa recalls boredom, exhilaration and grief in *Flights of Passage*. Fussell served as an infantry second lieutenant in Europe. His memoir, *Doing Battle*, describes his own growing callousness and fear. Late in the book, Fussell tells of encountering a woman a few years after the war; she stares fixedly at him across a restaurant in Cambridge, Massachusetts, where he is lunching alone. He is uncomfortable under her scrutiny.

". . .Did I know her? Had we met somewhere? Suddenly, without warning, she burst into uncontrollable tears.

"Did I remind her of her dead son?

"Had she been angry for a long time too?"

As I worked my way through these books, I grew afraid and angry myself. One rainy November morning I awoke and tried to imagine what it might be like for me if a particular little boy who lives down the street were to grow up and go to war. How would I imagine his experience and the life of his parents? What would I feel if he were killed or maimed? What would my wife and I and the boy's parents—we'd be older by then—say to each other and to ourselves? What if all of the boys in our neighborhood, including my two sons, grew up and went to war? What if our houses were bombed? What if we had to eat our dog—a gentle soul, a fast runner, part greyhound and part Labrador—to live? What if Jews (my wife and, by Jewish law, my sons are Jewish) were rounded up and sent away? My sons are beautiful, gifted creatures, smart, funny, handsome. What if my wife and I are raising one of them to kill someone else's child—a boy who is, say, nine years old now, who plays the piano, who has another nine years to live before my piano-playing son kills him? And what if we are raising one or both of our boys for someone else's child to shoot or blow to pieces in, say, the spring of the year 2010?

It didn't work: I couldn't imagine any of it, not really. Not at all.

And that's the problem. When one person dies or suffers, worlds collapse—a universe goes to pieces. It happened all the time in the war; collapsing worlds were routine. Not just for soldiers, of course. These stories show that everyone suffered: soldiers, civilians, children, babies, retirees, men, women, animals.

But we can't imagine it. Suffering is not an event to be summed up: a friend burns to death in a tank; your feet are blown off by a mine; your aunt starves in a camp; your brother is disintegrated by an artillery shell; 60 million people die. Suffering is an experience or a set of experiences: It must be lived, or at least described, as actual moments.

We cannot live the moments these writers did, but their descriptions offer us something more than facts. We read them out of interest— What was it like? How bad was it? How exciting? Could I have done it or borne it? But we also find in these stories a connection to the writers and the people they describe. At moments, disoriented and perhaps frightened by what we are asked to witness, we back into someone and turn and find ourselves: We find our compassion. Or it finds us.

More than half a century has passed since the war ended. Once again—despite Korea and Vietnam and literally countless other wars around the globe—we have grown, like the gunner's wife, "naive about pain and suffering." One popular newspaper columnist longs for "the nobility that illuminated the lives of our parents and grandparents . . ." who ". . . lived through wars and depressions, life and death, good stomping evil."

I know what the writer means. But such longings are shallow; they seem a lie about . . . I'm not sure about what—maybe about what we really want. Do we really want to die in holes in the ground and in ships? Send our children to war? Do without oranges? And just how enobling is any of that?

Our world offers its own opportunities to act nobly, if that really is what we want. (It even offers wars: Some 42 armed conflicts were going on as of late 1998.) But soldiers, my reading tells me, generally despise words like "nobility" and the people who use them too freely.

I imagine that many soldiers and other veterans of war sense that such words and the longings that inspire their use are dangerous. The work in this book reminds me that war is dangerous, and that so are attempts to glorify it or even to glorify its victims. We may want to believe that the people who died on Tarawa or in Normandy were nobler for it. But they were people like us: Pricked, they bled.

What did World War II mean? It made the world safer for democracy—our democracy, anyway, and some others. But what did the war mean to Kenjii Ogura, seven years old when his mother died of radiation sickness two weeks after the atomic bomb fell on Hiroshima? What did it achieve for William Manchester's friends who died on Okinawa—young men like Pip Spencer, 17, whose throat was cut while he slept in his foxhole? What would they say?

I don't know. Fortunately, meaning is not just a concept we invent to comfort ourselves; meaning exists for us whether we identify it or not. Whatever we may want to say that the war meant, it reminded many people that they would rather be doing something else—raising children, teaching mathematics, drinking Coke. Even at this great distance, the war in these stories reminds me that I love my peacetime life: wife, chocolate, blankets, children, books, friends, music.

That may not seem like much of a revelation: Of course life has some great things in it; of course we love some of those things; of course we want to live. But, you know, we forget.

My father fought in the war—he spent four years in the Pacific on battleships and other vessels, and saw action at places like Iwo Jima and Okinawa. Occasionally, as he grows older, I am tugged by an impulse to thank him. But for what, exactly? I worry that he would laugh at me.

So what can we say to these people—the writers of these stories, the others who experienced the war? It is too late, anyway: They are mostly dead now, or dying. Some have been gone for 60 years, beyond anyone's thanks or pity.

Listen: Their silence grows each moment, and it holds for them no memories, no comfort, no love to give meaning to what they endured. Soon there will be only silence in the space the war's victims—its dead and its survivors—once filled entirely, as clamorous and alive then as we are now.

—*Clint Willis*

from Goodbye, Darkness
by William Manchester

Biographer and historian William Manchester (born in 1922) writes that his experiences as a Marine sergeant fighting the Japanese transformed him from "a cheeky youth to a troubled man who, for over 30 years, repressed what he could not bear to remember." Manchester set out in 1978 to revisit the major battlefields of the Pacific war, including those where he had fought. Plagued by anxiety, guilt, and recurring nightmares, he aimed to "find what I had lost out there and retrieve it."

Our Boeing 747 has been fleeing westward from darkened California, racing across the Pacific toward the sun, the incandescent eye of God, but slowly, three hours later than West Coast time, twilight gathers outside, veil upon lilac veil. This is what the French call *l'heure bleue*. Aquamarine becomes turquoise; turquoise, lavender; lavender, violet; violet, magenta; magenta, mulberry. Seen through my cocktail glass, the light fades as it deepens; it becomes opalescent, crepuscular. In the last waning moments of the day I can still feel the failing sunlight on my cheek, taste it in my martini. The plane rises before a spindrift; the darkening sky, broken by clouds like combers, boils and foams overhead. Then the whole weight of evening falls upon me. Old memories, phantoms repressed for more than a third of a century, begin to stir. I can almost hear the rhythm of surf on distant snow-white beaches. I have another drink, and then I learn, for the hundredth time, that you can't drown your troubles, not the real ones, because if they are real they can swim.

One of my worst recollections, one I had buried in my deepest memory bank long ago, comes back with a clarity so blinding that I surge forward against the seat belt, appalled by it, filled with remorse and shame.

I am remembering the first man I slew.

There was this little hut on Motobu, perched atop a low rise overlooking the East China Sea. It was a fisherman's shack, so ordinary that scarcely anyone had noticed it. I did. I noticed it because I happened to glance in that direction at a crucial moment. The hut lay between us and B Company of the First Battalion. Word had been passed that that company had been taking sniper losses. They thought the sharpshooters were in spider holes, Jap foxholes, but as I was looking that way, I saw two B Company guys drop, and from the angle of their fall I knew the firing had to come from a window on the other side of that hut. At the same time, I saw that the shack had windows on *our* side, which meant that once the rifleman had B Company pinned down, he could turn toward us. I was dug in with Barney Cobb. We had excellent defilade ahead and the Twenty-second Marines on our right flank, but we had no protection from the hut, and our hole wasn't deep enough to let us sweat it out. Every time I glanced at that shack I was looking into the empty eye socket of death.

The situation was as clear as the deduction from a Euclidian theorem, but my psychological state was extremely complicated. S. L. A. Marshall once observed that the typical fighting man is often at a disadvantage because he "comes from a civilization in which aggression, connected with the taking of life, is prohibited and unacceptable." This was especially true of me, whose horror of violence had been so deepseated that I had been unable to trade punches with other boys. But since then life had become cheaper to me. "Two thousand pounds of education drops to a ten rupee," wrote Kipling of the fighting on India's North-West Frontier. My plight was not unlike that described by the famous sign in the Paris zoo: "Warning: this animal is vicious; when attacked, it defends itself." I was responding to a basic biological principle first set down by the German zoologist Heini Hediger in his

Skizzen zu einer Tierpsychologie um und im Zirkus. Hediger noted that beyond a certain distance, which varies from one species to another, an animal will retreat, while within it, it will attack. He called these "flight distance" and "critical distance." Obviously I was within critical distance of the hut. It was time to bar the bridge, stick a finger in the dike—to do *something.* I could be quick or I could be dead.

My choices were limited. Moving inland was inconvenient; the enemy was there, too. I was on the extreme left of our perimeter, and somehow I couldn't quite see myself turning my back on the shack and fleeing through the rest of the battalion screaming, like Chicken Little, "A Jap's after me! A Jap's after me!" Of course, I could order one of my people to take out the sniper; but I played the role of the NCO in Kipling's poem who always looks after the black sheep, and if I ducked this one, they would never let me forget it. Also, I couldn't be certain that the order would be obeyed. I was a gangling, long-boned youth, wholly lacking in what the Marine Corps called "command presence"—charisma—and I led nineteen highly insubordinate men. I couldn't even be sure that Barney would budge. It is war, not politics, that makes strange bedfellows. The fact that I outranked Barney was in itself odd. He was a great blond buffalo of a youth, with stubby hair, a scraggly mustache, and a powerful build. Before the war he had swum breaststroke for Brown, and had left me far behind in two intercollegiate meets. I valued his respect for me, which cowardice would have wiped out. So I asked him if he had any grenades. He didn't; nobody in the section did. The grenade shortage was chronic. That sterile exchange bought a little time, but every moment lengthened my odds against the Nip sharpshooter. Finally, sweating with the greatest fear I had known till then, I took a deep breath, told Barney, "Cover me," and took off for the hut at Mach 2 speed in little bounds, zigzagging and dropping every dozen steps, remembering to roll as I dropped. I was nearly there, arrowing in, when I realized that I wasn't wearing my steel helmet. The only cover on my head was my cloth Raider cap. That was a violation of orders. I was out of uniform. I remember hoping, idiotically, that nobody would report me.

Utterly terrified, I jolted to a stop on the threshold of the shack. I could feel a twitching in my jaw, coming and going like a winky light signaling some disorder. Various valves were opening and closing in my stomach. My mouth was dry, my legs quaking, and my eyes out of focus. Then my vision cleared. I unlocked the safety of my Colt, kicked the door with my right foot, and leapt inside. My horror returned. I was in an empty room. There was another door opposite the one I had unhinged, which meant another room, which meant the sniper was in there—and had been warned by the crash of the outer door. But I had committed myself. Flight was impossible now. So I smashed into the other room and saw him as a blur to my right. I wheeled that way, crouched, gripped the pistol butt in both hands, and fired.

Not only was he the first Japanese soldier I had ever shot at; he was the only one I had seen at close quarters. He was a robin-fat, moon-faced, roly-poly little man with his thick, stubby, trunklike legs sheathed in faded khaki puttees and the rest of him squeezed into a uniform that was much too tight. Unlike me, he was wearing a tin hat, dressed to kill. But I was quite safe from him. His Arisaka rifle was strapped on in a sniper's harness, and though he had heard me and was trying to turn toward me, the harness sling had him trapped. He couldn't disentangle himself from it. His eyes were rolling in panic. Realizing that he couldn't extricate his arms and defend himself, he was backing toward a corner with a curious, crablike motion.

My first shot had missed him, embedding itself in the straw wall, but the second caught him dead-on in the femoral artery. His left thigh blossomed, swiftly turning to mush. A wave of blood gushed from the wound; then another boiled out, sheeting across his legs, pooling on the earthen floor. Mutely he looked down at it. He dipped a hand in it and listlessly smeared his cheek red. His shoulders gave a little spasmodic jerk, as though someone had whacked him on the back; then he emitted a tremendous, raspy fart, slumped down, and died. I kept firing, wasting government property.

Already I thought I detected the dark brown effluvium of the freshly slain, a sour, pervasive emanation which is different from anything else you have known. Yet seeing death at that range, like smelling it, requires no previous experience. You instantly recognize the spastic convulsion and the rattle, which in his case was not loud, but deprecating and conciliatory, like the manners of civilian Japanese. He continued to sink until he reached the earthen floor. His eyes glazed over. Almost immediately a fly landed on his left eyeball. It was joined by another. I don't know how long I stood there staring. I knew from previous combat what lay ahead for the corpse. It would swell, then bloat, bursting out of the uniform. Then the face would turn from yellow to red, to purple, to green, to black. My father's account of the Argonne had omitted certain vital facts. A feeling of disgust and self-hatred clotted darkly in my throat, gagging me.

Jerking my head to shake off the stupor, I slipped a new, fully loaded magazine into the butt of my .45. Then I began to tremble, and next to shake, all over. I sobbed, in a voice still grainy with fear: "I'm sorry." Then I threw up all over myself. I recognized the half-digested C-ration beans dribbling down my front, smelled the vomit above the cordite. At the same time I noticed another odor; I had urinated in my skivvies. I pondered fleetingly why our excretions become so loathsome the instant they leave the body. Then Barney burst in on me, his carbine at the ready, his face gray, as though he, not I, had just become a partner in the firm of death. He ran over to the Nip's body, grabbed its stacking swivel—its neck—and let go, satisfied that it was a cadaver. I marveled at his courage; I couldn't have taken a step toward that corner. He approached me and then backed away, in revulsion, from my foul stench. He said: "Slim, you stink." I said nothing. I knew I had become a thing of tears and twitchings and dirtied pants. I remember wondering dumbly: *Is this what they mean by "conspicuous gallantry"?*

from Doing Battle:
The Making of a Skeptic
by Paul Fussell

Literary critic and historian Paul Fussell won the 1976 National Book Award for The Great War and Modern Memory, *a study of World War I and its impact on our culture. Fussell's account of his own service as an infantry officer in Europe during World War II is among the most openly angry of war memoirs. The young lieutenant—Fussell entered the army in 1944 at age 19—endured a series of harrowing engagements before a shell burst wounded him and killed two companions.*

On the night of November 10, we were introduced into the line in a forest overlooking the city of St. Dié, relieving a filthy, battle-beat-up company of the Third Division. The Germans we were facing had been in the war for five years. We were all new to it, and our inexperience, despite our affectations of adequacy, was the most conspicuous thing about us. I was so dumb that I was wearing my costly officer's short overcoat, with gold bars winking on and off on the shoulders. Experienced troops know that a night relief is among the most difficult of infantry procedures. Especially in a forest, where contact between leaders and led is a frustrating problem even in daylight. As beginners, we expected the night relief to go according to plan, but when we stumbled forward in the pitch black trying to find our assigned places, we were astonished to be cleverly and severely shelled: it was as if the Germans a few hundred yards away could see us in the dark and through the thick pine growth. When the shelling finally stopped, at about midnight, we realized that although near the place we were supposed to be, until daylight we would remain hopelessly lost. The order came down to stop where we were, lie down among the trees, and get some sleep: we would finish the relief at first light. Scattered over several hundred yards, the two hundred of us in F Company lay down in a darkness so thick you could see nothing at all but black. Despite the shock of our first shelling (and several people had been hit), we slept as soundly as babes.

At dawn, I awoke, and what I now saw all around me were numerous objects I'd miraculously not tripped over in the dark. These were dozens of dead German boys in greenish gray uniforms, killed a day or two before by the company we were replacing. If darkness had mercifully hidden them from us, dawn disclosed them with staring open eyes and greenish white faces and hands like marble, still clutching their rifles and machine pistols in their seventeen-year-old hands. One body was only a foot or so away from me, and I found myself fascinated by the stubble of his beard, which would have earned him a rebuke on a parade ground but not here, not anymore. Michelangelo could have made something beautiful out of these forms, in the tradition of the *Dying Gaul*, and I was astonished to find that in a way I couldn't understand, at first they struck me as awful but beautiful. But after a moment, no feeling but horror. My boyish illusions, largely intact to that moment of awakening, fell away all at once, and suddenly I knew that I was not and would never be in a world that was reasonable or just. To transform silly conscripts into cold marble after passing them through unbearable humiliation and fear seemed to do them an interesting injustice. I decided to ponder these things. In 1917, shocked by the ghastliness of the Battle of the Somme and recovering from a nervous breakdown, Wilfred Owen was seeking relief by reading a life of Tennyson. He wrote his mother: "Tennyson, it seems, was always a great child. So should I have been but for Beaumont Hamel." So should I have been but for the forest overlooking St. Dié.

Until that moment in the woods, the only dead people I'd seen had been Mother's parents, placid, dignified, cosmeticized, and decently on display in their expensive caskets at Turner and Stevens Mortuary in Pasadena. Unlike these ill-treated youths, they had been gathered full of years, cooperative participants in the inexorable process by which the universe deals with its superannuated organisms. These boys were different. They had been not fulfilled but cheated. But worse was to come almost immediately. The captain called for me, and as I ran toward him down a forest path, I met a sight even more devastating. The dead I'd seen were boys. Now I saw dead children, rigged out as soldiers. On the path lay two youngsters not older than fourteen. Each had taken a bullet in the head. The brains of one extruded from a one-inch hole in his forehead, pushing aside his woolen visor cap so like a schoolboy's. The brains of the other were coming out of his nostrils.

At this sight, I couldn't do what I wanted, go off by myself and cry. I had to pretend to be, if not actually gratified, at least undisturbed by this spectacle of our side victorious. Such murders, after all, were precisely what my platoon and I were there for. Here for the first time I practiced a defense against visible signs of emotion. I utilized it often during the coming months. I compressed my lips very tightly and kept them that way for some time. This ritual tightening-up constituted my sole defense against all my natural impulses to weep, scream, or run away.

At Sevastopol, almost exactly a hundred years earlier, Leo Tolstoy was a young officer like me, and I can thus adapt his version of first combat to make it uncannily like mine:

> *A lad fresh from [the Infantry School] finds himself [on the line in Alsace]. A few months ago he was as merry and happy as girls are the day after marriage. It seems but yesterday that he first donned the officer's uniform an expert tailor had skilfully padded with wadding, arranging the thick cloth and the shoulder-straps to mask the boyish and still undeveloped chest and give it a brave appearance. . . . It is no longer he who has to be on the watch lest he fail to notice and salute some passing officer; it is now his approach that is looked out for by the privates, and he carelessly raises his hand to his cap and commands 'at ease.' . . . Was it not yesterday . . . his mother was so touched that she wept*

for joy, kissing and caressing him . . . ? It was only yesterday that he met a lovely girl . . . and he knew that she (and not only she, but hundreds of other girls a thousand times better) might, and must, love him. It all seems to have happened but yesterday. It may have been trivial and absurd and conceited, but it was all innocent and therefore pleasing.

And now he is in [the line], and suddenly sees that something is not right, something is happening that is not at all as it should be. His commander calmly tells him that he—whose mother so loves him, and from whom not she alone but everyone expected so much that is good—that he, with all his special and incomparable physical and mental excellences, is to go where men are being killed and crippled. . . . His heart contracts with a double fear: the fear of death and the fear of shame. . . . He goes to the place where men are killed, and hopes it is only said that men are killed there, but that that is not really the case and things will turn out otherwise. But half an hour [in the line] is ample to show that the reality is more terrible and more unbearable than he expected.

Tolstoy's boy officer now realizes that he is precisely as vulnerable as the boys he's seen killed, and he thinks,

'Why should [the enemy] try to do it to me—to me who was so good, so nice, so dear, . . . not only to my mother . . . but to so many people—to almost everybody?'

It wasn't long before I could articulate for myself the message the war was sending the infantry soldier: "*You* are expendable. Don't imagine that your family's good opinion of you will cut any ice here. You are just another body to be used. Since *all* can't be damaged or destroyed as they are fed into the machinery, some may survive, but that's not my fault. Most must be chewed up, and you'll probably be one of them. This is regrettable, but nothing can be done about it."

Exhorting me, "Be careful! For God's sake, be careful!" the captain ordered me to sneak out between our woods and the Germans, occupying another woods a few hundred yards away, and to position myself in a two-story farmhouse out there, where through the binoculars I was to observe enemy behavior and by sound-powered phone give the warning if an attack seemed imminent. I took with me a sergeant and three or four men, and by keeping the house between us and the Germans we got there without being seen. But of course they knew that the house, the only one in the valley, must serve as an important observation post in our outpost line. From a window on the top floor, staying well back as I'd been taught, I examined the forest across the the little no-man's-land between us and the enemy. (We always called the Germans "Krauts," doubtless to bolster our sense that we were killing creatures very odd and sinister and thus appropriate targets of contempt. The more experienced troops of the Wehrmacht, not needing such bluster, referred to the Americans less offensively as "Amis," *Ah-mees*.) Although I could see only trees, I knew that somewhere over there was an 88-millimeter gun, because earlier it had fired at Sergeant Hudson and me when, frantically trying to get our platoon organized and positioned, we'd carelessly shown ourselves for a few seconds at the edge of our woods. This immediately drew a shell whose concussion knocked Hudson out for a few seconds, while a fragment cut a gash in the thick cloth of my stylish overcoat. By the time the Germans could reload, we'd scuttled back into the woods. The fact that one .88 shell was expended on a mere two men was a bad sign, suggesting no enemy ammunition shortage and plenty of acute observation.

The woods opposite were to be attacked next morning by another regiment of the 103rd Division, which would pass through us, and as it grew dark, I focused more and more intently on the German woods, searching for signs of German preparations.

And then an absolute gift, the result of a terrible mistake unworthy of experienced soldiers. One elementary infantry principle is never at all costs silhouette oneself on a hilltop. While I was watching, the Germans began to burn the city of St. Dié behind them, presumably to deny us its shelter during the coming winter. The flames leapt up, and I saw the silhouettes of about a dozen Germans digging emplacements at the top of their hill. They didn't know that they were silhouetted from my position, and with a proud conviction that we amateurs had caught the pros in this elementary gaffe, I grabbed the phone.

"Fox Six, this is Fox Two."

"Yes, do you see something?"

"Boy, do I! Can you get me connected with the eighty-one-millimeter mortars? Fast."

"I'll try."

(Pause and clicks.)

"How company."

"Can you get me the mortar section?"

"Mortars, Lieutenant Crow."

"Hey, Crow, this is Fussell, observing from a house between the lines. I've got a great target, about a dozen Krauts digging in on top of a hill four hundred yards away. I'll give you an azimuth from where I am. Fire a round and I'll adjust."

(A minute's pause. It seemed too long. I was afraid the Germans would wake up and scent their danger, but as the flames flickered in the distance behind them, they worked stolidly on. Then, a muted *pop* from behind me. Ahead, a sudden crack and a smoke cloud to the left of the Germans. To my wonder, they seemed to notice nothing and kept digging.)

"Range is OK. Move it two hundred yards to the right and fire for effect." (Would the Germans hear the unmistakable sounds of the mortars firing and vacate the scene fast? But they still didn't catch on. They continued working like obedient soldiers. Suddenly, with no warning at all, the heavy-mortar shells arrived on them virtually all at once, and bodies and limbs flew up into the air.)

"Wonderful! You've hit them exactly! Great shooting, Crow!"

As we became more experienced, we learned not to do such showy things anymore. They inevitably brought retribution, and both we and the Germans found that in the absence of orders to the contrary, the best policy was to leave well enough alone. This attitude used to infuriate General Patton, who insisted on constant aggression everywhere. "We must be eager to kill," he emphasized, "to inflict on the enemy, the hated enemy, all possible wounds, death, and destruction." He went on: "Do not say, 'I have done enough.' See what else you can do to raise hell with the enemy." He also tried to forbid signs of prudence that seemed to border on cowardice, like officers concealing their insignia to avoid the special attention of snipers, and tankers augmenting their front armor with rows of sandbags. Proud of my success so far, I ignored the possibility of enemy revenge. In this first encounter, my cleverness had outwitted them so badly that I was sure I could beat them forever.

I was now hungry, and I went downstairs to the kitchen where the French farm family and my men were busy preparing food. Suddenly, a deafening *crack!* from above. An .88 shell had hit my window exactly. It was as if they'd known all along that I was observing there but had decided not to waste a shell on a single pismire—until it seemed absolutely necessary. If I'd stayed two minutes longer, I'd now be a mess of bloody bits. This, merely the first of my many close calls, left me white and shaken. One shell fragment had come through the kitchen ceiling and lodged in the thigh of one of the French girls. We tied up her wound as well as we could, and her father, trembling with fury, ordered us out of the house. We compromised by moving for the rest of the night into a part of the cellar the family was not occupying. The father kept a sharp and hostile eye on us all night, clearly expecting rape next from this gang of careless, brutal foreigners.

That night I was ordered to send the sergeant and a couple of men on a patrol to find out the depth of a stream the troops attacking in the morning would have to cross. In due course the patrol returned with an encouraging report: the stream was so shallow that it could be crossed with ease. Because I always obeyed orders, I assumed that others did so too. It was only after the war, drinking beer with a member of that patrol, that I learned the truth. "You didn't actually think we went all the way out to that stream in the pitch dark, did you?" I answered that yes, I actually did. Terrified, they'd gone about twenty yards from the house and after a plausible interval, returned with their agreed-upon lie. But luckily they'd guessed right, and it turned out that the stream was shallow.

In the morning the attack went forward all around us, and watching from the farmyard, we had our first experience of the most awful thing you can see in combat—your fellow GIs savaged by machine-gun and mortar fire, screaming, bleeding, thrashing about on the ground in agony, crying, calling on Mother. We stared horrified, helpless to do anything. Later, returning through the forward edge of our woods, one of my men saw something he'll never forget, if he still lives. He saw on the ground a bloody liver or kidney or similar organ, blown out of one of our attacking soldiers.

From what I'd seen so far, and I'd been on the line only two days, I realized that Mencken would be very little help here. For all his wit and penetration, he was limited by a very American malady: skilled as he was with comic irony, he was deficient in the tragic sense. He didn't respond to the classical understanding that all human life is destined to failure, and that only tragic irony is capable of offering a grown-up vision.

And as I became more familiar with war up front I perceived that in addition to being a theater of terror and mortality, war is an exemplary theater of the absurd. Witness what I found as, looking for hidden Germans, I explored the downstairs of that farmhouse between the lines. Entering a small private chapel, properly furnished with altar and lace altar-cloth, what did I see but a live, fused artillery shell five inches in diameter, resting ridiculously on the carpet. There was no visible way it could have entered through wall or window. Someone had carried it in, and it was simply stupidly, mysteriously there. Was the object to sell it some day for scrap? A total mystery.

Similarly absurd was an occasion on the march some days later. For a couple of weeks we engaged in no large attacks but took part in a number of small-scale actions in the Vosges Mountains—patrols, raids, reconnaissance. The official history of the 103rd Division provides the context:

> *The scourge of the infantryman—the 'G.I.'s—hit the 103rd*
> *about its second week of combat. Theories concerning the cause of*

this strength-draining, stomach-sickening diarrhea were varied—
dirty canteen cups, unwashed apples given by the French, overly
sweet 'D' ration chocolate bars, mouldy 'K' crackers.

During this epidemic, which reached its peak in late
November and early December, it was not uncommon to see
platoons of men fall out of a marching column and run for
the brush.

One night I was marching with my platoon toward a town where we were to be billeted. Suddenly, with no warning at all, my stomach churned and terrible cramps forced out a cascade of liquid shit before I could scuttle to the side of the road and drop my trousers. While the company marched stolidly on, I spent fifteen minutes in a rutabaga patch trying to clean myself up. I first used my trench knife to cut off my soaking, stinking long underwear. I then tried to wipe off my legs, not with toilet paper, which I'd not yet learned never to be without, but with the only paper I had, some fancy stationery I'd bought in a town we'd passed through. That exhausted, I had recourse, finally, to the pages of my official Field Message Book, a useless Benning item some of us were still naive enough to carry. This cleanup was only barely successful: socks and shoes were still wet, brown, and offensive, and when I finally got myself more or less together again (three pairs of trousers, two shirts, two sweaters, raincoat, then over the whole, belt with canteen, first-aid packet, and extra clip for carbine), I went on to follow the company, long disappeared. I prowled the blacked-out town until I finally found the company billet. The first thing one of my men said was not "Where've you been, Sir?" but "Lieutenant, you stink!" "You're so right" was the only thing I could say. I have not often been so miserable, so humiliated, so profoundly unable to put on an impressive front. In the next few days, I somehow found washing water and a few clean articles of uniform. But there was a bright side: this episode, illustrating my comical vulnerability, quite cemented my relations with the platoon. Many of the men had suffered similarly, and my mishap reinforced the impression that we were all, really, equals, closer to each other than we'd ever thought before. Needless to say, Benning had in no way prepared me for an event like this, nor offered any sort of School Solution.

The narrative structure of "war stories," even mild and comic ones like that, has caused skeptics to suspect that raw events have been managed, and even invented, to point a moral or to heighten irony or melodrama. Tim O'Brien, who fought in Vietnam as an infantry sergeant, has gone so far as to declare, "A true war story is never moral. It does not instruct, nor encourage virtue, nor suggest models of proper human behavior." He concludes: "If a story seems moral, do not believe it." But I can offer a couple of factual reports for which, in different ways, the term *redemption* seems the only way to suggest their literary themes and their permanent attractiveness.

Back at Camp Howze one man in Company F was convicted of stealing money from a barracks mate and was properly punished by court-martial, after which he became the company pariah. Men turned away as he walked down the company street, and his bunk was distant from others'. Later, in France, a call came down for three enlisted men to volunteer with an officer for a hazardous twenty-four-hour patrol behind the German lines. One of our officers, our former first sergeant who had won a field commission, volunteered: none of the rest of us did. The author of a moral short story would have to invent at this point the motive of the pariah in volunteering for this dangerous mission—to "clear his name". But that would be the truth. He did volunteer, he did go on the patrol, and he was effective and brave during it. He returned to become one of our few company heroes, his disgrace entirely forgotten. To talk with him now and walk beside him was recognized as a privilege. It is impossible not to notice how often actual military situations approximate fictional melodrama or can be understood and made useful by sensing the melodramatic content in them.

The case of Second Lieutenant Abe Goldman is also instructive. He had joined F Company at Howze in April and was assigned to lead the third platoon. His arrival brought joy to every anti-Semite in the battalion, for Lieutenant Goldman seemed an absolute slob. He was short and fat, and he wheezed when marching. His khakis were not just ill-fitting and unpressed. They were dirty. His stumpy legs were encased in puttees too large, and his trouser legs were never bloused. On his collar his gold bar and crossed rifles were cheap and unpolished, as well as carelessly pinned on. His teeth were awful, he smiled all the time and chewed with his mouth open. He had come from the National Guard, and the officers from colleges regarded him with mingled astonishment and disdain. Why was he in the infantry instead of where he belonged, the Quartermaster Corps, the Finance Department, or the Medical Administrative Corps? Although we were often amused by him, regarding him as a cheerful company mascot, we were really deeply ashamed to be associated with him, and many times the company commander tried to get him transferred. But the news had spread, and it seemed that getting rid of Lieutenant Goldman was impossible. He shipped out with us, he came on the line with us, and he was with us still.

Fighting in Alsace in the fall kept us too busy to take much unfavorable notice of him, but he did seem more plausible as an infantry officer once he'd exchanged his filthy garrison uniform for the slovenly grease-stained dark green fatigues with helmet nets we wore now all the time. When we all looked crappy, he seemed almost to fit in. On November 30 we were to attack in the afternoon a German-occupied town called Nothalten, located just where the Vosges give way to the Rhine plain. Following the Benning received wisdom, which called for reconnaissance before an attack, the captain gathered a group of about ten officers and NCOs, with a few riflemen and an automatic rifle man as bodyguards, to go forward and look over the scene.

Led by the captain, we sauntered out, gaping about us, trying to locate "terrain features" on the map and the aerial photographs, just as we'd been taught. We assumed that the Germans were some distance in front of us and we talked and joked in normal voices. Suddenly, just as we approached a low mound with a small tree and some scraggly bushes growing on top of it, rifle shots cracked directly in front of us, and terribly close. No one was hit, by some miracle, or more likely because the Germans, terrified at seeing this heavily armed gang coming so near, couldn't shoot straight. We all threw ourselves down behind the mound, which provided a bit of cover. As I hit the ground I had a quick glimpse of a short trench about fifty yards ahead with two German-helmeted heads peering up out of it.

We were now all on the ground, paralyzed by surprise and fear into total inaction. It was the perfect moment for a "leader" to appear, but none of us elected to play that role. "Anybody got a grenade?" asked the captain fuzzily, his face pressed to the dirt. No one did. He finally ordered the automatic rifle to lay down fire, but the soldier in charge of it luckily found it "jammed," and he soon had it stripped down, ostentatiously looking for the cause of the stoppage, while the captain cursed and swore at him. Did one of the lieutenants resolve the situation with a crisp and brave Benning decision? No, no one did anything but lie there and hope.

Except Abe Goldman. He suddenly said, "Let's get those sons of bitches," and crawled forward with his carbine to the top of the mound. Just as he settled himself to fire, an immense crack split the air and Abe gave a little sigh and settled back behind the mound again. The back of his field jacket was ripped open from neck to waist, and out of that long rip steam was rising and blood was welling. As the person next to him, I inspected the damage while keeping my head well down. The bullet had somehow missed his head, but it had entered his fleshy back just below his neck and torn a straight two-foot-long bloody channel down his back from his shoulders to his ass. It must have hurt terribly, but except for an occasional quiet "Ohhhhh," Abe said nothing.

Aware that at any moment I might be called upon to return fire and invite Abe's fate, I set to work instantly at the self-appointed diversionary task of helping Abe Goldman, my equivalent of the mythical repair work conducted by the automatic rifle man. With impressive verisimilitude, he was now searching in the grass for dropped parts and blowing into the weapon's interstices to dislodge fictive dirt particles. Meanwhile, I was conveying the impression that without my total attention to his wound, Abe might bleed to death. Reaching under him, I managed to find his first-aid packet, to extract the rectangular metal box, and to open it. I took out the envelope of white sulfanilamide powder, tore off a corner, and sprinkled it like a condiment into the long bloody wound down Abe's back. When I opened out the white bandage pad, I found that it covered only about a quarter of Abe's wound, which was now bleeding freely all down its long course.

"Fussell, take Abe back and get help," said the captain. Turning Abe around toward the rear—that took five minutes, he was so heavy—I very slowly, moving one knee and one elbow at a time, crawled back, guiding and pulling Abe along with one arm across his back and being careful not to be seen from the other side of the mound. During this antlike progress, I whispered to Abe, encouraging him to crawl as well as he could and assuring him that he was going to be all right. I believed this, for my view of the wound disclosed no bones or internal organs, only bloody meat. During this clumsy, agonizing passage back, he uttered no word or sound of complaint.

We must have crawled together for fifty yards before I felt far enough from danger to kneel and pull him up onto his knees and guide him into a little clump of trees. There I left him while I ran back to the company several hundred yards to the rear. I found that our little recon group had not been missed at all and that no emergency was expected. After dispatching litter bearers for Abe, I sent a squad with a bazooka and grenades around to the right flank of the German trench. Almost immediately they blasted it, killed the two Germans, and released the pinned-down group. Relieved that the problem had been solved so satisfactorily, I sat down and ate a small can of K-ration cheese. My hands were still red with Abe's blood, but of course there was no place to wash them, and I eagerly consumed a mixture of cheese and blood. One of my sergeants told me later that it was the most brutal and insensitive thing he'd ever seen me do. Later, in deep winter, I had to go to the rear on some errand for the company. The only transportation available was a truck in the service of the Graves Registration outfit, and the only place I could sit during the hour-long drive was atop a pile of stiff German corpses, frozen hard as stones. The truck unloaded them at the Graves Registration depot, where I passed the time with the soldiers in charge. They were hopelessly drunk, and they had been for many weeks. It was the only way, they explained, they could do their work. Among their collected cadavers, it emerged, was one of a member of our Pomona College ROTC unit. I regarded it entirely unmoved, by this time conscious only of a feeling of relief that the cold body was not I. As time went on, there were fewer and fewer moments when I had to clamp my lips tightly together. I was becoming a fighting lieutenant in every respect.

Abe's instructive courage was not wasted. The anti-Semitic innuendos stopped dramatically. We all knew that Abe's behavior, both before and after being shot, did encourage virtue and constitute a model of proper human behavior. Six weeks after the war in Europe ended, I took a jeep into Innsbruck on some errand and caught a quick glimpse of his squat little figure on the sidewalk. Abe was just disabled enough not to return to a line company but was now doing some work with a motor pool or something like that, perhaps in the Quartermaster or Medical Administrative Corps. His uniform was still a mess and his gold bar was still dull and scratched. I stopped to chat. He said how much he missed the company and his soldiers and his fellow platoon leaders, and when he said how much he wanted to be back on the line again, I had no trouble believing him.

Abe was not the only one of us damaged in that attack on Nothalten. We fought on its vineyard-covered hills from midafternoon until pitch dark, and when we'd finished, of our six officers only two remained. I was one and the company executive officer and second-in-command was the other. Because the captain had had his knee shot off, the exec replaced him as company commander. My platoon, once forty strong, was reduced to twenty-seven men. Anxious to do well, I had led them so far into enemy territory that I had to be stopped and ordered not to bring them back until darkness could cover our return. There was a great deal of machine-gunning that day. Running gung ho to the attack at a vineyard corner, I passed one of the company's sergeants, a tough olive-skinned Italian American, writhing in agony. He'd been machine-gunned through the leg and had had enough. The little battle concluded with our pot-shotting a few middle-aged Germans trying to flee in their long, clumsy overcoats up a steep hill. Sharpshooting, we brought down a couple with pride and delight.

I perceived that despite my unwillingness to act the hero behind the mound in the morning, I had plenty of courage when violently attacking, worked up to anger and high physical excitement. This is why I felt fully adequate, even enthusiastic, when around this time I was ordered to lead my platoon in a night seizure of a town reputed to have been recently vacated by the Germans. I hadn't yet learned that when undertaken by my battalion, night operations inevitably failed. I might have understood that from our experience the first night on the line, near St. Dié. Regardless, brimming with confidence and a high sense of adventure, we set off late at night on this mission. And within an hour we were hopelessly lost. Sergeant Hudson and I huddled with the map under a raincoat and lit match after match without discovering where we were. The town at issue was there on the map all right, a few miles away, but where were we? We spent most of the night in a ditch, scratching our heads. When I finally began to get light, a nearby hill covered with woods offered at least the hope of elevated observation in daylight, and we got up there as fast as we could move. On the hill we split into two parties to search in different directions. Hudson took a large group, leaving me near a tree with a smaller group, which I sent off to explore for a few minutes. I was now alone. After fifteen minutes, I saw some soldiers returning and to make sure they recognized me, I greeted them with a wave. Three of them, who had their rifles slung, looked at each other wonderingly, and as they turned their heads I saw that their helmets were square cut on the sides, not rounded. Fortunately, some of my men had gone off without their rifles—moving around unarmed was the worst military sin, but we, being new, didn't know that yet—and they had leaned their guns against the tree where stood. Now the question was: could I kneel down, grab a stranger's rifle, and fire before the Germans could get theirs off their shoulders and aim at me? Miraculously, I won this little speed and agility contest.

The rifle I grabbed had, luckily, a round in the chamber. I knelt, snapped off the safety, and fired the whole clip of eight at the three Germans. One fell, one limped away at speed, and one ran—and ran straight into my men, who returned at a rush with their prisoner, alerted by my frenzied rapid firing to something ominous going on.

It was another close call for me, and afterward I trembled for hours, prompting one of my squad leaders to counsel me quietly and gently, over and over, "Take it easy, Lieutenant. Take it easy." Convinced that these three Germans were a mere patrol and that there were no others nearby, we went forward to look at the one I'd killed two hundred yards away, exactly as if we were hunters going up to inspect the game we'd shot. The dead one was a large NCO, hit about five times, three times in the head, which was bleeding copiously. "Stuck pig" would suggest the appropriate image. He stared at me with dead, as if reproachful eyes, as I removed his papers from his pocket. I'd won because I was faster than he. If I were rewriting the motto of the United States Military Academy, I'd add to *Duty*, *Honor*, and *Country* a fourth charge, *Celerity*. It was just as well, by the way, that we got lost that night. It turned out that the town we were to capture in the dark was swarming with the enemy, of whom the patrol that ran into me was a tiny representation.

Before we'd finished in Europe we'd seen hundreds of dead bodies, GIs as well as Germans, civilians as well as soldiers, officers as well as enlisted men, together with ample children. We learned that no infantry-man can survive psychologically very long unless he's mastered the principle that the dead don't know what they look like. The soldier smiling is not smiling, the man whose mouth drips blood doesn't know what he's doing, the man with half his skull blown away and his brain oozing onto the ground thinks he still looks OK. And the man whose cold eyes stare at you as if expressing a grievance is not doing that. He is elsewhere. The bodies are props on a set, and one must understand that their meaning now is that they are props, nothing more.

But there was one exception. One such prop did convey invaluable meaning. In Pasadena before the war, "Negroes" had seemed creatures quite alien, comical and harmless, not to be teased or tormented but also not to be taken on as intimates and hardly to be imagined as social equals. That is, they were not like us. Once, back in December 1944, I found myself alone, a bit behind the line, walking up a hillside path looking for a good position for a machine gun. Beside the path I suddenly came upon a six-foot-deep slit trench, dug earlier by the Germans. It seemed empty as I approached, but as I came closer and looked into it more carefully, I saw lying on the bottom the facedown body of a black American soldier. I knew he was dead because his skin was no longer dark brown but blue-black, or rather, dark brown with a dark blue, almost fluorescent, tinge. As I contemplated this sight, it came to me that Negroes were not at all what I'd thought them before. In important things, they were like us. In fact, they were us. The lucky among us, black or white, survived; the unlucky, black and white together, died in the open or under trees or at the bottom of slit trenches. Where it mattered at all, we were quite the same.

"The most extreme experience a human being can go through," says historian Stephen Ambrose, "is being a combat infantryman." Part of that experience involves, of course, intense fear, long continued. But another part requires a severe closing-off of normal human sympathy so that you can look dry-eyed and undisturbed at the most appalling things. For the naturally compassionate, this is profoundly painful, and it changes your life. In the First World War, platoon leader Wilfred Owen confesses at one point, "My senses are charred. I don't take the cigarette out of my mouth when I write Deceased over their letters." I don't wash Abe Goldman's blood off my hands before I eat the cheese.

And it was both illuminating and humbling to realize that I was not unique in what I was doing and in the way it was changing me. In Europe then there were 1,200 American rifle companies with 4,800 second lieutenants leading platoons like mine. Impossible for me, once so Pasadena-special, not to feel as murderous and cool as the other young officers. Earlier, there had occurred in F Company the event known as the Great Turkey Shoot. In a deep crater in a forest, someone had come upon a squad or two of Germans, perhaps fifteen or twenty in all. Their visible wish to surrender—most were in tears of terror and despair—was ignored by our men lining the rim. Perhaps some of our prisoners had recently been shot by the Germans. Perhaps some Germans hadn't surrendered fast enough and with suitable signs of contrition. (We were very hard on snotty Nazi adolescents.) Whatever the reason, the Great Turkey Shoot resulted. Laughing and howling, hoo-ha-ing and cowboy and good-old-boy yelling, our men exultantly shot into the crater until every single man down there was dead. A few tried to scale the sides, but there was no escape. If a body twitched or moved at all, it was shot again. The result was deep satisfaction, and the event was transformed into amusing narrative, told and retold over campfires all that winter. If it made you sick, you were not supposed to indicate. I was beginning to understand what a marine sergeant told Philip Caputo during the Vietnam War: "Before you leave here, Sir, you're going to learn that one of the most brutal things in the world is your average nineteen-year-old American boy."

Although many in my platoon were killed and wounded, not one was ever captured or ever ran away, and that was true of F Company as a whole. What did we think we were doing, and why would we never flee or give up? Some few may have been following the higher morality and offering their lives and limbs for the Allied cause and the Four Freedoms, but 90 percent of us were engaged in something much less romantic and heroic. We were maintaining our self-respect, protecting our manly image from the contempt of our fellows. By persisting without complaint, we were saving our families from disgrace. We were maintaining our honor by fulfilling an implied contract. We were not letting the others down. All of us desperately wanted to be removed from danger, but we now sensed that the war would not end in a few days and that only death or wounds would be likely to grant us our respite. We kept on, there being nothing else we could do. We knew the Germans had lost the war, and they knew it too. Our inexorable, if snail-like advance, told the story, as did the daily streams of dotlike silver bombers flying toward Germany with none coming in the other direction. It was the terrible necessity of the Germans' pedantically, literally *enacting* their defeat that we found so disheartening. Since it was clear that we we going to win, why did we have to enact the victory physically and kill them and ourselves in the process?

As we went on, we became always more aware that the idea of war is synonymous with the idea of mortal blunders. Experience taught us that being shot by one's own people was as great a hazard as being shot by the enemy, and at night we moved around carefully, clearly announcing our identity very often. Sometimes others were the victims of our blunders. F Company was once ordered to advance in a town at the bottom of a beautiful valley in the Vosges. The town was said by battalion intelligence to be occupied by Germans. To frighten them into leaving before we arrived, we dropped in a couple of 60-millimeter mortar shells. When we finally entered, we met a distraught woman wailing and wringing her hands. We had just killed her middle-aged husband, an architect working in his studio in the top floor of their house. There were no Germans in the town.

Of course we were all astonished and shocked to hear of the immense German attack in the Ardennes, and immediately the 103rd and other Seventh Army divisions traveled north to fill the space left by the Third Army as it rushed up to Bastogne. While the fighting there was going on, from mid-December to mid-January, we held a thin line near Sarrequemines, so thin that occasional patrols connecting a few strong points were our sole defense. My platoon spent most of the time trying to keep warm in a half-underground concrete bunker left over from the First World War. In the trees in front I set out elaborate booby traps and flares connected to trip wires. Typical of our lazy, careless, irresponsible procedures, I made no written plan of them, leaving it a possibility that in due course French men, women, or children would stumble into their deaths in the woods.

We had so few means of defending this line that we relied heavily on mines, especially antitank mines. This meant that Lieutenant Matt Rose, the child antitank officer from Camp Howze, had a lot to do, laying out his mines and from time to time checking on them. On one quiet morning, with nothing whatever going on and the Germans across the way more quiescent than usual, we heard an extraordinarily loud explosion several hundred yards off to our right. Soon there were hysterical shouts, getting closer and closer.

"Where's an officer? Lieutenant Rose has been killed!"

Taking along a couple of my men and heavily armed myself, I invited the shouter, quietly weeping by this time, to lead us back to the trouble. There at the edge of the woods, his body all loose and twisted like a blood-covered rag doll, lay Matt Rose. His head, neck, and the top of his shoulders hung behind him like a very red riding hood. Something had literally blown his head off. What had happened? We speculated at first that a single German shell had violated the local peace and scored a lucky direct hit. But the large black stain on the snow told the truth. Matt Rose had accidentally blown himself up with his own antitank mine, as his assistant, ordered prudently to kneel many yards away, confirmed. It was typical of the boy Matt Rose, and admirable, that he chose to do the hazardous work himself. As the winter went on, we gradually learned that the fuse in the American antitank mine, or its explosive, grew extremely unstable in subfreezing weather. Later, when I was in a hospital, a fellow patient was a young officer whose face was being rebuilt after it had been torn up by shattered glass. He had been looking out a picture window when a passing truck loaded with antitank mines hit a bump and the whole package blew up in front of him. The volatility of these mines remains generally unknown, and their devisers, manufacturers, and inspectors remain unnamed.

If the savaging of baby Matt Rose was awful—men from F Company had to remove his body, and they were sick at the sight—there were moments of coarse comedy equally crude that winter. Our gas masks were normally stored back with the company kitchens, well behind the lines, together with such other useless impedimenta as officers' heavy bedrolls. But at the beginning of January some authority came up with the rumor that the Germans might use poison gas as a last-ditch weapon, and the gas masks were sent up to us on the line, where for a week we carried them. During that week one of my sergeants told me that a man in his squad had thrown his mask away and was using the carrying case as a repository for candy bars. We agreed to punish that man and create some amusement as well, and we let the rest of the men in on our plot.

Installed for twenty-four hours of duty in the front-line bunk, I affected to be talking to company headquarters on the phone and receiving frightening news of an imminent German gas attack. The sergeant and I ordered gas masks on and watched with delight as one soldier sat on the straw glumly, his gas-mask carrier unopened. We asked him mock-innocently what the trouble was and made him announce that at the moment he had lots of candy but no gas mask. He was beginning to get scared too. To calm him, I declared that it had been found that a hand-kerchief soaked in urine and tied tightly across the nostrils would serve as an effective emergency mask, and he hastened to apply this expedient. By this time the whole group, faces covered by gas masks, was snorting and puffing with laughter, which finally gave away the joke. But we'd at least had a quarter hour of comedy, involving a brief welcome satire of the war itself, its dangers and its solemnity. The miscreant finally forgave us our collegiate practical joke, but he was careful of his equipment afterward.

His Ardennes counterattack having failed, Hitler tried one more time to break out of the Western Front. He didn't expect to win the war, but he did hope to put himself in a better posture to negotiate with the West and perhaps persuade the Americans and the British to turn on the Russians. This time he projected Operation "Nordwind," a large attack on the American Seventh Army, including the 103rd Division, holding the southern part of the line. It was still deep winter, the coldest in Europe for decades, and this would be a battle in snow and ice, the German troops clad in white camouflage suits and wearing white-painted helmets, supported by white tanks. The importance of this desperate attack became clear when the officers unhappily destined to command it were called back in late December to be harangued by Hitler himself at Bad Nauheim, in the presence of Heinrich Himmler and Martin Bormann, together with such important military figures as Field Marshal Keitel and Colonel-General Jodl. In his fifty-minute speech, Hitler proclaimed, "I haven't the slightest intention of losing the war." He went on to emphasize that the Allied front in the south was now so weak as a result of stretching north to assist in the Ardennes defense that it was more vulnerable than usual. East of the Vosges, only four or five American divisions remained. He proposed to wipe them out with eight divisions, including some first-rate SS units. He concluded: "It must be our absolute goal to settle the matter here in the west offensively; that must be our fanatical goal." The commanders on the ground were not at all enthusiastic, but loyally determined to do their best. One said in confidence to a colleague, "Two things are being overlooked: we have no air superiority and nothing equivalent to set against the massive U. S. artillery. Our men are spent and the replacements have no experience." (Many were sixteen years old.)

Although our replacements were older than that, they were equally inexperienced, and they were shocked beyond measure when the Germans attacked all along our Alsace line on New Year's Day, 1945. The Americans retreated everywhere. Whole battalions were wiped out. Many men were captured. Quite a few deserted. The roads were icy and it was snowing much of the time. When the snow let up, the temperature dropped to twenty below zero. Pushed back and back, by January 20 F Company was in the town of Niederbronn-les-Bains, which we abandoned at night for a nine-mile march in a raging snowstorm back to the River Moder. There we set up what we hoped would be a final defense line between the towns of Mulhausen and Bischoltz. The retreat in the snow and ice was a nightmare: tanks and trucks skidded off the road and had to be abandoned—to the Germans. We had a day or so to slow them down as they pursued us, and at one point someone laid out on the road a number of inverted dinner plates, hoping that when covered with a bit of snow they'd resemble antitank mines and cause a brief German delay. While we were struggling back, our positions along the Moder were being prepared by engineers. The ground being frozen too solid for digging, they used blocks of TNT to blast out three- and four-man holes roofed with railroad ties. Three feet of snow quickly covered these emergency emplacements, leaving nothing visible from the front but a dark slit two inches high and ten inches long. Through such a slit for the next five days I watched the Germans on the other side of the river getting ready to attack us. I reported back regularly by phone to company headquarters, located in a hole an enviable four hundred yards behind us. Crowded into the hole with me (we dignified it by the designation Platoon Headquarters) were Sergeant Hudson, platoon medic Juan Medillin, and the platoon messenger, Larry Bishop. The only entrance was through a slippery slide at the rear, which became increasingly nasty because there we had to throw out our excrement, deposited first on a spread-out K-ration carton. To appear outside the hole in daylight was to be shot instantly.

What an attack would mean for us was too frightening to dwell on. We could fire only forward, out of the slit, and only one man could fire at a time. If the German attack were to come during snow or fog, we couldn't fire effectively at all. All the Germans would have to do would be to approach invisibly from a flank and toss in a grenade, either through the slit or the rear entrance. At night one of us was always on guard at the slit. It was terribly cold. The only warmth we had came from burning the K-ration cartons and lighting the little heat tablets we warmed coffee over. We tried various expedients to survive the cold: there was disagreement over whether sleeping with the hands in the crotch or the armpits was the best way to avoid frostbite.

On January 25 the attack came. It followed a really terrifying artillery preparation. We cowered at the bottom of the hole, dreading a direct hit, and dreading equally a German attack during the barrage, which would catch us utterly unprepared to repel it. In his pep talk to his generals, Hitler had emphasized that the main purpose of this attack in Alsace was not the recovery of lost ground but the reduction of American "man-power." The object was "the destruction of enemy forces." That meant us, trembling in our ice-cold hole. Juan the Medic happened to be a serious Christian and a gifted amateur minister. He consoled us with prayers, in which, believers or not, we others occasionally joined. Juan's favorite morale-raising passages were from the Ninety-first Psalm:

> *I will say of the Lord, He is my refuge and my fortress: my God, in Him will I trust. . . .*

A thousand shall fall at thy side, and ten thousand at thy right hand; but it shall not come nigh thee.

He was also fond of quoting Romans 8:31: "If God be for us, who can be against us?"

The troops of the Sixth SS Mountain Division soon indicated that they were the ones against us. Stimulated by schnapps, shouting slogans and abuse, they swarmed toward us—to be torn to pieces by our machine guns. But thank God, who perhaps had heard Juan's prayers, the axis of the attack was five hundred yards to our right, and our hole remained unassaulted. Indeed, we watched proceedings from our filthy rear entrance. On the right the SS burst through our line, capturing a town behind, from which they were finally ejected after a brutal struggle. These SS men were the best troops we ever fought. They behaved as if they actually believed that their wounds and deaths might make a difference in the outcome of the war.

The SS attacks having failed, with corpses left all over our snow-covered hills, in our hole we resumed our quiet life of watchful terror until we were relieved by another battalion on January 27. Throughout, our problem had been less how to help win the war than how to survive the cold. The war was being won, actually, by the Russians, who at this moment were moving inexorably toward us, even if they were a thousand miles to the east. Since January 12, they had been exerting powerful pressure on their front, making dramatic daily advances of many miles. If they seemed not yet likely to appear at any moment coming over the mountains we were facing, wearing fur caps with red stars on the front and brandishing submachine guns, we could raise our morale by thinking of them as very near, and we gathered renewed strength from realizing the German dilemma, hopelessly trapped between two converging fronts. Why didn't they surrender? Why did we and they have to proceed with this nonsensical ordeal, repetitively killing ourselves, since the issue of victory in the war was already decided? When we were finally back in a town behind the lines, washing and shaving for the first time in many weeks, I came down with pneumonia, and with a temperature of 104 degrees was evacuated to a hospital where I spent the next two weeks imbibing antibiotics. It was warm and quiet and safe, and I hoped I'd never have to return to the line. But I did, and the winter war went on.

Probably because I was growing increasingly snotty and sarcastic toward the battalion staff, I always seemed to be the officer assigned to lead their patrols and raids, often at night. When I rejoined the company, the battalion staff chose me to go back to our just vacated battlefield to lead a night patrol of twenty-five men in an assault on the town of Mulhausen. Why, no one seemed to know. I was issued a Verey-light pistol containing a colored flare with which to call down artillery fire on the town if needed. With my experience of botched night operations, I could have foretold what was going to happen. We tried to enter the town by the most obvious route, insisted upon by the battalion staff. Machine guns at the edge of town stopped us immediately, and I decided to fire the planned signal flare. But the Verey-light pistol didn't work, no matter how often and how violently I pounded on its firing pin. We retreated in disorder, carrying one man with a bullet wound in his thigh.

It was while retreating this night up the silent, snowy slopes that I saw a wonderfully absurd, bizarre, and unforgettable sight quite surpassing the keepsake artillery shell in the farmhouse near St. Dié. There was some moonlight that night, perhaps one of the reasons our raid so conspicuously failed. Climbing slowly up the hill, draped with a long belt of machine-gun ammunition like a German soldier in a cheap patriotic illustration, I came upon a perfectly preserved dead waxwork German squad. By this time the whole front was silent. There was no rifle or machine-gun firing, no artillery, no mortars, not even clanking tank treads or truck motors to be heard in the distance. The spectacle that caused my mouth to open in wonder, and almost in admiration, consisted of five German soldiers spread out prone in a semicircular skirmish line. They were still staring forward, alert for signs of the Amis. Behind them, in the center of the semicircle, was an equally rigid German medic with his Red Cross armband who had been crawling forward to do his work. In his left hand, a roll of two-inch bandage; in his right, a pair of surgical scissors. I could infer a plausible narrative. One or more men in the group had been wounded, and as the medic crawled forward to do his duty, his intention was rudely frustrated by an unspeakably loud sharp crack overhead, and instantly the lights went out for all of them. The episode was doubtless a tribute to our proximity artillery fuse, an invaluable invention which arrived on the line that winter, enabling a shell to explode not when it struck something but when it came near to striking something. Here, it must have gone off five or ten yards above its victims. Or perhaps the damage had been done by the kind of artillery stunt called time-on-target—a showy mathematical technique of firing many guns from various places so that regardless of their varying distances from the target, the shells arrive all at the same time. The surprise is devastating, and the destruction immediate and unimaginable. Whichever, the little waxwork squad, its soldiers unbloody and unmarked, had all left life at the same instant.

For a minute I stood and contemplated this weird tableau. It was a sight that somehow brought art and life into strange relation. If an artist had arranged these figures this way, with the compelling narrative element, an audience could hardly have refrained from praise. It was so cold that the bodies didn't smell, and they'd not begun visibly to decompose, but their open eyes were clouded, and snow had lodged in their ears and the openings in their clothes and the slits in their caps. Their flesh was whitish green. Although they were prone, their knees and elbows were bent, as if they were athletes terribly surprised while sprinting. They looked like plaster simulacra excavated from some chill white Herculaneum. No one but me, apparently, saw this sight in the moonlight. Had I hallucinated the whole thing? Or was it some kind of show put on for my benefit? Was I intended somehow to interpret it as an image of the whole war and its meaning, less a struggle between good and evil than a worldwide disaster implicating everyone alike, scarcely distinguishing its victims in the general shambles and ruin? Whatever it meant, this experience remained with me as a prime illustration of modernism, not that it occurred but that it seemed so normal, and that no one seemed to care. Pasadena seemed very far away indeed.

By the time I'd been in the serious war for a couple of months, I'd learned quite a bit. I'd learned for one thing that the proper function of a rifle platoon leader was much less exalted than I'd wanted to believe at Benning. I knew now that a platoon leader made practically no tactical decisions except on a patrol or raid, nor did much of anything that elevated him above the status of a passer-on of orders and information from the company commander to the squad leaders. His job was essentially to be there, physically, and to censor letters, serve as an authoritative backer-up of the platoon sergeant, intervene occasionally in disputes among the men that the sergeant couldn't handle, and "lead" the platoon in company attacks, which meant being visible and conspicuous and shouting a lot. The platoon leader's main function seemed to be that of an emblem, a visible testimony that officers shared the hardships of the men, an example of manly phlegm and "official" sanction. I'd also learned that there's one emotion a junior officer can never indulge, and that's self-pity. Combat makes you realize how unspeakably lucky you are to have lost, as yet, no limbs, to eat and sleep daily, and to be on the winning side. F. Scott Fitzgerald and Hemingway agreed that if you're any good, you understand that *everything* that happens to you is your own damn fault and you embrace that knowledge and go on from there.

More practically, I learned never to trust novel, exotic equipment but to keep things simple. It took no more than a week to discover that the classy little Handie-Talkie radios we'd been equipped with wouldn't work: in ideal conditions they might, but not in forests, mountains, or any of the places we were. We threw them away and regarded their use by others as evidence of dangerous incompetence and naïveté. Instead, we relied on sound-powered telephones, or even more simply, runners and messengers. Similarly, we got rid of all but essentials in our personal kits. I ended up carrying nothing but a rifle and a light sleeping bag, suspended from my shoulder by a piece of tent rope, like a tramp. The only item you needed for eating was a spoon, carried in the breast pocket. Mess kits, backpacks, and musette bags were simply an impediment and a bore. Anything you couldn't carry in a pocket you shouldn't be carrying. That's where we carried extra socks and gloves and cigarettes and matches and K rations and toilet paper and letters from home and V-mail forms for writing back and a pen to write with. That's where I carried the company's mail-censoring rubber stamp and stamp pad when it was my turn, and I plied them busily whenever we halted and settled down for a moment in holes or houses. Carrying a toothbrush was regarded as effeminate. My greasy field-jacket pockets were large enough to hold the food treats my parents sent from Pasadena. I asked them to send more or less exotic things to counterbalance the rigors of the line, and they sent stuffed olives in bottles, malted milk tablets, Mexican tamales in jars, and candy. Now and then a box of homemade cookies would survive the passage, but more often arrived shrapnel-nicked and snow-soaked. Most of us also carried amulets and charms as secret protection against wounds and death, but few ever talked about them or showed them to others. Although entirely a skeptic, I carried as if "faithfully" a small brown leatherette-bound New Testament in the left-hand breast pocket of my shirt. I conceived that even if it didn't provide magical, supernatural safety, it at least—it was a half-inch thick—might slow down shell and grenade fragments and deflect a bayonet thrust to my chest. I did look into it from time to time, noting the unequivocal Commandment, "Thou shalt not kill," and enjoying the poetic skill of Henry F. Lyte's "Abide with Me."

In addition to learning to live out of our pockets, we learned many simple survival techniques. One was never to assume that a friendly soldier knew who you were at night and in his nervousness would refrain from shooting you. We learned that "passwords" were seldom efficacious: you had to raise your voice to speak them, risking arousing the enemy a hundred yards away, and it was very likely that the password had been forgotten by one or both of you anyway. Officially, the password was changed daily, but if you were out of contact with your company for a few days, you knew no passwords and had to hope for recognition and goodwill, which were not always vouchsafed. As we grew more experienced, which meant less "GI," we became more aware of not just the danger but the probability of intimate "friendly fire," and moving about in a woods at night, for example, we spoke softly our own names repeatedly, loudly enough to be heard but not by the enemy. "Fussell approaching," one would say, and without any comic intent. We had long ago disused the honorifics "Lieutenant" and "Captain," persuaded that they would draw immediate fire just like the shining gold and silver bars on our collars, which we covered with wool scarves. The only time we spoke with normal volume was when we were well behind the lines. Up front, we spoke very quietly or whispered. The Germans, appallingly clever at concealment, and patient at waiting for you to blunder, were always very close, at least in our imaginations. They were our boogeymen and, like children, we believed in them.

A couple of months of war taught us a lot about courage too. We came to understand what more have known than spoken of, that normally each man begins with a certain full reservoir, or bank account, of bravery, but that each time it's called upon, some is expended, never to be regained. After several months it has all been expended, and it's time for your breakdown. My reservoir was full, indeed overflowing, at St. Dié, and so certain did I feel that no harm could come to me—me— that I blithely pressed forward, quite enjoying the challenges and the pleasures of learning a new mode of life. At Nothalten, a lot of courage remained in my reservoir, and even the portent of Abe Goldman's blood didn't scare me badly. But at the Moder River line in the snow hole, some courage leaked away, and it was distinctly hard for me to leave the hole at night to go out and check on my men.

And some serious leakage occurred after I'd been back in the hospital with pneumonia. That seemed to break the rhythm and set me to thinking seriously about the physical risks I had been taking. I was really scared the night the flare-pistol didn't work: I was afraid the SS, knowing now how many and where we were, would counterattack and chase us back over the hills, intent on massacring the lot of us. But worse was ahead. I had not yet come to grips with the full force of President Roosevelt's words in his D-Day Prayer, where he referred to the assault troops as "Our sons, pride of our nation," and warned: "They will be sore tried, by night and by day, without rest. . . . The darkness will be rent by noise and flame. Men's souls will be shaken with the violences of war." He prayed, "Let our hearts be stout, to wait out the long travail, to bear sorrows that may come, to impart our courage unto our sons wheresoever they may be." That was the courage I was soon going to need.

As the days grew warmer and the snow began to melt, it became clear except to wild optimists that soon the Seventh Army would have to attack, this time en masse and seriously. No more of those little piecemeal attacks we'd been mounting. Nor could there be any escape or evasion: the war had to be won, and it had to be won by the infantry and the armor, at whatever cost. The whole Seventh Army, all twelve divisions of it, had to advance and keep going until the war was won.

But before attacking we had to capture prisoners to learn the strength of the immediate German defenses. A man I came to despise, a fat first lieutenant who was the battalion intelligence officer, charged me and my platoon with the task of locating a machine gun said to be operating at night just in front of the German line. And if possible, to bring back a prisoner or two. This lieutenant had never himself gone on a combat mission, preferring to remain in the rear marking his maps.

In deep darkness, the whole thirty of us set off down a convenient draw leading a couple of hundred yards to the ditch where we were to dispose ourselves in line and wait for the machine gun to manifest itself. I was carrying a phone and a reel of telephone wire, which squeaked loudly as the wire unwound, and we couldn't believe that the Germans weren't vividly aware of our clownish approach. Installed in the ditch, we looked for the German position but saw nothing. Suddenly, as in melodramatic fiction, a shot rang out. It came from one of my own men, whose rifle, he said, had gone off accidentally. Our position now obvious, there was nothing for it but to hightail it home and report the failed patrol to battalion.

This was the fourth time I'd been involved in a night operation that went awry, and most had ended in near disaster. I was learning from these mortal-farcical events about the eternal presence in human affairs of accident and contingency, as well as the fatuity of optimism at any time or place. All planning was not just likely to recoil ironically: it was almost certain to do so. Human beings were clearly not like machines. They were mysterious congeries of twisted will and error, misapprehension and misrepresentation, and the expected could not be expected of them.

Others in the war were learning this new, un-American view of the instability of human hopes and the unpredictability of human actions. A D-Day observer of the surprising sinking of the clever dual-drive tanks off the Normandy beaches, which went down like stones with the helpless, puzzled crews inside, said later that for him this catastrophe "diminished forever the credibility of the concepts of strategic planning and of tactical order; it provided me instead with a sense of chaos, random disaster, and vulnerability." Curiously, there seems something in the American character that makes it easy to believe that night operations can succeed. In the Normandy invasion, dropping the paratroops from the 82nd and the 101st Airborne Divisions at night practically guaranteed a fiasco, to the general astonishment of the planners.

Reporting our failed patrol at battalion headquarters, I was ordered, as if in punishment, to repeat the procedure the next night, and to use the same path leading to the same ditch. This in violation of an elementary infantry principle: never invite ambush by repeating the same patrol along the same route. I protested this plan but got nowhere. We were being forced to violate one of Patton's wise axioms, the fruit of knowing about, among other things, the fuckup called the Battle of the Somme. "Plans," he declared, "should be made by the people who are going to execute them." The battalion intelligence officer saw us off the next night, fantasizing that we were going to return with a string of prisoners, while we saw ourselves walking directly into a vicious ambush. But neither happened. The Germans must have been as scared as we, and if they knew we had moved that close to them, they decided to leave us alone. After two hours of waiting, we returned, with of course no prisoner.

The prisoners we did collar from time to time we usually took with-out effort. Most were pitiful youths who came across willingly, per-suaded that the war was lost, and tired and wet and hungry and scared as well. I found that the productive way to deal with them was to treat them kindly. It was not just fun to witness their astonishment at being offered a cigarette first thing, but such an act, if at all visible across the way, helped encourage others to give themselves up too. And the ciga-rette lit and a couple of smiles and pats on the back awarded, they were often not unwilling to tell a bit about details on their side of the line. The technique applied by the stout young intelligence officer was sig-nificantly different, and I doubt that it worked so well. If he found a prisoner resistant to interrogation, he had him remove boots and socks and stand outside in the snow until he changed his mind. I once passed battalion headquarters and saw one poor wretch, eyes and nose dripping, standing barefoot on a sheet of ice. He had apparently declined to violate his soldierly code requiring him to tell the enemy only his name, rank, and serial number. The safe bellicosity and facile cruelty of that battalion intelligence officer were not unusual in those who stayed well to the rear of the fighting. My memory of the relation of staffs to combat troops, at least in the mediocre units where I gained my experience, stayed with me long enough to color my views about that relation in my subsequent books about both the First and the Second World Wars.

So it was as a tiny, insignificant part of the Seventh Army's attack on March 15 that I found myself lying atop a German bunker in the woods next to Sergeant Hudson and Lieutenant Biedrzycki, listening inertly to the shells coming systematically closer and closer until one went off right above us. Its intolerably loud metallic *clang!* did more than deafen me. It sent red-hot metal tearing into my body. One piece went into my right thigh. Another entered my back. When I got my hearing and my senses back, the first thing I did was take a deep breath to see if my lung had been penetrated. When I found it had not, I felt less panicky and, despite the indescribable pain, able to look about me. Hudson, lying a few inches to my left, let out a couple of subdued groans and was silent. I saw his face turn from "flesh color" to white, and then to whitish green as his circulation stopped. One of my men looked down at me with distress and dragged me to the rear. Juan the Medic patched me up, scissoring my trouser leg off and cutting a large hole in my jacket and shirt over the back wound. He shook in the sulfa powder and injected morphine. When I asked him how Hudson and Biedrzycki were, he answered quietly, "Both dead." I shouted No! and felt a black fury flow over me. It has never entirely dissipated. Juan himself had a bullet through his leg. He received no medal for his cool heroism.

By now efficient new shelling had done us such damage as to put out of the question any continuation of our attack that day. As it began to grow dark, all we could do was to feel profound dismay and to await a counterattack, which never came. The many wounded were gathered in a small nearby dugout, equipped with chicken-wire bunks. On one of these I lay down—keeping my painful right leg draped over the side because I couldn't raise it into the bunk. The wounded in that dugout waiting to be, somehow, evacuated, lay in silence. There was no crying, moaning, or complaining. Except for one man, who had distinguished himself earlier in the day by an obvious attempt to escape the attack by simulating symptoms of appendicitis. Hearing his phony groans and cries, I became furious, shouting in his direction, "Look. There are people here hurt much worse than you are, so SHUT UP!" I think this was well received by the rest.

Conscious that I had a disgrace to overcome and suspecting that others knew why the lieutenant colonel had spoken to me so angrily, I was expiating by affecting extreme nobility. I insisted that I be the last to be removed and conveyed to the aid station. By the time all the others had been taken away, it was completely dark, and I was carried to a spot in the forest where the stretcher bearers promised to return in the morning. During the night, the morphine helped me sleep painlessly on the pine needles, although I was careful to stay on my back and not move so the leg wound wouldn't start bleeding again. To keep the opening in my back closed up, I pressed my left elbow against my left back muscles. (I later found my New Testament blood-stained as a result. The stains are still there, although now white instead of red.) During the night out there, all was quiet except for occasional moans from a very badly wounded German who had been laid a few feet from me. He died during the night.

In the morning, a most welcome sight: four German prisoners, led by a GI I didn't know, arrived with a litter. I was borne shoulder high out of the woods. The long-haired, dirty youth carrying one of my handles at my feet I recognized as one whose ass I had kicked very hard the day before. Overcome with guilt and embarrassment, I managed to unbutton one of the pockets of my field jacket and pull out a K-ration box, which I presented to him. Not recognizing me at all, he was puzzled, and probably imputed my action to lunacy. At the battalion aid station, set up in a nearby house on the road I had hesitated to run across, I was greeted as a hero. In their instinctive generosity, Americans have never understood, God bless them, that the cowardly are wounded as readily as the brave. Shell fragments don't care about the current moral status of the men they penetrate. Thus the Purple Heart remains a misleading and highly popular emblem of noble behavior. The obverse reads, "For Military Merit." No wonder experienced troops consider it a joke.

Fifty-five of us, virtually half our understrength company, were killed or wounded that memorable day in the woods. Before that day, it had been possible for me to imagine that the title of William L. White's popular book of 1942, *They Were Expendable*, about PT boat action in the Pacific, contained some legitimate exaggeration. Now I knew the truth. The fate of Hudson hadn't hit me yet, but it would before long. From the aid station I was taken by litter jeep to regiment, where my tag was checked and more morphine injected. Then, into a four-litter ambulance, with blood dripping down on me from the man above. After a ridiculously bumpy journey, it arrived at a field hospital, established in a large building with a once grand courtyard, now entirely filled with men on stretchers. It was like the scene of the aftermath of the Battle of Atlanta in *Gone with the Wind*. There was no noise but the rustling here and there of medics with syringes and extra pads and bandages and the murmuring of chaplains hearing confessions and counseling courage. Although we didn't know it, triage was going on. The hopeless were being removed to the dying area and the morgue. Those needing immediate operations were hustled into the operating theater. And those like me in no mortal danger were moved aside until the worst of the pressure was off. Because of the magnitude of the Seventh Army attack, which produced an unprecedented number of wounded, the least damaged had to wait their turn. Soon I found myself on an operating table, one of a half dozen under bright lights in a large room. My clothes were now entirely cut off, I was turned over and examined for additional wounds, and my wallet and insignia—someone knew how proud I still was of my gold bar and crossed rifles—were placed in a little cloth bag stuffed into my armpit. From now on a blanket was my only clothing. Before the sodium pentathol began to work its magic ("Count slowly backward from one hundred"), I heard a woman crying as if her heart would break, and I turned my head to behold a nurse weeping uncontrollably over a boy dying with great stertorous gasps a table away.

When I came to, my wounds had been cleaned out, dead flesh had been cut away, and they had been loosely bandaged: it had been found that the way to lessen the risk of gangrene and infection was to leave wounds open for a while instead of suturing them directly. I now hurt, and badly, for the medics were very careful not to overdo the delightful morphine. (Twenty years after the war, in a small Spanish town I came upon an American morphine junkie addicted during his wartime treatment for a ghastly stomach wound. There were many such.)

Next stop: an evacuation hospital, where "delayed closure," as the medics' term went, occurred. Here I underwent delayed emotional reaction too. Up to now, I'd been able to accommodate the shock of losing Hudson and half my men. But now, realizing intensely what had happened and dwelling on it, I began to cry. In my view, I had failed and disgraced myself. Hudson's death was my fault. The Germans were not to blame, nor the war. I had killed him, and Biedrzycki too. Poor Biedrzycki! He'd been an officer no more than a month, and his reward for the assiduity, skill, and loyalty that had earned him his field commission was to be killed instantly by shell fragments in a meaningless little forest in a trivial little battle in a war already won. It was all my fault, for afraid of giving more evidence of being a confirmed coward, I hadn't run for the entrance of the bunker when the shelling started. They would have followed and would still be living. Turning over and over these convictions and images, I gradually loosened emotionally and bawled like a small boy. For a half hour my noisy sobs echoed through the ward. The other patients, as if accustomed to such embarrassments, and even worse, kindly paid no attention, and I finally stopped and went to sleep.

from The Longest Day
by Cornelius Ryan

Cornelius Ryan (1920–1974) witnessed the June 6, 1944 Normandy landing as a young correspondent for the London Daily Telegraph. *He interviewed hundreds of veterans and other D-Day participants after the war for his 1959 book,* The Longest Day, *still the most gripping account of that invasion. This excerpt describes the Americans' initial assault on Utah and Omaha Beaches—a horrifying descent into the maelstrom.*

B y now the long, bobbing lines of assault craft were less than a mile from Omaha and Utah beaches. For the three thousand Americans in the first wave, H Hour was just fifteen minutes away.

The noise was deafening as the boats, long white wakes streaming out behind them, churned steadily for the shore. In the slopping, bouncing craft the men had to shout to be heard over the roar of the diesels. Overhead, like a great steel umbrella, the shells of the fleet still thundered. And rolling out from the coast came the booming explosions of the Allied air forces' carpet bombing. Strangely, the guns of the Atlantic Wall were silent. Troops saw the coastline stretching ahead and wondered about the absence of enemy fire. Maybe, many thought, it would be an easy landing after all.

The great square-faced ramps of the assault craft butted into every wave, and chilling, frothing green water sloshed over everyone. There were no heroes in these boats—just cold, miserable, anxious men, so jam-packed together, so weighed down by equipment that often there was no place to be seasick except over one another. *Newsweek*'s Kenneth Crawford, in the first Utah wave, saw a young 4th Division soldier, covered in his own vomit, slowly shaking his head in abject misery and disgust. "That guy Higgins," he said, "ain't got nothin' to be proud of about inventin' this goddamned boat."

Some men had no time to think about their miseries—they were bailing for their lives. Almost from the moment the assault craft left the mother ships, many boats had begun to fill with water. At first the men had paid little attention to the sea slopping about their legs; it was just another misery to be endured. Lieutenant George Kerchner of the Rangers watched the water slowly rise in his craft and wondered if it was serious. He had been told that the LCA was unsinkable. But then over the radio Kerchner's soldiers heard a call for help: "This is LCA 860! . . . LCA 860! . . . We're sinking! . . . We're sinking!" There was a final exclamation: "My God, we're sunk!" Immediately Kerchner and his men began bailing.

Directly behind Kerchner's boat, Sergeant Regis McCloskey, also of the Rangers, had his own troubles. McCloskey and his men had been bailing for more than an hour. Their boat carried ammunition for the Pointe du Hoc attack and all of the Rangers' packs. The boat was so waterlogged McCloskey was sure it would sink. His only hope lay in lightening the wallowing craft. McCloskey ordered his men to toss all unnecessary equipment overboard. Rations, extra clothing and packs went over the side. McCloskey heaved them all into the swells. In one pack was $1,200 which Private Chuck Vella had won in a crap game; in another was First Sergeant Charles Frederick's false teeth.

Landing craft began to sink in both the Omaha and Utah areas—ten off Omaha, seven off Utah. Some men were picked up by rescue boats coming up behind, others would float around for hours before being rescued. And some soldiers, their yells and screams unheard, were dragged down by their equipment and ammunition. They drowned within sight of the beaches, without having fired a shot.

In an instant the war had become personal. Troops heading for Utah Beach saw a control boat leading one of the waves suddenly rear up out of the water and explode. Seconds later heads bobbed up and survivors tried to save themselves by clinging to the wreckage. Another explosion followed almost immediately. The crew of a landing barge trying to launch four of the thirty-two amphibious tanks bound for Utah had dropped the ramp right onto a submerged sea mine. The front of the craft shot up and Sergeant Orris Johnson on a nearby LCT watched in frozen horror as a tank "soared more than a hundred feet into the air, tumbled slowly end over end, plunged back into the water and disappeared." Among the many dead, Johnson learned later, was his buddy, Tanker Don Neill.

Scores of Utah-bound men saw the dead bodies and heard the yells and screams of the drowning. One man, Lieutenant (j.g.) Francis X. Riley of the Coast Guard, remembers the scene vividly. The twenty-four-year-old officer, commanding an LCI, could only listen "to the anguished cries for help from wounded and shocked soldiers and sailors as they pleaded with us to pull them out of the water." But Riley's orders were to "disembark the troops on time regardless of casualties." Trying to close his mind to the screams, Riley ordered his craft on past the drowning men. There was nothing else he could do. The assault waves sped by, and as one boat carrying Lieutenant Colonel James Batte and the 4th Division's 8th Infantry Regiment troops threaded its way through the dead bodies, Batte heard one of his gray-faced men say, "Them lucky bastards—they ain't seasick no more."

The sight of the bodies in the water, the strain of the long trip in from the transport ships and now the ominous nearness of the flat sands and the dunes of Utah Beach jerked men out of their lethargy. Corporal Lee Cason, who had just turned twenty, suddenly found himself "cursing to high heaven against Hitler and Mussolini for getting us into this mess." His companions were startled at his vehemence—Cason had never before been known to swear. In many boats now soldiers nervously checked and rechecked their weapons. Men became so possessive of their ammunition that Colonel Eugene Caffey could not get a single man in his boat to give him a clip of bullets for his rifle. Caffey, who was not supposed to land until 9:00 a.m., had smuggled himself aboard an 8th Infantry craft in an effort to catch up with his veteran 1st Engineer Brigade. He had no equipment and although all the men in the boat were overloaded with ammunition, they were "hanging on to it for dear life." Caffey was finally able to load the rifle by taking up a collection of one bullet from each of eight men.

In the waters off Omaha Beach there had been a disaster. Nearly half of the amphibious tank force scheduled to support the assault troops had foundered. The plan was for sixty-four of these tanks to be launched two to three miles offshore. From there they were to swim in to the beach. Thirty-two of them had been allotted to the 1st Division's area—Easy Red, Fox Green and Fox Red. The landing barges carrying them reached their positions, the ramps were dropped and twenty-nine tanks were launched into the heaving swells. The weird-looking amphibious vehicles, their great balloonlike canvas skirts supporting them in the water, began breasting the waves, driving toward the shore. Then tragedy overtook the men of the 741st Tank Battalion. Under the pounding of the waves the canvas water wings ripped, supports broke, engines were flooded—and, one after another, twenty-seven tanks foundered and sank. Men came clawing up out of the hatches, inflating their life belts, plunging into the sea. Some succeeded in launching survival rafts. Others went down in the steel coffins.

Two tanks, battered and almost awash, were still heading for the shore. The crews of three others had the good fortune to be on a landing barge whose ramp jammed. They were put ashore later. The remaining thirty-two tanks—for the 29th Division's half of the beach—were safe. Officers in charge of the craft carrying them, overwhelmed by the disaster they had seen, wisely decided to take their force directly onto the beach. But the loss of the 1st Division tanks would cost hundreds of casualties within the next few minutes.

From two miles out the assault troops began to see the living and the dead in the water. The dead floated gently, moving with the tide toward the beach, as though determined to join their fellow Americans. The living bobbed up and down in the swells, savagely pleading for the help the assault boats could not tender. Sergeant Regis

McCloskey, his ammunition boat again safely under way, saw the screaming men in the water, "yelling for help, begging us to stop—and we couldn't. Not for anything or anyone." Gritting his teeth, McCloskey looked away as his boat sped past, and then, seconds later, he vomited over the side. Captain Robert Cunningham and his men saw survivors struggling, too. Instinctively their Navy crew swung the boat toward the men in the water. A fast launch cut them off. Over its loudspeaker came the grim words, "You are not a rescue ship! Get on shore!" In another boat nearby, Sergeant Noel Dube of an engineer battalion said the Act of Contrition.

Now the deadly martial music of the bombardment seemed to grow and swell as the thin wavy lines of assault craft closed in on Omaha Beach. Landing ships lying about one thousand yards offshore joined in the shelling; and then thousands of flashing rockets whooshed over the heads of the men. To the troops it seemed inconceivable that anything could survive the massive weight of firepower that flayed the German defenses. The beach was wreathed in haze, and plumes of smoke from grass fires drifted lazily down from the bluffs. Still the German guns remained silent. The boats bored in. In the thrashing surf and running back up the beach men could now see the lethal jungles of steel-and-concrete obstacles. They were strewn everywhere, draped with barbed wire and capped with mines. They were as cruel and ugly as the men had expected. Back of the defenses the beach itself was deserted; nothing and no one moved upon it. Closer and closer the boats pressed in . . . 500 yards . . . 450 yards. Still no enemy fire. Through waves that were four to five feet high the assault craft surged forward, and now the great bombardment began to lift, shifting to targets farther inland. The first boats were barely 400 yards from the shore when the German guns—the guns that few believed could have survived the raging Allied air and sea bombardment—opened up.

Through the din and clamor one sound was nearer, deadlier than all the rest—the sound of machine-gun bullets clanging across the steel, snout-like noses of the boats. Artillery roared. Mortar shells rained down. All along the four miles of Omaha Beach German guns flayed the assault craft.

It was H Hour.

They came ashore on Omaha Beach, the slogging, unglamorous men that no one envied. No battle ensigns flew for them, no horns or bugles sounded. But they had history on their side. They came from regiments that had bivouacked at places like Valley Forge, Stoney Creek, Antietam, Gettysburg, that had fought in the Argonne. They had crossed the beaches of North Africa, Sicily and Salerno. Now they had one more beach to cross. They would call this one "Bloody Omaha."

The most intense fire came from the cliffs and high bluffs at either end of the crescent-shaped beach—in the 29th Division's Dog Green area to the west and the 1st Division's Fox Green sector to the east. Here the Germans had concentrated their heaviest defenses to hold two of the principal exits leading off the beach at Vierville and toward Colleville. Everywhere along the beach men encountered heavy fire as their boats came in, but the troops landing at Dog Green and Fox Green hadn't a chance. German gunners on the cliffs looked almost directly down on the waterlogged assault craft that heaved and pitched toward these sectors of the beach. Awkward and slow, the assault boats were nearly stationary in the water. They were sitting ducks. Coxswains at the tillers, trying desperately to maneuver their unwieldy craft through the forest of mined obstacles, now had to run the gauntlet of fire from the cliffs.

Some boats, unable to find a way through the maze of obstacles and the withering cliff fire, were driven off and wandered aimlessly along the beach seeking a less heavily defended spot to land. Others, doggedly trying to come in at their assigned sectors, were shelled so badly that men plunged over the sides into deep water, where they were immediately picked off by machine-gun fire. Some landing craft were blown apart as they came in. Second Lieutenant Edward Gearing's assault boat, filled with thirty men of the 29th Division, disintegrated in one blinding moment three hundred yards from the Vierville exit at Dog Green. Gearing and his men were blown out of the boat and strewn over the water. Shocked and half drowned, the nineteen-year-old lieutenant came to the surface yards away from where his boat had gone down. Other survivors began to bob up, too. Their weapons, helmets and equipment were gone. The coxswain had disappeared and nearby one of Gearing's men, struggling beneath the weight of a heavy radio set strapped to his back, screamed out, "For God's sake, I'm drowning!" Nobody could get to the radioman before he went under. For Gearing and the remnants of his section the ordeal was just beginning. It would be three hours before they got on the beach. Then Gearing would learn that he was the only surviving officer of his company. The others were dead or seriously wounded.

All along Omaha Beach the dropping of the ramps seemed to be the signal for renewed, more concentrated machine-gun fire, and again the most murderous fire was in the Dog Green and Fox Green sectors. Boats of the 29th Division, coming into Dog Green, grounded on the sandbars. The ramps came down and men stepped out into water three to six feet deep. They had but one object in mind—to get through the water, cross two hundred yards of the obstacle-strewn sand, climb the gradually rising shingle and then take cover in the doubtful shelter of a seawall. But weighed down by their equipment, unable to run in the deep water and without cover of any kind, men were caught in crisscrossing machine-gun and small-arms fire.

Seasick men, already exhausted by the long hours spent on the transports and the assault boats, found themselves fighting for their lives in water which was often over their heads. Private David Silva saw the men in front of him being mowed down as they stepped off the ramp. When his turn came, he jumped into chest-high water and, bogged down by his equipment, watched spellbound as bullets flicked the surface all around him. Within seconds, machine-gun fire had riddled his pack, his clothing and his canteen. Silva felt like a "pigeon at a trap shoot." He thought he spotted the German machine gunner who was firing at him, but he could not fire back. His rifle was clogged with sand. Silva waded on, determined to make the sands ahead. He finally pulled himself up on the beach and dashed for the shelter of the sea wall, completely unaware that he had been wounded twice—once in the back, and once in the right leg.

Men fell all along the water's edge. Some were killed instantly, others called pitifully for the medics as the incoming tide slowly engulfed them. Among the dead was Captain Sherman Burroughs. His friend Captain Charles Cawthon saw the body washing back and forth in the surf. Cawthon wondered if Burroughs had recited "The Shooting of Dan McGrew" to his men on the run-in as he had planned. And when Captain Carroll Smith passed by, he could not help but think that Burroughs "would no longer suffer from his constant migraine headaches." Burroughs had been shot through the head.

Within the first few minutes of the carnage at Dog Green one entire company was put out of action. Less than a third of the men survived the bloody walk from the boats to the edge of the beach. Their officers were killed, severely wounded or missing, and the men, weaponless and shocked, huddled at the base of the cliffs all day. Another company in the same sector suffered even higher casualties. Company C of the 2nd Ranger Battalion had been ordered to knock out enemy strongpoints at Pointe de la Percée, slightly west of Vierville. The Rangers landed in two assault craft with the first wave on Dog Green. They were decimated. The lead craft was sunk almost immediately by artillery fire, and twelve men were killed outright. The moment the ramp of the second craft dropped down, machine-gun fire sprayed the debarking Rangers, killing and wounding fifteen. The remainder set out for the cliffs. Men fell one after another. Private First Class Nelson Noyes, staggering under the weight of a bazooka, made a hundred yards before he was forced to hit the ground. A few moments later he got up and ran forward again. When he reached the shingle he was machine-gunned in the leg. As he lay there Noyes saw the two Germans who had fired looking down on him from the cliff. Propping himself on his elbows he opened up with his Tommy gun and brought both of them down. By the time Captain Ralph E. Goranson, the company commander, reached the base of the cliff, he had only thirty-five Rangers left out of his seventy-man team. By nightfall these thirty-five would be cut down to twelve.

Misfortune piled upon misfortune for the men of Omaha Beach. Soldiers now discovered that they had been landed in the wrong sectors. Some came in almost two miles away from their original landing areas.

Boat sections from the 29th Division found themselves intermingled with men of the 1st Division. For example, units scheduled to land on Easy Green and fight toward an exit at Les Moulins discovered themselves at the eastern end of the beach in the hell of Fox Green. Nearly all the landing craft came in slightly east of their touchdown points. A control boat drifting off station, a strong current running eastward along the beach, the haze and smoke from grass fires which obscured landmarks—all these contributed to the mislandings. Companies that had been trained to capture certain objectives never got near them. Small groups found themselves pinned down by German fire and isolated in unrecognizable terrain, often without officers or communications.

The special Army-Navy demolition engineers who had the job of blowing paths through the beach obstacles were not only widely scattered, they were brought in crucial minutes behind schedule. These frustrated men set to work wherever they found themselves. But they fought a losing battle. In the few minutes they had before the following waves of troops bore down on the beaches, the engineers cleared only five and a half paths instead of the sixteen planned. Working with desperate haste, the demolition parties were impeded at every turn—infantrymen waded in among them, soldiers took shelter behind the obstacles they were about to blow and landing craft, buffeted by the swells, came in almost on top of them. Sergeant Barton A. Davis of the 299th Engineer Combat Battalion saw an assault boat bearing down on him. It was filled with 1st Division men and was coming straight in through the obstacles. There was a tremendous explosion and the boat disintegrated. It seemed to Davis that everyone in it was thrown into the air all at once. Bodies and parts of bodies landed all around the flaming wreckage. "I saw black dots of men trying to swim through the gasoline that had spread on the water and as we wondered what to do a headless torso flew a good fifty feet through the air and landed with a sickening thud near us." Davis did not see how anyone could have lived through the explosion, but two men did. They were pulled out of the water, badly burned but alive.

But the disaster that Davis had seen was no greater than that which

had overtaken the heroic men of his own unit, the Army-Navy Special
Engineer Task Force. The landing boats carrying their explosives had
been shelled, and the hulks of these craft lay blazing at the edge of the
beach. Engineers with small rubber boats loaded with plastic charges
and detonators were blown apart in the water when enemy fire
touched off the explosives. The Germans, seeing the engineers working
among the obstacles, seemed to single them out for special attention.
As the teams tied on their charges, snipers took careful aim at the
mines on the obstacles. At other times they seemed to wait until the
engineers had prepared whole lines of steel trestles and tetrahedra
obstacles for blowing. Then the Germans themselves would detonate
the obstacles with mortar fire—before the engineers could get out of
the area. By the end of the day casualties would be almost fifty percent.
Sergeant Davis himself would be one. Nightfall would find him aboard
a hospital ship with a wounded leg, heading back for England.

It was 7:00 a.m. The second wave of troops arrived on the shambles
that was Omaha Beach. Men splashed ashore under the saturating fire
of the enemy. Landing craft joined the ever growing graveyard of
wrecked, blazing hulks. Each wave of boats gave up its own bloody
contribution to the incoming tide, and all along the crescent-shaped
strip of beach dead Americans gently nudged each other in the water.

Piling up along the shore was the flotsam and jetsam of the invasion. Heavy equipment and supplies, boxes of ammunition, smashed
radios, field telephones, gas masks, entrenching tools, canteens, steel
helmets and life preservers were strewn everywhere. Great reels of wire,
ropes, ration boxes, mine detectors and scores of weapons, from broken rifles to stove-in bazookas, littered the sand. The twisted wrecks of
landing craft canted up crazily out of the water. Burning tanks threw
great spirals of black smoke into the air. Bulldozers lay on their sides
among the obstacles. Off Easy Red, floating in and out among all the
cast-off materials of war, men saw a guitar.

Small islands of wounded men dotted the sand. Passing troops
noticed that those who could sat bolt upright as though now immune
to any further hurt. They were quiet men, seemingly oblivious to the

sights and sounds around them. Staff Sergeant Alfred Eigenberg, a medic attached to the 6th Engineers Special Brigade, remembers "a terrible politeness among the more seriously injured." In his first few minutes on the beach, Eigenberg found so many wounded that he did not know "where to start or with whom." On Dog Red he came across a young soldier sitting in the sand with his leg "laid open from the knee to the pelvis as neatly as though a surgeon had done it with a scalpel." The wound was so deep that Eigenberg could clearly see the femoral artery pulsing. The soldier was in deep shock. Calmly he informed Eigenberg, "I've taken my sulfa pills and I've shaken all my sulfa powder into the wound. I'll be all right, won't I?" The nineteen-year-old Eigenberg didn't quite know what to say. He gave the soldier a shot of morphine and told him, "Sure, you'll be all right." Then, folding the neatly sliced halves of the man's leg together, Eigenberg did the only thing he could think of—he carefully closed the wound with safety pins.

Into the chaos, confusion and death on the beach poured the men of the third wave—and stopped. Minutes later the fourth wave came in—and they stopped. Men lay shoulder to shoulder on the sands, stones and shale. They crouched down behind obstacles; they sheltered among the bodies of the dead. Pinned down by the enemy fire which they had expected to be neutralized, confused by their landings in the wrong sectors, bewildered by the absence of the sheltering craters they had expected from the Air Force bombing, and shocked by the devastation and death all around them, the men froze on the beaches. They seemed in the grip of a strange paralysis. Overwhelmed by it all, some men believed the day was lost. Technical Sergeant William McClintock of the 741st Tank Battalion came upon a man sitting at the edge of the water, seemingly unaware of the machine-gun fire which rippled all over the area. He sat there "throwing stones into the water and softly crying as if his heart would break."

The shock would not last long. Even now a few men here and there, realizing that to stay on the beach meant certain death, were on their feet and moving.

from The Long Walk
by Slavomir Rawicz
as told to Ronald Downing

When the Germans and the Soviets divided Poland between them in 1939, cavalry officer Slavomir Rawicz fell captive to the Red Army, which shipped him to Siberia. He and six comrades from various countries escaped from their labor camp —they were later joined by a young woman—then faced a 4,000-mile walk to British India. Rawicz after the war told his story to British newspaperman Ronald Downing. We find the party crossing the Gobi Desert.

T wo days without water in the hillocky, sand-covered, August furnace of the Gobi and I felt the first flutterings of fear. The early rays of the sun rising over the rim of the world dispersed the sharp chill of the desert night. The light hit the tops of the billowing dunes and threw sharp shadows across the deep-sanded floors of the intervening little valleys. Fear came with small fast-beating wings and was suppressed as we sucked pebbles and dragged our feet on to make maximum distance before the blinding heat of noon. From time to time one or other of us would climb one of the endless knolls and look south to see the same deadly landscape stretching to the horizon. Towards midday we stuck our long clubs in the sand and draped our jackets over them to make a shelter. Alarm about our position must have been general but no one voiced it. My own feeling was that we must not frighten the girl and I am sure the others kept silent for the same reason.

The heat enveloped us, sucking the moisture from our bodies, putting ankle-irons of lethargy about our legs. Each one of us walked with his or her own thoughts and none spoke, dully concentrating on placing one foot ahead of the other interminably. Most often I led the way, Kolemenos and the girl nearest to me and the others bunched together a few yards behind. I was driving them now, making them get to their feet in the mornings, forcing them to cut short the noon rest. As we still walked in the rays of the setting sun the fear hit me again. It was, of course, the fundamental, most oppressive fear of all—that we should die here in the burning wilderness. I struggled against a panicky impulse to urge a return the way we had come, back to water and green things and life. I fought it down.

We flopped out against a tall dune and the cold stars came out to look at us. Our bone-weariness should have ensured the sleep of exhaustion but, tortured with thirst, one after another twisted restlessly, rose, wandered around and came back. Some time after midnight I suggested we start off again to take advantage of the cool conditions. Everybody seemed to be awake. We hauled ourselves upright and began again the trudge south. It was much easier going. We rested a couple of hours after dawn—and still the southerly prospect remained unaltered.

After this one trial there were no more night marches. Makowski stopped it.

"Can you plot your course by the stars?" he asked me. The others turned haggard faces towards me.

I paused before answering. "Not with complete certainty," I confessed.

"Can any of us?" he persisted. No one spoke.

"Then we could have been walking in circles all through the night," he said heavily.

I sensed the awful dismay his words had caused. I protested that I was sure we had not veered off course, that the rising sun had proved us still to be facing south. But in my own mind, even as I argued, I had to admit the possibility that Makowski was right. In any case, the seed of doubt had been sown and we just could not afford to add anything to the already heavy burden of apprehension.

So we went on through the shimmering stillness. Not even a faint zephyr of air came up to disperse the fine dust hanging almost unseen above the desert, the dust that coated our faces and beards, entered into our cracked lips and reddened the rims of eyes already sore tried by the stark brightness of the sun.

The severely-rationed dried fish gave out on about the fifth day and still we faced a lifeless horizon. In all this arid world only eight struggling human specks and an occasional snake were alive. We could have ceased to move quite easily and lain there and died. The temptation to extend the noonday halt, to go on dozing through the hot afternoon until the sun dropped out of sight invited our dry, aching bodies. Our feet were in a pitiable state as the burning sand struck through the thin soles of our moccasins. I found myself croaking at the others to get up and keep going. There is nothing here, I would say. There is nothing for days behind us. Ahead there must be something. There must be *something*. Kristina would stand up and join me, and Kolemenos. Then the others in a bunch. Like automatons we would be under way again, heads bent down, silent, thinking God knows what, but moving one foot ahead of the other hour after desperate hour.

On the sixth day the girl stumbled and, on her knees, looked up at me. "That was foolish of me, Slav. I tripped myself up." She did not wait for my assistance. She rose slowly from the sand and stepped out beside me. That afternoon I found to my faint surprise and irritation I was on my knees. I had not been conscious of the act of falling. One moment I was walking, the next I had stopped. On my knees, I thought . . . like a man at prayer. I got up. No one had slackened pace for me. They probably hardly noticed my stumble. It seemed to take me a very long time to regain my position at the head again. Others were falling, too, I noticed from time to time. The knees gave and they knelt there a few unbelieving seconds until realization came that they had ceased to be mobile. They came on again. There was no dropping out. These were the signs of growing, strength-sapping weakness, but it would have been fatal to have acknowledged them for what they were. They were the probing fingers of death and we were not ready to die yet.

The sun rose on the seventh day in a symphony of suffused pinks and gold. Already we had been plodding forward for an hour in the pale light of the false dawn and dully I looked at Kristina and the other shambling figures behind me and was struck with the unconquerable spirit of them all. Progress now was a shuffle; the effort to pick up the feet was beyond our strength.

Without much hope we watched Kolemenos climb laboriously to the top of a high mound. One or other of us did this every morning as soon as the light was sufficient to give clear visibility southwards to the horizon. He stood there for quite a minute with his hand over his eyes, and we kept walking, expecting the usual hopeless shrug of the shoulders. But Kolemenos made no move to come down, and because he was staring intently in one direction, a few degrees to the east of our course, I dragged to a stop. I felt Kristina's hand lightly on my arm. She, too, was gazing up at Kolemenos. Everybody halted. We saw him rub his eyes, shake his head slowly and resume his intent peering in the same direction, eyes screwed up. I wanted to shout to him but stayed quiet. Instead I started to climb up to him. Zaro and the girl came with me. Behind came the American and Marchinkovas. The two Poles, Paluchowicz and Makowski, leaned on their clubs and watched us go.

As I reached Kolemenos I was telling myself, "It will be nothing. I must not get excited. It surely can't be anything." My heart was pounding with the exertion of the slight climb.

Kolemenos made no sound. He flung out his right arm and pointed. My sight blurred over. For some seconds I could not focus. I did what I had seen Kolemenos do. I rubbed my eyes and looked again. There was *something*, a dark patch against the light sand. It might have been five miles distant from us. Through the dancing early morning haze it was shapeless and defied recognition. Excitement grew as we looked. We began to talk, to speculate. Panting and blowing, the two Poles came up to us. They, too, located the thing.

"Could it be an animal?" asked the Sergeant.

"Whatever it is, it is not sand," Mister Smith replied. "Let's go and investigate."

It took us a good two hours to make the intervening distance. Many times we lost sight of the thing we sought as we plunged along in the sandy depressions. We climbed more often than we would otherwise have done because we could not bear the idea that somehow the smudge on the landscape might disappear while we were cut off from view of it. It began to take shape and definition and hope began to well up in us. And hope became certainty. There were *trees*—real, live, growing, healthy trees, in a clump, outlined against the sand like a blob of ink on a fresh-laundered tablecloth.

"Where there are trees there is water," said the American.

"An oasis," somebody shouted, and the word fluttered from mouth to mouth.

Kristina whispered, "It is a miracle. God has saved us."

If we could have run we would have done so. We toiled that last half-mile as fast as we could flog our legs along. I went sprawling a few times. My tongue was dry and swollen in my mouth. The trees loomed larger and I saw they were palms. In their shade was a sunken hollow, roughly oval-shaped, and I knew this must be water. A few hundred yards from the oasis we crossed an east-west caravan track. On the fringe of the trees we passed an incongruous pile of what looked like rusting biscuit tins like some fantastic mid-desert junk yard. In the last twenty yards we quickened our pace and I think we managed a lope that was very near a run.

The trees, a dozen or more of them, were arranged in a crescent on the south side of the pool, and threw their shadow over it for part of the day. The wonderful cool water lay still and inviting in an elliptical depression hemmed round with big, rough-worked stones. At this time, probably the hottest season, the limits of the water had receded inwards from the stone ring, and we had to climb over to reach it. The whole, green, life-giving spot could have been contained inside half-an-acre.

Zaro had the mug but we could not wait for him to fill it and hand it round. We lay over the water lapping at it and sucking it in like animals. We allowed it to caress our fevered faces. We dabbed it around our necks. We drank until someone uttered the warning about filling our empty bellies with too much liquid. Then we soaked our food sacks and, sitting on the big stones, gently laved our cracked and lacerated feet. For blissful minutes we sat with the wet sacking draped about our feet. With a mugful of water at a time we rinsed from our heads and upper bodies some of the accumulated sand and dust of the six-and-a-half days of travail. The very feel and presence of water was an ecstasy. Our spirits zoomed. We had walked out of an abyss of fear into life and new hope. We chatted and laughed as though the liquid we had drunk was heady champagne. We wondered what hands had brought these stones and planted these palms to make of this miraculous pool a sign that could be seen from afar by thirst-tortured men.

The full extent of our good fortune was yet to be discovered. Some twenty yards east of the pool, on the opposite side from which we had approached, there were the remains of a still-warm fire and the fresh tracks of camels and many hoof-marks, telling of the recent halt of a big caravan. It had probably departed at sunrise. These men, whoever they were, had cooked and eaten meat, and the bones, as yet quite fresh and untainted, were scattered around the wood ashes. They were the bones of one large and one small animal and the meat had been sliced from them with knives, leaving small, succulent pieces still adhering. We shared out the bones and tore at them with our teeth, lauding our luck. Poor toothless Paluchowicz borrowed the knife from me and did as well as anybody. When there was no more meat we cracked each bone with the axe and sucked out the marrow.

For two or three hours during the heat of the afternoon we lay stretched out near the water under the blessed shade of the palms. Kolemenos, who had that rare gift of complete relaxation in any situation, snored with his arms behind his head and his cap pulled down over one eye. The sun's rays began to slant and I came out of a sleep haunted by blazing light and never-ending desert. I picked up the mug, climbed over the stones, scooped up water and drank again. The American stood up, stretched and joined me. Soon we were all up and about.

Zaro moved away. "I'm going to have a look at that pile of tins," he called back. "Maybe we'll find one we can carry water in."

The puzzle of that dump of civilised junk in the heart of the South Gobi must remain unsolved. There were about a hundred of the box-like metal containers and they had been there so long that, even in the dry air of that place, they had rusted beyond use. We turned them over one by one but could find nothing to indicate what they had contained or from where they had come. As we examined them we stacked them on one side. Beneath the pile, half-buried in the sand, Zaro pulled out a complete coil of rust-covered quarter-inch wire held together by circlets of thinner wire which broke away at a touch. I held a handful of sand in a fold of my sack and rubbed away at the heavy wire until I cleared the rust. The coating was thin; the wire was strong and sound.

That night we made a low-walled shelter from the tins, searched around for small pieces of wood and lit a fire. I lay awake for a long time trying to decide how long we should remain in this place, but the answer would not come. Sleep when it did come was dreamless and complete. I opened my eyes, according to the habit of the desert, about an hour before dawn, and Zaro was already pottering around, tugging tentatively at the free end of the coil of wire.

A conference of suggestion and counter-suggestion developed about that length of wire. We lugged it over to the pool and began pulling it out and rubbing it down with sand. No one had any clear notion what to do with it but there was unanimity on its probable usefulness to us some time in the future. Any metal object was precious. We just could not bring ourselves to leave treasure behind. Since we had to take it with us, the discussion finally boiled down to shaping it into an easily-portable form. That was how we came to spend hours of that day cutting off about four-feet lengths, turning the ends into hooks and making loops which could be slung around the neck. The metal was tough and bending it caused hard work with the back of the axe-head while the wire ends were jammed and firmly held in interstices between the close-set stones. When each of us had been supplied with a loop, Zaro and a couple of others made a few metal spikes about two feet long, one end beaten out to a point and the other looped to hang on the belt. Plenty of wire still remained when we had finished, but we thought we had all we could conveniently carry. The operation gave us a sense of achievement. To use our hands and our skill again was stimulating and there was, too, the prisoner's fierce pride of possession, be the object only a loop of discarded wire.

Inevitably came the question of when to depart. Two of our problems were insoluble. The oasis had water but no food. We had nothing in which to carry water, except our metal mug. Makowski argued that if we waited here a few days we stood a chance of meeting a caravan and securing ourselves a stock of food for the next stage. But I wanted to go. I said that, as we had just missed one caravan, there might not be another for weeks. We would wait on for days until we were too weak from lack of food to move at all and the next travellers might find us dead from starvation. In the light of what was to come, I hope I may be forgiven for my insistence. Yet I think I may have been right. But there is no way of judging the issue now, nor was there then. There was no acrimony about the debate. We were in desperate straits and we had to decide immediately one way or the other. The thing was decided late that evening. We would set out before dawn.

We were on our way when the sun came up and for half a day we could look back and see the trees of the oasis. I was glad when I could no longer see their shape against the skyline. For hours Zaro carried the mug, one hand underneath, the other over the top. He had filled it with water after we had all taken our final drinks and as he walked it slopped warm against his palm and little trickles escaped down the sides. When we halted at midday he had lost nearly half the quantity through spillage and evaporation and was complaining about the cramping of his arms in holding so tightly to the can. So, very carefully, sitting up under the small shade of our jackets slung over our clubs, we handed the water round and disposed of it a sip at a time.

This was the pre-oasis journey all over again, but this time we were deprived of even the scant sustenance of a few dried fish. For the first three days I thought we moved surprisingly well. On the fourth day the inescapable, strength-draining heat began quite suddenly to take its toll. Stumbles and falls became increasingly frequent, the pace slowed, speech dried up into short grunted phrases. I remember Makowski saying, "Hell can't be hotter than this bloody desert."

On the fifth day Kristina went to her knees. I turned slowly round to look at her, expecting her to get to her feet as she had done before. She remained kneeling, her fair head bowed down on her chest. She was very still. I moved towards her and Kolemenos stepped back at the same time. Before we could reach her she swayed from the hips and slumped forward, her face in the sand. We reached her at the same time and turned her on her back. She was unconscious. I opened the neck of her dress and started talking to her, gently shaking her, while Mister Smith set to with sticks and *fufaikas* to make shade for her.

She came to quickly. She looked at our anxious ring of faces, sat up, smiled through split lips and said, "I feel better now. I must have fallen over—I don't know how it happened."

"Don't worry," I consoled her. "We'll rest here a while and then you'll be all right again."

She leaned forward and lightly patted the back of my hand. "I won't fall down again."

We sat there a while. Kristina reached down to scratch her ankle and my eyes idly followed the hand. The ankle was swollen so that the skin pressed outward against the narrow-fitting ends of her padded trousers.

"Has anything bitten you, Kristina?"

"No, Slav. Why?"

"Your leg looks swollen."

She pulled up the trouser leg and looked, turning her foot about as she did so. "I hadn't noticed it before," she said.

We struggled on for a couple more hours. She seemed to be refreshed. Then she fell again and this time her knees buckled and her face hit the sand in almost one movement without even the action of putting her arms out to break the fall.

We turned her over again and wiped away the sand which had been forced into her nose and mouth. We put up the shelter. She lay with eyes closed, breathing in harsh gasps through her mouth. I looked at her ankles and they were a pitiful sight. Both were badly discolored and so swollen that it seemed they would burst the restricting bottoms of the trousers. I took out my knife and slit the cloth upwards. The skin appeared to be distended by water right up to the knees. I touched the swelling and the mark of my fingers remained for some seconds.

Kristina was unconscious for an hour while we tried to stifle our gnawing anxiety with banalities like, "It must be just a touch of sunstroke." I had a feeling like lead in the pit of my stomach. I was frightened.

She was quite cheerful when she came round. "I am becoming a nuisance," she said. "What can be the matter with me?" We fussed around her.

Kristina got to her feet. "Come on. We are wasting time."

I walked alongside her. She stopped suddenly and glanced down at her legs, her attention attracted by the flapping of slit trousers about her legs.

"My legs are getting quite thick, Slav."

"Do they hurt you, Kristina?"

"No, not at all. They must be swelling because I have walked so far."

The time was afternoon on the fifth day. She walked on for hours without more than an occasional small stumble and was still keeping up with Kolemenos and I when the sun had gone and we stopped for the night. Sitting there among us she stole frequent looks at her legs. She said nothing and we affected not to notice.

It was a disturbed night. All except Kolemenos seemed too weary and worried for sleep, Kristina lay still but I sensed she remained awake. I chewed on the pebble in my mouth. My teeth ached, my gums were enlarged and tender. Thoughts of flowing water constantly invaded my mind. I had clear pictures of the sampans I had seen on those northern rivers. I had little fits of shivering that made me stand up and walk around. My head felt constricted. I ached from head to foot.

For the first two hours of the sixth day the air was cool and walking was as pleasant as ever it can be in the desert. But soon the sun began to blaze at us out of a sky empty of clouds.

I took Kristina's elbow. "Can you keep going in this?"

"Yes, I think so."

Five minutes later she had folded up and was out, face down in the sand. Again we ministered to her and waited for her to open her eyes. She appeared to be breathing quite normally, like a tired child.

I stood a few steps away from her and the others came over to me. "She is very swollen," I said. "Do any of you know what that means?" Nobody knew the symptoms. We went back to her and waited. I flapped my cap over her face to make some air.

She smiled at us. "I am being a trouble again." We shook our heads. "I am afraid you had better leave me this time."

We all broke into protest at once. Kolemenos dropped down on his knees beside her. "Don't say that. Don't be a silly little girl. We shall never leave you." She lay there for another half-an-hour and when she tried to force herself up on her elbows she fell back again.

I spoke to Kolemenos. "We must give her a hand." We lifted her to her feet. "I can walk if you stay near me," she said.

Amazingly she walked, Kolemenos and I lightly holding her elbows. After a quarter of a mile we felt her start to fall forward. We steadied her and she went on again. She pulled herself erect and there was not a sound of distress, not a whimper. The next time she slumped forward we could not hold her. She had played herself utterly out and even the gallant will in that frail body could not produce another torturing effort. We were all in a bunch around her as the sun climbed up over our heads. Kolemenos and I each put an arm about her and, half-carrying, half-dragging her, set off again. A mile or so of that and I had no reserve of strength to give her. We stopped and I bent double fighting for breath.

"Stick beside me, Slav," said Kolemenos. "I am going to carry her." And he lifted her into his arms, swayed for a moment as he adjusted himself to the weight, and staggered off. He carried her for fully two hundred yards and I was there to ease her down when he paused for a rest.

"Please leave me, Anastazi," she begged. "You are wasting your strength." He looked at her but could not bring himself to speak.

We made a shelter there and stayed for perhaps three hours through the worst heat of the day. She lay still—I do not think she could move. The ugly swelling was past the knees and heavy with water. Kolemenos was flat on his back, restoring his strength. He knew what he was going to do.

The sun began to decline. Kolemenos bent down and swung her

into his arms and trudged off. I stayed with him and the rest were all about us. He covered fully a quarter of a mile before he put her down that first time. He picked her up again and walked, her head pillowed on his great shoulder. I can never in my life see anything so magnificent as the blond-bearded giant Kolemenos carrying Kristina, hour after hour, towards darkness of that awful sixth day. His ordeal lasted some four hours. Then she touched his cheek.

"Put me on the ground, Anastazi. Just lay me down on the ground."

I took her weight from him and together we eased her down. We gathered round her. A wisp of a smile hovered about the corners of her mouth. She looked very steadily at each one of us in turn and I thought she was going to speak. Her eyes were clear and very blue. There was a great tranquillity about her. She closed her eyes.

"She must be very tired," said Sergeant Paluchowicz. "The poor, tired little girl."

We stood around for several minutes, dispirited and at a loss to know what to do next. The shoulders of Kolemenos were sagging with exhaustion. We exchanged glances but could think of nothing to say. I looked down at Kristina. I looked at the open neck of her dress, and in a second I was down at her side with my ear over her heart. There was no beat. I did not believe it. I turned my head and applied the other ear. I lifted my head and picked up her thin wrist. There was no pulse. They were all looking at me intently. I dropped her hand and it thumped softly into the sand.

The American spoke, hardly above a whisper. I tried to answer but the words would not come. Instead the tears came, the bitter salt tears. And the sobs were torn from me. In that God-forsaken place seven men cried openly because the thing most precious to us in all the world had been taken from us. Kristina was dead.

I think we were half crazy there beside her body in the desert. We accused ourselves of having brought her here to her death. More personally, Makowski, speaking in Polish, blamed me for having insisted on leaving the shelter of the oasis.

The American intervened, his voice cold and flat. "Gentlemen, it is no use blaming ourselves. I think she was happy with us." The talk ceased. He went on, "Let us now give her a decent burial."

We scraped a hole in the sand at the base of a dune. Little pieces of stone that we sifted from the grains as we dug deeper we laid apart. I slit open a food sack and laid the double end gently under her chin. We lowered the body. On her breast lay her little crucifix. We stood around with our caps in our hands. There was no service, but each man spoke a prayer in his own language. Mister Smith spoke in English, the first time I had heard him use it. I opened out the sacking and lifted it over her face and I could not see for tears. We covered her with sand and we dotted the mound round with the little stones.

And Kolemenos took her tall stick and chopped a piece off it with his axe and bound the one piece to the other with a leather thong to make a cross.

So we said goodbye to her and went our empty way.

The awful thing was that there was so little but the girl to think about. Walking was sheer painful habit—it required no thought to perform. The sun beating down hour after hour would addle my brains and check the orderly sequence of thinking. I found I could imagine she was still there, just behind my shoulders and I could scuff along for miles seeing her. But there always came a time when the idea of her presence was so strong that I must turn my head, and bitter grief would knife at me all over again. I came slowly out of a troubled, thirst-ridden sleep that night and I was sure once more that she remained with us. And each fresh realization of her death renewed dumb agony.

It took another tragedy to dull the sharp edges of our memory of her. Oddly, too, it relieved some of the load of guilt I felt about her death.

On the eighth day out from the oasis Sigmund Makowski pitched over into the sand. His arms were still at his sides when his face thumped down and he had made no effort to use his stick to prevent the fall. He lay there a minute or two and was barely conscious. We looked down at him and saw the tell-tale sign. Over the top of his moccasins the flesh was soft and puffy. We exchanged glances and said nothing. We turned him round and flapped our sacks in his face and he recovered quickly. He got to his feet, shook his head from side to side, grabbed his stick and plunged off. He keeled over again and again, but he kept going. And all the time the sickening flabby swelling grew upwards and weighed upon his legs.

Makowski lasted longer after the first onset than Kristina had done. On the ninth day he must have slumped down half-a-dozen times in a couple of hours. Then, lying flat and heaving desperately with his arms to get himself to his knees, he called out the name of Kolemenos. Both Kolemenos and I knelt down beside him.

"If you give me a hand to get to my feet, I can keep going."

Kolemenos took one arm, I took the other. We got Makowski upright. Feebly he shook our hands off and stood swaying. I felt myself choking as he staggered off like a drunken man, still going forward, but weaving from side to side, stabbing his stick into the yielding sand as he went. The six of us stood there hopelessly and watched him go.

"Mustn't let him fall again," Kolemenos said to me.

It was not difficult to catch up with him. Kolemenos took his stick from him and we took an arm each. We put his arms about our shoulders and stepped out. He swung his head round to each of us in turn and gave a bit of a smile. He kept his legs moving, but progressively more weakly so that towards the end of the day he was an intolerable, sagging burden about our necks.

That night he seemed to sleep peacefully and in the morning of the tenth day he was not only still alive but appeared to have regained some strength. He set off with the rest of us dragging his feet but unaided. He moved for half-an-hour before his first fall, but thereafter he pitched over repeatedly until Kolemenos and I again went to his rescue. When the time came to make our noon-day halt he was draped about our shoulders like a sack and his legs had all but ceased to move. Mister Smith and Paluchowicz eased his weight away from us and gently laid him down on his back. Then we put up the shelter and squatted down around him. He lay quite still and only his eyes seemed to be alive.

After a while he closed his eyes and I had thought he had gone, but he was still breathing quietly. He opened his eyes again. The lids came down and this time he was dead. There was no spasm, no tremor, no outward sign to show that life had departed the body. Like Kristina, he had no words for us at the end.

The dossier for Sigmund Makowski, aged 37, ex-captain of the Polish frontier forces, *Korpus Ochrony Pogranicza*, was closed. Somewhere in Poland he had a wife. I would like her some day to know he was a brave man. We buried him there in the Gobi. The first grave we scratched out was too small and we had to lift out the body and enlarge the hole. We laid his sack, empty of food for so long, that he had carried with him for two thousand or more miles, over his face, and scooped the sand over him. Kolemenos made another small wooden cross, we said our prayers and we left him.

I tried hard to keep count of the days. I tried, too, to remember if I had ever read how long a man can keep alive without food and water. My head ached with the heat. Often the blackest pall of despair settled on me and I felt we were six doomed men toiling inevitably to destruction. With each hopeless dawn the thought recurred: Who will be next? We were six dried-out travesties of men shuffling, shuffling. The sand seemed to get deeper, more and more reluctant to let our ill-used feet go. When a man stumbled he made a show of getting quickly on his legs again. Quite openly now we examined our ankles for the first sign of swelling, for the warning of death.

In the shadow of death we grew closer together than ever before. No man would admit to despair. No man spoke of fear. The only thought spoken out again and again was that there must be water soon. All our hope was in this. Over every arid ridge of hot sand I imagined a tiny stream and after each waterless vista there was always another ridge to keep the hope alive.

Two days after Makowski's death we were reaching the limits of endurance. I think it was about the twelfth day out from the oasis. We walked only for about six hours on that day. We moved along in pairs now. There was no effort to choose partners. The man next to you was your friend and you took each other's arms and held each other up and kept moving. The only life we saw in the desert about us were snakes which lay still, heads showing and the length of their bodies hidden in deep holes in the sand. I wondered how they lived. They showed no fear of us and we had no desire to molest them. Once we did see a rat, but generally the snakes seemed to have the desert to themselves.

At the end of that twelfth day I was arm-in-arm with Zaro. Mister Smith and Paluchowicz were helping each other along and Kolemenos walked with Marchinkovas. In the middle of the night I felt a fever of desire to get moving again. I think I knew that if the miracle did not happen within the next twenty-four hours we could not expect to survive. I stuck it out until a couple of hours before dawn. Marchinkovas, Zaro and the American were awake, so I shook Kolemenos and Paluchowicz. I rasped at them through my dry and aching throat. I stood up. No one argued. As I started away they were with me. Paluchowicz stumbled a little at first because he was still not quite awake and his legs were stiff, but soon we were paired off again and making distance south.

It was easy to imagine in those pre-dawn hours that we were re-covering ground we had trudged over before, but the first light of the rising sun showed we were on course. We tacked from side to side as we walked, two by two, but it seemed to me we had made a remarkable number of tortured miles by the time the heat forced us to stop and rest. It was almost too much trouble to erect our flimsy canopy, but we did it because it was by now one of the habits of survival.

We sweated it out for about three hours in throbbing discomfort, mouths open, gasping in the warm desert air over enlarged, dust-covered tongues. I eased the sticky pebble round my sore gums to create a trickle of saliva so that I could swallow. I was at my lowest ebb, working on the very dregs of stamina and resolution. It was the devil's own job to haul ourselves upright again. We were all perilously weak and dangerously near death.

All my visions of water had been of exquisite cool ponds and murmuring streams. The water that saved our lives was an almost dried-out creek, the moisture compounded with the mud at the bottom of a channel not more than a couple of yards wide. We came over the last ridge and failed to see it. We were looking for water and this was no more than a slimy ooze which the killing desert was reluctant to reveal to us. We were almost on it before we saw it. We fell on our faces and sucked at the mud and dabbled our hands in it. For a few minutes we acted like demented men. We chewed mud for the moisture it contained and spat out the gritty residue.

It was the American who got the right idea. He swung his sack off his back and thrust a corner of it down into the mud. He waited some minutes, pulled out the sack and sucked at the damp corner. We followed his example. The amount of water we obtained in this way was infinitesimal compared with our raging, thirteen-day-old thirst, but it was something and it gave us hope. We began to talk again for the first time for days, to exchange suggestions. We decided to walk along the watercourse with the idea that if at this point there was dampness, somewhere there must be real water.

The creek narrowed until it was a mere crack in the ground and here we found water collected in tiny pools in the mud. By pressing down our cupped hands, palms uppermost, we were able to drink, really to drink again, to feel water trickling down our parched throats. We drank it, sand, mud and all, in ecstasy. It was probably as well that we were prevented from gulping it down in large quantities. After each drink there was a waiting period of several minutes before the little hollows filled again with up-seeping water. My split, puffed and bleeding lips burned as the water touched them. I held the water in my mouth before swallowing and washed it about my tongue, my tender gums and aching teeth.

For a couple of hours we lay sprawled out exhausted close against the creek. Then we drank some more. Late in the afternoon Zaro pulled off his moccasins and sat with his feet deep in the cool mud. He smiled through his broken lips at the bliss of it and called out to us to join him. We sat round in a rough circle. After those never-ending hot days with blistered and cracked feet being pushed on and on through the burning sand, this was an experience of wonderful relief. After a while I felt the water slowly trickling through into the depressions made by my feet. The balm of it seemed even to ease the aching bones. Now and again I pulled out my feet just for the joy of dropping them back again into the squelching mud.

Sitting there in the only comfort we had known since the far distant oasis, we began to talk, to face up to our still bleak future and to plan. The first fact was that we were starving and near the end of our strength. The second was that, in spite of this God-sent ribbon of moisture, we were still in the desert and the prospect was unchanged for as many miles ahead as we could see. The first decision reached was that we would stay here for a night and a day. This night we would sleep and in the morning we would make an extended exploration along the creek, hoping to find at some point flowing water. Where there was water, we reasoned, there might be life, something we could eat.

Early next morning we piled our *fufaikas* in a mound, split into two trios and set off in opposite directions along the creek. Kolemenos, the American and I in one party walked a mile or more eastward and found nothing. At times the watercourse disappeared entirely, as though it had gone underground. When we found it again it was still only a damp trail. Reluctantly we concluded that if there were flowing water it must be in some spring below ground and inaccessible to us. Two remarkably healthy-looking snakes were the only sign of life we encountered. We turned back and arrived at the meeting point. We had some time to wait for Zaro, Marchinkovas and Paluchowicz, and had begun to entertain some hopes that their delayed return might mean good tidings when we saw them approaching. Zaro stretched out his hands palms downwards to indicate that the investigation had produced nothing.

"No luck," said Marchinkovas as they came up to us.

"We found nothing, either," I told them.

We drank more of the brown, turgid water. We bathed our feet again and watched the sun mounting in the sky.

Kolemenos spoke. "All this bloody desert and only us and a few snakes to enjoy it. They can't eat us and we can't eat them."

"Only half-true, that statement." It was Mister Smith. "It is not unknown for men to eat snakes."

There was an immediate ripple of interest.

Mister Smith stroked his greying beard thoughtfully. "American Indians eat them. I have seen tourists in America tempted into trying them. I never tried to eat snake myself. I suppose it's a natural human revulsion against reptiles."

We sat in silence a while thinking over what he had said.

He broke in on our thoughts. "You know, gentlemen, I think snakes are our only chance. There's hardly anything a starving man can't eat."

The idea fascinated and repelled at the same time. We talked for a while about it but I think we all knew we were going to make the experiment. There was no choice.

"We need a forked stick to catch then," said Marchinkovas, "and we haven't got one."

"No difficulty about that," I told him. "We'll split the bottoms of a couple of our sticks and jam a small pebble into the cleft."

Kolemenos got up off his haunches. "Let's make a start with the sticks straightaway."

We decided to use Zaro's and Paluchowicz's. The splitting was done by Kolemenos with the axe. The wood was bound with thongs above the split and the small stones rammed home. The result was two efficient-looking instruments.

"How shall we know if the snakes are poisonous? Shall we be able to eat the poisonous kind?" This was Paluchowicz, and he was echoing a doubt that existed in most of our minds.

"There is nothing to worry about," said the American. "The poison is contained in a sac at the back of the head. When you cut off the head you will have removed the poison."

Apart from catching our meal, there remained one problem—fuel for a fire to do the cooking. We turned out our bags for the bits of tinder we always carried. Heaped together the pile was bigger than we had expected. From the bottom of his sack Zaro brought out three or four pats of dried animal dung and solemnly placed them on the collection of hoarded fuel: On another occasion we might have laughed, but smiling through split lips was painful.

"I picked it up at the oasis," said Zaro. "I thought it might be needed for fires some time."

I was sorry that we all had not done as Zaro had done back there. This dried animal waste was excellent fuel which burned slowly and produced fair heat. There had been occasions, too, since the oasis when we had come across little heaps of sun-dried debris deposited by the swirling, dancing whirlwinds which we had seen spiralling across the desert. But we had been too intent on our plodding progress to stop and gather these tiny harvests of the wind. From now on the search for tinder was to be a preoccupation ranking almost in importance with the hunt for snakes.

Smith and I got down to the job of preparing a fire while the others went off with the two forked sticks. We scratched down through the powdery top sand to the layer of bigger grains below and through that to the bed of small stones beneath. We were looking for a thin flat stone on which to cook our snake. It was fully an hour before we found one. Among the surrounding dunes we had glimpses of the others creeping quietly around in their quest for some unsuspecting reptile. In the way of things in this life, they spent a couple of hours without seeing a sign of one. When we cared nothing for them we seemed always to be finding them.

The fire was laid. In the blazing sun the flat stone seemed already hot enough for cooking (certainly I think it would have fried an egg easily). Marchinkovas came back to us droop-shouldered. "The snakes must have heard we had changed our minds about them," he said wryly. The three of us sat around the unlighted fire in silence for about another half-an-hour. There came suddenly a great yell from Zaro. We could not see him but we saw Kolemenos and Paluchowicz running in the direction of the sound. We got up and ran, too.

About fifty yards away Zaro had his snake. His stick was firmly about the writhing body a couple of inches behind the head and Zaro was sweating with the exertion of holding it there. We could not judge the size of the creature because all but about six inches of it was hidden in a hole in the sand and the wriggling power of the concealed length was slowly inching the stick back towards the hole. We were tired, weak, slow and clumsy and we ran around and got in one another's way in an effort to help Zaro. Then Paluchowicz jabbed his stick a couple of inches behind Zaro's. I pulled a thong from about my waist, slipped a loop about the snake against the hole and heaved. But there was too much snake inside and too little outside. It was stalemate.

Kolemenos settled the issue. The bright blade of his axe swished down and separated the snake's head from its body. The still wriggling length was hauled into the sunlight. The thing was nearly four feet long. It was as thick as a man's wrist, black above, with a creamy-brown belly lightening to a dull cream-white at the throat.

Zaro struck a pose. "There's your dinner, boys."

The thing still twitched as we carried it back to the fire. We laid it on my sack and, under the direction of the American, I started to skin it. The beginning of the operation was tricky. Smith said the skin could be peeled off entirely but I could get no grip at the neck. Eventually I slit the skin a few inches down and with difficulty started to part the snake from its tight sheath. I had never seen an unclothed snake before. The flesh was whitish at first but in the sun it turned a little darker while we waited for the fire to bring the flat stone to the right heat. We cut the body lengthwise and cleaned it out.

There was still a little reflex of life left as we curled the meat up on the stone over the fire. It sizzled pleasantly. Fat trickled down off the stone and made the fire spit. We streamed sweat as we sat around the fire. We could not take our eyes off the snake. With our sticks we lifted the stone off, turned the meat and put it back for the final stage of grilling. When we thought it was ready to eat we lifted it, stone and all, on to the sand to cool a little.

It lay eventually on my sack a yard or two away from the dying fire. We squatted round it but nobody seemed in a hurry to start carving it up. We looked at one another. Kolemenos spoke. "I am bloody hungry." He reached forward. We all went for it at the same time. Paluchowicz, the man without teeth, stretched his hand out to me for the knife. We ate. It was not long before the snake was reduced to a skeleton. The flesh was close-packed and filling. I had thought the taste might be powerful, even noxious. It was in fact mild, almost tasteless. It had no odor. I was faintly reminded of boiled, unseasoned fish.

"I wish I had thought of snakes earlier," said Mister Smith.

We drank some more of the muddy water. We watched the sun drop from its zenith. We knew that soon we must move again, and we were reluctant to go, to leave this precious ribbon of moisture and launch out again into the unknown, heat-baked country ahead. Sprawled out there, my stomach rumbling as it contended with its barbaric new meal, I longed for a smoke. We still had newspaper but the tobacco had long gone.

No one wanted to bring up the subject of when we should leave, so we talked about other things. For the first time we exchanged ideas freely about Kristina and Makowski. Why should death have overtaken them and left the rest of us still with the strength to carry on? There was no answer to this question, but we mulled it over. We talked of them with sadness and affection. It was, I suppose, an act of remembrance for two absent friends. And it took some of the heavy load of their great loss from us.

I found myself looking at the five of them, taking stock of them, trying to assess our chances. We were all sick men. Kolemenos had his moccasins off and I could see the inflamed raw patches where blisters had formed on punctured blisters, and I knew he was no worse off in this respect than any other of us. All our faces were so disfigured that our nearest relatives would have had difficulty in recognizing us. Lips were grotesquely swollen and deeply fissured. Cheeks were sunk in. Brows overhung red-rimmed eyes which seemed to have fallen back in their sockets. We were in an advanced state of scurvy. Only the toothless Paluchowicz escaped the discomfort of teeth rocking loose in sore gums. Already Kolemenos had pulled two aching teeth out between finger and thumb for Marchinkovas and he was to practise his primitive dentistry several times more in the future for others of the party.

Lice, scurvy and the sun had played havoc with our skin. The lice had multiplied with the filthy prolificacy of their kind and swarmed about us. They fed and grew to an obscenely large size. We scratched and scratched at our intolerably irritated bodies until we broke the skin and then our sweat-soaked clothes and untended dirty finger-nails caused the tiny cuts to become septic. This unclean affliction, superficial though it was, was a constant source of depression and misery. I killed the lice when I caught them with savage joy. They were pre-eminently the symbol of our fugitive degradation.

In the end no one took the initiative over our departure. There came a time when Kolemenos and Zaro stood up together. We all rose. We adjusted the wire loops about our necks, picked up our sacks. Into my sack went the flat cooking stone. The American carefully stowed away the little pile of fuel. Grimacing, Kolemenos pulled on his moccasins. We drank a little more water. And in the late afternoon we started off.

Many miles we walked that day, until the light of day faded out and until the stars came out in a purple-black sky. We slept huddled close together and were awake before dawn to start again.

Half-an-hour later Paluchowicz stopped with a groan, clutching his belly, doubled up. In the next hour we were all seized with the most violent, griping pains. All of us were assailed with diarrhoea of an intensity that left us weak and groaning. With the frequent stops we could not have covered more than five miles by late afternoon, when the attacks began to subside.

What had caused it—the snake-meat or the water? We asked one another this question.

Said Mister Smith, "It might well have been the dirty water. But most probably it arises simply from the fact that our empty stomachs are reacting against the sudden load of food and water."

"There's one good way to find out," Kolemenos said. "We'll eat some more snake. I am still hungry."

Marchinkovas shrugged his shoulders. "It will be snakes or nothing."

Paluchowicz gasped with another spasm of stomach ache.

"May God help us," he said, fervently.

Unquestionably the snakes of the Gobi saved us from death. We caught two within minutes of each other the next day. One was like the common European grass snake, the other arrayed in the brilliance of a silver-grey skin marked down the back with a dull red broad stripe flanked closely parallel with two thin lines of the same color. Profiting by the experience of my difficulty in skinning the first specimen, we clubbed these two to death and held the heads in Zaro's forked stick while I stripped off the skins.

We did not like these two colored snakes as much as we had the first capture. They were thinner-bodied and we imagined they tasted less pleasantly. I think the colors affected our judgment. The big black was not unlike a conger eel in appearance and in the texture of the flesh. Thereafter we sought specially for this species and counted ourselves lucky when we found one.

The clear fat which oozed out over the heat of the fire we used as a balm for our lips, our sore eyes and our feet and the soothing effect lasted for hours.

Two days after leaving the creek we had visitors. First there wheeled lazily over us half-a dozen ravens. They stayed with us throughout the morning and then made a leisurely departure as we erected our shelter at midday. We were wondering what had prompted their departure when two great shadows skimmed along the sand. We looked up and saw not twenty feet above a pair of magnificent, long-necked eagles, their plumage looking black against the sun. They passed over us several times and then alighted on the top of a sandy hillock twenty yards away and looked down on us. The spread of wings as they came in to land was enormous.

"What do you think *they* want?" someone asked.

The American considered. "It's fairly obvious, I think, that they saw the ravens and came to investigate the prospects of food."

Zaro said, "Well, they're not having *me*."

"Don't worry," I assured him. "They won't attack us."

Zaro stood up and shouted at the great birds. He made motions of throwing. The pair disdained to notice his antics. He scratched away at the sand and produced a couple of pebbles. He aimed carefully and threw. The stone sent up a puff of sand a yard short of them. One held its ground and the other did an ungainly single hop. Zaro hurled the second stone wide of its mark and the two eagles sat unmoved. They took off in their own good time as we dismantled the shelter and followed us for about an hour, high in the sky, before swinging away to the south and disappearing.

"Eagles live in mountains," said the American. "Perhaps we haven't far to go to get out of the desert."

We could see a long way ahead and there were no distant mountains. "They can also fly great distances," I said.

For three or four days we were tormented with stomach pain and its attendant diarrhoea; then, as we began to long for water again, the stomach trouble passed away. As we trudged on there were days when we caught not a glimpse of a snake. Another day and we would pick up a couple basking in the sun in a morning's search. We ate them as soon as we found them. There was a red-letter day when we caught two of the kind we called Big Blacks within half-an-hour. The days dragged by. We were inspected again by both the ravens and the eagles. We were able now to make a fix on a couple of bright stars and sometimes walked long after dark. We began again to dream longing dreams of water.

I lost count of the days again. My fitful sleep was invaded by visions of reptiles so tenacious of life that though I beat at them with my club in a frenzy they still hissed at me and crawled. All my fears came bursting through in dreams. Worst of all was the picture of myself staggering on alone, shouting for the others and knowing that I should never see them again. I would wake shivering in the morning cold and be happily reassured to see Smith, Kolemenos, Zaro, Marchinkovas and Paluchowicz close about me.

Almost imperceptibly the terrain was changing. The yellow sand was deepening in color, the grains were coarser, the smooth topped dunes taller. The sun still burned its shrivelling way across the blue, unclouded heavens but now there were days when a gentle breeze sighed out from the south and there was a hint of coolness in its caress. The nights were really cold and I had the impression that we were day by day gradually climbing out of the great heat-bowl.

It might have been a week or eight days after leaving the creek that we awoke to discover in a quickening of excitement and hope a new horizon. The day was sharply clear. Far over to the east, perhaps fifty miles away, shrouded in a blue haze like lingering tobacco smoke, a mountain range towered. Directly ahead there were also heights but they were mere foothills compared with the eastward eminences. So uninformed were we of Central Asian geography that we speculated on the possibility that the tall eastern barrier could be the Himalayas, that somehow we had by-passed them to the west, that we might now even be on the threshold of India. We were to learn that the whole considerable north-to-south expanse of Tibet, ruggedly harsh and mountainous, lay between us and the Himalayas.

We plodded on for two more exhausting, heart-breaking days before we reached firm ground, a waste of lightly-sanded rocks. We lay there in the extremity of our weakness and looked back at our tracks through the sand. There were no defined footmarks, only a dragging trail such as skis make in snow. Lifeless and naked the rocky ridge sloped easily into the distance above us. In my mind was the one thought that over the hump there might be water. We rested a couple of hours before we tackled the drag upwards. We took off our moccasins and emptied them of sand. We brushed the fine dust from between our toes. Then we went up and out of the Gobi.

Over the ridge there was more desolation. By nightfall we had dropped down into a stone-strewn valley. We might have struggled on longer but Marchinkovas fell and banged his knee. In the morning he showed us a big bruise and complained of a little stiffness but was able to walk. The pain passed off as he exercised it and he experienced no more trouble from the injury. We climbed again. There was no talking because none of us could spare the breath and movement of the lips was agony. We hauled ourselves along through a faint dawn mist and did not reach this next summit for several hours. From the top there was the view again of the great range to the east, looking even more formidable than at our first sight of it. Ahead there seemed to be an unbroken succession of low ridges corrugating the country as far as we could see. Below us the floor of the valley appeared to be covered with sand and we decided to get down before dark to search for snakes.

It was the merest accident that we did not miss the water on our way down. We had all passed it when Zaro turned round and yelled the one wonderful word. It was no more than a trickle from a crack in a rock but it glinted like silver. It crept down over the curve of a big round boulder and spread thinly over a flat rock below. Kolemenos and I had been picking our way down the slope some twenty yards ahead of Zaro when his shout arrested us. We turned quickly and scrambled back. We found that the source of the little spring was a crack just wide enough to take the fingers of one hand. The water was sparkling, clean and ice-cold. We channeled the tiny stream to a point where we could lead it into our battered and much traveled metal mug and sat down impatiently to watch it fill. The operation took fully ten minutes.

I said to Zaro, "You had passed this point. What made you turn round and find it?"

Zaro spoke quite seriously. "I think I must have smelt it. It was quite a strong impulse that made me turn my head."

The water tinkled musically into the mug until it was brimming. Carefully Zaro lifted it away and I noticed his hand was trembling a little so that some of the water spilled over. He faced Smith and with a bow, and, in imitation of the Mongolian etiquette of serving the senior first, handed him the water. The mug was passed round and each man took a gulp. No nectar of the gods could have tasted so wonderful. Again and again we filled the mug and drank. And then we left it, full and running over, under the life-giving spring so that any of us could drink whenever he felt like it.

The time was around the middle of the day. We agreed readily that we should stay close to the spring for another twenty-four hours, but up here on the hillside nothing lived—and we were very hungry. I volunteered to go down into the sandy valley to search for a snake and Zaro said he would come with me. We took the two forked sticks and set off, turning at intervals to look back and fix the position of the squatting group about the spring.

The descent took us over an hour and the heat shimmered off the sandy, boulder-strewn floor of the valley. Our hopes were immediately raised by seeing a snake about a yard long slither away at our approach and disappear under a rock but we foraged around well into the afternoon after that without seeing another living thing. Then we parted and went opposite ways and I had almost decided it was time to give up the quest when I heard Zaro let out a whoop of triumph. I ran to him and found him pinning down a Big Black which was thrashing about desperately in an effort to break free. I reversed my stick and battered it to death. I put my arm about Zaro's shoulders and congratulated him. He was always our Number One snake-catcher.

Zaro wore his capture like a trophy about his neck as we toiled back up the hillside. We were soaked with sweat and exhausted by the time we reached the spring and Kolemenos took over my usual job of skinning and preparing the snake for the fire. Paluchowicz had laid a fire from our few remaining sticks on which was placed the last piece of camel dung which Zaro had gathered at the oasis. There was not enough heat to cook the meat thoroughly but we were too hungry to be squeamish. We ate and we drank as the sun went down. Only Kolemenos slept well that night; for the rest of us it was too cold for comfort.

The next morning we were on our way again. This time there were no stomach cramps, which led us to believe that we owed at least some of the previous trouble to the muddy creek. We travelled down the long slope, across the hot valley and up the hillside facing us—a total of at least fifteen miles. From the top of the ridge we took fresh bearings. Directly ahead were some formidable heights, so we set our course over easier ground about ten degrees east of the line due south. Towards evening we were heartened by the discovery of the first vegetation we had seen since the oasis. It was a rough, spiky grass clinging hardily to dry rootholds in fissures between the rocks. We pulled up a clump, handed it round and closely examined it like men who had never seen grass before.

The wearing trek went on day after day. Our diet was still confined to an occasional snake—we lived on them altogether for upwards of three weeks from the time of our first sampling back in the desert. The nights set in with a chill which produced a frosty white rime on the stones of the upper hillsides. In vain we looked for signs of animal life, but there were birds: from time to time a pair of hovering hawks, some gossiping magpies and our old acquaintances the ravens. The wiry mountain grass grew more abundant with each passing day and its colour was greener. Then the country presented us with struggling low bushes and lone-growing dwarf trees, ideal fuel for the fires which we now started to light every night. The spectre of thirst receded as we found clear-running rivulets. It was rare now that we had to go waterless for longer than a day.

There came a day when we breasted the top of a long rise and looked unbelievingly down into a wide-spreading valley which showed far below the lush green of grazing grass. Still more exciting, there were, crawling like specks five miles or more distant from and below us, a flock of about a hundred sheep. We made the descent fast, slipping and sliding in our eagerness to get down. As we got nearer we heard the bleating and calling of the sheep. We had about a quarter of a mile to go to reach the flock when we saw the two dogs, long-coated liver-and-white collie types. They came racing round the flock to take up station between us and their charges.

Zaro called out to them, "Don't worry, we won't hurt them. Where's your master?" The dogs eyed him warily.

Kolemenos growled, "I only need to get near enough to a sheep for one swing of my old axe. . . ."

"Don't get impatient, Anastazi," I told him. "It is fairly obvious the shepherd has sent his dogs over here to intercept us. Let us swing away from the flock and see if they will lead us to their master."

We turned pointedly away. The dogs watched us closely for a couple of minutes. Then, apparently satisfied, they had headed us away from the sheep, ran off at great speed together towards the opposite slope of the valley. My eyes followed the line of their run ahead of them and then I shouted and pointed. A mile or more away rose a thin wisp of smoke.

"A fire at midday can only mean cooking," said Marchinkovas hopefully.

The fire was burning in the lee of a rocky outcrop against which had been built a one-man shelter of stones laid one above the other as in an old cairn. Seated there was an old man, his two dogs, tongues lolling, beside him. He spoke to his dogs as we neared him and they got up and raced off back across the valley to the flock. Steaming over the fire was a black iron cauldron. The American went to the front and approached bowing. The old man rose smiling and returned the bow and then went on to bow to each of us in turn.

He was white-bearded. The high cheek-bones in his broad, square face showed a skin which had been weathered to the color of old rosewood. He wore a warm goatskin cap with ear-flaps turned up over the crown in the fashion of the Mongols we had met in the north. His felt boots were well made and had stout leather soles. His unfastened three-quarter-length sheepskin coat was held to the body by a woven wool girdle and his trousers were bulkily padded, probably with lamb's-wool. He leaned his weight on a five-feet-tall wooden staff, the lower end of which was iron-spiked and the upper part terminating in a flattened "V" crutch formed by the bifurcation of the original branch. In a leather-bound wooden sheath he carried a bone-handled knife which I later observed was double-edged and of good workmanship. To greet us he got up from a rug of untreated sheepskin. There was no doubt of his friendliness and his pleasure at the arrival of unexpected visitors.

He talked eagerly and it was a minute or two before he realised we did not understand a word. I spoke in Russian and he regarded me blankly. It was a great pity because he must have been looking forward to conversation and the exchange of news. I think he was trying to tell us he had seen us a long way off and had prepared food against our arrival. He motioned us to sit near the fire and resumed the stirring of the pot which our coming had interrupted. I looked into the stone shelter and saw there was just room for one man to sleep. On the floor was a sleeping mat fashioned from bast.

As he wielded his big wooden spoon he made another attempt at conversation. He spoke slowly. It was no use. For a while there was silence. Mister Smith cleared his throat. He gestured with his arm around the group of us. "We," he said slowly in Russian, "go to Lhasa." The shepherd's eyes grew intelligent. "Lhasa, Lhasa," Smith repeated, and pointed south. From inside his jacket the old fellow pulled out a prayer-wheel which looked as if it had been with him for many years. The religious signs were painted on parchment, the edges of which were worn with use. He pointed to the sun and made circles, many of them, with his outstretched arm.

"He is trying to tell us how many days it will take us to reach Lhasa," I said.

"His arm's going round like a windmill," observed Zaro. "It must be a hell of a long way from here."

We bowed our acknowledgment of the information. From his pocket he produced a bag of salt—good quality stuff and almost white—and invited us to look into the cauldron as he sprinkled some in. We crowded round and saw a bubbling, greyish, thick gruel. He stirred again, brought out a spoonful, blew on it, smacked his lips, tasted and finally thrust out his tongue and ran it round his lips. He chuckled at us like a delighted schoolboy and his good humor was so infectious that we found ourselves laughing aloud in real enjoyment for the first time for months.

The next move by the old man had almost a ritualistic air. From his shack he produced an object wrapped in a linen bag. He looked at us, eyes twinkling, and I could not help thinking of a conjuror building up suspense for the trick which was to astound his audience. I think we all looked suitably impressed as he opened the bag and reached into it. Into the sunlight emerged a wooden bowl about five inches in diameter and three inches deep, beautifully turned, shining with care and use, of a rich walnut brown color. He blew on it, brushed it with his sleeve and handed it round. It was indeed a thing of which a man could be proud, the work of a craftsman. We handed it back with murmurs of appreciation.

Into the bowl he ladled a quantity of gruel and laid it on the skin rug. He disappeared into the shack and came out holding an unglazed earthenware jar, dark-brown and long-necked. It held about a gallon of ewe's milk, a little of which he added to the gruel in the bowl. He made no attempt at working out our seniority but handed the bowl and spoon to Zaro, who was seated nearest to him. Zaro ate a spoonful, smacked his lips and made to pass the bowl around, but the shepherd gently held his arm and indicated he was to finish the portion.

Zaro made short but evidently highly enjoyable work of it. "By God, that tastes wonderful," he exclaimed.

It was my turn next. The main ingredient seemed to be barley, but some kind of fat had been added. The sweet, fresh milk had cooled the mixture down a little and I fairly wolfed it down. I could feel the soothing warmth of it reaching my ill-treated stomach. I belched loudly, smacked my lips and handed back the bowl.

He saw to the needs of each of us in turn before he ate himself. To what was left in the cauldron he added several pints of milk and started stirring again, making enough extra to give us each another bowlful.

He took the cauldron off the fire to cool off, moving it with some difficulty because it had no handle, although I noticed there were the usual two holes in the rim. To our unspeakable joy he then produced tobacco from a skin pouch and handed us each enough for two or three cigarettes. Out came the pieces of hoarded newspaper. We lit up with glowing brands from the fire. We were happy in that moment and brimming over with gratitude towards a supremely generous host. And he, bless him, sat there cross-legged and basked in our smiles.

Away he went after about half-an-hour, refusing offers of help, to wash the cauldron and the precious bowl at a nearby spring. He came back, stoked up the fire and made us tea, Tibetan style, and this time we even faintly approved the taste of the rancid butter floating in globules on the surface.

I felt I wanted to do something for the old man. I said to Kolemenos, "Let's make him a handle for his cauldron out of one of the spare wire loops." Everybody thought it an excellent idea. It took us only about thirty minutes to break off a suitable length, shape it and fasten it. Our host was delighted.

We tried to think of some other service we could render. Someone suggested we forage for wood for the fire. We were away about an hour and came back with a pile of stuff, including a complete small tree which Kolemenos had hacked down with his axe. The shepherd had been waiting for our return. As we came in he was finishing sharpening his knife on a smooth piece of stone. He had his two dogs with him again. He made us sit down and, with his dogs at his heels, strode off.

He returned shortly dragging by the wool between its horns a young ram, the dogs circling him in quiet excitement as he came. In something like five minutes the ram was dead, butchered with practiced skill. He wanted no help from us on this job. He skinned and gutted the carcass with a speed which made my own abilities in this direction seem clumsy. The carcass finally was quartered. Salt was rubbed in one fore and one hind quarter, which were hung inside the stone hut. He threw the head and some other oddments to the dogs.

Half the sheep was roasted on wooden spits over the blazing fire that night and we ate again to repletion. We made signs that we would like to stay overnight and he seemed only too willing that we should. The six of us slept warm around the fire, while the shepherd lay the night inside his hut.

From somewhere he produced the next morning a batch of rough barley cakes—three each was our share. There was more tea and, to our astonishment, because we thought the limit of hospitality must already have been reached, the rest of the ram was roasted and shared out, and a little more tobacco distributed.

We left him in the early afternoon, after first restocking his fuel store. We did not know how to thank him for his inestimable kindness. Gently we patted his back and smiled at him. I think we managed to convey to him that he had made half-a-dozen most grateful friends.

At last we stood off a few feet from him and bowed low, keeping our eyes, according to custom, on his face. Gravely he returned the salute. We turned and walked away. When I turned he was sitting with his back to us, his dogs beside him. He did not look round.

from Heroic Heart: The Diary and Letters
of Kim Malthe-Bruun 1941-1945

edited by Vibeke Malthe-Bruun

Merchant seaman Kim Malthe-Bruun (1923-1945) joined the Danish resistance in September 1944. He was captured three months later, and executed on April 6, 1945; he was 21. Kim's mother, Vibeke Malthe-Bruun, published his letters and journal entries after the war; some passages are reminiscent of German poet Rainer Maria Rilke's prose. This excerpt opens with notes Kim wrote soon after he had been tortured by the Gestapo.

3 March 1945

Yesterday I was sitting at the table. I looked at my hands in amazement. They were trembling. I thought about it for a moment. There are some things which produce a purely physical reaction. Suddenly, as I was sitting here, I was possessed by the desire to draw something. I got up and started to sketch on the wall. I was fascinated and became more and more absorbed. Under my hand suddenly appeared a farmer, standing by a barbed-wire fence. I sat down, got up and made some changes, sat down again and felt much better. This was much better than anything I'd ever done before. All day I worked on it. There were so many things which I couldn't make come out the way I wanted them to. I studied it, stretched my imagination to the utmost and was suddenly completely exhausted. I erased all of it and since then even the idea of drawing makes me sick.

I've been thinking about this strange experience a good deal. Right afterwards I had such a wonderful feeling of relief, a sense of having won a victory and such intense happiness that I felt quite numb. It seemed as if body and soul became separated, one in a wild and soaring freedom beyond the reach of the world, and the other doubled up in a horrible cramp which held it to the earth. I suddenly realized how terrifically strong I am (but perhaps I only tried to talk myself into this). When the body and soul rejoined forces, it was as if all the joys of the world were right there for me. But it was as with so many stimulants; when the effect wore off the reaction set in. I saw that my hands were shaking, something had given inside. It was as if there had been a short circuit in the roots of my heart which drained it of all strength. I was like a man hungry for pleasure and consumed by desire. But still I was calm and in better spirits than ever before.

Although I feel no fear, my heart beats faster every time someone stops outside my door. It's a physical reaction although it's caused by a sensory perception.

Right afterwards I realized that now I understood something else about Jesus. It's the period of waiting that is the real test. I'm sure that to have a few nails driven through one's hands and to die on a cross is only a physical ordeal; the spirit is in a state of elation which can't be compared with anything else. But the period of waiting in the garden causes red blood to flow.

Strange, but I didn't feel any resentment or hatred at all. Something happened to my body, which is only the body of an adolescent, and it reacted as such, but my mind was elsewhere. It was aware of the small creatures who were busying themselves with my body, but it was in a world of its own and too engrossed to pay much attention to them.

I've learned something by being alone. It is as if I'd reached rock bottom in myself, which usually can't be seen for all the layers of egotism, conceit, love, and all the ups and downs of daily life. It is this which makes me feel as if I'd had a short circuit within me. When I'm with other people, their interests, their conversation, act as a balm, covering the rock bottom in myself with a warm compress. When I'm alone, it is as if layers of skin were being scraped away. Your mind is not at ease, you can't concentrate on reading, the spirit as well as the body must keep on pacing up and down. I suddenly understood what insanity must be, but I knew that this was like everything else which has happened to me, and in a couple of days I'll be myself again.

Sometimes a beautiful scene flashes before my eyes, but none of you are in it. I see myself riding on horseback out in the fields. But I must have children around me, not adults. I've been longing for the sea, but it has to be calm, because I couldn't stand being seasick at the moment. It was funny seeing that horse; it brought my whole childhood back again.

21 March 1945

My dearest little love,

On Wednesday, February 21st, at midnight I was sent to Police Headquarters for questioning, and on Wednesday, the 28th, I was sent back to Vestre. On Thursday I was placed in solitary confinement and forbidden to write letters. I was only allowed to go to the toilet morning and night with a guard when there was no one in the corridors. My food was brought by the soldiers. I was happy to be alone in my cell. I took off all my clothes and had a good wash and it gave me such a sense of freedom. That night I slept in a bed with sheets and a mattress.

I did some thinking and meditating, and the days passed very pleasantly. I had opened my window, and the sun was shining. I could smell spring in the air, the grass shooting out of the ground, the moist earth. I could hear the birds singing, and such a big streak of sunshine came in through the bars that I could sit on the bench and let it warm my face.

On Monday, March 5, I was transferred to Police Headquarters and put in Detention. On Wednesday they allowed me to receive my blanket.

Have been in the following cells: December 19, 1944 to February 2, 1945, in 252; from the same day at 8 o'clock, in 585 (dark cell); February 7 to 11, Froeslev. From February 12 to March 1 occupied the following cells in Vestre: 286, 284, 282, 276, 270. From March 1 to 5 in 586. Was then transferred to Police Headquarters: March 5 to 12, cell 50, March 12 to —? cell 37.

Twice I've been waiting in the cells of the Shell Building to be questioned so I think that I've been living a rather varied cell life. The cell I had when I sat in Detention was on the small side—6 feet, 3 inches by

4 feet—with a small bench and a table. I walked up and down—one and a half paces in each direction; twenty-four hours and all alike, only broken by the opening of the door when two slices of rye bread were handed to me. This was a real event. In the toilet they allowed me to wash, and it was wonderful. Then I paced up and down again, very much surprised that I didn't suffer. I thought of the days spent in solitary confinement and how rewarding they had been. I had the sun, the blue sky, and once in a while a little white cloud, and if I really made an effort I could see a plowed field, grass, people, and lots of other fascinating things. I could smell the earth and feel the coming of spring. It made me choke up inside and I felt very happy. All this had such a sound and soothing effect on my mind.

They say that the Shell Building was bombed yesterday and this upset me very much. Your school is so close by. Something could have happened to you, you might even have been killed, and here I sit writing to you not knowing if you're alive or if you will ever read this. How will I be able to find out how you are! But there are so many possibilities—perhaps you weren't even there yesterday.

We have been talking about what is really meant by art. I know what it means to me, but how could I possibly put it into words. Isn't an artist a person who can produce riches from the depths of himself and put them before people so that their lives will in turn be enriched by his art? But the minds of people must be prepared and fertilized in order to be able to accept it. One has to be a part of this era, be inspired by it, and in turn freely give of oneself to it. Only then can the untapped sources of man be reached—the forces that constitute a true artist.

Jesus lives among us, but he is much older and much more mature than the Jesus who lived at the time of the Apostles. He is like every other human being who has lived and grown spiritually, and I'm deeply convinced that he went through what every artist does—in fact, every human being. When I meet an old man, I can see in him the truth around which his life was formed, and which was awakened with his birth.

Jesus has grown older, and many people ask themselves if he ever really lived and if he wasn't simply the culmination of the Hebrew doctrine. I think I know what they mean but can't help asking myself, "This old man, has he ever been a child?"

I've caught lice, but I hope that I've gotten rid of them again. I had an awful lot of bites, and the itching almost drove me mad. Today I examined my clothes, which haven't been off my back for three weeks since I sleep on the floor with only a blanket over me. There were masses of eggs and lice. But now I've washed myself and my clothes so I hope this is the end of it.

I'm kept going by one thought: that nothing is impossible no matter how black things look at the moment. There are millions of possibilities which can't be foreseen, and no situation exists which can't be completely changed in a moment.

I'm lying on a mattress on the floor and letting the sun shine on my face. There are five of us in the cell. One of them is pacing up and down. Every time he comes toward me, his shadow falls on my face and again when he walks back. It is as if a switch was turned on and off inside me at regular intervals; like a little current of irritation which goes through me but completely vanishes when the sun touches my face again.

Today is Sunday and the weather is still perfect. How I would love to go for a walk in the woods with you, my darling! The sun has been shining since early morning and I've been lying here by the window watching the rays of light come through the blackout curtain and spreading out more and more. The air full of spring and morning came streaming down to me. A migration of birds flew over the rooftops and they must have been huge ones to judge by the flapping of their wings. This sound made something stir in me, and all of a sudden I felt so lighthearted. It was as if this migration held out a special promise for me, like spring itself, which is always full of promise of something new and fascinating for each of us. I didn't feel at all the way tame ducks do when their free brothers pass by up in the sky. My existence is much too quiet and peaceful for me to envy them, but I do know that the moment when I stand under a blue sky again my happiness will be without bounds.

As I was lying here happy that spring is here and that you and I are alive (I know now that you're safe and that nothing has happened to you), I was thinking about what this spring might have in store for us—certainly things far different from what we had imagined. Still, it may possibly be one of the happiest of our lives.

27 March 1945

I've been smoking some, and have noticed that it has a soothing effect when the nerves are on edge, but that the reaction is exactly the opposite when I'm calm. I don't think that I would ever smoke when I'm free. It makes me jittery, and seems to leave the mind empty. It is as if tobacco takes something out of you and leaves you feeling like a vacuum. I'm annoyed in the same way I am when I feel that I'm not making any progress.

I've often thought of the speech that Socrates made in his own defense, and also of the last time I was brought in for questioning. Socrates says in his introduction that he knows in advance what the outcome will be and that he will not be able, during the few hours at his disposal, to overcome the resentment they feel against him, a resentment which has worked into them like so many small, fine needle pricks during the years, so that it is now part of them. He knows that it would take a long time to erase an image and create a new one. I felt the same way. For many years the people I had to deal with had been taught to see things in a certain light and their minds were set against me. My hands were tied in every way so my only means of expressing myself was by the answers I had to give to the questions they asked. I know what Socrates must have gone through and I understand that a man as wise as he couldn't have acted in any other way.

Jesus has also been in my mind a lot of late. I can understand his boundless love for all humanity, and especially for those who put the nails through his hands. The moment he left Gethsemane he rose above every human passion. It was only during the period of waiting that he felt fear, the way Kaj Munk must have felt before he was taken out to the car, and before he came in contact with those who were to be his executioners. The moment he drove off with them he must have felt above it all, and this must have given him both dignity and strength.

The same with Jesus. At the moment when Judas kissed him on the cheek he had certainly regained all his peace of mind and his feeling of being above it all. Then he was swept up by an enormous wave which finally carried him to his death. It so filled his mind that he didn't have an instant's fear or hesitation. When he met his executioners they put him physically out of the material life. He felt so liberated, so uplifted, that he no longer saw them with the eyes of a human being, but with infinite wisdom and compassion, which creates understanding of the level on which the others find themselves.

The cleansing of the spirit makes you see the world from a new level way above what is known as pain or fear. You are already so far above the world and so immobile up there that the instinctive hatred which comes as a result of fear disappears. Those who are close to us in our lives can't reach us at a moment like this. They remain in the background, and it is only in passing that you send them a loving thought, whereas all that has been in the background of your life—your most sacred and unattainable ideals—suddenly grow into the main substance of the soul.

In a ray of light, Jesus saw for the last time his whole life pass before him. Fear comes from within, and if someone tries to produce a feeling of fear in another human being, he only succeeds in freeing him from all fear and causing him to rise to a plane where he cannot be reached.

It's Easter, and I've received a package from Nis [sic] today—it was wonderful.

Yesterday I wrote that in a moment like this you rise to a level where those who are near and dear only receive a loving thought in passing while your innermost thoughts come to the foreground and fill your being. Please don't misunderstand me, because this isn't exactly true either, but keep it in mind as you read the rest of this, and afterwards try to merge these two thoughts into one. This will perhaps bring us a little closer to the real truth.

At a moment like this, you're a big, trembling animal, alive and absolutely pure. There isn't a shadow anywhere, not a drop of hatred or fury, because these feelings couldn't germinate and grow in such an atmosphere of purity and simplicity. At that moment there isn't the slightest restraint or obstacle in your mind, and that is probably why the feeling of purity and freedom fills your being. It is as if your heart opened and a marvelous little green bud began to grow.

The moment fills you with a feeling of peace and devotion and the arch above your head seems very high. From where you are the people around you appear in an entirely different light. Do you think that a father in church, seeing his beloved holding their first-born child over the baptismal, notices the people around him? Don't you think that his heart is so overflowing with tenderness and love that he feels only affection for everything around him?

When I went up for questioning, or perhaps when I was already there, I said to myself all of a sudden, "If you could only come out in the woods with me as woodcutters, away from everything, even if only for a short time, a change would come about in you—perhaps not a permanent change because you are made of different material—but so that you would see and feel, for a little while at least, how profound life is and how rich is the world around you which you refuse to understand. This also flashed through my mind: "Have these men ever seen the reflection of the moon in a little pond in the forest, or have they ever seen the wind playing in the grass on the dunes before it drifts out over the edge and down toward the sea?"

Last night I had a long discussion with my cellmates and for the first time I felt that I would have liked to write something for the theatre, and I also know what it would have been. I could see the dark cell where the bars cast their black shadows on the wall bathed in moonlight. Four men are stretched out on the floor talking, each one with his ideals and ideas, each one with his own convictions, each with a different point of view. Suddenly I realized how much is still needed before we can consider ourselves a free people. Perhaps we'll be liberated, but will we be free? A country where every man has his personal opinion and has the courage to be responsible for it before God and man; where man isn't only an echo of the opinions and the reflection of his environment?

Just think how different Denmark could have been today.

VESTRE PRISON
GERMAN SECTION, CELL 411
4 April 1945

My own little darling,

Today I was taken before the military tribunal and condemned to death. What a terrible blow this is for a little girl of twenty! I've been given permission to write this farewell letter, but what shall I write? How shall I formulate my swan song? Time is short and there is so much to say.

What is the final and most precious thing I can give you? What do I possess that I can leave you as a parting gift so that in spite of your loss you will smile and go on living and developing?

We sailed on a stormy sea, we met in the trusting way of playing children and we loved each other. We still love each other and always will, but one day a storm separated us. I went aground while you were washed up on shore, and you are going to continue living in a new world. I don't expect you to forget me. Why should you forget something so beautiful as that which existed between us? But you mustn't become a slave to this memory. You must keep on going with the same easy and graceful approach to life as before and twice as happy because on your way Life gave you one of its greatest gifts. Free yourself—let this greatest of joys be everything to you, let it shine brighter and clearer than anything else, but let it be only one of your most treasured memories. Don't let it blind you and keep you from seeing all the wonderful things life has in store for you. Don't be unhappy, my dearest one. You must mature and grow rich in inner resources. Do you understand this, my beloved?

You will live on and you will have other beautiful adventures, but promise me—this you owe to everything I have lived for—that never will the thought of me come between you and Life. Remember, I will continue to live in your heart, but the part of me which remains there should be sound and natural and mustn't take up too much room. Gradually as bigger and more important things appear, I shall glide into the background and be a tiny speck of the soil out of which your happiness and your development will keep on growing.

Now you are heartbroken and this is what is known as sorrow, but Hanne, look beyond this. All of us are going to die and it isn't for us to judge whether my going a little earlier is good or bad.

I keep on thinking about Socrates. Read him and you will find Plato expressing what I feel at this moment. My love for you is without bounds, but not more so now than before. It's not a love which causes me pain. This is the way it is, and I want you to understand it. There is something inside me alive and growing—an inspiration, a love—call it what you like; something which I still haven't been able to define. Now I'm going to die and I still don't know if I have started a little flame in another being, a flame which will survive me. But still, my mind is at rest because I've seen the richness and abundance of nature. No one takes notice if a few seeds are trampled under and die. When I see all the riches that still live on, why should I despair?

Lift up your head, my most precious love, and look! The sea is still blue, the sea which I loved and which has enveloped us both. Now you will live for the two of us. I am gone and what remains is not a memory which will make you into a woman like S., but mold you into a woman living and warm, mature and happy. This does not mean that you are to try to rise above sorrow, because then you will become rigid and assume a saintly attitude with regard to your faith in me and in yourself, and you will lose what I most loved in you—that you are first and last and always a woman.

Remember—and I swear this is true—that all sorrow gradually turns into happiness. But few are those who admit it when the time comes. They cloak themselves in mourning; habit makes them think that it is sorrow, and so they continue to cloak themselves in it. The truth is that after suffering comes maturity and after this maturity the fruits are gathered.

You see, Hanne, one day you will meet the man who will be your husband. The thought of me will flash through you, and you will perhaps deep down have a vague, uneasy feeling that you are betraying me or something in you which is pure and sacred. Lift up your head once more, Hanne, look straight into my eyes which are smiling at you and you will understand that the only way to betray me is by not completely following your natural instincts. When you see him, let your heart go out to meet him—not to drown your sorrow but because you truly love him. You will be very, very happy because you now have a base on which feelings still unknown to you will nurture.

Greet Nitte for me. I've thought of writing her but don't know if I'll have the time. I seem to feel as if I could do more for you because all that is life to me is now concentrated on you. I would like to breathe into you all the life that is in me, so that it can go on and as little as possible of it go to waste. This is the way I was made.

Yours, but not for always.

VESTRE PRISON
GERMAN SECTION, CELL: 411
4 April 1945

Dearest Mother,

Today I went before the military tribunal together with Joergen, Niels and Ludwig. We were condemned to die. I know that you're strong and that you will be able to take this. But listen to me, Mother. It isn't enough that you are able to take it. You must also understand it. I'm not of importance and will soon be forgotten, but the ideas, the life, the inspiration which filled me will live on. You will find them everywhere—in the new green of spring, in people you will meet on your way, in a loving smile. Perhaps you will also find what was of value to me, you will love it and you won't forget me. I would have liked to grow and mature, but I will still live in your hearts and you will live on because you know that I am in front of you on the road and not behind, as you had perhaps thought at first. You know what has always been my greatest wish and what I thought I would become. Mother dear, come with me on my journey. Don't stop at the last stage of my life, but instead stop at some of the preceding ones and you may find something which will be of value to the girl I love and to you, Mother.

I have followed a certain path and I don't regret it. I've never betrayed what is in my heart, and now I seem to see the unbroken line which has run through my life. I'm not old, I ought not to die, and still, it seems so simple and natural to me. It's only the brutal way which at first terrifies us. I have so little time left; I don't quite know how to explain it, but my mind is completely at peace. I have always wanted to be like Socrates, but although I have no one to talk to as he had, I feel the same tranquility of spirit and very much want you, Hanne and Nitte to understand this. Remember me to Nitte; I love her dearly and meant every word I ever wrote.

How strange it seems to be writing this testament! Each word will stand; it can never be amended, never revoked, never changed. I'm thinking of so many things. Joergen is sitting here in front of me writing a letter to his daughter for her Confirmation—a document for life. We have lived together as friends and now we're going to die together. We have shared the same cell with Paul and we've had many differences but he knows me well by now and what I have to contribute.

Finally there are the children who have recently come to mean so much to me. I had so been looking forward to seeing them and being with them again. Just to think of them makes me happy and I hope they will grow up to be men who will be able to get more out of life than what lies on the surface. I hope that their character will develop freely and never be subjected to prejudice.

Give them my love, my godson and his brother.

I see what the situation in our country is leading up to and I know that Grandfather is right. But remember all of you that the aim shouldn't be to return to the period before the war, but that it is up to you, young and old, to create a broad, human ideal which everyone can recognize. This is the thing that our country needs; something that even a simple peasant boy can look up to and be happy in the thought that he is working and fighting for.

Then, finally, there is my Hanne. Make her see that the pilot stars are still shining and that I was only a beacon on her route. Help her to keep going. She can now become very happy.

In haste—your oldest and only son.

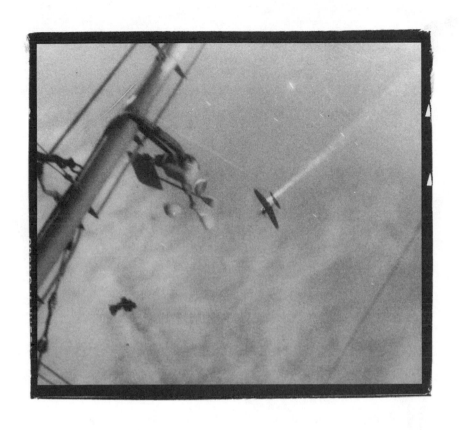

from Pacific War Diary 1942–1945
by James J. Fahey

James J. Fahey (1918–1991), a truck driver from Waltham, Massachusetts, served in the Pacific as a seaman, first class on the light cruiser USS Montpelier. *His diary entries from October 1942 through December 1945 offer firsthand impressions of life as a bluejacket. Fahey's observations are simple, unadorned and at times shocking. Here he returns to the war after two months' leave in "the good old U.S.A." Ahead lie the Philippines and one of the war's strangest horrors: the kamikaze.*

Wednesday, October 25, 1944: We left Mare Island, Calif. at 9:30 a.m. this morning, for the Pacific war. We pulled in here Aug. 22, 1944, after being out there 20 months. The two months we spent in the States really flew, it seems like we just returned and here we are on our way back again to take on the Japs again. This will be our last look at the U.S.A. until the war is over. Many of the men's wives and girl friends were at the pier to kiss them goodbye. We passed Alcatraz prison and the Golden Gate before we got out to sea. Our first stop will be Pearl Harbor.

Tuesday, October 31, 1944: This afternoon at 4:30 p.m. we pulled into Pearl Harbor, it took us 6 days to get here from Mare Island, Calif. I will try to cover what happened on the way here from the States. The weather was very cold and the sea was very rough until we were about one day from Pearl Harbor. Quite a few men got seasick, I did not. We ate our meals on the deck because the sea was too rough to set the benches and tables; they would have crashed into the bulkheads. We had to wear plenty of clothing on watch to keep warm. The other ships with us would almost go out of sight in the heavy big seas because the waters were so rough. The light cruiser *Astoria* and the heavy cruiser *Baltimore* also had left with us along with the other warships.

The *Baltimore* was the ship that carried President Roosevelt to the Aleutians and Pearl Harbor. We fired all guns on the way to Pearl Harbor. Also, the same day we pulled into Pearl Harbor, B–26 Bombers towed sleeves for us to shoot at. Our ship knocked down 12 sleeves without a strain. Our shooting was very good even if I do say so. When we pulled into Pearl Harbor we tied up to a buoy. The weather was warm and it felt good to go around in your shirtsleeves. Our mail went off the ship and movies were held topside the first night we got there.

Tuesday, November 7, 1944: This is what happened during our stay at Pearl Harbor. I got a special pass to visit my brother Joe on Ford Island. He censors mail 6 days a week. He has 1 day off, and no watches to stand. His hours are 8 a.m. to 4 p.m. He also showed me where he was on Dec. 7, 1941, when the Japs attacked Pearl Harbor. He came very close to being hit by Jap machine guns and bombs. You could still see the spot where the Japs hit. He also showed me around Honolulu and we took in a pro football game, we had a nice time. The climate here is very good, you can't beat it. Joe will have 9 years in the Navy, March 1945. He is going to put in 20 years and then retire, he will be 42 then. The people here are very small, the girls are good-looking. The war news for the last week of October said that our Navy knocked the Jap Navy out and our troops landed in the Central Philippines on Leyte. The Jap fleet lost many warships, all kinds. They called it the greatest sea battle in history, the Japs lost 64 warships. We will be out there soon. Today is election day, I think Roosevelt will get elected again. Everyone here thinks he will get in by a big margin. We left Pearl Harbor this morning at 8 a.m. for a couple of days of gunnery.

Wednesday, November 8, 1944: Yesterday we fired all day at targets on the beach and sleeves towed by planes, we also fired all night until 10 p.m. We were at General Quarters all day and night. Capt. Hoffman said whenever a ship gets new guns they have to be tested to see if they pass all the tests. Our 5 and 6 inch guns proved to be very good. We fired at targets on the beach that we could not see, spotters on the beach directed our fire. We also opened up on the beach with our machine guns. The Capt. said we might leave here for good in a couple of days. The Press News this morning said that Pres. Roosevelt is ahead by 2 million votes. The radio said the Japs subs sank 2 cargo ships between the States and Hawaii, they were 2 days behind us without escorts. Someone said they were supposed to meet us. Jap subs could have hit us easy at night because we did not have any escort. From now on though all ships will have destroyers or destroyer escorts with them. It was a little cloudy and we got some rain, but it turned out to be a warm day.

We also fired at radio-controlled planes, called drones, we will fire all day and night again.

At night we fired all guns at a sled towed by another ship. We fired by radar. We also fired by searchlight, the lights are connected with the radar and it gets on the target right away. We may go in tomorrow.

Thursday, November 9, 1944: This morning we finished our gunnery and pulled into Pearl Harbor at 9 a.m. I could not leave the ship because we had to carry ammunition all day and night until 4 a.m. the next morning, Friday. We got a lot of armor-piercing shell on, boy, are they heavy, about 135 lbs. each.

Friday, November 10, 1944: We worked so hard on ammunition that they let us sleep until 8:30 a.m. this morning. They never let us do that before. We left Pearl Harbor this morning, and on the way out, a light cruiser and 2 destroyers came in. They were all banged up from the sea battle Oct. 23, 1944, it will take some time to repair them. It looked like they were hit by shells from warships and strafing planes, they were also hit by torpedoes. The Bridge on one of the ships was blown off. They must have had a lot of casualties. In this sea battle the Jap and American warships slugged it out with each other. It took place in the dark and what a slugfest. When a battleship opens up on you it does not take long to put you to the bottom of the sea. Just as we got outside the nets Capt. Hoffman spoke and told us where we are going. He said that we are going to an island we took over last Sept. called Ulithi, it is about 125 miles N.E. of Yap and about 1,000 miles from Leyte in the Philippines where our troops invaded about 2 weeks ago. Yap is still held by the Japs. We expect to get there in 10 days. I suppose we will go to the Philippines from there. He said that we would have gunnery every day on the way to Ulithi. We also have the battleship *New Mexico* with us and 5 destroyers.

This morning we had drills against torpedo boats. A smoke screen was put up and the boats came at us from all directions at high speed. It was quite a show, they can really maneuver in the water. At a distance they are very hard to see and if it was getting dark, they would be very hard to hit. They can really take care of themselves. We also fired at sleeves towed by a B-26 bomber. I think the war will be over in 1945. On this Dec. 7, they should have a big raid on Japan. I hope the fleet is on it.

Saturday, November 11, 1944: Got off watch at 4 a.m. this morning, all hands up for General Quarters at 5:45 a.m., breakfast at 7 a.m. We did not do much today. We got the results of the Army–Notre Dame game. Army won 59 to 0, Army has not lost a game all season, they have the best team in the country. Everyone at Notre Dame must be in the service. We fired at a sleeve this afternoon. It was towed by our own seaplane S.O.C.

Sunday, November 12, 1944: Today we had church services in the mess hall. It was a nice sunny day, the sea was calm. We had our big meal at night. We set the clock back 1 hour at 5 p.m. They played music over the loudspeaker at 5 p.m. I hit the sack at 8 p.m.

Monday, November 13, 1944: We went to General Quarters at 5:30 p.m. It was pretty warm in the sack last night. I think I will sleep topside from now on. Today was the hottest day so far, like old times. The 5th div., that's us, got a lot of new cleaning stations. We are not going very fast, about 15 knots.

Ulithi is about 3400 miles from Pearl Harbor and 400 miles from Palau.

Tuesday, November 14, 1944: We passed the 180 meridan late tonight and we also gained a day this morning. It was Wed. instead of Tues. The new Executive Officer is not liked by the crew, he is too regulation for wartime. Before long everyone on board will be on report. You cannot put your hat on when topside, you have to do it below. He made a lot of new changes, if you lean on the life line you get extra duty. He thinks this is a peacetime Navy where you have liberty nearly every night. We are at war but he does not realize it. Men like him disorganize a ship and are responsible for the crew to go over the hill. In peacetime he would have an excuse but not now. When it comes to a little wisdom and everyday common sense, he is a complete failure. Pulling the stuff he pulls, no wonder so many men went over the hill and missed the ship. They call our ship "the floating jail," because nearly every day fellows have to go before him and he passes out the sentence. "The U.S.S. Concentration ship" is another name. Times have changed since the good old days in the Solomons. I don't think that we are running out of good officers. It is a good thing that we are not in the States because half the crew would go over the hill. I hope he gets on to himself but then again maybe he is a sick man, who knows?

Wednesday, November 15, 1944: No news, yesterday we fueled 2 destroyers, we also gave them food and ice cream. It was very hot today. It is too hot to sleep below.

Thursday, November 16, 1944: Hit the sack at 4 a.m. and got up at 5:30 a.m. We broke out the paravanes today and had practice clearing mines. They are put over the side of the ship and cut any mines we come in contact with. It looks like a big cigar, it has wings on it, it lays in the water. They also showed movies in the mess hall on 20 and 40 mm. machine guns today.

Friday, November 17, 1944: The Capt. spoke this evening and said we would pull into Ulithi early Tues. morning. He also said the Japs are sending suicide planes against our ships in larger numbers now, they crash their planes against our ships, the pilot stays in the plane also. The Japs did this before but on a small scale. A suicide plane with its bombs can do a lot of damage when it hits a ship, you have to destroy it before it reaches you. When we reach Ulithi we will receive more orders, telling us where to go. About 8 p.m. we were about 25 miles below the Marshalls, you could see a lot of lights coming from that direction. It must be from the movies topside. The Capt. said that Ulithi is just like the Marshalls. A big hole in the center full of water and coral and sand beaches all around it. There are some openings for ships to enter. It is a natural anchorage for ships. The land around it does not rise very high. At one time it was an island but a volcano came up through the center of it and now it is full of water. It was dark on watch today. It also rained very hard and the wind was very strong. I stand my watch on a different mount now, everyone has been changed around. This mount is smaller. There are so many men on report that they have to use the O.D.'s shack on the quarterdeck for another brig, the regular brig is full. The regular brig is nothing but a dark hole down in the bottom of the ship, it is very hot down there and you have very little room to move, the men look all washed out when they come out, you get bread and water and one full meal. You would think the men killed someone. If the Executive Officer has his way the crew would spend most of their time in the brig for the least thing. I got paid today, sent the rent money home, when we hit Ulithi it will go off. I had a working party in hangar deck, it was like an oven down there, we were covered with dirt and sweat when we finished. Hit the sack at 8:15 p.m.

Saturday, November 18, 1944: I got up at 4:30 a.m. had breakfast at 7:15 a.m. and had 8 to 12 noon watch. We had ham for dinner today. It did not rain today for a change, also a little cooler. One of the men was put on report because they found his hat on the deck, what a joke. We started water hours again this week. The water is on for 1 hour and off 4 or 5 hours. It is a nuisance. We have drinking water at all times. We sleep topside, too hot below, also put the clock back one hour at 5 p.m.

Sunday, November 19, 1944: Church services were held in the mess hall today. I had the church working party. Our new Chaplain is a Catholic Priest. All the other Chaplains we had were Protestant ministers. They were very friendly and everyone liked them very much. The new Chaplain's name is Fr. Wilson. The sea was very calm today, just like a pond. We were about an hour's airplane drive from Truk this afternoon. It is the Gibraltar of the Pacific. No white man has been on it in over 30 years. That would have been a very hard place to invade and capture. It was a good thing we bypassed it, it would have been a long, bloody campaign. Today is the 8th day since we left Pearl Harbor, 2 more days to go and we reach Ulithi. It was very hot today, also very hot in the mess hall, our shirts were soaking wet. You do not enjoy your meals, you want to get topside as soon as possible. It is getting like old times again, and we are also supposed to eat salt pills every day. I take them every day. We get a lot of radio programs from Japan, they tell an awful lot of lies to their people. They said that they sunk 11 aircraft carriers, 8 battleships and many other warships, 55 in all. This was to have taken place in the Philippine campaign. The Japs are the ones who took the big losses not us. Our forces are doing a job on them in the Philippines. In the European war they expect to drop 100,000 tons of bombs on Germany. In the first 15 days they dropped 50,000 tons of bombs. I bet we hit Japan on Dec. 7, from Tinian with our Big B-29's. It is a beautiful evening, just like a summer night back home. Everyone is topside sitting all over the ship. I will sleep topside and then go on watch, got midnight to 4 a.m. Hank Lawrence had his tonsils taken out yesterday. Last year this time this stretch of water was known as "no man's sea." It was Jap territory and it was very dangerous to send any ships here. But today it belongs to us. It is getting dark now as I sit topside and write. The time is 6:30 p.m. in the evening.

Monday, November 20, 1944: I hit the sack at 4 a.m. This morning all hands up at 5 a.m. for General Quarters. Today is our 9th day at sea. We should reach Ulithi tomorrow. There is a convoy behind us and it was attacked by Jap planes this afternoon. The planes must have come from Truk. This morning at 9 a.m. our destroyers picked up 3 Jap subs. The Japs sent word that 2 American battleships were on their way to the Jap-held island of Yap. The Japs thought we were battleships because we are very long, we are as long as the battleship *New Mexico*. The Japs are always watching us and we don't see them. The Japs must have thought that we were going to bombard their island of Yap, it is near Ulithi. I was told by a good friend of mine many months ago that we had broken the Jap code, but this was during the Solomons campaign. I did not pay much attention to him at the time. He knew what he was talking about after all. It is a warm, sunny day. Someone said Jap subs sank one of our ships the other day. They were quite a few miles ahead of us. There are a lot of Jap subs in these waters, because they know we have to use these waters to get to our destination. We turned the clock back at 5 p.m. this evening. I slept on the boat deck tonight, it was too hot to sleep below. Modock and I slept on some boxes of potatoes, they have an awful lot of them stored on the boat deck with a canvas over them. We lay down at 6:30 p.m. and chewed the fat for about an hour and then we fell asleep. It was a beautiful night, the moon was out for a while. Most of the nights this month had been very dark.

Tuesday, November 21, 1944: I got up at 3:15 a.m. to go on watch. At 5 a.m. this morning one of our planes was dropping flares. They said a Jap sub had surfaced. Today is the 10th day since we left Pearl Harbor, it is a 3400-mile trip.

At 9 a.m. this morning we pulled into Ulithi. It is 125 miles northeast of Yap, a Jap-held island. Ulithi looks like the Marshalls. When we pulled in we went alongside a tanker. It took about 3 hours to get the fuel. There are many ships here, all types, also numerous carriers. The big, powerful force of warships that we have here could do an awful lot of damage on the Japs. I was talking to one of the men on the tanker and he told me that a Jap sub sunk one of our tankers right in here in Ulithi. He said 4 Jap subs have been sunk here so far. They do not know how they got in here. Maybe followed our ships in. The Japs held Ulithi for a long time, they could have been hiding in here when we took over. Maybe they have a secret way of getting in. A couple of the Jap subs were small, they were manned by 8 men crews. Some of the Japs were picked up on the beach, the others killed themselves.

Our destroyers went all over the place dropping depth charges just in case more Jap subs were hiding here. They think that Jap subs are still hiding out in here. This is a very large place and covers quite a few miles. It is like one big circle surrounded by coral and sand beaches with coconut trees. The land does not rise very high. They think the reason the Jap sub sank the tanker instead of hitting a battleship or carrier was because they figured that would throw us off guard long enough for the Jap subs to sneak in and hit the battleships and carriers, but we were not distracted or fooled by their tricks. One sub tried to sneak out behind a net tender, but our destroyers sank it.

About 150 men were lost on the tanker the Japs sunk here, it was a mass of flames. He said quite a few of our damaged ships from the Philippine sea battle came in here. The light cruiser *Birmingham* had 190 men killed when it pulled alongside the carrier *Princeton* to take aboard the men, before it went down. The high octane gas and bombs went up and did quite a job on the *Birmingham*. The water is very calm here, there is also a good breeze. It is very hot in the ship. The Dr. inspected all living spaces today. We sent a working party to an LST for mail, and we got 3 bags of airmail. The LST is used as a post office. It was a beautiful evening to sleep topside, the air was dry. Many of the fellows did not want to sleep below because Jap subs might be hiding here. They said some of the Jap subs stay right under our ships. It gives you a funny feeling to be in a big lagoon surrounded by every kind of warship in the books and never knowing when one of them will be blown up by a Jap sub. The Jap subs are trapped in here, and in time they will be sunk like a bunch of drowned rats. I bet the men on the Jap subs must be talking to themselves when they see all these big, juicy targets and yet they cannot do anything about it. This is a situation submarine men always dream about, but never come across. I wonder what an American submarine would do in this sort of a situation.

Wednesday, November 22, 1944: The sun was shining at 5:30 a.m. this morning. We got ammunition and mail today. A Jap sub was sunk outside the net this morning. No news today, still at Ulithi.

Thursday, November 23, 1944: We left Ulithi at 1 p.m. this afternoon. Capt. Hoffman spoke to the crew. He said that we are on our way to Leyte, in the Philippines. Our troops invaded that big island Oct. 20, 1944. We expected to get there Sat. morning Nov. 25th. Our ship will be flagship of a task force of warships again, and we will join the Seventh Fleet. We still have Admiral Robert W. Hayler aboard, he was with us when we were out here before. The Seventh Fleet is the same fleet that defeated the Jap Fleet last Oct. at Surigao Strait in the central Philippines. The Japs lost battleships and every kind of a warship in this engagement. This was the greatest sea battle of all time. Admiral Oldendorf crossed the T on the Japs during this action, this is something that happens once in a lifetime. The Japs lost many ships and plenty were damaged.

Friday, November 24, 1944: The sea was calm and the air a little cooler today. About 6 p.m. tonight we were about 270 miles from Leyte Gulf. We had sunset General Quarters. I wrote some Christmas cards today.

Saturday, November 25, 1944: We pulled into Leyte Gulf in the Philippines at noon, this is a very big place, they say it is 60 miles long and 30 miles wide. We also passed the spot where our Navy and the Jap navy slugged it out at 3 a.m. in the morning. We will now be under the Supreme Command of General MacArthur. Our job is to patrol near the spot of the sea battle and destroy any Jap warships that try to attack our merchant ships and our troops on Leyte. Leyte is about in the center of the Philippines.

They say that there are over 7000 islands in the Philippines. Capt. Hoffman said the Japs have a force of 400 PT boats in these waters, they also have many airfields and they hit this place every day. We had sunset General Quarters, as usual the Jap air force came out and attacked the beach at Leyte, also our merchant ships. None of them attacked us. We could see the gunfire from where we were. Our troops inland also were attacked. I slept topside tonight.

Sunday, November 26, 1944: We had early General Quarters as usual. All hands went to battle stations at 10 a.m. this morning because of Jap planes, but no damage was done. At sunset General Quarters about 25 Jap planes hit the beach and transports in Leyte Gulf. They did not attack us, the all clear signal sounded at 9:30 p.m. but we were back again in 15 minutes, more Jap planes attacked. We stayed at battle stations until 11:45 p.m. The sky was full of red tracers as our guns fired at the Jap planes. I slept topside as usual.

Monday, November 27, 1944: All hands went to General Quarters at 5:30 a.m. this morning but no Jap planes attacked. The Press News said our bombers from Saipan hit Tokyo. This was the first time Saipan was used to hit Japan. We are still patrolling near Leyte. We got fuel from a tanker today. It was quite a sight to see the way our ships fueled from the tanker. Our task force consists of 18 warships, battleships, heavy and light cruisers and destroyers. While the tanker was refueling 2 ships from both sides, at the same time, all the other ships formed a big circle around the 3 ships. The ships kept circling at a good speed all during the operation. It was like the old Indian wars when the Indians used to keep circling our covered wagons. If Jap planes attacked while we were refueling we would throw up a wall of shells around the tanker so the Japs could not break through. In the meantime a sailor would be near the lines with an axe, ready to cut the lines so the ship could pull away from the tanker in a hurry. When a ship was finished refueling it would get in the circle so another ship could get fuel. It looked like the merry-go-round. It was a good day for the Japs to attack us because it was cloudy and the clouds were low with a little rain now and then. They could drop out of these low clouds and be on us very fast and be gone before we knew it. We were almost surrounded by Jap airfields.

At 10:50 a.m. this morning General Quarters sounded, all hands went to their battle stations. At the same time a battleship and a destroyer were alongside the tanker getting fuel. Out of the clouds I saw a big Jap bomber come crashing down into the water. It was not smoking and looked in good condition. It felt like I was in it as it hit the water not too far from the tanker, and the 2 ships that were refueling. One of our P-38 fighters hit it. He must have got the pilot. At first I thought it was one of our bombers that had engine trouble. It was not long after that when a force of about 30 Jap planes attacked us. Dive bombers and torpedo planes. Our two ships were busy getting away from the tanker because one bomb-hit on the tanker and it would be all over for the 3 ships.

The 2 ships finally got away from the tanker and joined the circle. I think the destroyers were on the outside of the circle. It looked funny to see the tanker all by itself in the center of the ships as we circled it, with our guns blazing away as the planes tried to break through. It was quite a sight, better than the movies. I never saw it done before. It must be the first time it was ever done in any war. Jap planes were coming at us from all directions. Before the attack started we did not know that they were suicide planes, with no intention of returning to their base. They had one thing in mind and that was to crash into our ships, bombs and all. You have to blow them up, to damage them doesn't mean much. Right off the bat a Jap plane made a suicide dive at the cruiser *St. Louis*, there was a big explosion and flames were seen shortly from the stern. Another one tried to do the same thing but he was shot down. A Jap plane came in on a battleship with its guns blazing away. Other Jap planes came in strafing one ship, dropping their bombs on another and crashing into another ship. The Jap planes were falling all around us, the air was full of Jap machine gun bullets. Jap planes and bombs were hitting all around us. Some of our ships were being hit by suicide planes, bombs and machine gun fire. It was a fight to the finish. While all this was taking place our ship had its hands full with Jap planes. We knocked our share of planes down but we also got hit by 3 suicide planes, but lucky for us they dropped their bombs before they crashed into us. In the meantime exploding planes overhead were showering us with their parts. It looked like it was raining plane parts. They were falling all over the ship. Quite a few of the men were hit by big pieces of Jap planes. We were supposed to have air coverage but all we had was 4 P–38 fighters, and when we opened up on the Jap planes they got out of the range of our exploding shells. They must have had a ring side seat of the show. The men on my mount were also showered with parts of Jap planes. One suicide dive bomber was heading right for us while we were firing at other attacking planes and if the 40 mm. mount behind us on the port side did not blow the Jap wing off it would have killed all of us. When the wing was blown off it, the plane turned some and bounced off into the water and the bombs blew part of the plane onto our ship. Another suicide plane crashed into one of the 5 inch mounts, pushing the side of the mount in and injuring some of the men inside. A lot of 5 inch shells were damaged. It was a miracle they did not explode. If that happened the powder and shells would have blown up the ship. Our 40 mm. mount is not too far away. The men threw the 5 inch shells over the side. They expected them to go off at any time. A Jap dive bomber crashed into one of the 40 mm. mounts but lucky for them it dropped its bombs on another ship before crashing. Parts of the plane flew everywhere when it crashed into the mount. Part of the motor hit Tomlinson, he had chunks of it all over him, his stomach, back, legs etc. The rest of the crew were wounded, most of them were sprayed with gasoline from the plane. Tomlinson was thrown a great distance and at first they thought he was knocked over the side. They finally found him in a corner in bad shape. One of the mt. Captains had the wires cut on his phones and kept talking into the phone, because he did not know they were cut by shrapnel until one of the fellows told him. The explosions were terrific as the suicide planes exploded in the water not too far away from our ship. The water was covered with black smoke that rose high into the air. The water looked like it was on fire. It would have been curtains for us if they had crashed into us.

Another suicide plane just overshot us. It grazed the 6 inch turret. It crashed into Leyte Gulf. There was a terrific explosion as the bombs exploded, about 20 ft. away. If we were going a little faster we would have been hit. The Jap planes that were not destroyed with our shells crashed into the water close by or hit our ships. It is a tough job to hold back this tidal wave of suicide planes. They come at you from all directions and also straight down at us at a very fast pace but some of the men have time for a few fast jokes, "This would be a great time to run out of ammunition." "This is mass suicide at its best." Another suicide plane came down at us in a very steep dive. It was a near miss, it just missed the 5 inch mount. The starboard side of the ship was showered with water and fragments. How long will our luck hold out? The Good Lord is really watching over us. This was very close to my 40 mm. mount and we were showered with debris. If the suicide plane exploded on the 5 inch mount, the ammunition should have gone up, after that anything could happen.

Planes were falling all around us, bombs were coming too close for comfort. The Jap planes were cutting up the water with machine gun fire. All the guns on the ships were blazing away, talk about action, never a dull moment. The fellows were passing ammunition like lightning as the guns were turning in all directions spitting out hot steel. Parts of destroyed suicide planes were scattered all over the ship. During a little lull in the action the men would look around for Jap souvenirs and what souvenirs there were. I got part of the plane. The deck near my mount was covered with blood, guts, brains, tongues, scalps, hearts, arms etc. from the Jap pilots. One of the Marines cut the ring off the finger of one of the dead pilots. They had to put the hose on to wash the blood off the deck. The deck ran red with blood. The Japs were spattered all over the place. One of the fellows had a Jap scalp, it looked just like you skinned an animal. The hair was black, cut very short and the color of the skin was yellow, real Japanese. I do not think he was very old. I picked up a tin pie plate with a tongue on it. The pilot's tooth mark was into it very deep. It was very big and long, it looked like part of his tonsils and throat were attached to it. It also looked like the tongue you buy in the meat store. This was the first time I ever saw a person's brains, what a mess. One of the men on our mount got a Jap rib and cleaned it up, he said his sister wants part of a Jap body. One fellow from Texas had a knee bone and he was going to preserve it in alcohol from the sick bay. The Jap bodies were blown into all sorts of pieces. I cannot think of everything that happened because too many things were happening at the same time.

These suicide or kamikaze pilots wanted to destroy us, our ships and themselves. This gives you an idea what kind of an enemy we are fighting. The air attacks in Europe are tame compared to what you run up against out here against the Japs. The Germans will come in so far, do their job and take off but not the Japs. I can see now how the Japs sank the two British battleships *Prince of Wales* and the *Repulse* at the beginning of the war at Singapore. You do not discourage the Japs, they never give up, you have to kill them. It is an honor to die for the Emperor. We do not know how many Jap planes were shot down or the total of planes that attacked us during all the action but they threw plenty of them at us. I have not heard how many planes our ship shot down but at one period of the attack our ship shot down 4 suicide planes within 2 minutes. I think most of the Jap planes that attacked us were destroyed. The attack lasted for 2 hours, we went to battle stations at 10:50 a.m. in the morning and secured at 2:10 p.m. in the afternoon. The action took place not too far from Leyte. Every ship had its hands full with the Jap planes during those 2 hours. The Japs started the attack with 30 planes but after that more planes kept joining them.

After we secured from General Quarters the men looked the ship over to see the damage. The ship was a mess, part of it was damaged, cables were down, steel life lines snapped and steel posts broken. Big pieces of Jap planes were scattered all over the ship, life rafts damaged. Our empty shell cases were everywhere. Some of the other ships were in worse condition than ours. The wounded were brought down to sick bay and some had to be operated on at once.

When it was all over the tanker was still in the middle of the circle and the Japs did not hit it.

Someone said a couple of rafts were in the water with some Japs in them and one of the Japs was in bad condition. We will get more information about this action later when all the reports are in. We had chow at 2:30 p.m. in the afternoon and at 6:30 p.m. we went to sunset General Quarters. The Japs did not come out tonight, guess they had enough action to hold them this afternoon for the day. We secured from General Quarters at 8 p.m. We got some rain this evening. I got the midnight to 4 a.m. watch. No sleep.

Mollie

by A. J. Liebling

A. J. Liebling (1904–1963) wrote about politics (The Earl of Louisiana), journalism (The Press), boxing (The Sweet Science), and the war (Mollie and Other War Pieces), all of which he covered for The New Yorker. Plump and nearsighted, he often tagged along on combat patrols. Liebling's celebrated wit, prose style, reporting skills, and sense of place and story are on display as he painstakingly reconstructs the history and eccentricities of a myterious dead private known as Mollie.

M ollie is a part of the history of La Piste Forestière, and La Piste Forestière is perhaps the most important part of the history of Mollie. La Piste Forestière, or the Foresters' Track, is a dirt road that connects Cap Serrat, on the northern coast of western Tunisia, with Sedjenane, a town twenty miles inland. The country it runs through is covered with small hills, and almost all the hills are coated with a ten-foot growth of tall bushes and short trees, so close together that once you leave the road you can't see fifty feet in front of you. From the top of any hill you can see the top of another hill, but, because of the growth, you can't tell whether there are men on it. This made the country hard to fight in. The hillsides that have no trees are bright with wild flowers in the spring, and two years ago, when some other war correspondents and I travelled back and forth along the Foresters' Track in jeeps, we sometimes used to measure our slow progress by reference to the almost geometrical patterns of color on such slopes. There was, for example, the hill with a rough yellow triangle of buttercups against a reddish-purple background of other blooms; it indicated that you were five miles from the road's junction with the main highway at Sedjenane. With luck you might reach the junction in two hours, but this was extremely unlikely, for the road was just wide enough for one truck—not for a truck and a jeep or even for a truck and a motorcycle. Only a man on foot or on a horse could progress along the margin of the road when there was a vehicle on it, and the horse would often have to scramble by with two feet off the road, like the sidehill bear of eastern Tennessee. When a jeep met a convoy, it sometimes had to back up for hundreds of yards to where there was room to get off the road and wait. Then, when all the heavy vehicles had passed, the jeep would resume its journey, perhaps to meet another convoy before it had recovered the lost yardage. Even when you got in behind trucks going your way, they were packed so closely together that they advanced at a crawl, so you did too. Bits of the war were threaded along the Foresters' Track like beads on a string, and the opportunity to become familiar with them was forced upon you. Mollie, for me, was the gaudiest bead.

The reason the Foresters' Track is such a miserable excuse for a road is that in normal times there is little need for it. There is a lighthouse at Cap Serrat and a forest warden's house about halfway between that and Sedjenane. The few Berbers in the district, who live in brush shelters in the bush, have no vehicles or need of a road. But in late April and early May of 1943, La Piste Forestière was an important military thoroughfare. The Allied armies, facing east, lay in a great arc with their right flank at Sousse, on the Gulf of Tunis, and this little road was the only supply line for twenty miles of front; that is, the extreme left flank of the Allied line. The actual front line ran parallel to the road and only a few hundred yards east of it during the first days of the offensive that was to end the Allies' North African campaign, but because of the hills and the brush, people on the road couldn't see the fighting. However, American artillery placed just west of the road—it would have been an engineering feat to get it any considerable distance into the brush—constantly fired over our heads as our jeeps piddled along. The gunners hoped that some of their shells were falling on the Germans and Italians who were trying to halt our infantry's advance with fire from hidden mortars and machine guns. The Luftwaffe in Africa had predeceased the enemy ground forces; the budget of planes allotted it for the African adventure was exhausted, I suppose, and the German High Command sent no more. This was lucky for us, because one good strafing, at any hour, would have jammed the road with burned-out vehicles and Allied dead. By repeating the strafing once a day, the Germans could have kept the road permanently out of commission. The potential danger from the air did not worry us for long, however. You soon become accustomed to immunity, even when you cannot understand the reason for it.

Trucks left ammunition along the side of the road to be carried up to the fighting lines on the backs of requisitioned mules and horses and little Arab donkeys, a strangely assorted herd conducted by an equally scratch lot of soldiers. The Washington army had decided years before that the war was now one-hundred-percent mechanized, so the field army, quite a different organization, had to improvise its animal transport as it went along. The wounded were carried down to the road by stretcher bearers. Ambulances, moving with the same disheartening slowness as everything else, picked up the casualties and took them out to a clearing station near the yellow-triangle hill I have mentioned, where some of the viable ones were patched up for the further slow haul out. Cruder surgical units, strung out along the road, took such cases as they were equipped to handle. These units were always right by the side of the road, since in that claustrophobe's nightmare of a country there was no other place for them to be. The advanced units were French and had women nurses with them. A French doctor I knew used to say that it helped the men bear pain if nurses were looking at them. "Since we have so little anesthesia," he said, "we rely upon vanity." Sometimes I would sit in my jeep and watch that doctor work. He had broken down a few saplings and bushes by the side of the road to clear a space for his ambulance, and next to the ambulance he had set up a campstool and a folding table with some instruments on it. Once a traffic jam stopped my jeep near his post when he had a tanned giant perched on the camp stool, a second lieutenant in the Corps Franc d'Afrique. The man's breasts were hanging off his chest in a kind of bloody ruff. "A bit of courage now, my son, will save you a great deal of trouble later on," the doctor said as he prepared to do something or other. I assumed, perhaps pessimistically, that he was going to hack off the bits of flesh as you would trim the ragged edges of an ill-cut page. "Go easy, Doctor," the young man said. "I'm such a softie." Then the traffic started to move, so I don't know what the doctor did to him.

The Corps Franc d'Afrique was a unit that had a short and glorious history. Soon after the Allied landings in North Africa, in October, 1942, the Corps Franc organized itself, literally, out of the elements the Darlanists in control of the North African government distrusted too much to incorporate into the regular French Army—Jews, anti-Nazis from concentration camps, de Gaullists, and other Allied sympathizers. A French general named Joseph de Goislard de Montsabert, who had helped plan the landings, had been thrown out by his collaborationist superiors, who, even after Darlan's agreement to play ball with the forces of democracy, had remained his superiors. De Montsabert, because he had a red face and snowy hair, was known to his troops as Strawberry in Cream. There had been among the French in North Africa a number of other professional officers and many reservists who, like the General, were apparently left out of the war because they were suspected of favoring de Gaulle or merely of being hostile to Germany. The Darlan regime had refused to mobilize the Jews because it clung to the Vichy thesis that they were not full citizens, and it did not want them to establish a claim to future consideration, and it was holding thousands of Spanish and German refugees and French Communists in concentration camps.

De Montsabert and a few of his officer friends, talking on the street in Algiers one rainy November day of that year, decided to start a "Free Corps" of men who wanted to fight but whom the government would not allow to. They took over a room in a schoolhouse on the Rue Mogador as headquarters and advertised in the *Echo d'Alger* for volunteers. The ad appeared once and then the Darlanist censorship, which was still operating under the Americans, like every other element of Vichy rule, suppressed it. But scores of volunteers had already appeared at the schoolhouse and de Montsabert sent them out with pieces of schoolroom chalk to write "Join the Corps Franc" on walls all over the city. Hundreds of new volunteers came in. General Giraud, who had arrived in Africa to command all the French but had subsequently accepted a role secondary to Darlan's, heard of the movement and interceded for it.

Giraud, whatever his limitations, considered it natural that anybody in his right mind should want to fight the Germans. Darlan and his Fascist friends began to think of the Corps Franc as a means of getting undesirables out of the way, so the government recognized it but at the same time refused it any equipment. The Corps began life with a miscellany of matériel begged from the British and Americans. Its men wore British battle dress and French insignia of rank, lived on American C rations, and carried any sort of weapons they could lay their hands on. The most characteristic feature of their appearance was a long beard, but even this was not universal, because some of the soldiers were too young to grow one. After the Corps Franc's arrival in Tunisia, it added to its heterogeneous equipment a great deal more stuff it captured from the enemy. The Corps went into the line in February of 1943, in the zone north of Sedjenane, and it remained there into the spring.

Late April in Tunisia is like late June in New York, and heat and dust were great nuisances to our men when they were attacking. In February and March, however, coastal Tunisia is drenched with a cold and constant downpour. The Foresters' Track was two feet deep in water when the Corps Franc began to fight along it. There were two battalions to start with—about twelve hundred men—to cover a sector twenty miles long. A third and fourth battalion had been added by the time the Americans began their offensive. The Corps, in the beginning, had only two ambulances, converted farm trucks owned by a Belgian colonist in Morocco. The Belgian and his son had driven the trucks across North Africa to join the Corps. But the trucks were unable to negotiate the flooded Track, so the men of the Corps carried their wounded out to Sedjenane on their shoulders. I once asked my doctor friend why they had not used mules. "The mules rolled over in the water and crushed the wounded men," he said. "We know. We tried it with wounded prisoners."

Now that the great attack was on, there were other troops along the Track with the Corps—the Sixtieth Infantry of the American Ninth Division, part of the American Ninth Division's artillery, an American tank-destroyer battalion, some Moroccan units, and some American motor-truck and medical outfits. The medics and the artillery made the French feel pampered and their morale got very high. One hot morning, I passed a lean, elderly soldier of the Corps Franc who was burying two of his comrades. He looked about sixty—there was no age limit in the Corps—and had a long, drooping mustache of a faded biscuit color. He had finished one grave and was sitting down to rest and cool off before beginning the other. The two dead men lay with their feet to the road. Blueflies had settled on their faces. I told my jeep driver to stop and asked the gravedigger what men these were. "One stiff was an Arab from Biskra," the old soldier said, "and the other a Spaniard, a nihilist from Oran." I asked him how his work was going. He wiped the sweat from his forehead and said happily, "Monsieur, like on roller skates."

A quarter of the men in the Corps Franc were Jews. A Jewish lieutenant named Rosenberg was its posthumous hero by the time I arrived in the Foresters' Track country. He had commanded a detachment of twenty men covering the retreat of his battalion during a German counterattack in early March. This was a sequel to the counterattack against the Americans at Kasserine Pass in late February, and both assaults were prototypes, on a small scale, of the counter-offensive the Germans were to launch in Belgium at the end of 1944—the last flurry of the hooked and dying fish. Rosenberg, holding one of the innumerable little hills with his men, had decided that it was not fitting for a Jew to retire, even when the Germans looked as though they had surrounded his position. He and his men held on until the rest of the battalion had made its escape. Then he rose, and, intoning the "Marseillaise," led his men in an attack with hand grenades. He and most of his men were, of course, killed.

Besides the Jews, the Corps had hundreds of political prisoners from labor camps in southern Algeria—Spanish Republicans who had fled to Africa in 1939, anti-Nazi Germans who had come even before that, and French "Communists and de Gaullists," to employ the usual Vichy designation for dissidents. The political prisoners had been released upon agreeing to enter the Corps Franc, which they did not consider an onerous condition. There were also hundreds of French-men who had joined because they distrusted the Vichy officers in the regular Army, or because they were "hard heads" who detested any species of regularity, or because they were too old or ill for more con-ventional fighting units. In the Corps Franc, they were at liberty to march and fight until they dropped. There were also a fair number of Mohammedans, good soldiers who had joined to earn the princely wage of twenty-three francs a day, ten times what they would have got if they had waited to be mobilized in their regular units. Whenever I had a chance, I asked Corps Franc soldiers what they had been in civil-ian life and why they had enlisted. I remember a former *carabiñero* who had fought in the Spanish Loyalist Army, and a baker of Italian parent-age from Bône, in Algeria, who said, "I am a Communist. Rich people are poison to me."

Other members of the Corps who made a special impression on me were a former admiral in the Spanish Republican Navy, who was now a company commander and would not allow junior officers to shout at soldiers; a Hungarian poet who had been studying medicine at the University of Algiers; a sixteen-year-old Alsatian from Strasbourg who had run away from home to avoid being forced to become a German citizen; and a French captain, a shipping broker in civil life, who proclaimed himself a Royalist. The captain's sixteen-year-old son was also in the Corps; the boy was a motorcycle dispatch rider. I also remember two tough Parisians who had not seen each other since one had escaped from jail in Dakar, where they had both been imprisoned for trying to join the Free French in Brazzaville. The other had escaped later. "Say, it's you, old pimp!" one of the men shouted joyously. "And how did you get out of the jug, old rottenness?" the second man shouted back. Once I shared a luncheon of C-ration vegetable hash, scallions, and medlars with a little fifty-three-year-old second lieutenant, one of those Frenchmen with a face like a parakeet, who until 1942 had been vice-president of the Paris Municipal Council, in which he represented the *arrondissement* of the Opéra. He had got out a clandestine paper and had helped Jewish friends smuggle millions of francs out of France. Betrayed to the Gestapo, he had been arrested and put in Cherche-Midi Prison; he had escaped with the aid of a jailer and come to Africa and the Corps Franc. The middle-aged soldier who waited on us spoke French with a farce-comedy Russian accent; he had been a waiter at the Scheherazade, a nightclub in Montmartre, and had often served the lieutenant when he was a civilian. A handsome young Viennese half-Jew, who had been on the Austrian track team in the last Olympic Games, once asked me for some sulfanilamide. He had been in a labor camp for six months without seeing a woman but had been allowed one night's leave in Oran before being sent on to the front. He wanted the sulfanilamide, he said, so that he could treat himself; he was afraid that a doctor might order him away from the firing line. And in a hospital tent at the clearing station I came across a man with a French flag wrapped around his waist; the medics discovered it when they cut his shirt away. He was a hard-looking, blondish chap with a mouthful of gold teeth and a face adorned by a cross-shaped knife scar—the *croix de vache* with which procurers sometimes mark business rivals. An interesting collection of obscene tattooing showed on the parts of him that the flag did not cover. Outwardly he was not a sentimental type.

"Where are you from?" I asked him.

"Belleville," he said. Belleville is a part of Paris not distinguished for its elegance.

"What did you do in civilian life?" I inquired.

That made him grin. "I lived on my income," he said.

"Why did you choose the Corps Franc?"

"Because I understood," he said.

The American soldiers interspersed with the men of the Corps Franc along the Foresters' Track found them a fantastic lot. Most of the men then in the Ninth Division came from New York, New Jersey, or New England, and their ideas of North Africa and Frenchmen had been acquired from films with Ronald Colman as Beau Geste or Charles Boyer as Charles Boyer. They thought the Frenchmen very reckless. The Ninth had had its first experience in battle on the road to Maknassy, in southern Tunisia, only a few weeks earlier, and it was not yet a polished division. The men of the Ninth in Germany recently took risks as non-chalantly as any Corps Franc soldier used to, but at the time I am speaking of they would sometimes call the Frenchmen "those crazy headhunters." This term reflected a tendency to confuse the Corps Franc with the Moroccans in the same zone; the Moroccans are not headhunters, either, but there is a popular American belief that they are paid according to how many enemy ears they bring in.

There were two tabors, or battalions, of Moroccans in the zone; a tabor consists of several goums, or companies, and each soldier who is a member of a company is called a goumier. For the sake of simplicity and euphony, Americans called the Moroccan soldiers themselves goums. The goums used to ride along the side of the road on bay mules or gray horses—sure-footed, mountain-bred animals—until they got near the place where they were going to fight. Then they would dismount and go off into the brush on bare feet, and return with their booty when they had finished their business. The goum's sole outer garment is the *djellabah*, which looks like a long brown bathrobe with a hood. It is made of cotton, wool, linen, goats' hair, or camels' hair and usually has vertical black stripes. It sheds water, insulates against heat and cold, is a substitute for a pup tent at night, and serves as a repository for everything the goum gloms, like the capacious garment of a professional shoplifter. In their Moroccan homeland the goums live with their wives and children in their own villages and are supposed to pay themselves with the spoils of tribes that resist the French government. In Tunisia the spoils were pretty well confined to soldiers' gear. As a goum killed or captured more and more enemies, he would put on layer after layer of tunics and trousers, always wearing the *djellabah* over everything. The girth of the goums increased as the campaign wore on. This swollen effect gave a goum an air of prosperity and importance, in his opinion; his standing as a warrior, he thought, was in direct ratio to his circumference. A goum who was doing well often wore, between sorties, one German and one Italian boot and carried a string of extra boots over his saddlebow. The funny part of it was that a goum wearing six men's clothing could slip noiselessly through a thicket that was impassable to a skinny American. The French officers commanding the goums assured me that their men were not paid by the ear; if a goum occasionally had a few dried ears concealed in a fold of his *djellabah,* one officer explained, it was because goums had discovered that such souvenirs had a trade value in G.I. cigarettes and chewing gum. "Far from paying for ears," this officer said, "we have recently been offering a small reward for live prisoners for interrogation. It is evident that a prisoner without ears is not a good subject for interrogation, because he does not hear the questions plainly." To hold the goums' respect, the officers had to be able to march, climb, and fight with them, and a goum is as inexhaustible as a mountain sheep and about as fastidious as a hyena. Most goums come from the Atlas Mountains and few of them speak Arabic, much less French, so the officers have to be fluent in the southern Berber dialects, which are all that the men know. The goums are trying companions in minefields, because, as one officer remarked, "They say, 'If it is the will of God, we go up,' and then they just push forward." Neither they nor the Corps Franc had mine detectors. An American captain named Yankauer, who was the surgeon at the clearing station near the yellow-triangle hill, was once digging scraps of steel out of a goum who had stepped on a mine. The man let out one short squeal—there was no anesthetic—and then began a steady chant. Yankauer asked a goum officer, who was waiting his turn on the table, what the goum was saying. The officer translated, "He chants, 'God forgive me, I am a woman. God forgive me, I am a woman,' because, you see, he has cried aloud, so he is ashamed." The goums' chief weapons were curved knives and long rifles of the vintage of 1871, and one of the supply problems of the campaign for the American G-4 was finding ammunition for these antediluvian small arms. Colonel Pierre Magnan, who had succeeded de Montsabert in command of the Corps Franc, was the senior French officer in the zone. I was with him one day when the commander of a newly arrived tabor presented himself for orders. "How are you fixed for automatic weapons, Major?" Magnan asked. "We have two old machine guns," the goum officer said. Then, when he saw Magnan's glum look, he added cheerily, "But don't worry, my Colonel, we use them only on maneuvers."

Magnan was a trim, rather elegant officer who, before the Allied landings, had commanded a crack infantry regiment in Morocco. On the morning of the American landings, he had arrested General Noguès, the Governor General of Morocco, and then asked him to prevent any fighting between the French and Americans by welcoming the invading forces. Noguès had telephoned to a tank regiment to come and arrest Magnan. Magnan, unwilling to shed French blood, had surrendered to the tankmen and become a prisoner in his turn. The liberated Noguès had then ordered a resistance that cost hundreds of French and American lives. Magnan was kept in prison for several days after Noguès, who was backed by our State Department, had consented to be agreeable to the Allies. Magnan had then been released, but he was deprived of his command and consigned to the Corps Franc. He now commands a division in France, and de Montsabert has a *corps d'armée,* so the scheme to keep them down has not been precisely a success.

The Axis forces north of Sedjenane must have been as hard put to it for supply routes as we were. I don't remember the roads the Intelligence maps showed behind the enemy's lines, but they could not have been numerous or elaborate. The Germans did not seem to have a great deal of artillery, but they occasionally landed shells on our road. Once, I remember, they shot up a couple of tank destroyers shortly after the jeep I was in had pulled out to let them pass. Throughout, it was a stubborn, nasty sort of fighting in the brush, and casualties arrived in a steady trickle rather than any great spurt, because large-scale attacks were impossible. Our men fought their way a few hundred yards further east each day, toward Ferryville and Bizerte. Eventually, when Rommel's forces crumpled, men of the Corps Franc, in trucks driven by American soldiers, got to Bizerte before any other Allied troops.

On Easter Sunday, which came late in April, I was out along the Track all day, riding in a jeep with Hal Boyle, a correspondent for the Associated Press. At the end of the afternoon we headed home, hoping to get back to the press camp before night so that we wouldn't have to buck a stream of two-and-a-half-ton trucks and armored vehicles in the blackout. Traffic seemed, if anything, heavier than usual along the Foresters' Track, as it always did when you were in a hurry. The jeep stopped for minutes at a time, which gave Boyle the opportunity to climb out and get the names and home addresses of American soldiers for his stories. Sometimes he would stay behind, talking, and catch up with the jeep the next time it was snagged. We could have walked along the Track faster than we rode. Finally we came to a dip in the road. Fifty yards below and to our right there was a shallow stream, and there was almost no brush on the slope from the road down to the water. This, for the Foresters' Track country, was a considerable clearing, and it was being used for a number of activities. Some goums were watering their mounts in the stream, some French and American soldiers were heating rations over brush fires, a number of vehicles were parked there, and Colonel Magnan and some officers were holding a staff meeting. As we approached the clearing, we were stopped again for a moment by the traffic. A dismal American soldier came out of the brush on our left, tugging a gaunt, reluctant white horse. "Come along, Horrible," the soldier said in a tone of intensest loathing. "This goddam horse got me lost three times today," he said to us, looking over his shoulder at the sneering, wall-eyed beast. He evidently thought the horse was supposed to guide him.

We moved downhill a bit and stopped again, this time behind an ambulance that was loading wounded. There was a group of soldiers around the ambulance. Boyle and I got out to look. There were four wounded men, all badly hit. They were breathing hard and probably didn't know what was going on. Shock and heavy doses of morphia were making their move easy, or at least quiet. The four men were all from the Sixtieth Infantry of the Ninth Division. A soldier by the road said that they had been on a patrol and had exchanged shots with a couple of Germans; the Germans had popped up waving white handkerchiefs, the Americans had stood up to take them prisoners, and another German, lying concealed, had opened on them with a machine gun. It was the sort of thing that had happened dozens of times to other units, and that undoubtedly has happened hundreds of times since. Such casualties, a Polish officer once said to me, are an entry fee to battle. That doesn't make them easy to take, however. The soldiers had been told about this particular trick in their training courses, but they had probably thought it was a fable invented to make them hate the enemy. Now the men around the ambulance had really begun to hate the enemy. While Boyle was getting the names and addresses of the men, I saw another American soldier by the side of the road. This one was dead. A soldier nearby said that the dead man had been a private known as Mollie.

A blanket covered Mollie's face, so I surmised that it had been shattered, but there was no blood on the ground, so I judged that he had been killed in the brush and carried down to the road to await transport. A big, wild-looking sergeant was standing alongside him—a hawk-nosed, red-necked man with a couple of front teeth missing—and I asked him if the dead man had been in the patrol with the four wounded ones. "Jeez, no!" the sergeant said, looking at me as if I ought to know about the man with the blanket over his face. "That's Comrade Molotov. The Mayor of Broadway. Didn't you ever hear of him? Jeez, Mac, he once captured six hundred Eyetalians by himself and brought them all back along with him. Sniper got him, I guess. I don't know, because he went out with the French, and he was found dead up there in the hills. He always liked to do crazy things—go off by himself with a pair of big field glasses he had and watch the enemy put in minefields, or take off and be an artillery spotter for a while, or drive a tank. From the minute he seen those frogs, he was bound to go off with them."

"Was his name really Molotov?" I asked.

"No," said the sergeant, "he just called himself that. The boys mostly shortened it to Mollie. I don't even know what his real name was— Warren, I think. Carl Warren. He used to say he was a Broadway big shot. 'Just ask anybody around Forty-fourth Street,' he used to say. 'They all know me.' Me, I'm from White Plains—I never heard of him before he joined up."

"I had him with me on a patrol that was to contact the French when the regiment was moving into this zone last Thursday," a stocky blond corporal said. "The first French patrol we met, Mollie says to me, 'This is too far back for me. I'm going up in the hills with these frogs and get me some Lugers.' He was always collecting things he captured off Germans and Italians, but the one thing he didn't have yet was a Luger. I knew if I didn't let him go he would take off anyway and get into more trouble with the C.O. He was always in trouble. So I said, 'All right, but the frogs got to give me a receipt for you, so I can prove you didn't go A.W.O.L.' One of the soldiers with me could speak French, so he explained it and the frog noncom give me a receipt on a piece of toilet paper and Mollie went off with them." The corporal fished in one of the pockets of his field jacket and brought out a sheet of tissue. On it, the French noncom had written, in pencil, *"Pris avec moi le soldat américain Molotov, 23 avril, '43, Namin, caporal chef."*

"Mollie couldn't speak French," the American corporal went on, "but he always got on good with the frogs. It's funny where those big field glasses went, though. He used to always have them around his neck, but somebody must have figured they were no more good to him after he was dead, so they sucked them up. He used to always say that he was a big-shot gambler and that he used to watch the horse races with those glasses."

By now the four wounded men had been loaded into the ambulance. It moved off. Obviously, there was a good story in Mollie, but he was not available for an interview. The driver of the truck behind our jeep was giving us the horn, so I pulled Boyle toward the jeep. He got in, still looking back at Mollie, who said nothing to keep him, and we drove away. When we had gone a little way, at our customary slow pace, a tall lieutenant signalled to us from the roadside that he wanted a hitch and we stopped and indicated that he should hop aboard. He told us his name was Carl Ruff. He was from New York and thought I might know his wife, an advertising woman, but I didn't. Ruff was dog-tired from scrambling through the bush. I said something about Mollie, and Ruff said that he had not known him alive but had been the first American to see his body, on Good Friday morning. The French had led him to it. "He was on the slope of a hill," Ruff said, "and slugs from an automatic rifle had hit him in the right eye and chest. He must have been working his way up the hill, crouching, when the German opened on him and hit him in the chest, and then as he fell, the other bullet probably got him in the eye. He couldn't have lived a minute."

It was a month later, aboard the United States War Shipping Administration steamer *Monterey*, a luxury liner that had been con-verted to war service without any needless suppression of comfort, that I next heard of Molotov, the Mayor of Broadway. The *Monterey* was on her way from Casablanca to New York. On the passenger list were four correspondents besides myself, a thousand German prisoners, five hundred wounded Americans, all of whom would need long hospital-ization, and a couple of hundred officers and men who were being transferred or were on various errands. It was one of the advantages of being a correspondent that one could go to America without being a German or wounded, or without being phenomenally lucky, which the unwounded soldiers on our boat considered that they were. The cross-ing had almost a holiday atmosphere. We were homeward bound after a great victory in the North African campaign, the first the Allies had scored over Germany in a war nearly four years old. The weather was perfect and the *Monterey*, which was not overcrowded and had wide decks and comfortable lounges, had the aspect and feeling of a cruise ship. The wounded were glad, in their sad way, to be going home. The prisoners were in good spirits, too; they seemed to regard the journey as a Nazi Strength through Joy excursion. They organized vaudeville shows, boxing matches, and art exhibitions with the energetic cooperation of the ship's chaplain, who found much to admire in the Christian cheerfulness with which they endured their increased rations. A couple of anti-Nazi prisoners had announced themselves on the first day out, but the German noncoms had knocked them about and set them to cleaning latrines, so order had soon been restored. "That's an army where they really have some discipline!" one of the American officers on board told me enviously. The prisoners had to put up with some hardships, of course. They complained one evening when ice cream was served to the wounded but not to them, and another time they didn't think the transport surgeon, a Jew, was "sympathetic" enough to a German officer with a stomach ache.

The hospital orderlies would wheel the legless wounded out on the promenade deck in wheelchairs to see the German boxing bouts, and the other wounded would follow them, some swinging along on crutches or hopping on one foot, some with their arms in slings or casts, some with their broken necks held stiffly in casts and harnesses. They had mixed reactions to the bouts. An arm case named Sanderson, a private who wore the Ninth Division shoulder patch, told me one day that he wished he could be turned loose on the prisoners with a tommygun, because he didn't like to see them jumping about in front of his legless pals. Another arm case, named Shapiro, from the same division, always got a lot of amusement out of the show. Shapiro was a rugged-looking boy from the Brownsville part of Brooklyn. He explained how he felt one day after two Afrika Korps heavyweights had gone through a couple of rounds of grunting, posturing, and slapping. "Every time I see them box, I know we can't lose the war," he said. "The Master Race—phooey! Any kid off the street could of took the both of them."

Shapiro and Sanderson, I learned during one ringside conversation with them, had both been in the Sixtieth Infantry, Molotov's old regiment. They had been wounded in the fighting around Maknassy, in southern Tunisia, early in April, the first serious action the regiment had been in. Molotov had been killed late in April, during the drive on Bizerte, and until I told them, the boys hadn't heard he was dead. I asked them if they had known him.

"How could you help it?" Shapiro said. "There will never be anybody in the division as well known as him. In the first place, you couldn't help noticing him on account of his clothes. He looked like a soldier out of some other army, always wearing them twenty-dollar green tailor-made officers' shirts and sometimes riding boots, with a French berrit with a long rooster feather that he got off an Italian prisoner's hat, and a long black-and-red cape that he got off another prisoner for a can of C ration."

"And the officers let him get away with it?" I asked.

"Not in the rear areas, they didn't," Shapiro said. "But in combat, Mollie was an asset. Major Kauffman, his battalion commander, knew it, so he would kind of go along with him. But he would never have him made even a pfc. Mollie couldn't of stood the responsibility. He was the greatest natural-born foul-up in the Army," Shapiro added reverently. "He was court-martialled twenty or thirty times, but the Major always got him out of it. He had the biggest blanket roll in the Ninth Division, with a wall tent inside it and some Arabian carpets and bronze lamps and a folding washstand and about five changes of uniform, none of them regulation, and he would always manage to get it on a truck when we moved. When he pitched his tent, it looked like a concession at Coney Island. I was with him when he got his first issue of clothing at Camp Dix in 1941. 'I've threw better stuff than this away,' he said. He never liked to wear issue. He was up for court-martial for deserting his post when he was on guard duty at Fort Bragg, but the regiment sailed for Morocco before they could try him, and he did so good in the landing at Port Lyautey that they kind of forgave him. Then he went over the hill again when he was guarding a dock at Oran in the winter, but they moved us up into the combat zone before they could try him then, so he beat that rap, too. He was a very lucky fellow. I can hardly think of him being dead."

"Well, what was so good about him?" I asked.

Sanderson, who was a thin, sharp-faced boy from Michigan, answered me with the embarrassed frankness of a modern mother explaining the facts of life to her offspring. "Sir," he said, "it may not sound nice to say it, and I do not want to knock anyone, but in battle almost everybody is frightened, especially the first couple of times. Once in a while you find a fellow who isn't frightened at all. He goes forward and the other fellows go along with him. So he is very important. Probably he is a popoff, and he kids the other guys, and they all feel better. Mostly those quiet, determined fellows crack up before the popoffs. Mollie was the biggest popoff and the biggest screwball and the biggest foul-up I ever saw, and he wasn't afraid of nothing. Some fellows get brave with experience, I guess, but Mollie never had any fear to begin with. Like one time on the road to Maknassy, the battalion was trying to take some hills and we were getting no place. They were just Italians in front of us, but they had plenty of stuff and they were in cover and we were in the open. Mollie stands right up, wearing the cape and the berrit with the feather, and he says, 'I bet those Italians would surrender if somebody asked them to. What the hell do they want to fight for?' he says. So he walks across the minefield and up the hill to the Italians, waving his arms and making funny motions, and they shoot at him for a while and then stop, thinking he is crazy. He goes up there yelling '*Veni qua!*' which he says afterward is New York Italian for 'Come here!' and '*Feeneesh la guerre!*,' which is French, and when he gets to the Italians he finds a soldier who was a barber in Astoria but went home on a visit and got drafted in the Italian Army, so the barber translates for him and the Italians say sure, they would like to surrender, and Mollie comes back to the lines with five hundred and sixty-eight prisoners. He had about ten Italian automatics strapped to his belt and fifteen field glasses hung over his shoulders. So instead of being stopped, we took the position and cleaned up on the enemy. That was good for the morale of the battalion. The next time we got in a fight, we said to ourselves, 'Those guys are just looking for an easy out,' so we got up and chased them the hell away from there. A disciplined soldier would never have did what Mollie done. He was a very unusual guy. He gave the battalion confidence and the battalion gave the regiment confidence, because the other battalions said, 'If the Second can take all those prisoners, we can, too.' And the Thirty-ninth and the Forty-seventh Regiments probably said to themselves, 'If the Sixtieth is winning all them fights, we can also.' So you might say that Mollie made the whole division." I found out afterward that Sanderson had oversimplified the story, but it was essentially true and the tradition endures in the Ninth Division.

"What kind of a looking fellow was Mollie?" I asked.

"He was a good-looking kid," Shapiro said. "Medium-sized, around a hundred and sixty pounds, with long, curly blond hair. They could almost never get him to have his hair cut. Once, when it got too bad, Major Kauffman took him by the hand and said, 'Come along with me. We'll get a haircut together.' So he sat him down and held onto him while the G.I. barber cut both their hair. And everything he wore had to be sharp. I remember that after the French surrendered to us at Port Lyautey, a lot of French officers gave a party and invited a couple of officers from the battalion to it, and when the officers got there they found Mollie was there, and the Frenchmen were all bowing to him and saluting him. He was dressed so sharp they thought he was an officer, too—maybe a colonel."

Another boy, a badly wounded one in a wheelchair, heard us talking about Mollie and rolled his chair over to us. "It was the field glasses I'll always remember," he said. "From the first day we landed on the beach in Morocco, Mollie had those glasses. He told some fellows once he captured them from a French general, but he told some others he brought them all the way from New York. He told them he used to watch horse races with the glasses; he was fit to be tied when he got to Morocco and found there was no scratch sheets. 'Ain't there no way to telegraph a bet on a race?' he said, and then he let out a howl. 'vot a schvindle!' That was his favorite saying—'Vot a schvindle!' He was always bitching about something. He used to go out scouting with the glasses, all alone, and find the enemy and tip Major Kauffman off where they were. He had a lot of curiosity. He always had plenty of money, but he would never tell where he got it from. He just let people understand he was a big shot—maybe in some racket. When we were down at Fort Bragg, he and another fellow, a sergeant, had a big Buick that he kept outside the camp, and they used to go riding all around the country. They used to get some swell stuff."

"He never shot crap for less than fifty dollars a roll when he had the dice," Shapiro said, "and he never slept with any woman under an actress." The way Shapiro said it, it was as if he had said, "He never saluted anybody under the rank of brigadier general."

During the rest of the voyage, I heard more about Mollie. I found nobody who was sure of his real name, but the majority opinion was that it was something like Carl Warren. "But he wasn't American stock or Irish," Sanderson said one day in a group discussion. "He seemed to me more German-American." Another boy in the conversation said that Mollie had told him he was of Russian descent. Sanderson was sure that Molotov wasn't Russian. "Somebody just called him that because he was a radical, I guess," he said. "He was always hollering he was framed." "He used to have a big map of the eastern front in his tent in Morocco," another soldier said, "and every time the Russians advanced he would mark it with pins and holler, 'Hey, Comrade, howdya like that!'" One boy remembered that Mollie had won fifteen hundred dollars in a crap game at Fort Bragg. "He had it for about three days," he said, "and then lost it to a civilian. When he got cleaned in a game, he would never borrow a buck to play on with. He would just leave. Then the next time he played, he would have a new roll. Right after we landed in Morocco, he was awful flush, even for him, and he told a couple of guys he'd climbed over the wall of an old fort the French had just surrendered and there, in some office, he found a briefcase with fifty thousand francs in it. The next thing he done was hire twelve Arabs to cook and clean and wash dishes for him."

"I was inducted the same time with him, at Grand Central Palace," an armless youngster said, "and him and me and the bunch was marched down to Penn Station to take the train. That was way back in

January, 1941," he added, as if referring to a prehistoric event. "He was wearing a blue double-breasted jacket and a dark-blue sport shirt open at the neck and gray flannel trousers and a camel's-hair overcoat. They took us into a restaurant on Thirty-fourth Street to buy us a feed and Mollie started buying beers for the whole crowd. 'Come on, Comrades,' he says. 'Plenty more where this comes from.' Then he led the singing on the train all the way down to Dix. But as soon as he got down there and they took all his fancy clothes away from him, he was licked. 'Vot a schvindle!' he says. He drew K.P. a lot at Dix, but he always paid some other guy to do it for him. The only thing he could ever do good outside of combat was D.R.O.—that's dining-room orderly at the officers' mess. I've seen him carry three stacks of dishes on each arm."

When I told them how Mollie had been killed, Shapiro said that that was just what you'd have expected of Mollie. "He never liked to stay with his own unit," he said. "You could hardly even tell what battalion he was in."

I was not to see the Army's official version of what Mollie had done in the fight against the six hundred Italians until last summer, when I caught up with the Second Battalion of the Sixtieth Infantry near Marigny, in Normandy. Mollie's protector, Major Michael S. Kauffman, by then a lieutenant colonel, was still commanding officer. "Mollie didn't capture the lot by himself," Kauffman said, "but he was instrumental in getting them, and there were about six hundred of them all right. The battalion S-2 got out a mimeographed training pamphlet about that fight, because there were some points in it that we thought instructive. I'll get you a copy." The pamphlet he gave me bears the slightly ambitious title "The Battle of Sened, 23 March, '43, G Co. 60th Infantry Dawn Attack on Sened, Tunisia." The Sened of the title was the village of Sened, in the high *djebel* a couple of miles south of the Sened railroad station. It was country I remembered well: a bare plain with occasional bunch grass, with naked red-rock hills rising above it. The Americans had fought there several times; I had seen the taking of the railroad station by another regiment at the beginning of February, 1943, and it had been lost and retaken between then and March 23rd.

On the first page of the pamphlet there was a map showing the Italian position, on two hills separated by a narrow gorge, and the jump-off position of the Americans, two much smaller hills a couple of miles to the north. Then there was a list of "combat lessons to be learned," some of which were: "A small aggressive force can knock out a large group by determined action," "Individuals, soldiers with initiative, aggressiveness, and courage, can influence a large battle," and "Confusion is normal in combat." I have often since thought that this last one would make a fine title for a book on war. The pamphlet told how an Italian force estimated at from thirty men to three thousand, according to the various persons interviewed in advance of the fight by S-2 ("Question civilians," the pamphlet said. "Don't rely on one estimate of enemy strength. Weigh all information in the light of its source"), had taken refuge in the village of Sened. G Company, about a hundred and fifty men, had been ordered to clean out the Italians. It had artillery support from some guns of the First Armored Division; in fact, a Lieutenant Colonel MacPherson, an artillery battalion commander, was actually the senior American officer in the action. This colonel, acting as his own forward observer, had looked over the situation and at four in the afternoon of March 22nd had ordered the first platoon of the company to attack. It was soon apparent, judging by the defenders' fire, that the lowest estimate of the enemy's strength was very wrong and that there were at least several hundred Italians on the two hills. Then, in the words of the pamphlet, "Private Molotov"—even his officers had long since forgotten his civilian name—"crawls to enemy position with Pfc. De Marco (both are volunteers) and arranges surrender conference. C.O. refuses to surrender and fire fight continues. Individual enemy riflemen begin to throw down their arms. First platoon returns to Sened Station at dark with 147 prisoners, including 3 officers."

"De Marco was a friend of Molotov's," Colonel Kauffman told me. "It was Mollie's idea to go up to the enemy position, and De Marco did the talking. It must have been pretty effective, because all those Italians came back with them."

"G Company," the pamphlet continued, "attacks again at dawn, first and third platoons attacking. Entrance to town is deep narrow gorge between two long ridges. Town lies in continuation of gorge, surrounded on all sides by 1,000–12,000 foot *djebels* as shown in sketch. (Possible enemy escape route was used by Ancient Romans as park for wild animals used in gladiatorial matches.) Approach to gorge entrance is terraced and well concealed by a large olive-tree grove; five (5) or six (6) field pieces in grove have been knocked out by previous day's artillery fire."

Although the pamphlet didn't say so, the olive groves had once covered all the plain. That plain is now given over to bunch grass, but it was carefully irrigated in the days of the Roman Empire. The "wild animals used in gladiatorial matches" were for the arena at the splendid stone city of Capsa, now the sprawling, dried-mud Arab town of Gafsa, fifteen miles from Sened.

"Company attacks as shown on sketch," the pamphlet continued, "third platoon making steep rocky climb around right, first platoon (Molotov's) around left. Light machine guns and mortars follow close behind by bounds, grenadiers move well to front with mission of flushing enemy out of numerous caves where he has taken up defensive positions. Left platoon, commanded by Sergeant Vernon Mugerditchian, moves slowly over ground devoid of concealment, and finally comes to rest. Molotov goes out alone, keeping abreast of faster moving platoon on right, and assists Lt. Col. MacPherson in artillery direction by shouting."

The combined artillery and infantry fire made the Italians quit. The pamphlet says, in closing, "Italian captain leads column of prisoners out of hills, bringing total of 537 (including officers). Total booty includes 2 large trucks, 3 small trucks, several personnel carrier motorcycles, 200 pistols, machine guns, rifles, and ammunition."

"Mollie liked to go out ahead and feel he was running the show," Colonel Kauffman said. "We put him in for a D.S.C. for what he did, but it was turned down. Then we put in for a Silver Star, and that was granted, but he was killed before he ever heard about it. He was a terrible soldier. He and another fellow were to be tried by a general court-martial for quitting their guard posts on the docks at Oran, but we had to go into action before court could be held. The other fellow had his court after the end of the campaign and got five years."

The officers of the battalion, and those at division headquarters, knew that I was going to write a story about Mollie sometime. Whenever I would encounter one of them, in a country tavern or at a corps or Army headquarters, or on a dusty road behind the lines, during our final campaign before Germany's surrender, he would ask me when I was going to "do Mollie." I am doing him now.

Even after I had been back in the States for a while that summer of 1943, I had an intermittent interest in Mollie, although La Piste Forestière assumed a curious unreality after I had been living on lower Fifth Avenue a couple of weeks. I asked a fellow I knew at the *Times* to check back through the casualty lists and see if the death of a soldier with a name like "Carl Warren" had been reported, since I knew the lists gave the addresses of the next of kin and I thought I might be able to find out more about Mollie. The *Times* man found out that there hadn't been any such name but that there was often a long interval between casualties and publication. I took to turning mechanically to the new lists as they came out and looking through the "W"s. One day I saw listed, among the Army dead, "Karl C. Warner, sister Mrs. Ulidjak, 230 E. Eightieth Street, Manhattan." The juxtaposition of "a name like Warren" with one that I took to be Russian or Ukrainian made me suspect that Warner was Molotov, and it turned out that I was right.

A couple of days later, I went uptown to look for Mrs. Ulidjak. No. 230 is between Second and Third Avenues, in a block overshadowed by the great brute mass of the Manhattan Storage & Warehouse Company's building at the corner of Eightieth. Along the block there were a crumbling, red-brick elementary school of the type Fusion administrations like to keep going so that they can hold the tax rate down, a yellowish, old-fashioned Baptist church, some boys playing ball in the street, and a banner, bearing a number of service stars, hung on a line stretched across the street. As yet, it had no gold stars. No. 230 is what is still called a "new-law tenement," although the law governing this type of construction is fifty years old: a six-story walkup with the apartments built around air shafts. Ulidjak was one of the names on the mailboxes in the vestibule. I pushed the button beside it, and in a minute there was an answering buzz and I walked upstairs. A thin, pale woman with a long, bony face and straight blond hair pulled back into a bun came to the apartment door. She looked under thirty and wore silver-rimmed spectacles. This was Mrs. Ulidjak, Private Warner's sister. Her husband is in the Merchant Marine. She didn't seem startled when I said I was a correspondent; every American expects to be interviewed by a reporter sometime. Mrs. Ulidjak had been notified of her brother's death by the War Department over a week before, but she had no idea how it had happened or where. She said he had been in the Sixtieth Infantry, all right, so I was sure Warner had been Mollie. "Was he fighting the Japs?" she asked me. When I told her no, she seemed slightly disappointed. "And you were there?" she asked. I said I had been. Then, apparently trying to visualize me in the context of war, she asked, "Did you wear a helmet, like Ernie Pyle? Gee, they must be heavy to wear. Did it hurt your head much?" When I had reassured her on this point, she led me into a small sitting room with a window opening on a dark air shaft. A young man and a young woman, who Mrs. Ulidjak said were neighbors, were in the room, but they went into the adjoining kitchen, apparently so that they would not feel obliged to look solemn.

"Was your name Warner, too, before you were married?" I asked Mrs. Ulidjak.

"No," she said, "Karl and I were named Petuskia—that's Russian—but he changed to Warner when he came to New York because he thought it sounded sweller. We were from a little place called Cokesburg, in western Pennsylvania. He hardly ever came up here. He had his own friends."

"Did he go to high school in Cokesburg?" I asked.

The idea amused Mrs. Ulidjak. "No, just grammar school," she said. "He was a pit boy in the coal mines until we came to New York. But he always liked to dress nice. You can ask any of the cops around the Mall in Central Park about him. Curly, they used to call him, or Blondy. He was quite a lady's man."

Then I asked her the question that had puzzled Mollie's Army friends: "What did he do for a living before he went into the Army?"

"He was a bartender down to Jimmy Kelly's, the nightclub in the Village," Mrs. Ulidjak said.

She then told me that her brother's Christian name really was Karl and that he was twenty-six when he was killed, although he had looked several years younger. Both parents are dead. The parents had never told her, as far as she could remember, what part of Russia they came from. When I said that Mollie had been a hero, she was pleased, and said he had always had an awful crust. She called the young neighbors, who seemed to be of Italian descent, back into the sitting room and made me repeat the story of how Mollie captured the six hundred Italians (I hadn't seen the official version of his exploit yet and naturally I gave him full credit in mine). "Six hundred wops!"" Mrs. Ulidjak exclaimed gaily. She got a lot of fun out of Mollie's "big shot" stories, too. She showed me a large, expensive-looking photograph of him "addressing" a golf ball. He was wearing light-colored plus-fours, white stockings, and brogues with tassels, and there was a big, happy grin on his face that made it plain that he was not going to hit the ball but was just posing. He had a wide, plump face with high cheekbones and square white teeth, and the hair about which I had so often heard looked at least six inches long. "He had a room at 456 West Forty-fourth Street, and a little Jewish tailor down in that neighborhood made all those nice things for him special," she said admiringly. She had never heard him called Molotov.

I went over to West Forty-fourth Street a few days later. The 400 block, between Ninth and Tenth Avenues, looks more depressing than the one the Ulidjaks live on. It is mostly shops dealing in the cheap merchandise that is used as premiums, and stores that sell waiters' supplies, and lodging houses favored by waiters and cooks. It was evident from the look of the house at No. 456 that though Mollie had spent a disproportionate share of his income on clothes, he had not wasted anything on his living quarters. No one at No. 456 remembered Mollie. The tenants and the janitor had all come there since his time. I couldn't find the little tailor. But on the north side of Forty-fourth Street, near Ninth Avenue, there is a building occupied by the Warner Brothers' Eastern offices, and I was sure that this had given Mollie the idea of calling himself Warner.

That evening I went down to Jimmy Kelly's, on Sullivan Street. Kelly's is the kind of club that never changes much but that you seldom remember anything specific about unless you have had a fight there. I had been there a few times before I had gone overseas, in 1941, but I couldn't even remember the bartender's face. Kelly's has a dance floor a little bigger than two tablecloths, and there is always a show with young, sometimes pretty girls imitating the specialties that more famous and experienced performers are doing at clubs uptown, and a master of ceremonies making cracks so old that they have been used in Hollywood musicals. The man behind the bar the night I showed up said he had been there several years and had known his predecessor, whose name was not Molotov. He had never heard of a bartender named Molotov or Warner or Mollie or Karl at Kelly's. After I had had a couple of Scotches and had told him the story, he said he wondered if the fellow I meant hadn't been a busboy. The description seemed to fit one who had worked there. "We all used to call this kid Curly," he said, "but Ray, the waiter who is the union delegate, might remember his real name."

Ray was a scholarly-looking man with a high, narrow forehead and shell-rimmed spectacles. "Curly's name *was* Karl C. Warner," he said after he had been told what I wanted to know. "I remember it from his union card. He was a man who would always stand up for his fellow-worker. Waiters and Waitresses Local No. 1 sent him down here in the summer of 1940 and he worked until late the next fall. He was outspoken but a hard worker and strong—he could carry three stacks of dishes on each arm. A busboy has a lot to do in a place like this when there is a rush on—clearing away dishes, setting up for new parties, bringing the waiters their orders—and a stupid boy can spoil the wait-ers' lives for them. We had another boy here at the same time, an Irish boy, who kidded Curly about the fancy clothes he wore, so they went down in the basement and fought for a couple of hours one afternoon. Nobody won the fight. They just fought until they were tired and then stopped. Curly had wide interests for a busboy," Ray continued. "When there was no rush on, he would sometimes stop by a customer's table, particularly if it was some man who looked important, and talk to him for ten minutes or so. The customers didn't seem to mind. He had a nice way about him. He had a kind of curiosity."

The Army stories about Mollie's wealth made Ray and the bartender laugh. "He used to come back here now and then during the first year he was in the Army," Ray said, "and always he would borrow ten or twenty dollars from one of us waiters. We would lend it to him because we liked him, without expecting to get it back." A busboy at Kelly's is paid only nominal wages, Ray told me—just about enough to cover his laundry bill—but the waiters chip in a percentage of their tips for the boys. "I guess Curly averaged about forty a week here," he said. "If he was anxious to get extra money, he might have had a lunch job some-place else at the same time, but I never heard about it. A tailor like he had probably made those suits for about twenty-five per. What else did he have to spend money on? His night life was here. He used to tell us he had worked at El Morocco, but we used to say, 'What's the differ-ence? Dirty dishes are the same all over.'"

At the union headquarters, which are on the twelfth floor of a loft building on West Fortieth Street, Mollie was also remembered. The serious, chunky young woman in the union secretary's office said, "Warner was always a dissident. He would speak up at every meeting and object to everything. But we all liked him. He stopped paying dues a few months before he went into the Army, but at Christmas time in 1941 he came back here and said he heard that union members in the services were getting a present from the local, so he wanted one, too. So we gave it to him, of course. The secretary will be interested to know he is dead."

The young woman called the secretary, a plump, olive-complexioned man, from his desk in an inner room and said to him, "You remember Karl Warner, the blond boy with curly hair? He has been killed in Africa. He was a hero."

"Is that so?" the secretary said. "Well, get a man to put up a gold paper star on the flag in the members' hall right away and draw up a notice to put on the bulletin board. He is the first member of Local No. 1 to die in this war."

I thought how pleased Mollie would have been at being restored to good standing in the union, without even having paid up his dues. Then I thought of how much fun he would have had on the Mall in Central Park, in the summertime, if he could only have gone up there with his Silver Star ribbon on, and a lot of enemy souvenirs. I also thought of how far La Piste Forestière was from the kitchen in Jimmy Kelly's.

from The Thin Red Line
by James Jones

James Jones (1921–1977) served in the Pacific during the war; he rose to sergeant, won a Bronze Star, and was wounded. His 1962 novel, The Thin Red Line, is still shocking in its subversiveness: It shows not how war makes men, but how it humiliates them. In this passage, terrified infantrymen must assault a heavily defended Japanese position.

D awn came, and passed, and still they waited. The roses and blues of the dawn light changed to the pearl and misty grays of early morning light. Of course everyone had been up, and nervously ready, since long before dawn. But for today Colonel Tall had requested a new artillery wrinkle. Because of yesterday's heavy repulse, Tall had asked for, and got, an artillery time-on-target "shoot." This device, an artillery technique left over from World War I, was a method of calculating so that the first rounds of every battery hit their various targets simultaneously. Under TOT fire men caught in the open would suddenly find themselves enveloped in a curtain of murderous fire without the usual warning of a few shells arriving early from the nearest guns. The thing to do was to wait a bit, play poker with them, try to catch them when they were out of their holes for breakfast or an early morning stretch. So they waited. Along the crest the silent troops stared across a silent ravine to the silent hilltop, and the silent hill stared back.

C-for-Charlie, waiting with the assault companies on the slope below, could not even see this much. Nor did they care. They crouched over their weapons in total and unspeakable insularity, so many separate small islands. To their right and to their left A-for-Able and B-for-Baker did the same.

At exactly twenty-two minutes after first daylight Colonel Tall's requested TOT fire struck, an earthcracking, solidly tangible, continuous roar on Hill 210. The artillery fired three-minute concentrations at irregular intervals, hoping to catch the survivors out of their holes. Twenty minutes later, and before the barrage itself was ended, whistles began to blow along the crest of Hill 209.

. The assault companies had no recourse except to begin to move. Minds cast frantically about for legitimate last minute excuses, and found none. In the men themselves nervous fear and anxiety, contained so long and with such effort in order to appear brave, now began to come out in yelled exhortations and yelps of gross false enthusiasm. They moved up the slope; and in bunches, crouching low and carrying their rifles in one or both hands, they hopped over the crest and commenced to run sideways and crouching down the short forward slope to the flat, rocky ground in front. Men in the line shouted encouragement to them as they passed through. A small cheer, dwarfed by the distant mountains, rose and died. A few slapped some of them toughly on the shoulder as they went through. Men who would not die today winked lustily at men who, in some cases, would soon be dead. On C-for-Charlie's right fifty yards away A-for-Able was going through an identical ritual.

They were rested. At least, they were comparatively so; they had not had to stand watch one half of the night, and they had not been up on the line where jitters precluded sleep, but down below, protected. And they had been fed. And watered. If few of them had slept much, at least they were better off than the men on the line.

Corporal Fife was one of those who had slept the least. He still could not get over little Bead's having killed that Jap like that. What with that, the rain, the total lack of shelter from the rain, and his nervous excitation about the morrow, he had only dozed once for about five minutes. But the loss of sleep did not bother him. He was young, and healthy, and fairly strong. In fact, he had never felt *healthier* or in better shape in his life; and earlier in the day, in the first gray of early light, he had stood forth upon the slope and, exuding energy and vitality, had looked a long time down the ravine as it fell and deepened toward the rear until he wanted to spread wide his arms with sacrifice and love of life and love of men. He didn't do it of course. There were men awake all round him. But he had wanted to. And now as he dropped over the ridge and into the beginning of the battle, he shot one swift look behind him, one last look, and found himself staring head on into the wide, brown, spectacle-covered eyes of Bugger Stein, who happened to be right behind him. What a hell of a last look! Fife thought sourly.

Stein thought he had never seen such a deep, dark, intense, angrily haunted look as that which Fife bent on him as they dropped over the ridge, and Stein thought it was directed at him. At him, personally. They two were almost the last to go. Only Sergeant Welsh and young Bead remained behind them. And when Stein looked back, they were coming, hunched low, chopping with their feet, sliding down the shale and dirt of the slope.

Stein's dispositions had been the same today as in the two previous days. They had done nothing much and he saw no reason to change the march order: 1st Platoon first, 2d Platoon second, 3d in reserve. One of the two machine guns went with each forward platoon; the mortars would stay with the Company HQ and the reserve. That was the way they had moved out. And as Stein slid to the bottom of 209's short forward slope he could see 1st Platoon pass out of sight beyond one of the little folds of ground which ran across their line of advance. They were about a hundred yards ahead and appeared to be deployed well.

There were three of these little folds in the ground. All of them were perpendicular to the south face of Hill 209, parallel to each other. It had been Stein's idea, when inspecting the terrain with Colonel Tall the evening before, to utilize these as cover by shoving off from the right end of the hill and then advancing left across them and across his own front—instead of getting himself caught in the steeper ravine immediately between the two hills, as had happened to Fox Co. Tall had agreed to this.

Afterward, Stein had briefed his own officers on it. Kneeling just behind the crest with them in the fading light, he pointed it all out and they looked it over. Somewhere in the dusk a sniper's rifle had spat angrily. One by one they inspected it through binoculars. The third and furthest left of these three folds was about a hundred and fifty yards from the beginning of the slope which became the Elephant's Neck. This slope steepened as it climbed to the U-shaped eminence of the Elephant's Head, which from five hundred yards beyond commanded and brooded over the entire area. This hundred and fifty yard low area, as well as the third fold, was dominated by two lesser, grassy ridges growing out of the slope and two hundred yards apart, one on either side of the low area. Both ridges were at right angles to the folds of ground and parallel to the line of advance. With these in their hands *plus* the Elephant's Head, the Japanese could put down a terrible fire over the whole approach area. Tall's plan was for the forward elements to move up onto these two ridges, locating and eliminating the hidden strong points there which had stopped 2d Battalion yesterday, and then with the reserve company to reinforce them, work their way up the Elephant's Neck to take the The Head. This was the Bowling Alley. But there was no way to outflank it. On the left it fell in a precipitous slope to the river, and on the right the Japanese held the jungle in force. It had to be taken frontally. All of this Stein had lined out for his officers last evening. Now they were preparing to execute it.

Stein, at the bottom of the shale slope, could see very little of anything. A great racketing of noise had commenced and hung everywhere in the air without seeming to have any source. Part of course was due to his own side firing all along the line, and the bombardment and the mortars. Perhaps the Japanese were firing too now. But he could see no visual signs of it. What time was it, anyway? Stein looked at his watch, and its little face stared back at him with an intensity it had never had before. Six forty-five; a quarter to seven in the morning. Back home he would be just—Stein realized he had never really seen his watch. He forced himself to put his arm down. Directly in front of him his reserve 3d Platoon were spread out and flattened behind the first of the three little folds of ground. With them were the Company HQ and the mortar section. Most of them were looking at him with faces as intense as his watch's face. Stein ran crouching over to them, his equipment bouncing and banging on him, shouting for them to set up the mortars there, motioning with his hand. Then he realized that he could only just barely hear his own voice himself, with all this banging and racketing of doom bouncing around in the air. How could they hear him? He wondered how the 1st Platoon—and the 2d—were doing, and how he could see.

The 1st Platoon, at that particular moment, was spread out and flattened behind the middle of the three little folds of ground. Behind it the 2d Platoon was spread out and flattened in the low between the folds. Nobody really wanted to move. Young Lt. Whyte had already looked over the area between this fold and the third and seen nothing, and he already had motioned for his two scouts to proceed there. Now he motioned to them again, using an additional hand-and-arm signal meaning "speed." The booming and banging and racketing in the air was bothering Whyte, too. It did not seem to come from any one place or several places, but simply hung and jounced in the air, sourceless. He too could see no visual end results of so much banging and exploding. His two scouts still not having moved, Whyte became angry and opened his mouth and bellowed at them, motioning again. They could not hear him of course, but he knew they could see the black open hole of his mouth. Both of them stared at him as though they thought him insane for even suggesting such a thing, but this time, after a moment, they moved. Almost side by side they leaped up, crossed the crest of the little fold, and ran crouching down to the low where they flattened themselves. After a moment they leaped up again, one a little behind the other, and ran bent almost double to the top of the last fold and fell flat. After another moment and a perfunctory peek over its top, they motioned Whyte to come on. Whyte jumped up making a sweeping forward motion with his arm and ran forward, his platoon behind him. As the 1st Platoon moved, making the crossing as the scouts had: in two rushes the 2d Platoon moved to the top of the middle fold.

Back at the first fold of ground Stein had seen this move and been a little reassured by it. Creeping close to the top of the fold among his men, he had raised himself to his knees to see, his face and whole patches of his skin twitching with mad alarm in an effort to call his insanity to his attention. When nothing hit him immediately, he stayed up, standing on his knees, to see 1st Platoon leave the middle fold and arrive at the crest of the third. At least they had got that far. Maybe it wouldn't be so bad. He lay back down, feeling quite proud, and realized his flattened men around him had been staring at him intently. He felt even prouder. Behind him, in the low of the fold, the mortar squads were setting up their mortars. Crawling back to them through the internal racketing still floating loose in the air, he shouted in Culp's ear for him to make the left-hand grassy ridge his target. At the mortars Private Mazzi, the Italian boy from the Bronx, stared at him with wide, frightened eyes. So did most of the others. Stein crawled back to the top of the fold. He arrived, and raised himself, just in time to see 1st Platoon and then 2d Platoon attack. He was the only man along the top of the first fold who did see it, because he was the only man who was not flattened on the ground. He bit his lip. Even from here he could tell that it was bad, a serious tactical blunder.

If tactical blunder it was, the fault was Whyte's. First Whyte, and secondly, Lt. Tom Blane of the 2d Platoon. Whyte had arrived at the top of the third and last fold of ground without a casualty. This in itself seemed strange to him, if not highly overoptimistic. He knew his orders: he was to locate and eliminate the hidden strong points on the two grassy ridges. The nearest of these, the right-hand one, had its rather sharply defined beginnings about eighty yards to his right front. While his men flattened themselves and stared at him with intense sweating faces, he raised himself cautiously on his elbows till only his eyes showed, and inspected the terrain. Before him the ground fell, sparsely grassed and rocky, until it reached the beginnings of the little ridge, where it immediately became thickly grassed with the brown, waist-high grass. He could not see anything that looked like Japanese or their emplacements. Whyte was scared, but his anxiety to do well today was stronger. He did not really believe he would be killed in this war. Briefly he glanced over his shoulder to the ridge of Hill 209 where groups of men stood half-exposed, watching. One of them was the corps commander. The loud banging and racketing hanging sourceless in the air had abated somewhat, had raised itself a few yards, after the lifting of the barrage from the little ridges to the Elephant's Head. Again Whyte looked at the terrain and then motioned his scouts forward.

Once again the two riflemen stared at him as though they thought he had lost his mind, as though they would have liked to reason with him if they hadn't feared losing their reputations. Again Whyte motioned them forward, jerking his arm up and down in the signal for speed. The men looked at each other, then, gathering themselves on hands and knees first, bounced up and sprinted twenty-five yards down into the low area and fell flat. After a moment in which they inspected and found themselves still alive, they gathered themselves again. On hands and knees, preparing to rise, the first one suddenly fell down flat and bounced; the second, a little way behind him, got a little further up so that when he fell he tumbled on his shoulder and rolled onto his back. And there they lay, both victims of well-placed rifle shots by unseen riflemen. Neither moved again. Both were obviously dead. Whyte stared at them shocked. He had known them almost four months. He had heard no shots nor had he seen anything move. No bullets kicked up dirt anywhere in front. Again he stared at the quiet, masked face of the deserted little ridge.

What was he supposed to do now? The high, sourceless racketing in the air seemed to have gotten a little louder. Whyte, who was a meaty, big young man, had been a champion boxer and champion judoman at his university where he was preparing himself to be a marine biologist, as well as having been the school's best swimmer. Anyway, they can't get all of us, he thought loyally, but meaning principally himself, and made his decision.

"Come on, boys! Let's go get 'em!" he yelled and leaped to his feet motioning the platoon forward. He took two steps, the platoon with their bayonets fixed since early morning right behind him, and fell down dead, stitched diagonally from hip to shoulder by bullets, one of which exploded his heart. He had just time enough to think that something had hurt him terribly, not even enough to think that he was dead, before he was. Perhaps he screamed.

Five others of his platoon went down with him almost simultaneously, in various states of disrepair, some dead, some only nicked. But the impetus Whyte had inaugurated remained, and the platoon charged blindly on. Another impetus would be needed to stop it or change its direction. A few more men went down. Invisible rifles and machine guns hammered from what seemed to be every quarter of the globe. After reaching the two dead scouts, they came in range of the more distant left ridge, which took them with a heavy crossfire. Sergeant Big Queen, running with the rest and bellowing incoherently, and who had only been promoted two days before after the defection of Stack, watched the platoon sergeant, a man named Grove, throw his rifle from him as though he feared it, and go down hollering and clawing at his chest. Queen did not even think about it. Near him Pfc Doll ran too, blinking his eyes rapidly as though this might protect him. His mind had withdrawn completely in terror, and he did not think at all. Doll's sense of personal invulnerability was having a severe test, but had not as yet, like Whyte's, failed. They were past the dead scouts now. More men on the left were beginning to go down. And behind them over the top of the third fold, suddenly, came the 2d Platoon in full career, yelling hoarsely.

This was the responsibility of 2d Lt Blane. It was not a particularly complex responsibility. It had nothing to do with envy, jealousy, paranoia, or suppressed self-destruction. He too, like Whyte, knew what his orders were, and he had promised Bill Whyte he would back him up and help him out. He too knew the corps commander was watching, and he

too wanted to do well today. Not as athletic as his fellow worker, but
more imaginative, more sensitive, he too leaped up and motioned his
men forward, when he saw 1st Platoon move. He could see the whole
thing finished in his imagination: himself and Whyte and their men
standing atop the bombed out bunkers in proper triumph, the position captured. He too died on the forward slope but not at the crest like
Whyte. It took several seconds for the still-hidden Japanese gunners to
raise their fire, and 2d Platoon was ten yards down the gentle little
slope before it was unleashed against them. Nine men fell at once. Two
died and one of them was Blane. Not touched by a machinegun, he
unluckily was chosen as target by three separate riflemen, none of
whom knew about the others or that he was an officer, and all of whom
connected. He bounced another five yards forward, and with three bullets through his chest cavity did not die right away. He lay on his back
and, dreamily and quite numb, stared at the high, beautiful, pure white
cumuli which sailed like stately ships across the sunny, cool blue tropic
sky. It hurt him a little when he breathed. He was dimly aware that he
might possibly die as he became unconscious.

2d Platoon had just reached the two dead 1st Platoon scouts when
mortar shells began to drop in onto the 1st Platoon twenty-five yards
ahead. First two, then a single, then three together popped up in unbelievable mushrooms of dirt and stones. Chards and pieces whickered
and whirred in the air. It was the impetus needed either to change the
direction of the blind charge or to stop it completely. It did both. In the
2d Platoon S/Sgt. Keck, watched by everyone now with Lt Blane down,
threw out his arms holding his rifle at the balance, dug in his heels and
bellowed in a voice like the combined voices of ten men for them to
"Hit dirt! Hit dirt!" 2d Platoon needed no urging. Running men melted
into the earth as if a strong wind had come up and blown them over like
dried stalks.

In the 1st Platoon, less lucky, reaction varied. On the extreme right
the line had reached the first beginning slope of the right-hand ridge,
long hillock really, and a few men—perhaps a squad—turned and dove
into the waist-high grass there, defilading themselves from the hidden

MGs above them as well as protecting them from the mortars. On the far left that end had much further to go, seventy yards more, to reach dead space under the lefthand ridge; but a group of men tried to make it. None of them reached it, however. They were hosed to earth and hiding by the machineguns above them, or bowled over stunned by the mortars, before they could defilade themselves from the MGs or get close enough to them to escape the mortars. Just to the left of the center was the attached machine gun squad from Culp's platoon, allowed to join the charge by Whyte through forgetfulness or for some obscure tactical reason of his own, all five of whom, running together, were knocked down by the same mortar shell, gun and tripod and ammo boxes all going every which way and bouncing end over end, although not one of the five was wounded by it. These marked the furthest point of advance. On the extreme left five or six riflemen were able to take refuge in a brushy draw at the foot of Hill 209 which, a little further down, became the deep ravine where Fox and George had been trapped and hit yesterday. These men began to fire at the two grassy ridges although they could see no targets.

In the center of 1st Platoon's line there were no defilades or draws to run to. The middle, before the mortars stopped them, had run itself right on down and out onto the dangerous low area, where they could not only be enfiladed by the ridges but could also be hit by MG plunging fire from Hill 210 itself. Here there was nothing to do but get down and hunt holes. Fortunately the TOT barrage had searched here as well as on the hillocks, and there were 105 and 155 holes available. Men jostled each other for them, shared them. The late Lt Whyte's 19th Century charge was over. The mortar rounds continued to drop here and there across the area, searching flesh, searching bone.

Private John Bell of the 2d Platoon lay sprawled exactly as his body had skidded to a halt, without moving a muscle. He could not see because his eyes were shut, but he listened. On the little ridges the prolonged yammering of the MGs had stopped and now confined itself to short bursts at specific targets. Here and there wounded men bellowed, whined or whimpered. Bell's face was turned left, his cheek pressed to the ground, and he tried not even to breath too conspicuously for fear of calling attention to himself. Cautiously he opened his eyes, half afraid the movement of eyelids would be seen by a machine gunner a hundred yards away, and found himself staring into the open eyes of the 1st Platoon's first scout lying dead five yards to Bell's left. This was, or had been, a young Graeco-Turkish draftee named Kral. Kral was noted for two things, the ugliest bent-nosed face in the regiment and the thickest glasses in C-for-Charlie. That with such a myopia he could be a scout was a joke of the company. But Kral had volunteered for it; he wanted to be where the action was, he said; in peace or in war. A hep kid from Jersey, he had nevertheless believed the four-color propaganda leaflets. He had not known that the profession of first scout of a rifle platoon was a thing of the past and belonged in the Indian Wars, not to the massed divisions, superior firepower, and tighter social control of today. First target, the term should be, not first scout, and now the big glasses still reposed on his face. They had not fallen off. But something about their angle, at least from where Bell lay, magnified the open eyes until they filled the entire lenses. Bell could not help staring fixedly at them, and they stared back with a vastly wise and tolerant amusement. The more Bell stared at them the more he felt them to be holes into the center of the universe and that he might fall in through them to go drifting down through starry space amongst galaxies and spiral nebulae and island universes. He remembered he used to think of his wife's cunt like that, in a more pleasant way. Forcibly Bell shut his eyes. But he was afraid to move his head, and whenever he opened them again, there Kral's eyes were, staring at him their droll and flaccid message of amiable goodwill, sucking at him dizzyingly. And wherever he looked they followed him, pleasantly but stubbornly. From above, invisible but there, the fiery sun heat of the tropic day heated his head inside his helmet, making his soul limp. Bell had never known such eviscerating, ballshrinking terror. Somewhere out of his sight another mortar shell exploded. But in general the day seemed to have become very quiet. His arm with his watch on it lay within his range of vision, he noticed. My God! Was it only 7:45? Defeatedly he let his eyes go back where they

wanted: to Kral's. HERE LIES FOUR-EYES KRAL, DIED FOR SOME-
THING. When one of Kral's huge eyes winked at him waggishly, he
knew in desperation he had to do something, although he had been
lying there only thirty seconds. Without moving, his cheek still pressed
to earth, he yelled loudly.

"Hey, *Keck*!" He waited. "Hey, *Keck*! We got to get out of here!"

"I know it," came the muffled answer. Keck was obviously lying with
his head turned the other way and had no intention of moving it.

"What'll we do?"

"Well . . ." There was silence while Keck thought. It was interrupted
by a high, quavery voice from a long way off.

"We know you there, Yank. Yank, we know you there."

"Tojo eats shit!'" Keck yelled. He was answered by an angry burst of
machinegun fire. "Roozover' eat shit!" the faraway voice screamed.

"You goddam right he does!" some frightened Republican called
from Bell's blind right side. When the firing stopped, Bell called again.

"What'll we do, Keck?"

"Listen," came the muffled answer. "All you guys listen. Pass it along
so everybody knows." He waited and there was a muffled chorus. "Now
get this. When I holler go, everybody up. Load and lock and have a
nuther clip in yore hand. 1st and 3d Squads stay put, kneeling position,
and fire covering fire. 2d and 4th Squads hightail it back over that little
fold. 1st and 3d Squads fire two clips, then scoot. 2d and 4th fire covering fire from that fold. If you can't see nothin, fire searching fire. Space
yore shots. Them positions is somewhere about halfway up them ridges.
Everybody fire at the righthand ridge which is closer. You got that?"

He waited while everyone muffledly tried to assure themselves that
everybody else knew.

"Everybody got it?" Keck called muffledly. There were no answers.
"Then—GO!" he bellowed.

The slope came to life. Bell, in the 2d Squad, did not even bother
with the brave man's formality of looking about to see if the plan was
working, but instead squirmed around and leaped up running, his legs
already pistoning before the leap came down to earth. Safe beyond the

little fold of ground, which by now had taken on characteristics of huge size, he whirled and began to fire cover, terribly afraid of being stitched across the chest like Lt Whyte who lay only a few yards away. Methodically he drilled his shots into the dun hillside which still hid the invisible, yammering MGs, one round to the right, one to the left, one to center, one to the left . . . He could not believe that any of them might actually hit somebody. If one did, what a nowhere way to go: killed by accident; slain not as an individual but by sheer statistical probability, by the calculated chance of searching fire, even as he himself might be at any moment. Mathematics! Mathematics! Algebra! Geometry! When 1st and 3d Squads came diving and tumbling back over the tiny crest, Bell was content to throw himself prone, press his cheek to the earth, shut his eyes, and lie there. God, oh, God! Why am I *here*? Why am I *here*? After a moment's thought, he decided he better change it to: why are *we* here. That way, no agency of retribution could exact payment from him for being selfish.

Apparently Keck's plan had worked very well. 2d and 4th Squads, having the surprise, had gotten back untouched; and 1st and 3d Squads had had only two men hit. Bell had been looking right at one of them. Running hard with his head down, the man (a *boy*, named Kline) had jerked his head up suddenly, his eyes wide with start and fright, and cried out "Oh!" his mouth a round pursed hole in his face, and had gone down. Sick at himself for it, Bell had felt laughter burbling up in his chest. He did not know whether Kline was killed or wounded. The MGs had stopped yammering. Now, in the comparative quiet and fifty yards to their front, 1st Platoon was down and invisible amongst their shell holes and sparse grass. Anguished, frightened cries of "Medic! Medic!" were beginning to be raised now here and there across the field, and 2d Platoon having escaped were slowly realizing that they were not after all very safe even here.

Back at the CP behind the first fold Stein was not alone in seeing the tumbling, pellmell return of the 2d Platoon to the third fold. Seeing that their Captain could safely stand up on his knees without being pumped full of holes or mangled, others were now doing it. He was

setting them a pretty good example, Stein thought, still a little astonished by his own bravery. They were going to need medics up there, he
decided, and called his two company aidmen to him.

"You two fellows better get on up there," Stein yelled to them above
the racket. "I expect they need you." That sounded calm and good.

"Yes, sir," one of them said. That was the scholarly, bespectacled one,
the senior. They looked at each other seriously.

"I'll try to get stretcherbearers to the low between here and the second fold, to help you," Stein shouted. "See if you can't drag them back
that far." He stood up on his knees again to peer forward, at where now
and then single mortar shells geysered here and there beyond the third
fold. "Go by rushes if you think you have to," he added inconclusively.
They disappeared.

"I need a runner," Stein bawled, looking toward the line of his men
who had had both the sense and the courage to climb to their knees in
order to see. All of them heard him, because the whole little line rolled
their eyes to look at him or turned toward him their heads. But not a
single figure moved to come forward or answered him. Stein stared
back at them disbelieving. He was aware he had misjudged them completely, and he felt like a damned fool. He had expected to be swamped
by volunteers. A sinking terror took hold of him: if he could be that
wrong about this, what else might he not be wrong about? His enthusiasm had betrayed him. To save face he looked away, trying to pretend
he had not expected anything. But it wasn't soon enough and he knew
they knew. Not quite sure what to do next, he was saved the trouble of
deciding: a wraithlike, ghostly figure appeared at his elbow.

"I'll go, sir."

It was Charlie Dale, the second cook, scowling with intensity, his
face dark and excited.

Stein told him what he wanted about the stretcherbearers, and then
watched him go trotting off bent over at the waist toward the slope of
Hill 209 which he would have to climb. Stein had no idea where he
had been, or where he had come from so suddenly. He could not
remember seeing him all day today until now. Certainly he had not

been one of the line of kneeling standees. Stein looked back at them, somewhat restored. Dale. He must remember that.

There were now twelve men standing on their knees along the little fold of ground, trying to see what was going on up front. Young Corporal Fife was not, however, one of these. Fife was one of the ones who stayed flattened out, and he was as absolutely flattened as he could get. While Stein stood above him on his knees observing, Fife lay with his knees drawn up and his ear to the soundpower phone Stein had given him care of, and he did not care if he never stood up or ever saw anything. Earlier, when Stein had first done it with his stupid pleased pride shining all over his face, Fife had forced himself to stand straight up on his knees for several seconds, in order that no one might tag him with the title of coward. But he felt that was enough. Anyway, his curiosity was not at all piqued. All he had seen, when he did get up, was the top two feet of a dirt mushroom from a mortar shell landing beyond the third fold. What the fuck was so great about that? Suddenly a spasm of utter hopelessness shook Fife. Helplessness, that was what he felt; complete helplessness. He was as helpless as if agents of his government had bound him hand and foot and delivered him here and then gone back to wherever it was good agents went. Maybe a Washington cocktail bar, with lots of cunts all around. And here he lay, as bound and tied by his own mental processes and social indoctrination as if they were ropes, simply because while he could admit to himself privately that he was a coward, he did not have the guts to admit it publicly. It was agonizing. He was reacting exactly as the smarter minds of his society had anticipated he would react. They were ahead of him all down the line. And he was powerless to change. It was frustrating, maddening like a brick wall all around him that he could neither bust through nor leap over and at the same time—making it even worse-—there was his knowledge that there was really no wall at all. If early this morning he had been full of self-sacrifice, he now no longer was. He did not want to be here. He did not want to be here at all. He wanted to be over there where the generals were standing up on the ridge in complete safety, watching. Sweating with fear and an unbelievable tension of double-mindedness, Fife looked over at them and if looks of hatred could kill they would all have fallen down dead and the campaign would be over until they shipped in some new ones. If only he could go crazy. Then he would not be responsible. Why couldn't he go crazy? But he couldn't. The unstone of the stone wall immediately rose up around him denying him exit. He could only lie here and be stretched apart on this rack of double-mindedness. Off to the right, some yards beyond the last man of the reserve platoon, Fife's eyes recorded for him the images of Sergeants Welsh and Storm crouched behind a small rock outcrop. As he watched, Storm raised his arm and pointed. Welsh snaked his rifle onto the top of the rock and checking the stock, fired off five shots. Both peered. Then they looked at each other and shrugged. It was an easily understood little pantomime. Fife fell into an intense rage. Cowboys and Indians! Cowboys and Indians! Everybody's playing cowboys and Indians! Just as if these weren't real bullets, and you couldn't really get killed. Fife's head burned with a fury so intense that it threatened to blow all his mental fuses right out through his ears in two bursts of black smoke. His rage was broken off short, snapped off at the hilt as it were, by the buzzing whistle of the soundpower phone in his ear.

Startled, Fife cleared his throat, shocked into wondering whether he could still talk, after so long. It was the first time he had tried a word since leaving the ridge. It was also the first time he had ever heard this damn phone thing work. He pushed the button and cupped it to his mouth. "Yes?" he said cautiously.

"What do you mean, 'yes'?" a calm cold voice said, and waited. Fife hung suspended in a great empty black void, trying to think. What had he meant? "I mean this is Charlie Cat Seven," he said, remembering the code jargon. "Over."

"That's better," the calm voice said. "This is Seven Cat Ace." That meant 1st Battalion, the HQ. "Colonel Tall here. I want Captain Stein. Over."

"Yes, Sir," Fife said. "He's right here." He reached up one arm to tug at the skirt of Stein's green fatigue blouse. Stein looked down, staring, as if he had never seen Fife before. Or anybody else.

"Colonel Tall wants you."

Stein lay down (glad to flatten himself, Fife noted with satisfaction) and took the phone. Despite the racketing din overhead, both he and Fife beside him could hear the Colonel clearly.

When he accepted the phone and pushed down the button, Bugger Stein was already casting about for his explanations. He had not expected to be called upon to recite so soon, and he had not prepared his lessons. What he could say would of course depend on Tall's willingness to allow any explanation at all. He could not help being a guilty schoolboy about to be birched. "Charlie Cat Seven. Stein," he said. "Over." He released the button.

What he heard astounded him to speechlessness.

"Magnificent, Stein, magnificent." Tall's clear cold calm boyish voice came to him—came to both of them—rimed over with a crust of clear cold boyish enthusiasm. "The finest thing these old eyes have seen in a long time. In a month of Sundays." Stein had a vivid mental picture of Tall's close-cropped, boyish Anglo-Saxon head and unlined, Anglo-Saxon face. Tall was less than two years older than Stein. His clear, innocent, boyish eyes were the youngest Stein had seen in some time. "Beautifully conceived and beautifully executed. You'll be mentioned in Battalion Orders, Stein. Your men came through for you beautifully. Over."

Stein pressed the button, managed a weak "Yes, Sir. Over," and released the button. He could not think of anything else to say.

"Best sacrificial commitment to develop a hidden position I have ever seen outside maneuvers. Young Whyte led beautifully. I'm mentioning him, too. I saw him go down in that first melee. Was he hurt very bad? But sending in your 2d too was brilliant. They might very well have carried both subsidiary ridges with luck. I don't think they were hurt too bad. Blane led well too. His withdrawal was very old pro. How many of the emplacements did they locate? Did they knock out any? We ought to have those ridges cleaned out by noon. Over."

Stein listened, rapt, staring into the eyes of Fife who listened also, staring back. For Fife the calm, pleasant, conversational tone of Col Tall was both maddening and terrifying. And for Stein it was like hearing a radio report on the fighting in Africa which he knew nothing about. Once in school his father had called him long distance to brag about a good report card which Stein had thought would be bad. Neither listener betrayed what he thought to the other, and the silence lengthened.

"Hello? Hello? Hello, Stein? Over?"

Stein pressed the button. "Yes, Sir. Here, Sir. Over." Stein released the button.

"Thought you'd been hit," Tall's voice came back matter-of-factly. "I said, how many of the emplacements did they locate? And did they knock any of them out? Over."

Stein pressed the button, staring into the wide eyes of Fife as if he might see Tall on the other side of them. "I don't know. Over." He released the button.

"What do you mean you don't know? How can you not know?" Tall's cool, calm, conversational voice said. "Over."

Stein was in a quandary. He could admit what both he and Fife knew, or perhaps Fife did not know, which was that he knew nothing about Whyte's attack, had not ordered it, and until now had believed it bad. Or he could continue to accept credit for it and try to explain his ignorance of its results. He could not, of course, know that Tall would later change his opinion. With a delicacy of sensibility Stein had never expected to see at all in the army, and certainly not on the field under fire, Fife suddenly lowered his eyes and looked away, half turned his head. He was still listening, but at least he was pretending not to.

Stein pressed the button, which was a necessity, but which was beginning to madden him. "I'm back here," he said sharply. "Behind the third fold.

"Do you want me to stand up? And wave? So you can see me?" he added with caustic anger. "Over."

"No," Tall's voice said calmly, the irony lost on him. "I can see where you are. I want you to do something. I want you to get up there and see what the situation is, Stein. I want Hill 210 in my hands tonight. And to do that I have to have those two ridges by noon. Have you forgotten the corps commander is here observing today? He's got Admiral Barr with him, flown in specially. The Admiral got up at dawn for this. I want you to come to life down there, Stein," he said crisply. "Over and out."

Stein continued to listen, gripping the phone and staring off furiously, though he knew nothing more was forthcoming. Finally he reached out and tapped Fife and gave it to him. Fife took it in silence. Stein rolled to his feet and ran crouching back down to where the mortars were periodically firing off rounds with their weird, other-world, lingering gonglike sound.

"Doing any good?" he bellowed in Culp's ear.

"We're getting bursts on both ridges," Culp bellowed back in his amiable way. "I decided to put one tube onto the right ridge," he said parenthetically, and then shrugged. "But I don't know if we're doin any damage. If they're dug in—" He let it trail off and shrugged again.

"I've decided to move forward to the second fold," Stein yelled. "Will that be too close for you?"

Culp strode three paces forward up the shallow slope and craned his neck to see over the crest, squinting. He came back. "No. It's pretty close, but I think we can still hit. But we're runnin pretty low on ammo. If we keep on firing at this rate—" Again he shrugged.

"Send everybody but your sergeants back for fresh ammo. All they can carry. Then follow us."

"They don't any of them like to carry them aprons," Culp yelled. "They all say if they get hit with one of those things on them . . ."

"God damn it, Bob! I can't be bothered with a thing like that at a time like this! They knew what they were gonna have to carry!"

"I know it." Culp shrugged. "Where do you want me?"

Stein thought. "On the right, I guess. If they locate you, they'll try to hit you. I want you away from the reserve platoon. I'll give you a few riflemen in case they try to send a patrol in on our flank. Anything that looks like more than a patrol, you let me know quick."

"Don't worry!" Culp said. He turned to his squads. Stein trotted off to the right, where he had seen Al Gore, Lt. of his 3d Platoon, motioning at the same time for Sgt. Welsh to come over to him. Welsh came, followed by Storm, for the orders conference. Even Welsh, Stein noticed parenthetically, even Welsh had that strained, intent, withdrawn look on his face—like a greasy patina of guilty wishful thinking.

While 3d Platoon and Stein's Company HQ were trooping forward in two parallel single files in their move to the second fold, the 1st Platoon continued to lie in its shellholes. After the first crash and volley and thunder of mortars they all had expected to be dead in five minutes. Now, it seemed unbelievable but the Japanese did not seem to be able to see them very well. Now and then a bullet or a burst zipped by low overhead, followed in a second or so by the sound of its firing. Mortar rounds still sighed down on them, exploding with roaring mushrooms of terror and dirt. But in general the Japanese seemed to be waiting for something. 1st Platoon was willing to wait with them. Leaderless, pinned down, pressing its hands and sweating faces to the dirt, 1st Platoon was willing to wait forever and never move again. Many prayed and promised God they would go to church services every Sunday. But slowly, they began to realize that they could move around, could fire back, that death was not a foregone conclusion and inevitable for all.

The medics helped with this. The two company aidmen, given their orders by Stein, had moved up amongst 2d Platoon along the third fold, and had begun little sorties out onto the shallow slope after wounded. In all there were 15 wounded men, and 6 dead. The two aidmen did not bother with the dead, but slowly they retrieved for the stretcherbearers all of the wounded. With insouciance, sober, serious and bespectacled, the two of them moved up and down the slope, bandaging and salting, dragging and half-carrying. Mortar shells knocked them down, MG fire kicked up dirt around them, but nothing touched them. Both would be dead before the week was out (and replaced by types much less admired in C-for-Charlie), but for now they clumped untouchably on, two sobersides concerned with aiding the sobbing, near-helpless men it was their official duty to aid. Eventually enough 1st Platoon men raised their heads high enough to see them, and realized movement was possible—at least, as long as they did not all stand up in a body and wave and shout "Here we are!" Not one of them had as yet seen a single Japanese.

The Escape of Mrs. Jeffries
by Janet Flanner

Janet Flanner (1892–1978) was The New Yorker's Paris correspondent for almost fifty years, beginning in 1925. "The Escape of Mrs. Jeffries" recounts an American woman's attempt to escape Nazi-occupied France and return to the United States. The piece is precisely observed: Flanner gets in all the detail she needs to convey the grimness, urgency, frustration and danger that the Occupation held for the people who endured and, in some cases, defied it.

Last September, Mrs. Ellen Jeffries, an American expatriate who had lived in France for twenty years because she was in love with it, tardily decided to leave Paris. Actually, Mrs. Jeffries is not her name; nor are any of the other names in this narrative the names of the people involved. In 1942, after two years of the German occupation, she was among the dozen or more diehards, all women, left over from that colony of about five thousand Americans to whom Paris, during the twenties and thirties, had seemed liberty itself. Since Pearl Harbor, however, detention, *résidence forcée*, or even a concentration camp looked like the inevitable expatriate American way. Or there was flight. By finally making up her mind, on September 1st, to leave, and by moving as rapidly, which in the end meant as illegally, as possible, Mrs. Jeffries managed to arrive in New York the second week of April, 1943. All things considered, including the fact that her travel problems included escapes across two French borders and that escapes are slow-moving projects demanding lots of careful talk first, Mrs. Jeffries, who is forty-five, statuesque, unmelodramatic, New Hampshire–born, a seasoned traveller, and nobody's fool, thinks she made fast time.

Certainly, by last September, it was already better, in Paris, to be conquered French than unconquered American, especially if you wanted to leave it. A trickle of Frenchmen, preferably those who were on food or collaboration business, were given German *Ausweise*, the *Kommandantur* exit visas, which allowed them to cross from Occupied into Vichy France. But no American in Paris last summer was given an exit visa for any reason whatever. The Germans had decided that all Americans were dishonorable. As proof, they pointed out that resident Americans, who before Pearl Harbor had been graciously granted passes merely to visit in the Unoccupied Zone, had from there impolitely run for the Spanish border and home. Even before Pearl Harbor, the Nazis, to keep closer tabs on those who were left in Paris and the environs, had ordered them not to set foot outside the Departments of the Seine and the Siene-et-Oise and to report once a week to their local police station to sign an alien ledger that contained their photographs and data on them. After Pearl Harbor, the ladies also had to register at the Chambre des Députés, where the Germans, ironically, had set up their alien-enemy *Büro*, and sign a new Nazi alien-enemy questionnaire that included the optimistic inquiry *"Avez vous un cheval?"* Two entire lines were reserved for this "Have you a horse?" question. There was no need for the Germans to wonder if American men had horses to donate to the Reichswehr, because all male Americans had been crowded into detention barracks at Compiègne a week after America had entered the war.

In the two years that had passed since the Germans had officially cut France in two, the first, wild seepage of refugees, members of separated families, and soldiers' wives and children across the Armistice demarcation line had settled down into an orderly but illicit commuting, organized, for patriotism or pay, by guides who shuttled back and forth two or three times a week with passengers in tow. Right now nobody seems to know if this smuggling of human beings is still going on, since the Nazis occupy both halves of France. All that is known is that early in February, 1943, the Germans, typically, declared that the demarcation line had been erased but that identification papers or passports, which are precisely what some people either do not possess or most want to hide, must still be shown in order to cross what no longer exists. Early in the spring of 1942 the French were still crossing, for fifty or a hundred francs a head, or for nothing, if poor and in trouble. Then, in May, there was a terrible, little-publicized *rafle*, or raid, on the remaining foreign Jews in Paris, which drastically worsened the chances of anyone's crossing the border. The Nazis ordered that non-French Jewish men, women, and children be separated from one another and sent off, in a new, triple form of segregation, to different camps. When the Gestapo arrived in the Belleville Jewish quarter of Paris to enforce the order, some parents threw themselves and their children, or pushed one another, out of the windows of their homes rather than be separated. A new wild flight of Jews from the rest of Occupied France stampeded the border guides. As a result, the guide fees for everybody, Jew or non-Jew, rose in the tragic competition for flight. Also, the Nazi border patrols, an especially venal lot, boosted their bribery rates or refused to cooperate at all. Then, after the Commandos made their first big Continental raid, on August 19th, at Dieppe, the Nazi restrictions on the movements of the population, which had slackened slightly in the course of two years, suddenly tightened. For passing Jews over the line, guides were shot; passing anybody became more difficult; and passing any English-speaking person became dangerous and thus even costlier. Mrs. Jeffries was automatically a bad proposition, from the guides' viewpoint, because, though a Presbyterian, she was a forty-five-year-old American female and therefore regarded as bothersome if everybody should have to cut and run from a Nazi patrol.

To start dickering for one of these crossings, the regular Parisian phrase was "*Connaissez-vous un passage?*" This was usually addressed to any of the ubiquitous, omniscient, and trusted café waiters who, since the German occupation, have performed a patriotic service and earned a little extra by purveying to Parisians certain anti-Nazi necessities, such as black-market food tips, contraband cigarettes, British radio news, and introductions to border guides. On September 1st, Mrs. Jeffries found her waiter. His first offer was an exorbitant demand for eleven thousand francs from a *type* who, upon a refusal, immediately came down to a bargain eight thousand. As was customary, this proposition was offered by a guide's Paris under-cover, or contact, man, who on an every-other-day schedule got together passage parties of a dozen or more people. The guide furnished transportation, exclusive of railroad accommodation, in the shape of hay carts or trucks for long detours on border side roads, and made arrangements for, but didn't pay for, food and lodging en route. For his aid, integrity, organization, and knowledge of the ropes, he charged an over-all service fee. Most of the guides operated in one of five or six topographically convenient crossing points, of which the eastern, being closer to Paris, were the more popular. The Nazis got around, in rotation, to each exit, for a spell methodically watched it like a cat, then went and eyed another place while the mice scurried out through the unplugged holes. During the first week in September, all the eastern passage points were suddenly reported *brûlé*, or hot. The guides got word, through their grapevines, that the Nazi patrols were searching all buses on roads approaching the eastern border crossings; at the same time the Paris Nazis had a temporary fit of checking the identity papers of all travellers leaving by the Gare de Lyon and the Gare d' Austerlitz. Mrs. Jeffries lay low and passed up the eight-thousand bargain.

By the middle of September the coast looked clear again. Through a second and better-connected waiter, Mrs. Jeffries paid a rock-bottom five-thousand-franc fee to a bold, brown-eyed, young de Gaullist named René, the contact man for a guide, a big farm-owner in the district through which she was to cross. She sent her luggage to Lyons, the first city in the Unoccupied Zone she was aiming for, by train; it is one of the anomalies of life under the Nazis that property has more right of way than people. For the crossing, René advised her to travel light, with only a rucksack on her back, in case she had to run. On September 16th, he told her to meet him at a certain railroad station the next morning at six in order to fight for a seat on the eight o'clock train, and for the love of God not to talk in public, as her American-accented French was *formidable*. At seven o'clock, by which time Mrs. Jeffries had silently struggled into her seat, René appeared and, busy with last-minute details, asked her to find an extra seat for what he called a friend, who was going with them. Largely by sign language, she wangled a seat in the next coach for the friend, who, from the brief view she had of him, looked to be French, fortyish, pale, and nervous. After the train had started and she had painfully watched the Tour Eiffel fade from her life and view, she began, irresistibly, to enjoy her journey through rural France. She had not been allowed to travel for nearly two years. Also, she had a fine shoe-box lunch with her. A French woman friend who owned a little place outside Paris had brought her, the day before, three precious fresh hard-boiled eggs, two *pâté maison* sandwiches, and a nearly ripe home-grown pear.

Well before noon and well inside the demarcation border, Mrs. Jeffries, according to plan, got off the train at a small town and walked down the main street to the foot of a hill, where René had said she would find a *bistro*. She found five and, being thirsty, chose the nicest and ordered the customary glass of bad beer. René eventually rolled up in an old Citroën, and with him was the guide. When René introduced her to the guide, Joseph, her stomach, which had turned over in terror whenever she thought about making the crossing, was quieted. Joseph was a middle-aged, bull-necked countryman, paternal, polite, and bustling. René, it developed, was in a hurry to get on to Marseille. The two men had a confidential conversation, but she could not help overhearing some of it, and she gathered that René was on a gun-running job for de Gaulle and that Joseph planned to hide him in the back of the Citroën under some vegetables and drive him to a railway station on the other side of the border, where René would get back on the train he had just got off. The train, she knew, would be held up for hours at the border while the French and German police inspected *Ausweise* and civil papers—which René apparently never fussed with—hunted in the toilets and under the seats for refugees, and searched passengers for contraband. Contraband was anything portable, precious, and personal left after two years of German occupation; it could be love letters, family messages, trinkets, old furs, more money than your visa said you possessed, or fine jewels.

René and Joseph left on their mission, Joseph promising to return as soon as possible. As Mrs. Jeffries sat alone, drinking her beer, the pale Frenchman of that morning's journey came up and introduced himself as Monsieur Georges. Then he introduced what seemed to be the rest of Joseph's crossing party—three French provincial matrons who said they were sisters, a Jewish Frenchwoman with a sick-looking little boy, three melancholy young Dutch Jews, and a French sailor in uniform. As if France had never been defeated or divided, the sailor had spent his leave, as usual, visiting his mother in Paris and was now on his way back to his ship in Toulon. Georges begged Mrs. Jeffries, on account of her accent, not to talk, and then invited her to play *belote*, a talkative card game. Since she didn't know how, he told her the story of his recent life. He had wanted to fight on the side of noble-hearted Russia and so had volunteered to be smuggled from Paris across the border near Lyons and thence to London to join the de Gaulle army as a mechanic. She asked in a whisper whether he was an airplane or a tank mechanic. He said he was neither; he was an expert maker of frames for ladies' petit-point handbags, the sort formerly sold to the American and now to the German tourist trade. He proudly said that it cost the de Gaulle movement twenty thousand francs to smuggle a man like him from Paris to London. He had false teeth, limp gray hair, spots on his vest, and delicate, artisan's hands. Because Mrs. Jeffries was polite, she didn't say she thought that the Fighting French had made a poor buy.

Late in the afternoon, Joseph returned and moved his party to a second *bistro*, one farther up the hill and near a church. Four Gestapo agents were drinking beer at the *zinc*. Joseph claimed that he could spot them a mile off, because the Gestapo invariably wore ersatz tweeds of either a bilious brown or an unpleasant gray, apparently the only choice left to the Germans, and they always shaved their necks and carried briefcases, neither of these habits French. The waiter at the new *bistro* warned Joseph's party not to talk over their drinks and then cracked off-color jokes, which made the three Gallic matrons laugh hysterically. At five o'clock, Joseph led Mrs. Jeffries around the corner to a photographer, who took her picture and made out a false French civilian's identification paper that she would get, complete with her picture, the next day on the other side of the border. He told her that the paper was made out in a Gallic version of her name and warned her not to forget that she was to become, temporarily, Madame Hélène Geoffroi.

Shortly afterward, behind the church, Joseph and Mrs. Jeffries joined the rest of the party, who were huddled against the choir door. Joseph hurriedly piled them all into a waiting butcher's camion and pulled a pair of black curtains tight across the back. Inside they found fragments of suet and dried blood and three more Jews. The camion started off. Five minutes later, Joseph, who was driving, was stopped for questioning by two German patrolmen. Behind the black curtains the three new Jews whispered nervously, which made everybody else even more nervous. Then the Germans said, *"Heil Hitler und merci,"* and the truck set off again. After an hour's drive, the truck stopped, Joseph unbuttoned the curtains, and they climbed out. They were in the country, behind a building that will here be described as an old blacksmith's shop. They hurried inside and were put in a new annex, where apparently machine parts were being manufactured. This part of the shop was not yet entirely roofed over, and for the next few hours the party watched the darkening sky and then the stars. As they sat, they could hear an unseen little river frothing against boulders. Joseph had told them that the river, which marked the border, was where they were to cross into the Unoccupied Zone that night and that the rocks were what they were to cross on. No one, not even Monsieur Georges, talked much. It was better not to say anything about where you came from and it was certainly too soon to discuss where you thought you would eventually arrive. Finally they heard two members of the German night patrol approach the shop on their first round. Over the noise of the water and their own thumping hearts, the hidden party listened to the German voices lifted in puffing, pidgin French. Apparently the two Nazis were hungry only for conversation, though Mrs. Jeffries heard Joseph offer them chocolate. He did not offer them cigarettes or money, the two other things German soldiers have an appetite for.

The party was to cross at nine. At ten minutes to nine, Joseph brought in a young peasant whom he called his nephew. He looked nothing like Joseph. He was big, stalwart, and dressed only in swimming trunks. Joseph explained that the river was no more than four feet deep and that if anyone fell in, not to scream, because his nephew, who would be standing in the middle, would come to the rescue. "We have him here to tranquillize the ladies," Joseph added gravely. Then, less confidently, he said that the Nazi patrol ought to be a quarter of a mile away by then but that one never could tell about those monsters. Everyone was instructed to crouch while crossing the river, in order to be less visible and a smaller target in case the Nazis came back and started to fire. The party was to cross rapidly and one by one.

Everybody filed out of the blacksmith shop and to the edge of the river. Mrs. Jeffries followed the French sailor. Crossing the river, she could see, on the far side, the pompon of his cap silhouetted against the stars. As she stepped, crouching, on the third boulder, she put one foot on the hem of her raincoat and almost fell in. The unlikely nephew, chest-deep in the water, laughed and whispered, *"Courage."* When Mrs. Jeffries got to the other side of the little river, she ran, still crouching, for a quarter of a mile through a field of stubble. Finally she came to a dirt road that led to a village. Then, as already instructed by Joseph, she turned to the right and knocked at the door of the second cottage. A fat, red-faced young woman opened the door. When Mrs. Jeffries asked if she were Joseph's aunt, she nodded indifferently. Falsehoods and the pounding heart of someone who had just run the line meant nothing to her. Fugitives were a business. Without being asked, she said that Mrs. Jeffries could have a bed to herself for fifty francs. Apparently Joseph, like a capitalist carefully splitting up his investments, had distributed his party all over the neighborhood.

Mrs. Jeffries inspected the bed. It looked filthy and stank in memory of other refugees who had lain on it, maybe trembling the way Mrs. Jeffries trembled now. From her rucksack she took out a bottle of perfume and sprinkled the pillow, and then tried, unsuccessfully, to eat one of the hard-boiled eggs. She went to bed with her clothes on. The combination of the bed smell and the perfume made her sick, but there was nothing in the room to be sick in, so she forced herself to go to sleep. In the morning the fat young woman gave her acorn coffee and a slice of sour gray bread. She took the fifty francs agreed upon and absorbed another fifty as tip because she had not asked Madame to sign a lodger's slip, as the law demands. For fugitives, every evasion of the law is a luxury that must be paid for extra, though unofficial kindnesses often come free of charge.

Joseph had told Mrs. Jeffries to go to the local *épicerie* after breakfast and ask the owner for her false French civilian paper. Like a prestidigitator, the grocer obligingly pulled it out of the inside of his old hat. Then he pointed down the empty road and said, "Joseph said to walk that way. You'll meet a truck." After walking a mile in the mild sun, she sat down under a tree to smoke, to wonder what had happened to the truck, and to look at herself, and her new life history, as Madame Hélène Geoffroi. The photograph was nothing like her and the paper said that she had been born in Normandy in a town she had never heard of. A truck rattled by, stopped, and backed up; it contained Joseph and the rest of his party. "You will never get to New York sitting down like that," he called, and they all laughed excitedly. Everyone, even the melancholy Jews, seemed united by a temporary sort of gaiety because of the success of what they had been through together the night before.

At noon they pulled up at one of those modest country inns famed for generations for its cuisine. The black-market luncheon proved to be finer than anything Mrs. Jeffries had sampled since France fell—multiple hors-d'oeuvres, delicious local trout (it being Friday), grilled chops, two vegetables, ripe cheese, fruit compote, and a serious Burgundy. Monsieur Georges, who sat beside her, remarked how wise he had been to put his false teeth in his breast pocket before the crossing. He had been afraid that, as he jumped for the rocks, the teeth might fall out of his face. Mrs. Jeffries paid a luncheon check of seven hundred francs, or seven dollars. The waiter had regarded Georges as her husband and had put him on her bill. After the tasty barley coffee, the chef-owner of the place came in to receive compliments on his food. He said that he had run a *fin bec* restaurant at Menton until the Italians came but that he did not like macaroni cooking. Being both an artist and a patriot, he had moved away.

After lunch, Mrs. Jeffries and Georges, who were bound for Lyons, said goodbye to the rest of the party. Where the others were going, or trying to go, they alone knew. On saying goodbye to Joseph, Mrs. Jeffries thanked him with real emotion. He must have been used to that. All he said was *"Ce n'est rien, Madame. A votre service."* He was going back to the *bistro* on the hill and tomorrow night he and another party would be crossing the river. A local guide named Jean, who did odd jobs for Joseph, was detailed to the Lyons contingent, which was joined by an elderly Serb underground worker. They were to sit up in the restaurant until three in the morning, walk to the nearest railway station, and catch an early train for Lyons. There Jean would introduce them to a certain café, where a patriot (as in French Revolutionary times, today all the pals among *le peuple* are patriots) would tip them off to some safe rooms to live in. As Madame Hélène Geoffroi, Mrs. Jeffries tried to show her false paper to the ticket taker at the station next morning. Though under orders from the Vichy police to check up on all travellers, he didn't bother to glance at her forgery, which disappointed her.

Owing to a saboteur's wreck on the main line, their train was four hours late, and they wearily arrived at eleven in the morning at the Lyons café. There a peppery young Fighting Frenchman, Marcel, who had expected only Jean, and him on time, flew into a temper at the sight of an unexpected American woman, an unexplained old Serb, and the unwelcome Georges. As one of the local Fighting French authorities, Marcel ordered Georges back to Paris because he considered him something de Gaulle would not have as a gift. Suspicious and arrogant, Marcel then shut up like a clam, refusing aid to any of them.

Apologetically, the Serb offered Mrs. Jeffries the address of a compatriot's boarding house that was reported to have nice food. With her rucksack still on her back, she took three wrong trams to the outskirts of Lyons, walked up four long, wrong streets, and finally managed to arrive, weeping with fatigue, at what turned out to be an ordinary French lodging house for men workers. "Ah, if Madame were only not a woman," the patriot proprietor wailed. He nevertheless offered to give her lunch in his barracklike dining room, where about a hundred workmen were already feeding. However, as the Serb had prophesied, the stew was excellent. While Madame was still reviving herself on it, he walked in. He apologized for intruding and said he had worried about her. It occurred to Mrs. Jeffries at that moment that for the past two years in Paris she had lived her quiet, expatriate, familiar existence without difficulties and also without anyone's help. In Lyons she was a stranger and in a bad way. It was over her stew that she realized that the war had indeed reclassified people; that to those in trouble people had now become very kind or very cruel or as indifferent as stones. At the Serb's kindness she started crying again.

Like friendly homing pigeons, Mrs. Jeffries and the Serb returned to the café. It was closed. From behind the door the owner shouted that the police were expecting an anti-Vichy riot and to get off the streets, quick. Mrs. Jeffries and the Serb ran down the street. At the first hotel they came to, he pushed her in and, still running, disappeared. When she asked for lodging, the woman at the desk calmly offered her a bathroom to sleep in. The city was jammed; the annual commercial fair, the famous Foire de Lyon, was opening that week, just as if war and riots were routine and just as if the fair would show something besides ersatz. When Mrs. Jeffries handed over her false French civilian paper, which, if she spent the night even in a bathroom, would have to be copied on a *fiche* to be presented to the police the next morning, the woman said sharply, "French? With that accent?" Mrs. Jeffries, a poor liar, lamely murmured that she had been brought up in America. "You should say that with more conviction," the woman replied, and put the *fiche* into a desk drawer. Alarmed, Mrs. Jeffries casually strolled out onto the street, then ran back to the café, where, on the deserted sidewalk, the Serb and the angry Marcel were arguing. Marcel became even angrier when she told him of the suspicion that her false French paper had aroused. He declared that since she was an American she hadn't needed such a paper in the first place, that her Parisian *carte d'identité* sufficed in Vichy France, and that if the woman squealed, all of Joseph's papers forged by that particular photographer for foreigners who did need them would become hot. While tearing up her Geoffroi paper, he forbade Mrs. Jeffries to return to the hotel. When she said that she had to sleep somewhere and that she hadn't had her clothes off for two nights, he unexpectedly apologized. Rather grudgingly, he invited her to stay the night with him, explaining that he was sleeping, *sub rosa*, in a collaborationist uncle's flat, and that both he and she would have to be up and out before seven the next morning, when the uncle was returning from a big business trip. Marcel said that his family were bitterly divided; half were de Gaullists like himself and the other half were like the rich, Pétainist, avuncular swine. While they were still talking, the café reopened, and she was able to get a much-needed glass of weak beer. Apparently the riot had been called off.

That evening, after dinner, she took a Saturday-night bath in the collaborationist's luxurious bathtub. Next morning, early, she made both beds, as womanly thanks for the hospitality, and by seven Marcel had installed her in the center of Lyons in what called itself a hotel but was really three floors of furnished rooms over a side-street shop. The hotel did not register its lodgers on any *fiche* and had no breakfasts, hot water, or closets. The clothes cupboard in her room was a length of pink cretonne stretched diagonally across one corner on a string, not nearly big enough to hold her clothes when she picked up her trunk, which had come through more easily than she had. She was to live in this room for the next eight weeks, which was the length of time it would take her to get the solemn, legal papers necessary for her to leave France illegally. The Nazis have upset the law, the logic, and the sense of humor of all Europe.

◆ ◆ ◆

After the dramas of German occupation that were constantly shaking Paris, Mrs. Jeffries had expected to find life dull in Lyons. However, once she had accepted the difference between the French attitude toward recent history that she had known in Paris and the attitude that she found in Lyons, she had an undeniably stimulating sojourn. In Paris the French had been against the Germans. In Lyons, which the Germans were not to march into until nine days before she left, the French were still enjoying being against other French. Lyons proudly rated itself the most excited and exciting city in Unoccupied France. Certainly bombs in the Royalists' Action Française newspaper offices, in Pétain's Legion headquarters, and in Laval's recruiting stations, where French workmen were being enrolled for labor in Germany, were regarded as commonplaces, and so were street riots and clashes between the silk-mill hands, the brutal Darlan police (modelled on the Gestapo), the Vichy police, and the Lyons police, in all possible combinations, and so, too, were arrests, escapes, denunciations, plots, and counterplots. The Lyonnais subsisted on the violences indigenous to their city, which was the Unoccupied receiving end of whatever was shipped out of Germany on the Mulhouse express and whatever sneaked out of Paris on the P.L.M. *rapide.* For the underground anti-Nazi groups in France, Lyons was the reckless halfway house between northern France and Marseille. In Lyons gun smugglers dictated reports to their confidential secretaries and provided the customary fifty-thousand-franc fees to complacent guards who would wink at a lucky comrade's escape from some Occupied prison, saboteurs held conferences like good businessmen, and draftsmen made blueprints for railway wrecks.

Lyons was the first Unoccupied stop for the escaping Jews, old and young, who never ceased rolling down from the north. The Cathedral's archbishop, Monseigneur Gerlier, boldly adopted a hundred of the foreign Jewish children who had been torn from their parents and sent to concentration camps after a Vichy roundup that had netted ten thousand Jews. French prisoners from Germany who had been wounded by the R.A.F. bombers arrived at the Lyons railway station in coaches which the Germans had carefully labelled *"Blessés par les avions anglais."* One day, in the station, a trainload of returned French war prisoners just arriving from Germany patriotically threw stones, with all their weak strength, at a trainload of French workmen who, with what even the non-collaborationist French at first esteemed equal patriotism, were just starting off to Germany in exchange for the incoming prisoners.

The various patriots' cafés in Lyons functioned as forums, check-rooms, and occasionally dormitories for patriots' out-of-town friends, their suspicious-looking packages, and their girls. In one of the cafés there circulated a young patriot who was, for his underground group, the official killer of members who squealed. He was green-eyed and handsome, had been a gigolo in a well-known Montmartre *boîte* formerly enjoyed by American tourist ladies, had nervous, beautiful hands that itched at the sight of money, and was, his comrades reported, excellent at what they called serious jobs but unreliable at details or organization, which bored him. He dressed in what he thought was the perfect English manner, but he always looked a little too neat. His father was an electrician. The killer dreamed of a France of the future in which, after the Americans had won, he and his father would install expensive American radios in every house in the nation.

In the patriot groups, generosities were fantastic and not uncommon. Among those who were really working for *la patrie*, aid and money were handed around as if both were magnificently uncostly. The traditional French grip on the banknote seemed finally to have been loosed in a gesture of desperate, tardy patriotism. A thousand francs, or five or ten thousand, could always be raised to send some Frenchman on one of the many militant jobs of *les services* (which is what the underground movements are called), in which the success of a man's assignment could often be proved only by his being imprisoned or shot. Because resistance needs equipment, especially scarce in a land where the conqueror has swept the shelves bare, the cash boxes of *les services* had to be kept overflowing. Even to hire a rope long and strong enough to help a comrade escape from the third story of a prison cost twenty thousand francs, or two hundred dollars at the black-market rate of exchange. Wild and naïve schemes flourished among the patriots, and often worked. One morning, Mrs. Jeffries was wakened at her rooming house by a youth who claimed to be an American and said that his father had been a Yankee soldier in the last war. And did the American lady want to go back to New York in a submarine or on a bomber? He could send her free in either one if she could leave in a half hour. She felt that she could not dress so quickly.

When the Americans finally, in the invasion of Africa, on Sunday, November 8th, took their first strategic step toward Europe, Mrs. Jeffries, who had then been in Lyons seven weeks, got the news at breakfast in her favorite patriots' café. The owner came to her table to tell her and offer his felicitations. The clients cheered her. Americans were rare in Lyons and together she and the good news made it a great occasion. "Pétain ordered us to retreat! If we'd only retreated far enough, now we would be in Africa with the Yanks!" one Frenchman shouted to her. When she took out a package of old, bootlegged Lucky Strikes, she was cheered again. To the Lyonnais the Luckies seemed positive proof that the Americans had actually arrived from across the Atlantic.

During the next two days, Lyons seethed with excitement and what turned out to be mistaken preparation for its new role in France's history. The city, in response to a radioed appeal from General de Gaulle in London, busily prepared a reckless Fighting French street demonstration for Wednesday, which was Armistice Day. Instead, on Wednesday, the Germans marched in, en route for Marseille and eventually Toulon. At ten o'clock that morning, when Mrs. Jeffries walked out of her rooming house to have breakfast, she found, instead of a de Gaulle parade on the Place Bellecour, Vichy police circling in a protecting ring around a dozen Germans with machine guns, ready, if necessary, for the sullen crowd that had gathered. All day the Germans poured through in camions with equipment which looked old and used and "nothing like 1940" the Lyonnais jeered with satisfaction. But the Germans continued to pour through the city all night, and what was rushed past after curfew in the dark was, as anyone who dared peer out from behind his window curtains could see, powerfully shining and new. There were miles of unscarred tanks, trucks, and troop carriers packed with jolted, drowsing Nazis, gleaming swarms of buzzing motorcycles, and lumbering contingents of immaculate, stiff-necked guns. By morning, German *Kommissäre* were domiciled in requisitioned hotels, including the town's finest, the Grand-Nouvel. At first the Lyonnais would not believe their eyes and insisted that the Germans were only resting, *de passage*. Then the city realized that it was occupied. No one in Lyons had seen more than one egg a month for half a year. When the news got around that the Germans were really in residence, the black market unfroze, Lyons swarmed to its restaurants, and there was a binge of five-egg omelets which produced a municipal bilious attack. To make sure that the Nazis wouldn't get so much as one yolk, Lyons ate its entire stock of thousands of stale eggs in twenty-four hours flat.

Mrs. Jeffries had left Paris, on September 17th, just in time. On September 24th the Paris Nazis had arrested her remaining American women friends and shipped them for detention to a hotel in the Vosges spa town of Vittel. Now Mrs. Jeffries felt that the Germans, in occupying Lyons, were catching up with her too. On November 18th, a week after they had come, she went with her American passport to the Spanish Consulate and asked for a Spanish visa, the fourth and most difficult of a quartet of permits upon whose accumulation and synchronization a traveller's departure from France depended. These four legal treasures, coming in time, were wings on a refugee's feet, but late, they could be like stones around a refugee's neck, pulling him down to destruction. The first permit was dependent merely upon the possession of a *carte d'identité* and a passport, and each succeeding one upon the one before; the first, third, and fourth were good for only a month; and it could take three months to obtain the whole set, during which time, just as the fourth was granted, the first and third could expire, and the process, through a series of renewals, would have to start all over again. In despair, some refugees killed themselves after a losing race to make their *papiers* come out even, and others, who had enough money to live on through a first lengthy paper-stamping period of hope, became penniless during the second attempt and, unable to escape, eventually rotted in jails or concentration camps. In war-racked, refugee-ridden Europe, people are no longer people, they are their papers.

In the seven weeks she had been in Lyons, Mrs. Jeffries had with diligence accumulated and kept up to date the first three of her permits. The first was her *permis de séjour* from the Rhône prefecture, allowing her to remain in Lyons, where she had no business to be in the first place and where the Vichy police might nab her. Lyons was a refugee bottleneck, so European fugitives were denied *permis* by the hundreds every day, but Mrs. Jeffries, favored as an American by the municipal clerks, some of whom, from the Vichy viewpoint, hadn't yet got into line, obtained her *permis* after only a week of obstinate finagling. Once she had this No. 1 stamp, she could safely go to the Sûreté and ask for her stamp No. 2, a Vichy France *visa de sortie*. Vichy's visa took four weeks. Paper No. 3 was her Portuguese visa, good for only a month, which took two weeks to obtain and on the possession of which her subsequent Spanish visa, also good for only a month, depended. Spain, which is politically worried and physically undernourished, allows no foreigner to enter unless he has stamped proof that he means to hurry right out again, usually to Lisbon and its airport, Europe's last exit. On November 18th, when Mrs. Jeffries asked the Spanish Consulate clerk for her visa, he informed her that (a) Spain had that day mobilized its army, (b) he had heard that the Spanish border was in consequence closed, (c) he had heard that it was open twice a week, but that the trains were booked so solidly that no one could get on one for six months, (d) he had heard it was open for one hour every afternoon to pass mail and telegrams only, and (e) he knew it would take ten days for the *señora* to obtain a Spanish visa unless she wished to make him, as she had implied she would, a gracious gift of five hundred francs for the Spanish poor, in which case she could have her visa the day after tomorrow.

Mrs. Jeffries gave him the five hundred francs and two days later he gave her the visa and the official information that the border was indeed closed tighter than a trap. However, he reminded her that in

Spain, as in most of contemporary Europe, her visa, paradoxically, would be honored even though she entered the country by stealth. He kindly suggested that she go and look around in the French border city of Pau. Pau, Mrs. Jeffries knew, was the trading center for the mountaineer guides who, for a terrific price, walked their refugee clients over the Pyrenees into Spain.

On November 20th, a little over two months out of Paris, Mrs. Jeffries unhooked her rucksack from underneath the pink cretonne curtains in her rooming house and started for Pau. Her train trip from Lyons to Pau, which would have taken about sixteen hours in peacetime, took the wornout French locomotives twenty-four hours on France's dilapidated railroad tracks. Mrs. Jeffries was lucky; she had a seat for the entire journey. The late November rain, which are southern France's version of early winter, had set in. Her second-class coach was overcrowded, unheated, and damp. Whenever her feet felt congealed in her inadequate, wooden-soled sandals, which are what most women in France now have to wear, she sat on her feet, like Buddha, which most French women have of late learned how to do.

In Pau the only place she could find to sleep was a maid's room under the mansard of a third-class hotel. For two years all the first-class hotels of Pau, the capital of the Basses-Pyrénées, like those of the so-called Unoccupied key cities, had been occupied by the German Gestapo and Armistice Commission. Now, since the Nazis had made the occupation official, the second-class hostelries had been booked for the oncoming German Army *Kommandanturen*. Her first three days in Pau, Mrs. Jeffries found no French face which she wanted to trust with her peculiarly personal question, "Pardon me, but do you know anyone who could smuggle me across the Spanish border?" After the rebellious air of Paris and the violence of Lyons, the sullen atmosphere of bourgeois, once-fashionable Pau was not encouraging. The city seemed indifferent to the war, which had never really touched it; hardened to its Germans, who had come with defeat; and annoyed at America's North African invasion, whose first military achievement, as far as Pau could see, was the cutting off of the city's best black-market green-vegetable supply.

Mrs. Jeffries hoped to avoid walking across the mountains into Spain. She had tried to find in Pau one of the local patriot *cheminots*, who, like thousands of their fellow railroad workers all over France, were helping to resist the Germans by helping anybody who hated them, and by carrying messages for underground *services*, transporting their agents, sidetracking shipments to Germany, chalking tortoises (the symbol of slowdowns) on every piece of freight, sabotaging, passing fugitives in good standing, and the like. Mrs. Jeffries hoped to arrange for a ride across the Pyrenees to Spain in a nice freight car. But the superb, skillful patriotism of the *cheminots*, which everyone in France knew about, had finally become too familiar to the Nazis, and, in a typical, Hydra-headed plan, they had decided to kill the French railroad men's resistance movement, and further paralyze the French people's ability to move about, by inviting twelve thousand French railway workers to go to Germany, since too many German railroad men were on duty in Russia. By the time Mrs. Jeffries began to get her bearings in Pau, dozens of the district's *cheminots* were already in concentration camps for turning down the German invitation to travel, the railroad grapevine was in disorder, and the stowing away of an American woman in a box car was out of the question.

All in all, for the first twelve days Mrs. Jeffries was in Pau, it seemed impossible to find someone to smuggle her out in any way whatever. The smuggling had to be done by guides, arrangements for whom were made by contact men, and no contact man was willing to load a woman onto his unsuspecting mountaineer guide. It was a tough walking trip over the Pyrenees, the Pyrenees' passes being on the whole higher than those in the Alps, and the guides wanted no females, especially one who was forty-five and an American to boot. No one really wanted to smuggle Americans of either sex, because for two years Americans had been as rare as hens' teeth around Pau and so were material for comment. In the first week, after getting a foothold in a good assortment of cafés, high and low, Mrs. Jeffries was refused admittance to over two dozen passage parties she'd heard about. The second week she concentrated on contact men who made appointments only at night; they seemed more responsible, as they usually held respectable office jobs by day. An insurance clerk pessimistically refused to try to pass her or anybody else, because fifty Frenchmen he had helped pass the week before had been caught by the Spaniards and were already back home again and under surveillance; they were white-collar men and students who, since the American invasion, had been eager to go to North Africa, join the French forces, and *"refaire la guerre avec les frères américains."* A kindly, hard-up Swede made a contact for her, and got an offer for an immediate crossing at twenty thousand francs. He thought the fee was too high, and while he was still haggling with the contact man, the party started off for the mountains.

Finally, in a lively café that specialized in B.B.C. news broadcasts, tuned down to a whisper, Mrs. Jeffries discovered a native waiter who had escaped from a prison-camp in Germany and who offered not only to seek a contact but, in his enthusiasm, to lend her the money, if necessary, for a passage, which he said ordinarily cost from two to ten thousand francs but for her would be astronomically higher. He was still looking for a passage at any price when, on November 24th, the German Army trucked in and occupied Pau. Three days later the French garrison there was demobilized. That night the waiter told her that after France fell the French soldiers had been mostly anti-British and pro-Vichy. Then, after the Dieppe Commando raid, he said, the men had turned around and wanted to *rejoindre les Alliés*, too late. The American invasion of Africa had added to their fever to fight the Germans again. As an answer to this pro-Allied sentiment, the Germans, in one swift blow delivered everywhere at once in Unoccupied France, in one day demobilized all that was left of what had once been France's army, thus scattering the men and their rebellious hopes and turning what had been men with guns into eighty thousand defenseless unemployed, ripe for shipping to Germany's labor camps. The waiter said that in Pau that morning, while some of the French officers wept, the Germans had simply ordered the French soldiers to fall in line, stack their arms, and fall out as civilians because the French Army no longer existed.

Back in their barracks, where they had providently hidden a cache of pistols, the soldiers tied the weapons under their ill-fitting, baggy breeches and got away with them, prepared for the great day when the Yanks would invade France. What uniforms the demobilized soldiers did not have on their backs were gathered up by the Nazis and sent to Germany to add to the Nazi wool pile.

On her twelfth day in Pau, Mrs. Jeffries decided that at least she would be ready and properly dressed for a crossing at a moment's notice, should an offer come. She had shipped her trunk there from Lyons, and it was still at the railway station, waiting baggage-car room on a train to Spain. An amenable porter let her open it and take out the warm clothes she wanted, change into them in the dirty ladies' toilet, and pack the light clothes she had taken off. With her ski boots in her hand, she walked out of the station dressed in a tweed skirt, wool stockings, sweater, scarf, topcoat, and mittens, and nearly roasted en route to a second-hand bookshop, where, it was reported, the proprietress ran a smugglers' travel agency on the side. There she got a too prompt, over-enthusiastic reply. The woman said *"Oui"* and in the same breath demanded fifty thousand francs for a crossing with a group leaving the next morning. She said that the trip would be deluxe, with donkeys to ride up the lower slopes and only two hours of what she called promenading on the peaks. Mrs. Jeffries, who had nearly forty thousand francs left in her pocketbook, declared, with equal airiness, that she had only thirty-five thousand francs on earth, and walked out. When she returned to her hotel, the concierge whispered to her that the Gestapo had called, requesting her to appear at the *Kommissäriat* the next morning. Mrs. Jeffries ran back, sweating, to the bookshop, and the woman big-heartedly accepted the thirty-five thousand francs.

The plan for crossing the Pyrenees into Spain was simple. All Mrs. Jeffries had to do was appear with her rucksack at the bookshop the next morning, pick up a contact man, go with him to the station, and board a certain southbound train, on which, before it started, the bookshop woman's husband, coming in on an earlier northbound train from border business, would find them. The husband would inform the contact man what town they were to get off at, which guide was to take the job, which taxi-man to trust, and other vital details. The husband's train was late. Mrs. Jeffries' train was about to depart and the contact man was hanging nervously out the window when the husband, from the window of his train, arriving on the next track, shouted, "Not now! Tomorrow night!" It was an additional letdown for Mrs. Jeffries to realize that she didn't have a room to spend the next thirty-six hours in. The bookshop woman warned her to keep out of the cafés, as that was where the Gestapo always looked first. She recommended a humble *pension* where no one asked questions or names. Mrs. Jeffries got a room that had a broken window, through which, as special preparation for the crossing, she caught cold.

Mrs. Jeffries and the contact man left Pau by another train the following evening, and in the last vestiges of daylight they got off at a way station and stepped into a waiting taxi and into the company of three men who apparently were to cross with her. All three spoke French with a slight accent and all three immediately protested that she spoke French with a heavy accent and was a woman besides. All three, furthermore, violently agreed that an American woman in the party made the crossing look like a dangerous job. After an hour's quarrelsome ride, the five of them stepped out in the dark into what smelled like a farmyard and fumbled their way into a low building. They were in a sheepfold, together with the warm sheep. The contact man departed. Ten minutes later he returned and said that the coast was clear. He led the party outdoors and, after a brief walk, into a cottage, pleasant and immaculate, which turned out to be the guide's. Their guide, a man named Boniface, who ran a speakeasy in his parlor, where he sold rum by the glass, had just said good night to his last customers. He was big, blond, and dignified. He accepted the surprise of having an American lady with taciturn calm. His young wife served the party a superb supper of black bean soup, an omelet of fresh eggs, a whole roasted baby lamb killed for them that day, goat cheese, strong mountain wine, and a warm loaf of home-made white bread. It was the first white bread Mrs. Jeffries had seen in two years and it tasted like manna.

The bookshop woman had talked of donkeys and a two-hour stroll on the peaks; at the station her husband had mentioned a truck and a four-hour walk. Now Boniface warned them that they would walk on their own legs for fifteen or twenty hours, from the time they left his front door until they slid downhill into Spain, that along the line there was an ascent of seven thousand feet, and that at least one or two nights would be passed in shepherds' huts, unoccupied because of the season of the year. Boniface himself was to take them about three-quarters of the way and then hand them over to a Spanish guide who would meet the party en route. One of the three male travellers, who before supper had formally introduced himself under a fancy French name, angrily declared that he was returning to Pau with the contact man to complain about the American woman, to complain about the distance over the mountains, and to demand his money back. After he had slammed the cottage door on his way out, one of the two remaining men, a dark little fellow, said sadly that his friend would unfortunately be back, that both his fine name and passport were false, that he was really named Fishbein and was a crooked Strasbourg Jew, and that he himself was a Polish Jew named Kowalski.

Kowalski was, he said, a watchmaker; he had become a naturalized Frenchman eighteen years ago and had spent his savings of a hundred thousand francs to get himself and his wife from Paris, via Toulouse, to Pau. Three days ago the Germans had literally kicked the Kowalskis out of their room in Pau, torn him from his wife, and said that she could sleep under the bridges. Madame Kowalski had a weak heart, which would not permit her to walk over the mountains. He could do nothing but leave her there, wondering if he would ever see her again. He was going to try to get to Tunisia and join up as a chauffeur for the American soldiers. The hitherto silent No. 3 of the party, a blond, blue-eyed young man, then said that he would not tell his name or nationality until they reached Spain. When Mrs. Jeffries laughed and said he was a German, he laughed, too, in self-conscious surprise. He said that he planned to tell the American consul at Madrid that he was an American and so get to Casablanca. Then, in broken English, he said to Mrs. Jeffries that his mother's sister lived in Yorkville and gave her name and address. After they had all retired for the night, Mrs. Jeffries was unable to sleep at first because there was only a thin partition between her room and the room occupied by the two men and the German kept her awake with his haranguing.

Next morning breakfast was brought up to the travellers. They ate together in Mrs. Jeffries' room, at her invitation. They were forbidden to go downstairs all day for fear the parlor grog customers, who twice daily were augmented by the Nazi patrol, would see them. Over their hot milk and grain coffee, the blond young man, who had weakened in his resolve at least to the point of calling himself Hans, was still talking. He declared that the whole thing looked like a middle-class swindle to him, that he was an anti-Nazi Socialist who had been in the Foreign Legion, that that cow of a woman in Pau had gypped them all, that he had paid her what she called a bargain price of thirty-five thousand francs because his cousin had paid the same the week before, that the two Jews, because they were Jews, had each had to pay fifty thousand francs, that God alone knew what Madame the American had had to pay, and that out of this fortune the noble Boniface, who did almost all the work and took almost all the risk, received only two thousand francs for the whole job. At noon the noble Boniface brought up a dozen fried eggs, with ham, and said that the other *monsieur*—Fishbein, or whatever his name was—had better return from Pau that day if he expected to cross into Spain before spring. A shepherd down from the uplands had just reported that snow was expected in two days; when it arrived, the pass would be closed for the winter. Fishbein, arrayed in a brand-new mountain-climbing outfit of glossy brown corduroy, turned up for a cold lamb supper.

On the following day, the party set off in the blackness just before dawn. The slopes of the foothills were steep, slippery with dried grass, and tiring. Mrs. Jeffries, who hadn't eaten as well in two years as she had during the past two days, was short of breath. Boniface vainly kept urging speed; until they reached their first stop, at a shepherd's hut, a few hours up, they would be in danger of encountering the French customs guard, a neighbor of Boniface and a law-abiding man. They came to the hut just before noon. Boniface forbade them to kindle a fire for fear his *douanier* would see the smoke. In the confused haste of departure, no one had remembered to take along water. A lunch of cheese and chocolate made them thirstier. While they rested, Boniface, who had to meet a rum-smuggling friend, walked off into the panorama of soaring granite slopes like a man going to keep a business engagement just around the corner. It was nearly dusk when he returned with a jug of icy mountain-torrent water and bad news. The Spanish guide, who was to meet them the next day, was *brûlé*; the Nazi patrol was after him and anyone else loose on the mountains. Boniface ordered the party to lie low and spend the night where it was. The hut contained a shelf on which the shepherd, when he was with his flock in the summer, slept on a pallet of bracken. It was too late in the year for bracken, so Mrs. Jeffries slept on the bare boards. The four men slept on the floor.

Daybreak was magnificent in the circus-shaped valleys below, but Boniface was too familiar with the view to waste time on it and was impatient to start the big climb. That day they walked nine hours single file, stopping twice to eat chocolate and bread. All morning the men begged Mrs. Jeffries not to hold them back but to walk faster. By noon only Boniface was still striding along easily. They had left the fan-ribbed plateaus for the Pyrenees' upper reaches and were ascending the gullies that marked the next portion of their route. Once Mrs. Jeffries lit a cigarette, but she quickly found that she was too busy walking to smoke. The gullies, which were the beds of torrents in spring, became rougher and steeper and the stones they walked on rolled in little avalanches underfoot. To maintain her balance, she had to keep her eyes on the toes of her boots and on the heels of the boots in front of her; this gave her something to concentrate on and steadied her. Like a man showing off the local sights to a visiting lady, Boniface politely pointed out to her evidences of his rum runners—the charred wood of a fire under a sheltering rock and later, in a gulch, a broken cask, which it made her thirsty to look at.

A soft rain started and then turned to sleet. Fishbein, who was hung about with small luggage, entreated Mrs. Jeffries to shelter under her topcoat a cardboard box that he said contained noodles, though it felt heavier to her. By four they entered the pass, seventy-five hundred feet above sea level, which Boniface had been aiming for. On the boulders beside a waterfall at which they stopped to drink, they found whiskers of ice that were refreshing to the throat. Here Fishbein emitted a series of questions he had apparently been storing up during the plodding, single-file silence of the day. Did Boniface know if you could get good prices for Moroccan food in the black market in Marseille? How much could you get for English gold sovereigns in Lisbon? Was it true that saccharine was selling for two thousand pesetas a kilo in Madrid, and did he know anybody on the other side of the border who had ever heard of the stuff? "We have heard enough, Monsieur," said Boniface, "to know that saccharine is so scarce in Pau that the cafés serve it already dissolved in bottles, like sugar water. Here in the mountains, when war comes, we use honey. From father to son we have smuggled rum. Ça, c'est notre droit. But we never smuggled dirty things like drugs, even sweet ones." He turned to Mrs. Jeffries. "Give him back his package," he ordered. She handed it over, saying she supposed that Fishbein, after all, was not fool enough to ask her to lug noodles over the Pyrenees and that the box was too light for gold but probably heavy enough for saccharine. Fishbein didn't look at the other men, but he laughed at her and took back his box with alacrity.

At sundown, an increasingly cold wind revived Mrs. Jeffries' New Hampshire blood and gave her second strength, but it seemed to exhaust the already weary men, who begged Boniface, at whose heels she was sturdily treading, to slow down, for the lady's sake. Just before nightfall they reached a second shepherd's hut, also vacant. It proved to be comfortably large; its shelf was big enough for all four travellers to throw themselves down together to rest, close, indifferent, exhausted. A while later, after cheese and chocolate, Mrs. Jeffries uncorked a flask of armagnac she had brought with her, Hans produced a jar of jam, and Kowalski passed around a box of biscuits. There was a spring by the hut but no bucket, so they leaned over the pool and drank from their dirty hands.

At four the next morning the Spanish guide arrived with his dog and a Basque friend. The three had walked all night in contempt of the Nazi patrols, who didn't know their way around in the dark. The Spaniard, who looked like an American Indian and was a taciturn man, grunted what little he had to say in a very limited French. The dog was affectionate. The Basque spoke fluent French and carried a hunting gun, forbidden in France since the armistice. He said that he had brought it along for any game birds he might encounter but that he preferred to shoot at the Nazi patrols; in the mountains their corpses were never found. In the dark and another rainstorm, they started off on their two ways, big Boniface to go alone back home and the crossing party on toward invisible Spain. The party now included two mountaineers, but in the damp darkness Mrs. Jeffries' real guide was whatever light neck scarf was visible in front of her. The Spaniard, who led the way, was nervous and stopped to listen a lot. Just before dawn they walked past a big stone house, inside which a dog barked. No one, however, came outdoors to see what was up. Long after sunup the gullies still gleamed with the ice that had formed in the night. By noon Mrs. Jeffries' pack—her rucksack and a small overnight case strapped to it with her belt—seemed so heavy that she could scarcely breathe in the thin mountain air. Apologetically she offered the mountaineers a thousand francs if they would carry her luggage. The Spaniard reluctantly took the money. The Basque refused at first to accept her banknote; *tout de même,* he said, he was only a friend, not a guide entitled to pay. Then he gave in.

By two o'clock the party had almost reached the Spanish border. The Spaniard then thought he heard a Nazi patrol and hastily ordered the travellers to slide down a series of gulches. The stones, as Mrs. Jeffries' skirt rolled up, cut her bare thighs. It took the party two more hours to

zigzag their way up the side of a mountain to get back on the trail
again. Just before they came to the border, their route was strewn with
morsels of torn paper. These were the fragments of passports that
escaping Frenchmen, who probably aimed to pass themselves off as
French-Canadians, had destroyed, as the last proof of their national
identity. Hans was not surprised to find a piece of his cousin's forged
French passport behind a rock. A tall, impressive stone monument,
with "France" carved on the north side and "España" on the south,
marked the border line. The party rushed a few feet into Spain and
started laughing. They had arrived and felt safe. Hysterically, the
German, the Pole, and the Alsatian began asking the American Mrs.
Jeffries' advice and shouting their immediate plans. Hans asked if he
might become her brother in Spain, since he was going to be American
anyhow. It seemed to her a good idea. Fishbein and Kowalski said that
they would declare themselves French-Canadians, since they spoke no
English. Fishbein said that Quebec was the popular birthplace these
days and Kowalski was enthusiastic, though he couldn't remember the
name and kept asking Mrs. Jeffries, "Where was it that I was born?"

Their gaiety vanished when their escorts refused to go any farther.
The Spaniard and his friend had walked all night, they lived over on
the next ridge, and they had to bring another party across the next day,
if the snow held off. Mrs. Jeffries, Kowalski, and Hans each offered first
the Spaniard and then his friend a thousand francs to continue, but
Fishbein wouldn't offer anything. Both escorts haughtily refused to
accept any more money, but they nevertheless accompanied the party
another mile to the brow of the mountain. There the guide pointed to
a settlement far below. He told his party to go to a house with a wire
fence and ask for the friend of José. The two mountaineers and the dog
then turned on their heels toward home.

In the scattered settlement, which the crossing party reached before
dusk, no one had heard of José or his friend, and the first three
dwellings Mrs. Jeffries and the men came upon all had wire fences. At
the third, a tall, elderly Spanish shepherd with two tall young sons hos-

pitably took them in. His cottage consisted of a single room, without illumination except for two resin torches stuck in iron rings beside the fireplace. The room opened into a haymow. While the sons stared in embarrassment, Mrs. Jeffries took off her sweater and skirt by the fire and changed to a rumpled flannel dress. The father gave the visitors bread and two bottles of dark wine, for which he would take no money. He and his sons then sat down at a small table and ate their frugal supper of cabbage soup from one pitifully small pot. There was apparently no other food in the house. The hungry party slept in the haymow and next morning washed in a brook.

By eight o'clock, Hans and Kowalski, who had gone forth to see what sort of hamlet they were in and how they could get out of it, had already been arrested. Fishbein came running into the cottage with the news, plucked his precious cardboard box and bags from the corner in which he had placed them, and plunged into the haymow. For a few minutes Mrs. Jeffries heard him burrowing. She never laid eyes on him again.

Two youthful, smiling members of the *guardia civil*, wearing cocked hats, walked in, quite sociably, with the arrested men. Mrs. Jeffries was not arrested, because she had a passport, but she was detained for questioning. She heard Hans, in Foreign Legion Spanish, tell the police that he was her *hermano*, Frank Jeffries, of Nuevo Hampshire. Kowalski said nothing; he merely looked sad and fatalistic. Neither of them had papers to prove or disprove anything they might say. Hans claimed that their papers had been stolen. Both believed the popular French legend that there were British and American consuls at the big, nearby town of X and that these officials had the magic power of transmuting men, willingly without a country, into British and American soldiers and transporting them to fight on the North African front. There was some discussion between the young policemen of whether it would be correct to let the three foreigners hire a cart to take them to the nearest village jail, ten kilometres distant, or whether they should walk. Kowalski, the only one who had any Spanish money, paid a hundred pesetas for the use of their host's cart. They reached the jail at four.

At the jail the two men were searched for dangerous instruments and Hans's nailfile was taken from him. He stuck to his story that he was Mrs. Jeffries' brother, young Jeffries; neither he nor Mrs. Jeffries had stopped to think, though the village police chief thought of it right away, that as a Jeffries he could at best be only her brother-in-law. The chief, who seemed to be in a dither, said that he had been swamped by ninety so-called French-Canadians in five days and that his jail was full. *Sotto voce*, the two members of the *guardia civil* suggested to the *americana*, whose pocketbook they had just searched for forbidden foreign monies, that if she wanted to rid herself of her two thousand illegal French francs, accommodations could perhaps be had in the village's crowded hotel for the night for her relative, friend, and self, and how many rooms would they want? Hans and Kowalski humbly whispered, "One room for us all would be fine." Mrs. Jeffries said oh, for the love of God, could she room alone for a change?

Mrs. Jeffries was granted the luxury of solitude. Her room contained an enlarged photograph of a young man whom the proprietress bitterly described as her last and littlest brother, shot by Franco. Three others, she said, had died as Loyalist soldiers during the Civil War. She advised Kowalski and Hans to write that night to the British and American consuls in Madrid and say that if they never turned up to look for them in the stinkhole jail in the town of X.

The bus to X the next morning contained Mrs. Jeffries, Hans, Kowalski, and eighteen arrested Frenchmen who still hoped to get to North Africa to fight alongside the Americans. Most of the eighteen were advance-guard men and had groups of followers waiting in France to start if and when the chiefs got safely through. An ex–Army officer on the seat beside Mrs. Jeffries was a de Gaullist volunteer who had been arrested in Dakar and sent to a prison camp in Pétain's France, where he had learned English and Spanish from other prisoners and, like them, lived on carrot tops. Thirteen of his comrades there had starved to death. When some food packages from home finally came through, five of the men gained enough strength to escape from the concentration camp. He said that the friends of the American lady were lucky not to have been arrested till morning; he and twelve of the others in the bus had spent the night in the village calaboose in a room with a privy in it; the room was so small that five men took turns standing up while eight men lay on the floor. They had been given no food for twenty-four hours. When the French officer discovered that Mrs. Jeffries was that rare traveller, one whose passport and papers were actually in order, she instantly became, in his eyes, a sort of emissary extraordinary. The unreasonable European conviction in a crisis that Americans are saviors who can think of everything and get anything done swept through the bus when the prisoners saw the officer start scribbling on bits of paper. As fugitives, and experienced rebels, they guessed what that meant; he was trusting her with the names and addresses of Spanish friends who might intercede for him if he was imprisoned. Immediately all the men tried to crowd around her in an eager, swaying mass, to give her their own touchstone addresses or their mothers' names. Would she write *Maman*, would she even write President Roosevelt? Most of the men were fliers. One ex-captain had five hundred pilots back in France waiting a chance to fly American fighting planes; the group in the bus included everything from two frightened students who didn't want to be sent to work in Germany to a retired artillery colonel. All the Frenchmen implicitly believed that the British and American consulates could get them through Axis Spain and over to Allied North Africa, which they admitted would be a miracle if it came off but a disgrace if it didn't.

The two amiable members of the *guardia civil* had told Mrs. Jeffries, probably to please a lady, that she was *en liberated* and that there was an American consul at X. At the X police station, which, Spanish fashion, reopened for business at ten o'clock at night, she learned that the nearest British and American consulates were at Madrid and that she certainly was not at liberty. Furthermore, as the police department's problem child, she was put at the end of the night's docket for special questioning, not because she had entered Spain illegally but because her papers were suspiciously O.K. She sat in the stationhouse till midnight, helplessly watching and hearing Hans and Kowalski and all eighteen militant Frenchmen from the bus interrogated into jail.

Seventeen of the eighteen declared, while the Spanish roared with laughter, that they were born in Quebec. The retired artillery colonel, who wanted to be different, said he had been born in Winnipeg. Mrs. Jeffries felt very sad when she said good night to Kowalski, whom she promised to visit in jail next day, and to Hans, whom she kissed on both cheeks to strengthen the brother and-sister story. The police, after studying her papers and questioning her, told her to return in the morning and sent her to a hotel, where a housekeeper was assigned to watch her closely. At 1 a.m. she took off all her clothes for the first time in four days. Her feet had bled when she was crossing the mountains and her thighs were still lacerated from sliding down gullies. Then she took her first bath since leaving Lyons.

The next morning Mrs. Jeffries discovered that though she was in Spain physically she was not there officially and that though she had money in her pocket she was penniless. She had crossed the border with exactly fifty dollars in American currency and a Banque de France draft for two hundred pesetas. No one in X would touch her greenbacks, American money being too illegal in provincial Spain even for the black market. No bank would cash her draft, which was drawn on a bank in the Spanish border town of Canfranc, across the Pyrenees from Pau. The Spanish police refused to admit that she was in Spain at all, because Canfranc, and not X, had also been put on her passport as her Spanish port of entry by the accommodating Lyons Spanish Consulate clerk, who was obliged to write down some entrance town and knew that she was planning to smuggle herself across somewhere in the neighborhood of Canfranc. This clerk had also told her that her draft would be good anywhere in Spain and that she need never set foot in Canfranc. Now it looked as if she wouldn't even be allowed to, since, on top of everything else, her hotel refused to let her leave town unless she paid her bill. The police, on the other hand, wouldn't let her stay in town unless her entry visa was stamped at Canfranc first. The police unsentimentally advised her to raise some cash by selling her wedding ring, which she still wore. That noon, in the hotel corridor, a courtly, middle-aged Spaniard made her a remarkable speech in French which began, "I am not very rich." In it, he explained that he had heard of her sad case and would she permit him to lend her the money for her hotel bill and her journey to Canfranc? When, in her gratitude, she offered him her ring as security to cover his fantastic offer, he refused it. His only request was that the American *señora* post from Lisbon a love letter to his fiancée, aged thirty-five, who for ten years had lived in Rio de Janeiro. At that moment he seemed to Mrs. Jeffries the most quixotic, romantic, and kind man in the world.

Spanish trains, because of a shortage of equipment, run into a terminal point one day and out of it the next. X was such a point and this was X's out day, so Mrs. Jeffries left that night at six for the town of Saragossa, which was south, and there she had to wait from midnight till six the next morning for a train to Canfranc, which was north. Two other hotel guests, who also had port-of-entry and money complications at Canfranc, made the trip with her. They were a German-Jewish couple travelling as Catholics on false French passports, which were nothing but sheets of typewriter paper stamped with visas for which, being Jews, they had been forced to pay ten times what Mrs. Jeffries had paid. The couple were desperate because their Portuguese visas, without which their entry visas into Spain were not valid, had just lapsed and they feared, with justification, that they would be sent back to the Nazis in France. By the time Mrs. Jeffries cashed her draft and arrived at the police station in Canfranc to get her passport stamped, the couple's Spanish visas had, indeed, been invalidated and they were speechless with terror. In this state they numbly refused to act as interpreters for an even more tragic female compatriot, just picked up by the police, who could not figure her out. Through Mrs. Jeffries' questionings in halting, high-school German, it was revealed that this woman was Jewish, from Frankfort, and sixty, and had four American dollars and thirty French francs to her name, plus a sister in New Jersey and a ticket to Palestine on a ship that had sailed from Barcelona the month before. The police had temporarily saved her life by arresting her in the border hills, she was in a daze, her feet were frozen, her luggage consisted of a string shopping bag, and she claimed that she had crossed the Pyrenees alone. Her mind was still wandering. She thought that Canfranc, which is in the mountains, was Barcelona, which is on the sea. Mrs. Jeffries took her to a restaurant and fed her. In the midst of the meal she whispered reproachfully, "I have never eaten any but kosher food," and hid some morsels of broken bread in her shopping bag. After coffee she tried to pay her half of the check. Later the police said that they had no choice but to return her to France, though Mrs. Jeffries cajoled, stormed, made a scene, and prophesied that they were sending the old woman back to a very disagreeable death.

From Canfranc, Mrs. Jeffries wearily took the train back to Saragossa. That evening, at the Saragossa station, where she was to catch the express for Madrid, she again met, to her surprise, the Jewish couple, shaken but hopeful. They had been able to "arrange things" with the Canfranc police. To pay for their tickets to Madrid, they were selling a heavy gold chain to the station lunch counter woman, who really did not want to buy it; she said that this sort of jewelry only reminded her of the troubles everybody had been through.

Mrs. Jeffries, at least, was fortunate enough to have three pesetas left when she arrived in Madrid, so she was able to take a tram to the American consulate. There she found a comforting letter of credit, a Clipper reservation, and loving, questioning letters from her worried New Hampshire family. Then the troubles of the world at large and of the Spaniards in particular, with civil war behind them and poverty ahead; the nightmare, somnambulistic existence of refugees, all trying to wake up outside of the continent of Europe; the xenophobia of embittered, hungry Madrileños; the Puerta del Sol prison across the street from one of the nicest cafés in town, and the fourteen other city prisons with anxious crowds hovering nervously at the gates; the sick faces and shabby clothes of the city's poor—the whole costly, cruel Fascist pattern of life began closing in on her again. In Madrid the penniless political prisoners were dying in rocky cells underground and up on the streets life was even more expensive than it had been under the German occupation in Paris. She spent a hundred and thirty dollars in eight days in Madrid, though all she did was pay her debt to the Quixote in the hotel in X, buy one necessary pair of bad stockings for $3.50, live *en pension* with poor meals and no butter at the second-class Hotel Nacional, and purchase food packages for the now-imprisoned middle-aged Jewish couple, who, whatever they had arranged for themselves in Canfranc, had not been able to make it stick in Madrid. She received a pathetic postal card from Hans, in a concentration camp with Kowalski at Campo de Miranda de Ebro, in the mountains. Like a man of the modern world, he said that it was not a bad concentration camp, as camps went, and that the American consul had sent him neither passport, uniform, nor food. In a faint, pencilled postscript in English he added, "I am kold. Write soonly. Your brother, Frank J."

It took a full eight days and ceaseless scurrying for Mrs. Jeffries to renew her Portuguese visa, which had lapsed, and to obtain a precious temporary extension of her Spanish visa until the new Portuguese stamp was obtained. The complications of special police papers, which the Franco administration had built up like a towering wall against foreigners, whom it was supposed to keep from staying in the country, in the end merely made it more difficult for then to leave. For forty-eight hours she stayed in her hotel because the Madrid police had taken and held her passport. In the Europe of today, to walk around without your passport buttoned in your pocket is as abnormal as it would be to walk around without your heart beating in your body.

Ignorance, revenge, and bureaucracy in all their contemporary European forms made Mrs. Jeffries' days in Madrid a seesaw of uncertainty. Until her last hour there she did not know when she would leave or why it could not have been sooner. No one in any country in Europe knows what is going on in the country next to it; international trains, whose movement formerly seemed as sure as the sun's, are now spoken of as if they could disappear off the face of the earth once they crossed a border. Officials themselves, who have people's lives, documents, and plans in their hands, know little that is exact, except that whatever they know can change by breakfast tomorrow. In place of certainty there is only a vast, tangled ball of rumor. In place of sensible, humane procedure, now destroyed by wars, revenge, suspicion, and power politics, petty official strictures have been built up against which the individual is as helpless as a caged animal. Because Mrs. Jeffries had lived in so-called Communistic France under the Front Populaire, which favored the Spanish Loyalists, a high-up Spanish Fascist official spitefully delayed signing one of her papers, which made her miss the night express she was scheduled to take to Lisbon. Because she had lived in non-interventionist France under the Radical Socialists, who had imprisoned refugee Loyalists, a lower-down Spanish Republican concierge maliciously made her miss the next night's train.

Mrs. Jeffries had been officially told that the Madrid-Lisbon sleeping compartments cost seventy pesetas and could be arranged for only with the porter on the train; rumor told her that the compartments actually cost thirty pesetas at the railway station but were sold there only to Spaniards. She got on the train Monday, December 21, 1942, with seventy-five pesetas in her pocket and discovered that the porter demanded eighty for a berth. Fortunately, an Englishman in the crowded day coach had the eighty and was willing to spend it, so at least she was able to get his seat. She had been officially told that she could take a hundred pesetas from Spain into Portugal. Next morning, at the Portuguese border, a Spanish customs inspector told her she could not take even her seventy-five pesetas out, that all of it had to be left behind for the poor of Spain. A jovial Spanish policeman advised her to spend her money for breakfast in the station. She spent her pesetas for her breakfast and for his, too. The policeman drank a cup of coffee and a bottle of anisette.

After the harshness of Madrid, Lisbon seemed soft. After the acute astringencies of the rest of Europe, Portugal seemed only pinched. The hotels and bars of Lisbon, the last diplomatic freehold on the Continent's all-important Atlantic coastline, were full of Turks, Americans, English, Poles, French, Germans, Scandinavians, Swiss, Iranians, South Americans, and a medley of decorated buttonholes, uniforms, medals, spies, oil men, ambassadors, black-market agents, legation attachés, political secretaries, and Berlin *Damen* who, if they had any chic at all, were sized up as tarts doubling as *agents provocateurs*. Mrs. Jeffries passed Christmas Day in bed, reading a second-hand copy of Voltaire s "Candide," which is now having a popular revival among Lisbon's international, war-worn misanthropes, possibly because it cynically describes the city's calamitous earthquake of nearly two hundred years back as being (like Europe's new disasters?) something that was "all for the best in the best of all possible worlds."

Mrs. Jeffries had supposed that she would leave Lisbon, and all Europe, shortly after New Year's Day. However, an early January Clipper reservation was cancelled, owing to the priorities of diplomats and generals. As the weeks went by, she was squeezed out again and again by diplomats' secretaries, lend-lease agents, and the military. Along with a growing crowd of patient, unimportant civilians, Mrs. Jeffries, awaiting her turn, saw the winter out and spring established in Lisbon before she was at last lucky enough to get another Clipper passage for the first week in April. Seven months after Mrs. Jeffries had left Paris, she left Europe and started flying, roundabout, toward the United States. To get to New York from Lisbon she flew to Portuguese Guinea, and from there to Fisherman's Lake in Liberia, where the passengers lunched on fried pork chops a few steps from the equator. From there she flew the South Atlantic to Natal in Brazil, then to Belém in the same country, then north to Port of Spain in Trinidad, on to San Juan in Puerto Rico, to Bermuda, and, on her fourth day in the air, to LaGuardia Field, wet but welcome in an April shower. She had never flown home before. It didn't seem quite right to land in New York without first sighting the Statue of Liberty.

from Parachute Infantry
by David Kenyon Webster

David Kenyon Webster parachuted behind German lines early on June 6, 1944 in support of the Normandy landing. Many of his fellow paratroopers did not survive the jump itself. Those who did often found themselves alone, lost and frightened in the dark countryside. Webster described the experience in a memoir written soon after the war.

C igarette?" Porter asked, on my left.

"No thanks," I smiled. With the lift from the ground, I had experienced a sudden, total change of feeling. The load of brooding worry had dropped off, leaving me light, reckless, resigned, and almost detached. Part of this feeling was due to the drowsy effect of the sleeping tablets, but most of it was sheer relief at the end of all the waiting.

I looked around to see how the others were reacting to the takeoff. Only the smokers, who were faintly lighted by the firefly glow of their cigarettes, were visible. When they inhaled, the flaring tips lit up their shadowy, blackened faces. They did not look happy.

The engines roared louder, as if for a grip on the sky. We were bucking and slamming around now in the rough air currents above the big Devonshire hills that had once seemed so lovely.

I turned stiffly and, staring out the window, saw, far below in the shifting moonlight, the dotted white perimeter lights of the field and the tiny red-and-green wing-tip lights of other C-47s taxiing and taking off and getting into formation. My God, I thought impatiently, we're still circling the airfield.

We banked again and continued round and round in a great, droning loop until the whole second Battalion was formed in a long V of Vs, nine planes wide.

While I watched, a red light crept up on us in the darkness outside. It was our wing plane moving into position. When it was almost abreast, it throttled down and rode alongside with a bouncing, yawing motion.

It's too close, I said to myself, my eyes fixed on the light. One dip, one twist, and we'll come together and both go down. But hell, why worry? There's nothing I can do about it.

The moon went behind a cloud, and I twisted back into position. Suspended in a rackety darkness lit only by cigarettes and a tiny blue ceiling light in the pilot's passageway, I felt as if I were in the wildest of bad dreams, riding a nightmare to a Goya hell. A night jump was always eerie, but this one seemed so utterly unreal and incredible and yet so final that it wrung the feeling out of me and left me passively indifferent. Impatience was now my greatest emotion.

The crew chief left his stand near the door and, stopping here and there to chat with the men, slowly worked his way back toward the bulkhead, where Sergeant Graham was sitting. Soon he made a return trip to the tail, clutching the anchor line that ran down the plane's ceiling, and stood by the open door. He beckoned to our lieutenant, who rose clumsily from a seat nearby and looked out, then nodded and smiled. Facing down the aisle, the lieutenant yelled, "Look, men, look! It's the fleet."

I turned stiffly to the window again, like a rusty robot, and gasped, "Man, oh man." Five hundred feet below, spread out for miles on the moonlit sea, were scores and scores of landing barges, destroyers, cruisers, and attack transports. They were bearing the infantry slowly east, like a flood of lava, to a dawn assault on the shingle shore of Normandy.

As the battalion passed overhead, a lamp blinked up at us from a command ship. All the planes' wing-tip lights flashed off. The blue lights went out in the pilots' passageways.

My shoulders swung away from the window. I stared at the men opposite me in the racketing, vibrating, oil-reeking, vomit-scented darkness. "Isn't it great?" I said to Nash. "Those guys are going in!"

There was no reply, so I turned and looked at Nash, who had said for months that he was going to die on D-Day and who by comparison made me seem like an optimist, and saw that he had not heard me. He looked very scared.

I started to tell him that everything was going to be all right, but as I shouted the first words, my ears tingled and the engines' pitch changed as they strained for altitude. It wouldn't be long now, I knew, and suddenly I lost interest in Nash. My stomach tightened and filled with ice, and a voice told me to get ready. "It's coming," the voice said, "it's coming."

The red light flashed on in the jump panel beside the door.

The plane lurched and roared as if in answer, and our lieutenant staggered erect, grabbed the anchor line with one hand, and snapped his static line to it. "Stand up and hook up!" he shouted.

These were the Channel Islands, Guernsey and Jersey, between which we were now flying. We knew they were the Channel Islands because we had been told that we would stand up and hook up when we reached them. With only twenty minutes to go, we stood up and hooked up over a hostile land of flak batteries and antiaircraft machine guns. As we passed between the islands, tiny red dashes of tracer fire floated up at us lazily from both sides.

The men rose woodenly from their seats, felt blindly for the anchor line, clicked their static-line snap fasteners to it, and held on. How did I ever get into this? we asked ourselves, and why?

Now we stood in one line, facing the tail, so crowded together that we could scarcely breathe. This was the line of departure—the Channel Islands.

"Push me," Nash said. "Push me when we go." He was clinging to the static line with both hands.

The plane went slower and slower; the motors got louder and louder. From the strain on them, I could tell that we were still climbing, gaining altitude for the run to the drop zone. A stream of tracer bullets floated up at us, speeded up as they passed the windows, and disappeared with a rattling burrat.

We had reached the mainland. It was a little after midnight. The infantry was due at six—"if they take the beach."

Someone threw up and cursed, and Porter had to catch me to keep me from falling in a sudden lurch as the pilot took evasive action to avoid another flak nest that had opened fire on the planes ahead.

Ten thousand Germans.

Oh God, I prayed, get me out of here. I don't want to blow up in the sky and burn to death. I don't want to die like a mouse in a can on a garbage dump fire. I want to die fighting. Let's jump, let's jump. Let's go, go, go!

"Check your equipment!" the lieutenant shouted.

I felt the snap fasteners on my leg straps. They were closed tightly and in place. How about the reserve snaps? Also good. And the belly-band? In place. I knew the chest buckle was snapped, for it had been digging into my ribs ever since I had put on my chute.

Now I checked Nash, who stood in front of me, while Porter checked my pack, for each man was responsible for himself and the man ahead. Yes, Nash's backpack was all right; the chute was in its cover, the rubber bands still held most of the static line in position.

Burrrrat! Another machine-gun burst crackled around the plane.

"Sound off for equipment check!"

Up by the pilot's passageway, where Graham had been crowded into the entrance, the lieutenant's command sounded like a child's whisper. The pilot gunned the engines and threw the craft from side to side.

An 88mm shell burst outside with a quick flash and a metallic bang. The blast tilted the plane, throwing men onto the seats. They clutched their way back up again.

"Sound off for equipment check!" the lieutenant shouted again.

"Number twenty OK!" Graham roared. "Like hell I'm OK," he confided. "I'm scared speechless." He slapped Porter's shoulder.

"Number nineteen OK!" cried Porter, slapping my shoulder as a signal for me to shout.

I yelled that I was OK, and then Nash took up the cry and passed it on. The plane dived toward the ground, passing under a string of three white flares that hung malevolently motionless in the sky. The pilot twisted and yawed and raced back up again.

I smelled the smoke and oil and puke and gagged on my supper as it rose in my throat. Nash whispered the Lord's Prayer, and Graham goddamned the pilot for using evasive action.

"Number fourteen OK!"

"Number thirteen OK!"

I shook my head and clamped my teeth shut. I was beyond all hope. If you have to die, you have to die—and what a way this is! If you have to jump, you have to jump. A man's life and death are decided by forces that he cannot fight. He can only question them and rebel against them, but in the end, he has to go with them. For Chrissake, let's get out of this firetrap!

The plane slammed up and down, zigzagged, rattled and roared, threw us from side to side with such violence that several of us fell down again, cursing the pilot. The muscle and fiber melted from my legs. It was all I could do to remain upright and not dissolve into a gutless, gibbering blob of fear. Too weak to stand, I clung to my static line with both hands. I felt like crying, screaming, killing myself.

A flash of light came in the window, and I glanced outside and saw wisps of cloud streaking by. Now and then a pale full moon, mocking in its serenity, appeared briefly among the long, thin, scudding black clouds. This is a night for murder, I thought. God must have planned it that way.

"Close up and stand in the door!" the lieutenant yelled. Left foot forward in a lockstep, each man pushed hard against the man before him. The plane bounced up and down and gasped for altitude.

I could feel Graham crowding Porter and Porter crowding me, but I had forgotten all about them. I had forgotten all about everything and everybody but Private David K. Webster, who wanted to get out of this plane more than anything else in the world.

The motors faded out somewhat, and the plane rustled through the air more slowly.

We're over the drop zone, we're over the drop zone! Let's *go*! I had an insane urge to jump.

"Go!" the lieutenant shouted. He bent over and lifted the ends of the parapaks, slid them out the door, and jumped after them. The line of men surged forward.

Two men fell down on the threshold. There was a wild, cursing tangle as others fought to lift them and push them out, and then the line moved again, sucked out the door like a stream of water. I shuffled up, glanced down, and stopped, dumbfounded.

All I could see was water, miles and miles of water. But this was D-Day and nobody went back to England and a lot of infantry riding open barges seasick to the low-tide beaches were depending on us to draw the Germans off the causeways and gun batteries, and so, as Porter hurled himself against me, I grabbed both sides of the door and threw myself at the water.

I fell a hundred feet in three seconds, straight toward a huge flooded area shining in the moonlight. I thought I was going to fall all the way, but there was nothing I could do about it except dig my fingers into my reserve and wait to be smashed flat. I should have counted "one thousand, two thousand, three thousand"—the general would have had me shout "Bill Lee," but that was expecting too much—and yet all I could do was gape at the water.

Suddenly a giant snapped a whip with me on the end, my chute popped open, and I found myself swinging wildly in the wind. Twisted in the fall, my risers were unwinding and spinning me around. They pinned my head down with my chin on the top of my rifle case and prevented me from looking up and checking my canopy. I figured that everything was all right, because at least I was floating free in the great silence that always followed the opening shock.

For several seconds, I seemed to be suspended in the sky, with no downward motion, and then all at once, the whole body of water whirled and rushed up at me.

Jesus, I thought, I'm going to drown.

I wrenched desperately at my reserve chute's snap fasteners as the first step in preparing for a water landing. I also had to undo two leg snaps, my chest buckle, and the bellyband. The next step would have been to drop the reserve and work myself into the seat of my harness, so that I could fling my arms straight up and drop from the chute when I was ten feet above the water. I didn't even have time to begin the procedure.

We had jumped so low—from about three hundred feet, instead of the scheduled seven hundred—that while I was still wrenching at the first reserve snap, I saw the water twenty feet below. I've had it, I thought. Goddamn Air Corps. I reached up, grasped all four risers, and yanked down hard, to fill the canopy with air and slow my descent. Just before I hit, I closed my eyes and took a deep breath of air. My feet splashed into the water.

I held my breath, expecting to sink over my head and wondering how I was going to escape from my harness underwater—and hit bottom three feet down. My chute billowed away from me in the light wind and collapsed on the surface. I went to work to free myself from my gear. Immensely relieved at the safe landing, I undid the reserve and discarded it, yanked loose the bellyband, unsnapped the leg straps and chest buckle, detached my rifle case, and let the harness sink into the swamp. I was on my own at last.

The silence ended abruptly with a long, ripping burst—burrrrrrrrp!— that made me look around in fright. That's a German machine gun, I told myself. They've seen me. The bullets cracked and popped in the air above, and as I stared open-mouthed and paralyzed with fright, I saw whiplike tracers darting at me from some faroff place. I dropped to my knees in the cold, black water, which tasted old and brackish, as if it had lain still for a long time, and passively waited to be killed.

Somebody wants to kill me, I thought. So this is what war is really like? I couldn't believe that somebody wanted to kill me. What had I done to them?

I wanted to go up to them and tell them that I didn't want to kill anybody, that I thought the whole war was a lot of malarkey. I don't want to hurt anybody, I would say. All I ask of the world is to be left alone. Why do you want to kill me? You've never seen me before. Why do you want to kill me?

The machine gun fired again, a longer burst that held me motionless. I shook my head to make sure it was all real, and it was. The bullets were not in my imagination. They were real, and they were seeking me out to kill me. The gunners wouldn't even let me get close enough to talk it over with them. They wanted to kill me right here in the swamp.

The machine gun searched the area again. Faroff in the night, others burped and spluttered. Enemy rifles added their pop, pop-pop.

I waited about five minutes for someone to walk up and kill me. Then my courage returned when I noticed that the shooting was all quite far away. I rose from the water, assembled my rifle and loaded it, and rammed on my bayonet. I was ready to go.

Burp . . . burrrrp . . . burrp . . . crack-crack . . . pop . . . pop-pop.

Lost and lonely, wrestling with the greatest fear of my life, I stood bewildered in the middle of a vast lake and looked for help. They've wrecked the invasion, I thought, hearing only enemy fire. Where are Porter and Nash and the lieutenant and the rest of my friends? Where is the drop zone? Where are the other regiments? Six regiments jumped tonight, and I am alone in Normandy.

I shivered convulsively and started to cry, then thought better of it. The hell with everything! I'm here for keeps; make the best of it. At least I can try to get out of this swamp before sunrise. But where will I go? Which way is out?

I took the little brass compass from my pocket and looked at it in the spell of the moonlight. The needle was frozen in position. I shook the compass and cursed, and holding it close, saw that it was filled with water. "Son of a bitch," I hissed, throwing it away. A wise guy probably made a fortune off those compasses in the States. And now men will die because somebody gypped the government. Sons of bitches.

A flare burst over the water several hundred yards away. I bowed my head and waited for the bullets to hit me like a baseball bat, but there were no bullets. The flare died out with the afterglow of a burnt match, and I looked around in the moonlight. I sought an orchard, three white lights, a crossroads village named Hébert, and five hundred men from the 2nd Battalion and all I saw was water and flares and tracers. I listened for our bugle call, and all I heard was enemy rifle and machine-gun fire.

Suddenly the whole thing struck me as ludicrous; all the preparations and briefings, all the maps and sand tables, and for what? Why had they bothered? For all the good it did, the army might as well have yanked us out of a pub and dumped us helter-skelter to find our own way to the Germans. Instead of a regiment of over fifteen hundred men carefully assembled on a well-defined drop zone, D-Day was one man alone in an old swamp that the Air Corps said didn't even exist.

The angry clatter of a plan gone wrong filled the air. Zigzag tracers arched through the sky, and there were red flares, green flares, white flares. Grenades and mortars thumped and blammed, while small arms continued their serenade to liberation. From inland came the strange tolling of a church bell. "Invasion, invasion," it seemed to clang to the Germans still in their billets. I stood transfixed, as at a great spectacle of nature. The uneasy moon shifted behind some dark, racing clouds, and black night fell again, but there was no peace.

My courage, which had flared up briefly, died down again. My God, I thought, only the Germans are shooting. They must have been expecting us. We're done for. The invasion will fail. We'll be rounded up and butchered by the SS.

Now a new noise came—the distant rumble of a massed flight of planes—and my spirits rose. The planes were coming toward me. I followed their progress by the fountains of tracer that splashed up at them. It's the 501, I thought excitedly. They're due now. Come on down and we'll get 'em together!

They jumped up in a moonlit moment in a Fourth of July sky laced with great fans of tracer bullets. The bullets lit the planes and the shadowy parachutes and the men tumbling out of them like strings of ball bearings and followed the men to the ground, fanning back and forth with a ferocious rattling. Sick at my stomach, I watched the men swing helpless in the heavy fire. I wanted to help them, but there was nothing I could do but watch with mounting anger and hate.

"Those freaking Krauts!" I whispered. I wanted to kill them all.

I threw away my gas mask and adjusted my musette bag on my back. The box of 30-caliber ammunition I had carried on the jump was dropped at my feet. Where was the machine gun that would use it now? I took my Hawkins mine from a big pants pocket and threw that away too, for there were no tanks in the flooded area. I had to travel light to reach the Germans before dawn.

Swish . . . swish . . . swish-swish: I heard the sound of wading. I held my breath and sank slowly into the water with my rifle ready. A flare rose in the distance, but it was no help, for all I could see was black night and black water. The swishing came closer.

With my finger tight on the trigger of my M-1, I reached for the cricket hanging from a string around my neck. The wader was very close now, but I still couldn't see him. I had a slight advantage, however, in that a person at night can see better looking up from ground level than looking down from a walking height. I squeezed the cricket, click-click, and waited.

The wader stopped. I held my breath until it was ready to burst from my chest in a gigantic pop. Bayonet, hell! I'm going to shoot this son of a bitch. One more step and I'm shooting.

Click-clack, click-clack.

"Who is it? Jesus Christ, who is it?"

"Lachute, Headquarters Company."

"Polecat! It's me, Webster." I jumped up with a splash, walked to him, and hugged him and pounded his back and told him how glad I was to see him. "I thought there were only Krauts down here," I said.

"Sure sounds like it, doesn't it, buddy?" He was as glad to see me as I was to see him. "Looks like they got us by the ass. Seen anybody else from the plane?"

"No. I've only been out of my chute ten or fifteen minutes. One more step and I would have shot you."

A small, slender young man from New Orleans, with liquid black eyes and a lively sense of humor, Lachute said that he hadn't even seen me, not even after he had heard my cricket. "What'll we do now?" he asked.

"Go to the high ground. There's no cover here. We have to get out of this swamp before daylight. Goddamn Air Corps sure made a mess of this one, didn't they? How's your compass?" Lachute searched his pockets and handed me his compass. It, too, was waterlogged. I threw it away with a curse.

We had to orient ourselves before we could go anywhere, and so crouched at water level and waited for the moon to reappear. In its light, I looked around slowly in a complete circle. There was a big, dark ridge about a mile away that was dotted with flares and gun flashes. Parallel to it, on the other side of the flooded area, was a lesser ridge. The flooded area was about a mile and a half wide. There was no action on the lesser ridge. "That must be the sand dunes behind the beach," I said.

I closed my eyes and tried to re-create the sand table in the S-2 tent. Evidently we had been dropped between Utah Beach and the mainland, in the low ground spreading out from the estuary of the Douse River. The thing to do now was to head for the big ridge and help shoot the Germans off it. The infantry was due at six. They couldn't cross the flooded area with Germans still on that ridge.

"Let's go," I whispered, standing up and starting off.

"Where to?"

"The high ground. That big ridge where all the shooting is. See those flares? See the trees? Man, they're killing troopers up there. What a sound those church bells make! It gives me the creeps."

"Yeah, it sounds like a funeral—our funeral," Lachute laughed.

We waded fifty yards, then stopped abruptly when we heard a number of men talking in the loud tones of irritated soldiers on a tedious field problem.

"Christ," one said. "Let's get out of here."

"Nah," another replied. "Stick around till morning. Then we can see where to go."

I clicked my cricket. The talking stopped, but there was no answer to the challenge, so I clicked again.

"Flash," someone whispered.

"Thunder," I replied. We walked up to a grassy hummock twenty yards long and almost a yard high.

Six men squatted there like chickens flooded out of their roost. There was a first sergeant from a 2nd Battalion line company, a Headquarters Company machine gunner who had lost an older brother at Anzio and had joined the paratroops to avenge him, two men from the 501, one from the 502, and an 82nd Airborne man from the 508. Four of the six regiments that had jumped were represented. Nobody knew where they were or what to do next. They had been debating the issue for almost half an hour, according to the machine gunner, a hotheaded eighteen-year-old from a large Italian family in Trenton, New Jersey. He told us that he was sick and tired of the whole damn bunch.

I went to the first sergeant, the senior noncom and theoretical leader, said hello, and asked if he knew where we were.

"Beats the hell out of me," he said cheerfully. "Nobody's compass works. I'm going to stay here till daylight, then take off."

I gaped at him. "You're crazy," I said. I had never liked him before, and now I wanted to spit on him. "They're killing troopers up there. We have to get those Krauts."

"Oh, hell . . ."

"On top of that, if you wait till daylight, the Krauts on the high ground will nail you before you go a hundred yards. There's no cover in this swamp. I'm going up to that big ridge. You can come if you want to, but I don't really give a damn, because I'm going anyway. But first I'm going to junk these ODs. They weigh a ton."

I removed my webbing and spread it carefully on the ground. A flare arched through the sky and burst almost directly over the hummock, lighting us all in its fierce glow. A machine gun followed the flare, and once again I had the sensation of being watched. "Jesus," somebody gasped, "they see us." The flare died out, and the machine gun, which had been shooting high, stopped firing. Everybody commenced arguing again, louder than before, over whether they should leave the island or stay and what direction they should take when and if they left and what they should do when they arrived wherever they were going.

Group action, I thought, undressing quickly and throwing away my water-soaked woolen shirt and pants. I'll do better on my own.

I took off my woolen underwear, wrung it out, rolled it up, and put it in my musette bag. I cut off the bottoms of my jump pants to keep them from holding water. Then I put my jump suit and webbing back on again. I threw away my jump rope and two cartons of cigarettes that I had brought along to trade with the friendly natives.

"Let's go," I said to Lachute. "The hell with these guys."

"OK, buddy."

"I'm with you," the young machine gunner said. He turned to the others and asked if they wanted to come along. They all rose except the first sergeant. He remained seated and told us to be careful and not get hurt. As we moved off, he rose uncertainly and watched us go, then sat down again.

A flare rose over the big ridge, and the Germans started shooting under it. A Thompson submachine gun pututted, and an M-1 joined its solid bamming in reply. I smiled. The troopers on the high ground were coming out of it. There was hope for us all.

Listening intently, freezing under flares, crouching and eyeing the night with distrust, our little column waded slowly across the flooded area. The lone M-1 and the Thompson died out, the enemy firing increased, the hope that had flared in us flickered low again. We all felt tired and depressed and discouraged, the usual reaction that set in an hour or so after a jump. I wanted to lie down and go to sleep, but there was no place to lie down.

Wading slowly across a field two feet in water, I pushed through a line of reeds and suddenly stumbled headlong into a hidden ditch six feet deep. Throwing my arms high to keep my rifle dry, I held my breath and drove forward underwater. After ten feet, I staggered up a steep bank and back into the air again. Lachute, who had stopped bewildered when I had vanished, stood on the far shore, awaiting developments.

"Watch it!" I whispered, as the other men came up. "That ditch is six feet deep."

"I can't swim," Lachute said.

"I'll help you," I replied. "Be right over." I took a deep breath and held it and went back underwater. He climbed on my shoulders, holding both our rifles, kicked his heels in my side, and yelled, "Giddyap!" I walked down into the ditch, staggered across, and forced my way up the other bank, where we waited, shivering, for the rest of the men to join us. When everybody was over, we set out again, hoping that our ammunition had not been dampened.

There was a deep drainage ditch like this on the edge of almost every field, and we had to make such a crossing every hundred yards or so. The process exhausted us, and we had to stop more and more frequently to lean on our rifles and gasp for air.

The sound of American firing grew more widespread, as scattered paratroopers on the high ground gradually came together and sought out the Germans in the fields and villages. The church bell rang no more, the flares diminished, and slowly the moon, which saw it all begin, dropped down in the west.

Two men from the 82nd waded up on us quickly from the right, accompanied us for several hundred yards, then drifted off as casually as they had come. Lachute threw away his gas mask, and the others discarded all their superfluous equipment. The ridge got bigger and longer and higher, the air suddenly turned very cold, and finally the sky lightened and dawn came with a gray drizzle.

Our group began to break up. The two 501 men, who were carrying all their company headquarters' maps, said good-bye and went off to seek their captain, and the others went to the side or continued forward. Lachute and I headed for a patch of young trees that offered some concealment in the final approach to the ridge. Finally we were the only ones left. We stopped and ate breakfast among the trees.

While we were eating, a massive group of A-20 light bombers came up behind us, following the coastline, and laid a string of bombs a mile long on the sand dunes behind Utah Beach. It was the preliminary bombardment; the infantry was ready to come ashore. The smoke rose a thousand feet into the air. We stood up and cheered as the kettledrum booming of the bombing came to us.

Lachute noticed a column of men wading parallel to the big ridge and decided to join them, even though they were dangerously exposed and appeared to be going into a firefight. I decided to follow the little trees closer and then cut across a tree-covered mound about fifty yards from the base of the ridge. We wished each other luck and set off on our separate ways.

As I came up to the tree-covered mound, I heard someone call my name. "Webster, Webster!" I looked around and saw Nash lying on the ground.

"What's the matter?" I inquired, kneeling beside him. He appeared to be hurt and in shock. "Are you wounded?"

"No, I wrenched my ankle on the jump. I can't move. God, it hurts."

I looked around at the ridge. It was only about fifty yards away. A channel of deep, black water about twenty yards wide lay at its base.

"Come on," I said. "I'll help you reach dry ground."

"No," he replied. "I'm going to die here. I'm hurt. I can't go any farther."

I looked at him and thought of what fun he had been in Aldbourne and of the time I had met him in London and of the raucous little songs he used to sing, and I felt like crying.

"Come on!" I said. "For Chrissake."

He shook his head. "I said this jump was going to be my last, Web, and it was. You go on. I'm staying here."

"They'll kill you. Better get out of here while the coast is clear."

"So long, buddy." He gave me his hand, and I shook it hard. I couldn't understand what had come over him.

I left the mound and, slinging my rifle over my back, swam to the edge of the big ridge. Nash waved to me when I got out, and I waved back and started off on a forest path with the safety catch off my rifle and my eyes scanning everything ahead. A hundred yards later, I came to a road that led out of the swamp. A band of men was milling about on its edge, near a little stone stable. They had just cleaned out a pocket of Germans, they said, and were about to follow after another group of paratroopers who had gone over the ridge. I sat down in the stable and fell asleep. An officer roused me in a few minutes and told me to go up the road with the rest of the men.

The road passed through a dense forest of trees so thick and lush with undergrowth that it looked like a jungle. After a while, it topped the ridge and came out in a little village. No civilians were on hand, but the place was full of life, as dozens of wild-eyed paratroopers in blackface ran about in the streets. One group found a German truck and piled into it. They immediately drove down a side street in search of the enemy. An E Company man passed by on a captured motorcycle, and two others from the 506th came up in a farm cart drawn by a fine brown horse. A lone paratrooper stood in the center of the village square, firing his rifle at the bronze rooster weathervane atop a very old church.

Stopping to watch the fun, I noticed men running up a side street with bottles in their hands. "Where'd you get the liquor?" I asked as the men came together and began to move out of the village in parallel columns.

"Third house down that way, buddy," one of them replied. "Door's open. Help yourself." I ran down and went in. The liquor cabinet, which had been broken open by an earlier liberator, stood in one corner of a dark living room with lots of lace and old furniture. Ashamed of myself for housebreaking and yet chilled through, I selected a fifth of Hennessy cognac and ran back to join the column.

I tried to dig the cork out with my bayonet, then smashed the top of the bottle against a rock and drank. The column I had joined was mostly 2nd Battalion—I was home again. Glad to be back with the outfit and bound I knew not where, I swallowed a huge mouthful of liquor. It seared its way down my throat and whirled around in my stomach like a blowtorch.

The warmth spread through my body, making me smile with pleasure. I was alive, and I intended to stay that way.

from The Normandy Diary of
Marie-Louise Osmont: 1940-1944
by Marie-Louise Osmont

Marie-Louise Osmont, a widow living in the Normandy village of Périers, was compelled to share her beloved Château Périers with first German and then British soldiers. Her journals exhibit a sturdy, compassionate character: Madame Osmont deplored the soldiers' greed and clumsiness, but she was touched by their youth and their unhappiness.

August 6, 1940

First occupation of the Château de Périers by the Germans; altogether, two noncommissioned officers and four enlisted men.

It seems terrible—for me they represent Invasion, Defeat. Seeing these six booted aviators move into three rooms (gray bedroom and small library room, left side as you go upstairs, and large room with two beds on the right side), I am heartbroken. The house (although by now I no longer have a maid) is spotlessly clean, polished up, each rare curio in its place, flowers in the vases. The garden is still pretty to look at, in spite of the fact that Antoine the gardener has left, a prisoner; there are flowers, vegetables, and fruit.

I find these six men extremely irritating, except for a certain Franz (from near the Dutch border), really very young and charming. As a matter of fact, they are all six well bred, discreet, and clean. They spend the whole day in their underwear, which is unaesthetic but not really malicious; they make noise, which is natural; they don't have much to eat, and Bernice makes them omelettes and fried potatoes with their purchases. They have almost no work to do, play cards. Young Franz follows me around like a puppy while I do the housework and jabbers bad French incessantly. He wants to teach me German and thinks that he knows French.

All six seem almost like waifs.

One day they asked me to let them come to the parlor at eight o'clock in the evening, to listen to a special radio broadcast for the German soldiers—I almost said no, that was my first impulse. Nevertheless I agreed. Each day they knock on the door at the precise time and settle in near the radio while I pretend to be intent on my knitting. One of them offers me an "English cigarette" (they deliberately emphasize). After listening, they leave again with profuse thanks. Well bred, discreet . . . and their presence is unbearable to me! (I have often thought of them since probably all killed—in the midst of the confusion, the filth, and the screams.)

August 15, 1940

An infantry officer, haughty, came to visit, relegated the six (annoyed) aviators to two rooms, and ordered me to empty the place of nearly everything except the immovable furniture: dining room, parlor, study, and part of the third floor; I still have my bedroom, along with the dressing room and the little boudoir.

I cried. Frantic and desperate, I moved all the pretty little fragile furniture to the third floor, into two bedrooms, hid the small treasures, the brasses, everything that seemed precious to me. I spent the afternoon and night at it.

The next morning, a company marching as if on parade made a circuit of the lawn and, on command, stacked their weapons in front of the house. I was overcome with emotion; so many things went through my mind! Fifty-two men in the house, Bavarians and Prussians. Indeed I quarreled with them all; I complained more than once. I was restless and light-headed with the spirit of battle, wanting to defend this house at any price. I was, above all else, desperate.

August 17, 1940

The big oak table from the dining room was carried into the garden. The clerk settled in, making check marks in his record books, then medics armed with pads and iodine, and finally the medical officer. A procession of more than one hundred bare-chested men, coming to be vaccinated against typhoid.

August 18, 1940

Small bombardment, not very far away, by airplane. Excitement among the men; the officer, still aloof, has trenches dug in the enclosed garden and the chicken coop (after long study to find the best place).

Departure of the six aviators.

Night alert drill and practicing rapid departure by truck. The truck bumps the right gatepost and knocks it to the ground (gate sprung and can no longer be closed). Repeated protests and complaints on my part. The Germans, after long examinations by the brass, put the post back up themselves (crooked).

I complain about the soldiers who are ransacking the vegetable garden. They are made to line up in two ranks in front of the stoop, and I go among them to identify and point them out. I'm rather nervous. One of them shows me a photo of a bombed-out house, telling me that "soon the château will look like this." I answer, "With you in it, so much the better." He answers I don't know what, looking nasty, while talking about "grapes." I was to understand later that he had stolen the grapes from the greenhouse. It's been like this for a month—an uneasy life, nights without sleep because of the noise, the repulsive filth of the garden and the house, the wretched staircase ravaged by hobnails, furniture full of jam and soup, men eating just about everywhere and throwing what they don't like on the floor. In the park one steps in . . . despite a special ditch dug under the trees.

The village has some of them in nearly every house.

September 15, 1940

Finally, they leave one night, taking their equipment (mattresses, blankets) with them. The greenhouse is ransacked, the panes broken, probably by the soldier with the photo.

October 12, 1940

German airplane shot down and catches fire on the ground at the Montblanc farm.

March 19, 1942

Four Germans to house for four days; officer almost invisible, men well behaved; a huge Bavarian, rather funny. No trouble.

Crashed at Périers: an English airplane in Lignoir's garden, still another in Montblanc's pasture.

_____ 1942

Is it quieter? Or am I going to get used to this state of affairs? It's gotten so that I meet the men, around the former lawn, almost without seeing them. They themselves seem almost happy, probably relieved when they compare themselves to those who are fighting. Sometimes they show me photos of comrades who have been killed. I've learned to shrug my shoulders and say, *"C'est la guerre"* [that's war], as they themselves do, even though it's horrible!

_____ 1943

House occupied by units whose sole occupation is to scribble ceaselessly on tons of paper and type. They are perhaps alarming, but quiet. Nothing picturesque. It's like living in a ministry (or an embassy). (Not much to eat; I'm hungry.)

_____ 1943

Met a man in the park, who had already spoken to me in almost-correct French. I ask him the name of the unit that's staying at my house and blackening so much paper. He puts a finger to his lips as a signal for silence, then with great mystery he says, "Police." —??
That doesn't tell me anything new—what's odd is that they know my maiden name! What good does that do them??

Bernice contrives to cook nettles in the style of chopped spinach; it isn't bad, but without any fat, it's certainly not very nourishing! I drink a lot of water several times a day; it quiets the rumbling of my stomach . . . I'm hungry . . .

February 9, 1944, Wednesday evening

I was staying at Caen. After dinner I went to the Rue de Geöle, to the Montards' house. They were shattered. The order had arrived to evacuate "immediately and without delay" the entire Château de Mathieu, including the outbuildings, and to turn over the vegetable garden. Huge house, occupied by the family ever since the Beauchamps' grandparents, where over the years they have amassed antique furniture, small collectors' items, the thousand objects needed by a large family, to say nothing of the enormous collection of archives, books, and scientific documents accumulated by Mr. Lignoir. House full of memories, full of the past.

I'm devastated. I understand and share their distress. For twenty years my life has run close to theirs, at times mixing with it. I respect them, I love them; they are like family. They decide to get everything out, to gather everything together in Caen, to do anything in order to keep the vegetable garden, which helps them live. Sleepless night. I think of them, and I fear for myself; I ask myself, whether, if I faced the same fate, I would have the same quiet courage.

February 11, 1944, Friday

Two mornings later, I go to Mathieu to try—along with so many others— to help them if possible. It's heartbreaking to see this house being emptied. Around eleven o'clock in the morning, in the middle of everybody's hurried coming and going, I hear the telephone ring in the hall. I'm nearby. I grab it. I hear Bernice's panic-stricken voice calling, "Madame," because ten of these gentlemen are inspecting Périers in order to occupy it. I answer, "I'm on my way." I jump on my bicycle, and in spite of a terrible, icy wind, I rush down the road. Car parked in front of the gate, group of officers and junior officers stopped in the little path, conferring with Bernice and the mayor. I come up to them, I greet the officer with a "Good day, sir," which I intend to be correct and which is probably icy. They tell me that they are going to billet men in the house. I ask whether I can keep my bedroom. They answer, "Of course," almost good-naturedly, as if it's the most natural thing in the world. My heart beats a little slower. They reinspect the different rooms, which they have done already in my absence. I go past my side, which is still locked, saying, "That is my room, sir." They don't ask to see it! By evening, everything has to be clear—that is to say the ground floor (except for the study, where I will pile the furniture), the second floor except for my side, the third floor except for the end bedroom and the big attic. They parley in front of the outbuildings, ask me to remove the car, to which I reply that it's impossible. They leave.

Working until the middle of the night (with the help of Bernice and Pierre), I emptied all the rooms of their contents, except for the bulky, immovable armoires.

I packed away as many things as possible, something I had never done before. The experience proved to me that I had not yet emptied out enough. I was supposed to give them absolutely bare rooms.

Around ten o'clock in the evening, a cariloe arrives. Two soldiers unload vegetables, bread, a Frigidaire, and begin to set themselves up in the dining room.

A noncommissioned officer of the *Kommandantur* [headquarters] arrives, sets up some crates in the parlor, carefully and mysteriously locks up, and asks me for a room.

February 12, 1944, in the morning

Six-ton trucks and yet more six-ton trucks, continually unloading in front of the house, on the grass, in the park, an unexpected and disturbing array of equipment. Where can they put all that? I try to talk to them, but I get nothing definite. I understand only (and very clearly) that they have decided to squeeze everything in, and my heart stops, since I am terribly afraid that they might tell me to empty the premises.

February 13, 1944

More trucks, now with the addition of carts, livestock carts, wagons. All of them full to overflowing: mattresses, beds, armoires, Louis XII armchairs, leather armchairs, mirrors, washbasins, bathtubs (stolen from just about everywhere), corrugated metal, timber, coal, potatoes, cases of ammunition, etc., etc.

I go through a succession of unpleasant emotions: panic, anger, dumb resignation, discouragement, with a kind of physical fatigue: rubbery legs, nausea, intense cold. It's hard having to fight alone, and yet it's so much better this way!

I realize, nevertheless, that I have become inured to it and that if, at the beginning of 1940, I had seen the invasion of the house taking this form, I would have suffered far more! One really does get used to many things. I also think that all this is beyond me, that I only have the will to fight for the little things, and especially to look like the proprietor, the landlady who wants to show that she is there . . . but that's all. The fate of this property is no longer in my hands; we are in the midst of chaos— heading toward a near and terrible unknown, and the preservation of rare furniture, antique tapestries, fragile curios, all that seems ridiculous. I will fight for the memory of the dead. I will fight largely out of sentimentality, a little bit out of habit, but without conviction, and that is perhaps what makes me the saddest. Neither enthusiasm nor faith in the future . . . where are we headed? "It is not at all necessary to hope in order to undertake, nor to succeed in order to persevere."

February 14, 1944

Same invading tide. I must turn over to them the outbuildings, the old damp cellars, full of the unspeakable rubbish that one keeps, not knowing why. Also the two rooms called the coachman's rooms, and that's not all: The attics are next! At the idea of having to empty this jumble of boxes, boards, broken furniture, tools of every sort, Bernice loses control and I am very near to doing the same. I wonder whether we aren't going to go crazy, and this morning will remain in my memory as a horrible time.

The second lieutenant had told me that he was going to give me two men to help me. Two civilians arrived, two Russians, one of whom spoke French marvelously and was profuse in his declarations of devotion, his manners as courtly as those of a great lord. He presented himself as a prince or a count! (I don't know which)! Originally from the Ukraine, former owner of a large estate, former court chauffeur, his mother a former lady-in-waiting to the empress (!?). According to him, he was tortured by the Bolsheviks, his family shot, he himself imprisoned, tied up with ropes, etc., etc. His companion, an ex-colonel of lancers (!?). Both of them in rags, dirty but, it must be admitted, with a polish and manners that suggested an origin well above the ordinary. That can't be improvised.

The self-styled prince helped give me a foretaste of madness. He advised me to leave, to flee, promised me the worst misfortunes, gave me atrocious details of today's Russia, predicted a deplorable future for the country. All that in a low voice, mysteriously, a finger to his lips. I came back to my room worn out and terrified. During the day, I got his civilian comrades to talk about him and learned that he had been interned for three years in an insane asylum. That explains quite a few things. Now I listen to him calmly; he amuses me, but from another point of view I don't trust him.

The ex-colonel of lancers has also been mad, it seems (what a pair); he is short, slight, and wears a little jacket of the Eton type, tight and too short, in which he is bound to shiver.

For this new invasion includes more than just German troops. We are in the very Tower of Babel: Parisian drivers (former taxi or delivery truck drivers)—pure Parisian accent, indescribable slang, a bit rough, but nice. Russians (most of them White Russians): sophisticated, polite, and disturbing; one of them, named Nicholas, has loafed around Paris almost all his life (thirty-two years), making cocktails at the Casanova, also as a taxi driver; indiscreet, impudent as the devil, very funny, but to be put in his place when necessary. Italians: prisoners of war; carried out the occupation of Monte Carlo and Nice, taken prisoner at the time of the armistice and the Italian betrayal (the second one); they're emaciated, sad, sluggish, and shivering; they're half starved. I have discovered an Armenian who comes from Constantinople, stranded here by I don't know what odd circumstance!

It's quite strange, all this mixture of faces. It's interesting to observe, worrisome, because all of them steal to improve an abnormal and deplorable existence, and when you consider the return in terms of work, it's absolutely nil. One wonders why the Germans encumber themselves this way, with men who, consistently, do not want to do anything.

—French paid 130 francs a day: they joke, laugh, don't respect the NCO; finagling, making the best of it.

—Russians very ably *pretend* to work.

—Italians: nothing; roll a wheelbarrow when they have no choice or wash a vehicle from time to time.

Another side of the matter: French women (and what women!!) come from seven o'clock in the morning to three o'clock in the afternoon to peel vegetables. Shouts, laughter, blatant behavior! One is ashamed, but that's how it is! Peeling potatoes is certainly not their principal occupation!

Unsuccessful attempt to move the Ciney stove from the parlor; it spends the night outside. In the morning it has disappeared. With the help of an Austrian who speaks French well, I complain. It's the Italians who have taken it. In the afternoon I see it come back on a wagon.

February 15, 1944

One of the women knocks at my door to ask me for sheets of paper for "the gentlemen." Moreover, she has an escort, and I hear muffled laughter behind the door. She introduces herself: "I am one of the kitchen ladies." If anyone had told me before that I would see that in the stairwell (I'm talking about the girl) . . .

There was also "that thing": a framed picture on the second floor—a life-size Hitler!!! Horrors! It stayed in the stairwell for twenty-four hours, in the place of honor on the chest of drawers. Disappeared. Fortunately, Hitler lasted only a short time at my house. I met an enlisted man, a peasant type, who is leaving the *Kommandantur*. He looked at me with a grand gesture toward the photo, puffed out his lips, and let out a "pffft" of disgust . . . there were at least two of us with the same opinion!

The second evening of the move, quarter to midnight, I wasn't asleep. Laughter and singing from two men arriving late, probably drunk. Two calls, one right after the other, and a rifle shot. Silence on the road and hubbub in the house. It was the guard posted at the gate who fired. Very distressing feeling, to think that perhaps a man is lying dead. The next morning I learn that it involved two Parisian drivers coming back to sleep at the farm. The bullet barely missed one of them. The guard was apparently trembling with fear!

There is also, all night long, a patrol that changes every three hours. A German escorted by a Frenchman, on whom they put a green over-coat, go around through the park, the garden, around the trucks and the house. For the moment, nothing to fear from the "terrorists."

Seven Matford four-seater cars are parked behind the house in good order. But that's not enough: In the grass sloping down from the veg-etable garden, they are going to dig large, deep recesses to shelter them (from what?). As to the six-ton trucks, they showed up first at the park, hiding under the trees, driving over the cyclamens (how sad!). One of them was even hidden under the roses, along the wall; it drove over the stalks of irises and lilies! Two became very nicely stuck in the spongy grass under the American walnut. An entire morning to get them out, with the help of metal gratings, and wasting quite a bit of gasoline.

February 16, 1944, morning
Mornings being always propitious for brilliant inspirations and vast plans, they decide first to put the trucks in the woods, then, a few hours later (orders and counterorders, the military life), in the drive. Great idea! "If you please, madame"; someone leads me politely in front of the gate. Explanations: They're going to remove the markers, they'll knock down the embankment, they'll make a ramp by piling up gravel on each side, under the trees. They'll dig (well, sure!), they'll

re-pile gravel (why not?) and they'll put the trucks in place. In 1940, '41, '42, if anyone had told me that, I would have been shattered; it was what I dreaded the most. Today I listen with perhaps a vague, tight-lipped smile.

February 17, 1944

Execution of this martial project.

Since it rained torrents the whole night, the path that circles what used to be the lawn has become, thanks to the many convoys, a mudhole as deep as a stream; water, liquid mud, a vile sludge. Some Russians are given the job of breaking up the stones of a small wall bordering the old pond, which was knocked down several months ago (I expected to have it put back up one day). These stones are carried in wheelbarrows, some into the deep rut, some onto the former lawn (on which the vehicles have in any case been driving for several days).

I ask the sergeant not to take down walls on the property to find the necessary materials.

Very nicely, he promises me they won't and explains to me that he will "find some in Périers."

In fact it is Mrs. Deforge's wall that is called to the sacrifice (it wasn't used for anything anyway, and was nothing but a ruin). Men take it down, and requisitioned carts carry it here, to make an entry into the drive and a solid path to the site laid out for the trucks.

February 18, 1944

Continued: They work without enthusiasm and without energy.

The second floors of the outbuildings are lit by electricity (they must be pretty astonished). An aluminum wire, badly insulated, brings the current directly from the road (no question of a meter).

It burst into flames today, in one of the coachman's rooms. Someone made a fire in the fireplace, embers fell onto the very old floor. A hole of two square meters is left; the cellar underneath, full of straw, narrowly escaped. The soldiers, rather annoyed, repair it, and I make a few comments.

It will all burst into flames one day; that will settle the question undecided for years: whether or not to destroy these decrepit, unhealthy, and inconvenient outbuildings . . .

February 19, 1944, Saturday

They continue to work in moderation; they aren't straining themselves. It will stop at noon, in any case, with rest in the afternoon. Sunday, too; I can therefore leave unconcerned for Caen, to come back Sunday evening. It has snowed; icy wind.

I'm dumbfounded to learn that the cook is a "shopkeeper." A Russian explains to me that he sells meat, butter, cognac, etc., to soldiers who want to send packages to their families or take some when they go on leave. He intends to buy some meat from him this very evening, to cook in his room. Will there come a day of great scarcity and very great hunger, suppressing any other feelings, when I will go, with my shopping basket, to buy meat at the door of "my" kitchen?? The irony of fate!! What will we see yet?

February 20, 1944

Saturday evening in Caen. Theater, to change my outlook. Le Regain plays Cinna, unusual sets and costumes, good interpretation. We shivered. Sunday, restaurant lunch with the old gang. Terrifically depressing! I leave at five o'clock in the afternoon; I arrive at Périers pierced through by this Siberian wind. I notice that the big gravel freshly placed around the lawn is thoroughly flattened. No more trucks around the house! Bernice appears and tells me about this bewildering departure: Announced late Saturday evening, the departure took place in good order at ten o'clock in the morning. Destination: Isigny or Carentan (?). Purpose unknown, of course. No more six-ton trucks, no more Matfords, no more Parisian drivers with their Montmartre gab, no more strange-looking Russian civilians. All that's left is the *Kommandantur* and its associated services: tack room in the outbuildings, cobbler on the third floor tapping constantly; tailor, barracks of soldiers in the parlor, and the kitchen—quiet, actually; the field kitchen has left as well.

After the insane hubbub of the past week, the house seems empty. Silence, no coming and going, a rest home for pensioners . . . Bernice, who had of course already established lots of relationships among the French and Russian drivers, is almost sad!! Incredible! And her husband is a prisoner . . .

The whole area around the house is clean and freshly picked up. They have taken away a lot of equipment; bathtubs and washbasins have disappeared (where to?), the gasoline depot is gone, the timber taken up.

They have also taken the rubber watering hose that the sergeant had asked me for and which, although in bad condition, belonged to me just the same. It's a small point.

We still have remaining, neatly stacked, the corrugated metal and, thank God, the enormous depot of cases of ammunition; we can defend ourselves or blow up, take your pick.

A peaceful evening by the fireside. At nine-thirty the electricity goes out, the fuses must have blown. Someone knocks at my door, twice, tries to open the door. I hesitate—uncertain, I don't move. They'll have to learn to get through the night without me. Ten minutes later, the lights come back on; they've found the meter.

February 21, 1944, Monday

Gray, cold day; nothing special.

Big decrease in the comings and goings in the second-floor stairwell. Someone comes to see the officer in a pretty four-wheeled phaeton-type carriage, two bay horses, nice harness. Style.

I go to ask the mayor to see that I am provided with a requisition slip. He would prefer, naturally, that I request it myself. I tell him that since he has directed the requisitioning in this area, it is up to him to do it and not me, a poor requisitionee. Then, too, he is the mayor; it's his "job." But he is a timid man, even a coward.

February 22, 1944

Apart from a violent and icy wind, dead quiet in the house. If this continues I may think I'm in a convent.

Quiet—minimum of noise—peaceful nights. I sleep like lead—except for the nightmares.

February 25, 1944

Don't trust the kitchen women.

The officer goes away on leave. A young NCO (?) comes to inspect, he's twenty years old. Everybody's heels clicking.

February 26, 1944

Visit to second floor of the outbuildings, transformed into repair shop and equipment depot.

It is really organized in a marvelous fashion, electricity, 220V current, meter, tools laid out in perfect order, shelves on the walls, workbench, welding equipment, etc.

The soldier, who in civilian life worked with locomotives (?), obviously adores his little cubbyhole, which he arranges lovingly and in which he works constantly on piles of repair jobs. He explained everything to me nicely, I expressed admiration for a lot of things, and meant it; he was delighted and I was very interested. I need to cultivate him, to get my bicycle repaired; it's becoming a piece of junk, with tires worn down to the cord.

Dead quiet.

March 7, 1944

Lock forced on the Norman armoire on the third floor.

March 8, 1944

During the night someone staves in the barrel of unstarted cider, probably hoping to find some wine. A lot of cider spilled.

Still, two guards circle the house all night long, and sometimes chatter a little too much under the windows. In these times of terrorists and armed attacks, it gives a reassuring feeling; I sleep like lead.

Little by little, you get to know the men living in the house and to figure out their characters. Bernice is on the best of terms with them and starts interminable conversations; she, who would find a way to talk to a tree, is in heaven, and her nervous condition has disappeared. I would single out the two cooks, Franz and Willy; the armorer Goula, who is a decent boy; the tailor, who one evening, with great mystery, gave me a gift of a loaf of bread. There is also a Pole who sifts flour, to Bernice's great joy (!). As for the *Spiess* [slang for top army sergeant], if you don't see him, you hear him! The drivers called him the Neapolitan singer.

Since the departure of the trucks and cars, there are now nine regimental carriages hidden in the park (the horses at Deforge's), along with nine small Russian wagons. Also an antiaircraft machine-gun carrier. To say nothing of the incessant coming and going of wagons between the cannons and the house, carrying the men's food for each meal and all sorts of other things.

My dogs are putting on weight before my eyes. Franz sends them all the bones that have cooked with the soup vegetables, and there are plenty! In addition, Bernice helps herself copiously from the little barrel used to collect the fatty water and scraps. Not everything goes to the battery's pigs (there are four of them at Deforge's).

March 30, 1944

This morning I hear, from my room, psalms being sung in chorus in the barracks room—that is to say, in the parlor—below. Then preaching, then more hymns, another little sermon—new hymns—it's the pastor, who has come to fulfill his mission. I see him leaving, very dignified, looking the part: French army-type cap, knitted scarf, escorted by soldiers, two of whom carry, naturally, the inevitable carbines.

From time to time the men shoot at the innumerable crows that nest in the park.

Odd conversation in the vegetable garden, in the sunshine, with two secretaries from the office.

April 1, 1944

Great stir around the kitchen in the morning. It's only April Fool exchanges, the inevitable jokes, childish and just alike in both countries (to judge by what I'm seeing). They send the Pole, urgently, to take a very heavy case of ammunition on his bicycle to the cannons, where nobody claims it, of course, and we watch him return with his unwieldy parcel. They hang cutout paper fish on the backs of the kitchen girls. I went by there myself, and I must admit I "fell for it." Franz comes to tell me very seriously that "the *Spiess* wants to talk" to me. Fortunately, I have the good sense not to ask him anything; I simply walk by him. He says nothing to me, but Franz delightedly declares me an April Fool. One amuses oneself as one can. (I learned later that in Germany they joke like this for three days, which may be a bit long!)

No more radio! I deposited it at the town hall, like Maltemps and the others. But now you can hear music on the second floor from the linen room, or rather the Kommandantur's day room, and on the third floor from Franz's room. Those who had radios no longer have them, and those who had none have found some.

April 3, 1944

Up until this time, Périers' trees had not been affected; the disaster began this morning. Bernice woke me by announcing that "they" were cutting trees in the drive and along the road (twenty or so already). I leaped up, armed with the paper from the prefect's office forbidding any cutting. The secretary of the *Kommandantur* was nice enough to listen to me, and after a long telephone call to his commander, he followed me down the drive, talked with the young lieutenant in charge of the forty men, infantry engineers, under his command. Obviously, "my" people had no desire to see their natural camouflage disappear. He was therefore sufficiently insistent, and the lieutenant gave the order not to continue any further in the drive or along the road. That much was saved, at least. But alas, they absolutely had to have trees, and without delay. The massacre therefore continued in the woods. All day long they chopped continually, and all day you could hear the falling of the locusts, the elms and alas, the pretty, graceful birches . . . that I loved so much!

It's horrible to see. You would think that a bombardment had raged in this spot. Trees lying on the ground—over a hundred already! Others cut but tangled up with their neighbors and resisting with all their branches, as if they refused to go. All of them in full strength, stock in full growth, good and straight, trunks clean and robust, in full vigor. Those are all they're taking, chosen for uniform diameter; they'll leave the old ones and the young ones that are still nothing more than saplings. Happy are the dead who do not see this sad thing!

April 4, 1944

Same work as yesterday; what will be the toll and the extent of the disaster? I don't dare think about it. It will all go away, perhaps! The trees are all destined to be buried half their length deep, in holes that are already being prepared for the purpose, to cut up the large, flat expanses in order to prevent airplanes from landing! And to keep these tree trunks from rotting too quickly—they are obviously expecting a long duration—they peel off the bark to a certain height and singe them with a burner. This operation is being carried out in one of the farm pastures, facing the woods. I couldn't watch for long. It seemed to me that these still-living trees were humans being tortured, and I thought I could feel their suffering. The men I interrupted yesterday morning looked at me half jeering, half snarling. What a crew! This morning the farmer spent his time fighting with them. Everything went away: straw, wood, crates, chickens.

Will we have to suffer this for a long time yet? The plain around us is broad, and if it all has to be bristling with trees stuck into the ground, how many will it take? Thousands. The whole woods will not be enough.

There is a certain restlessness in the command; they scour the whole district, most probably with an eye to future works! What is coming next?

April 8, 1944

Same work in the woods. They are not satisfied with the medium-sized stock, they are taking the saplings. Everything is piled along the road before being burned and loaded on the vehicles. In places, there are already completely open clearings. Many French workers from Blainville and Périers are needed to consummate this disaster. There is talk about using the women to dig the holes. (I think I may well be one of them!)

April 9, 1944—Easter Sunday

Dead quiet. Nobody is working. Capricious weather: heavy showers, rain and wind, followed by very warm sunshine.

April 11, 1944, Tuesday

Birth of two baby goats, Fanette's kids. What a hectic afternoon! I was by myself, Bernice having gone to Caen with her eldest son. About three o'clock I see that Fanette is beginning to suffer; she bleats, pants, acts unhappy. I let her off her tether and shut her up in her stable, where I go often to watch over her. Around four o'clock, everything starts happening: She's stretched out in a corner, cries piteously, and the little feet start to emerge. I bring straw and am there for the birth of two little kids, completely white, all sticky and weak. I am in the process of rubbing them down with straw and helping them come alive when I see Franz's head framed in the doorway. "Chief would like to see car to buy it." This is just the time! Irritated, I say to him, "Just a moment, Franz," and I continue my rather dirty little job. He disappears, and comes back escorted by the captain, the adjutant, Willy, Robert—I don't know who all—and everybody, leaning over the door, takes an interest in the event, contemplates with joy the two little animals that are beginning to shake themselves; they ask a hundred questions in the usual broken French: "How old is *madame* mama?" "In the *'babies'* is these one *monsieur* and one *madame*?" "They're going to be much cold," etc., etc.

Finally, seeing that the two little animals are alive and healthy, I leave them on their straw, explain that I am going to wash my hands—which is certainly necessary—and to take care of the chore that I've anticipated for several days. I get the keys to the garage. Now everyone is interested in the car. They walk around it as best they can, in the middle of all sorts of equipment hastily piled there, and they ask me another hundred questions of a different sort: how many miles per gallon, how fast, etc. A mechanic replacing Goula, who is on leave, raises the hood and notices certain "damage" to the Delco, no battery, no shutoff switch, etc. . . . I explain. . . . The captain seems to want it very badly, and examines tires and car with satisfaction. I close the garage and go back to my two little Mickeys, whom I put out in the sunshine and who rapidly dry off and become adorable, with their uncertain movements. The captain and the *Spiess* spend three quarters of an hour admiring them. My washing and bleaching work hardly progresses at all.

April 12, 1944

The cutting of the trees in the woods is proving to be a disaster! They are cutting everything: big locusts, elms in full vigor, the big firs, everything! Nothing will be left but the thicket, in a disarray and chaos that are wretched to behold!

April 13, 1944

Bad day, horribly depressed; all day long the mechanic busies himself at putting my poor little Rosengart in running condition, and succeeds. (And to think that I had stuffed the gasoline tank with powdered sugar . . . someone gave me the tip, but it didn't work!) I see her circling around what used to be the lawn, coming and going on the road, clean, shiny like before, when the weather was nice, and I am carried back five years, and I miss it, and my heart is so heavy that I can't keep myself from blubbering, right there in the road. My car prancing by, all spick-and-span and being driven by others, the woods that are disappearing, everything that is disappearing . . . it's too much for one day, and my courage disappears too.

Toward evening I get myself under control; I devote myself to scrounging a few logs, with Bernice's help, and the work does me good.

The hares, panicked by all these men setting posts in the plain, arrive, panicked, in large numbers around the houses, and are slaughtered by Robert, who has killed four of them today and given them to his girlfriend as presents. It's really a nasty day—perhaps someday this will seem like next to nothing. Let's expect the worst.

April 15, 1944, Saturday

Large-scale maneuvers in the sector. Since morning, invasion of the houses by men in complete battle gear. In a drenching rain, they circle around the house with the horses, the wagons, the cars. They're everywhere. They go into all the rooms to try to find some shelter. Young men, almost children, asleep on their feet, looking exhausted. Crackling of rifles and machine guns.

April 16, 1944

Death of the dog Boulot yesterday. He received a terrible blow, running after a female in the countryside. A brute clubbed him. He tried to get back to the house, in spite of his shattered shoulder, fell down along the [illegible], where Bernice went to get him and fortunately had him destroyed fairly quickly by Franz from the kitchen. I was away. I reamed the details from her when I got back today; she was crying, showed me his grave in a clump of bushes. None of this helps relieve my horrible depression.

April 17, 1944

Letter from J. O. about the house. What will become of poor Périers later? Is it worth the trouble for me to keep fighting? The French from the village plunder the woods, all delighted by this disaster. It makes my depression complete.

April 18, 1944

I call police headquarters to lodge a complaint against Merière, who is stealing and who answers me insolently that "all the wood" is his, that "it's the Germans who gave it" to him.

April 20, 1944

Nasty day—police—investigation—etc.

April 21, 1944

The car leaves, still without requisition papers. Tomorrow I shall go to Caen, to the *Feldkommandantur* [field headquarters].

April 23, 1944, Sunday

Warm sunshine. First appearance of bare torsos sprawled on the grass.

April 24, 1944

Complained to the *Kommandantur* about the car. Bourdon is really very pleasant—quite amusing conversations heard in the corridors.

April 25, 1944

Celebration of Hitler's name day, on the twentieth. In honor of the occasion, new ranks and decorations are awarded. The men go for a speech at the cannons and come back delighted. The menu is greatly enhanced, they drink not a little (but they don't talk about anything). That evening, a cannon shot.

Franz is made a corporal. Müller is made an *Unteroffizier* [noncommissioned officer]. Weruca and others, *Obergefreiter* [private first class]. He is delighted to get 1,600 francs a month.

April 27, 1944

First important conversation with the *Spiess*.

April 29, 1944

I return from Caen, where the streets are filled with a feverish activity, which makes you think that "something" is going to happen. On my arrival here I find preparations for departure: field kitchen in front of the house, boxes in the hall, papers burned, things put away, etc. In fact, by starting a few conversations I learn that they will leave "probably" on the first of May, that is to say the day after tomorrow. They are waiting for the order. The men are not happy, nor am I, actually. I was beginning to get used to this group, to get to know them all, and they were becoming pleasant. Everything must begin again. And what will the next ones be like? For of course there will be others. In Mathieu, six hundred of them arrived today, billeted in all the houses! What shall we see in the days to come? I am a little fearful, and very nervous!

April 30, 1944

Now it's official. They are going to leave, and are only awaiting the order by telephone. They will be replaced by a motorized unit! Périers has not yet hosted that branch; the collection will be complete!

They leave, without any enthusiasm, for Merville, where they will have to sleep in tents; for all of those from the office, who had good beds, this does not overwhelm them with joy.

On a path in the park I meet a sad-looking soldier, who obviously wants to talk. About the war, naturally, the ruins, the dead—as if it were our fault—he doesn't say it, though, and I don't know what he really thinks. Annoyed, I snap at him: "The war, always the war. Too bad for you, all you have to do is not obey your Hitler." Terrified, he looks in all directions, as if someone could hear us in this isolated spot, in the middle of the trees. Then, very low, with a finger to his lips, he confides something that is probably risky for him: "I'm not a National Socialist." And he leaves very quickly, worried, or perhaps relieved?

Long conversation this evening with the *Spiess* and Weruca, the latter forcefully demanding colonies.

They speak openly about the landing and say, "So much the better. Soon the war will be over."

Everything seems to indicate that the event cannot be far off. Airplanes go over continually, in imposing squadrons. [illegible] today, there is one alert after another, the road is furrowed by transports of all sorts. Today saw Riva Bella after this week's bombardment: impressive damage.

May 1, 1944

The preparations continue. Everything is buckled into sacks, the boxes are ready; they take down the maps and photos tacked to the walls or the armoire doors. French gas-generating trucks and regimental carts begin transporting the ammunition by way of Merville. None hide their disappointment. You don't hear anything but *"Grand malheur!"* and they are almost emotional. One feels that they are going to make the preparations last as long as possible. They will be replaced by "assault tanks," a large number of which are already quartered at Mathieu!

This evening I attend to their [animals], which are starving and filthy; I try to convince the tailor that out of compassion he should make them *"kaput"* tomorrow. He promises.

May 2, 1944

Quiet day. Ammunition continues to disappear for Gonneville-Merville. After dinner, sitting on the stone from the pond, indescribable conversation with Franz, Willy, and the cobbler.

May 3, 1944

Preparations are taking a new turn; they are emptying the kitchen's reserves, the supplies of canned food, Goula's equipment. In the evening, coming and going of new cars belonging to the area's new units. Nineteen-year-old kids, one of whom is a priest. A moonlit night. Today A.A. at Caen and Lébisey. Death of Brière! The traitor known and feared by all.

May 4, 1944

Catastrophic day, which was preceded by a sleepless night because of the incessant noise of cars, trucks, tracked vehicles, coming in and going out continually. Up early. I see the preparations for departure speed up briskly while the new men arrive. And once more there is the laborious, difficult installation of edgy, tired men, who have been traveling for two days and two nights without sleep, coming from Brittany. There are a lot of them—and since they are motorized, they have a lot of trucks, small tracked vehicles, and cars. All these machines move into the park on the cyclamens, hiding under the trees, damaging the young stock. In the drive ten other big trucks artfully lose themselves in the thicket, with what I must admit is consummate skill. You can pass ten paces from them without suspecting a thing, unless the men's voices give them away.

But a lot of men have to be lodged in the house, *Kommandantur* on the second floor, tailor and cobbler on the third—the same old story.

They are a long way from having the equipment that the last ones

had, and there are endless requests: a glass, tables, chairs, lamps, etc.—
there was even a question at one point of emptying an armoire in the
linen room! I avoid this first catastrophe. Noon arrives with a bewildering hubbub of men going up, coming down, nailing, carrying furniture from one room to the other as it suits them. I see the big table
from the dining room going up to the second floor, six men carrying it
briskly in spite of its weight.

After lunch I come close to total disaster. Doesn't the *Spiess* (very
pleased with himself) discover the closed study, full to bursting with
furniture, cooking utensils, books, porcelains—everything that I had
moved there—and doesn't he have the nerve to want me to move it all
to the coachman's rooms in the outbuildings, in order to transform the
study into a canteen?! I was insane, desperate, and Bernice was crying!
He insisted firmly—I felt that he would not give up—and at the moment
when I thought I was lost, I was saved by a warrant officer, speaking
remarkable French (two years in the Afrika), extremely nice and understanding. He felt my distress, and whether out of pity, innate courtesy,
or understanding of the beauty of the furniture and books—or something else entirely—he intervened, in a private conversation with this
terrible *Spiess*, and the dreadful project was suddenly abandoned. When
I thanked him later, he said a few very tactful words about the sadness
of these damaged houses! It's so extraordinary that on this day an unexpected and benevolent assistance should appear.

Until evening, continuation of this arduous installation. The mattresses from the big beds disappear into the outbuildings, etc. But one
can see that as a group they are under control, well managed, very
good discipline, interesting NCOs. Quite a big difference from the previous ones.

Actually, I don't detest all of these men in the same way. There are
two levels: When I see coming toward me officers full of arrogance,
self-satisfied, probably cruel, my hair stands on end! The enlisted men,
the NCOs, the lower they are on the social ladder, the more you can
look at them without hate. Apart from a few fanatics, they are simply
men like so many others. They are afraid, they are controlled like sheep

or like tools, they are often childish, sometimes stupid. Actually, like me they are *unhappy* (for reasons different from mine).

And when they show me their family photos!! Well, then they cry.

Cooking and supply are still here, with their field kitchen, and seem not to be able to decide to leave. Plan, in any case, to return in two weeks, when the motorized unit leaves, and they—supposedly— shouldn't be staying long. But who knows?

And what events may come to pass between now and then! The tiny village of Périers goes to sleep tonight with 220 foreign men. Who could have foreseen that a short time ago? I am exhausted and broken, as after an illness. What a life, what a fight! And always alone . . .

<small>from</small> The Bloody Battle for Suribachi
by Richard Wheeler

The most famous photograph of the war is a picture of Marines hoisting the flag over Mount Suribachi, a volcano on Iwo Jima. Richard Wheeler (born 1922) was badly wounded as a young Marine during the five-day assault on Suribachi. He survived to write a history of the 35-day Iwo Jima campaign (Iwo), as well as a riveting personal account of the fight for Suribachi. We join Wheeler as he moves forward to participate in the attack on the volcano's defenses.

I t was about 4:00 when we got the order to head for the front. We were to relieve our company's 1st Platoon, whose leaders were 1st Lieutenant George E. Stoddard and Platoon Sergeant Paul P. Paljavcsick. The unit had been on the line for some hours and had lost a number of men, Lieutenant Stoddard himself having been wounded.

Our battalion had made some gains during the afternoon, and the front was now about three hundred yards ahead of us. Since the trip would take us over wholly open ground and there would be no place for us to rendezvous before our deployment, Lieutenant Wells decided to make a personal reconnaissance of the line before having us come up. Platoon Sergeant Thomas, after waiting about fifteen minutes, was to start sending us up in small groups to be placed on the line as we arrived. Wells felt that this procedure would not only minimize the confusion of the deployment but would keep our unit less conspicuous than if we moved up in force.

The lieutenant covered about two-thirds of the distance to the front without much trouble. Then a machine gun on Suribachi opened up on him. As bullets began to cut into the sand beside him he veered away and jumped into a broad but shallow crater. Lying against one of its sides was a Marine with bloody chest wounds that appeared to be mortal. Still conscious, he was breathing heavily through his mouth.

It would seem a man in such a state would have thoughts only for himself. But this man yelled: "Get out of here! They've got this hole covered!"

As Wells sprang from the crater he dropped the poncho that had been folded in to the rear of his belt, and he glanced back to see it being chewed up by Japanese bullets. This spurred him to race for a nearby mound of sand, which he dived behind.

In the meantime Ernest Thomas had been ordered by a higher officer to take our entire platoon to the front immediately. And in spite of our lieutenant's instructions the sergeant had to do as he was told.

We left our parapet by filing around its left flank, and as soon as were in the open we felt naked and vulnerable. During our wait we had at times almost forgotten Mount Suribachi, but suddenly there it was again, smoking under our regiment's attack but looking bigger and more menacing than ever.

Within a few minutes we were engulfed by the action, and its noise and fury increased as we advanced. The sand around us held booming howitzers, tanks, halftracks and 37-millimeter guns. Also firing earnestly, though less visibly, were many of the mortars and machine guns of our weapons platoons. Because of the field's activity our move wasn't noticeable enough to invite a concentration of enemy fire, but we were conscious of some close shellbursts and the sporadic whine of bullets.

Wells was still pinned down behind the sand pile as we drew near him, and the unexpected sight of us made him furious. He said afterward that we came "not as I ordered but like a band of Comanches, with Thomas in the lead. I was never so mad in my life." He shouted and signaled for us to take cover and watched us scatter "like a bunch of goddamned quail."

Wanting to tell him what had happened, Thomas continued toward him. He ran first for the hole that held the dying Marine and the riddled poncho, and he didn't immediately comprehend the lieutenant's urgent warning that he avoid it. But at the last moment he altered his course and headed for the mound where Wells lay, shortly dropping beside him on the sand.

By this time one of our own machine gunners had spotted the source of the lieutenant's plight, and after a brief duel the Japanese gun fell silent.

Two tanks, having been ordered to cover the last hundred yards of our advance, now lumbered toward us from the direction of the front. We regarded their arrival with mixed feelings. Their atmosphere of power was comforting, but we knew they might at any second draw fire from the enemy's heaviest weapons.

We hadn't dispersed as widely as Wells feared, and he and Thomas were soon able to get us into two irregular columns behind the tanks. They began to grind forward clumsily, rising and falling on the uneven sand and throwing up sprays of it with their creaking tracks. As we slogged along in their wake they fired their 75-millimeter guns, trying to make the Japanese ahead keep under cover and keep their resistance at a minimum. After each blast a large shell casing was ejected out onto the sand. One of these brushed the hand of Pfc. Graydon W. "Grady" Dyce, a lean fair-skinned South Dakotan, and stung him with its heat.

Mount Suribachi's gray dome was now rising above us in staggering proportions. The sun had slipped behind it and we were moving in its shadow, and this magnified its forbidding aspect.

Some of us began to notice Japanese activity in the brush that covered the volcano's approaches. Now and then a man would stop briefly and let go a few ill-aimed shots. Several men at this time made the alarming discovery that their weapons were sand-jammed.

As we reached the first of the front-line troops I passed a rifleman who was lying on his stomach in a shallow hole and was sighting toward the brush.

"How's it going up here?" I shouted to him.

His answering shout was hardly reassuring: "We're getting shot to hell!"

When our advance at last halted and we took cover we were part of a line that was a scant two hundred yards from Suribachi's first defenses. But even at this distance there wasn't much discernible. We saw the same battered blockhouse walls we had seen from a distance and a few smaller concrete structures whose sand had been blown away, but that was about all. The majority of the caves were as obscure as the bunkers, pillboxes and trenches. Even those entrances on the volcano's steep slopes were most of them hidden by clefts and shadows. Judged by appearances Mount Suribachi was no more than an enormous green-skirted mound of rock and dirt. But we knew we were facing one of the most ingenious fortresses ever conceived.

For some unknown reason the Japanese gave us little trouble as we deployed. This surprised us, since we had assumed there once we were in this close it would be almost impossible for us to move without drawing fire.

The area held a generous scattering of bomb craters and shell holes, and we took to them in two- and three-man groups. We of Howard Snyder's squad, ordered into platoon reserve, settled about twenty-five yards behind the forward line. Wells probably picked us for the reserve spot because we had been grenaded the night before and had spent the hours even less restfully than his other squads.

While the lieutenant was setting up his command post he chanced to look toward the edge of Suribachi's brush and see the tops of several enemy heads in a hole he believed to be a mortar pit. He had discovered a job for a tank, but the two that had covered our approach had already withdrawn. There was one firing from a position in front of the platoon on our right, however, and he decided to run over to it.

He took with him Corporal Robert M. Lane, the leader of our 2nd squad. Lane, a red-haired Arkansan, was quiet and reserved, not easy to know; but he was a former raider, which was enough to assure us of his battlefield competence.

When the pair reached the tank they found two dead Marines lying beside it. Its telephone was on the sand with a mangled wire. The men had been shot down while informing the crew of a target, and the phone they dropped had been backed over.

Wells was carrying his Thompson, and he used its butt to pound on the side of the tank to get its crew's attention. Then he pointed toward the enemy emplacement, and the tank's gunner soon spotted the heads. After firing several rounds he made a direct hit, and Wells and Lane saw one of the Japanese fly into the air. They could only guess at the fate of the others.

Lane took the lead on the return run, the lieutenant following closely. Suddenly a heavy shell exploded right behind Wells. Its concussion threw him astride Lane's back, and both men sprawled to the sand. They were remarkably lucky. The shell had buried itself so deeply before bursting that Wells received only a few sandblast scratches and Lane wasn't touched. Relieved to find themselves unhurt, they rose and resumed running, and they were about recovered from the experience by the time they got back to the platoon.

With darkness now only an hour or two away, the attack on the volcano diminished. The last of our tanks were withdrawing to their night stations, and our planes were returning to their carriers. We infantrymen, left largely to our own resources, went on the defensive. Our assault would not be renewed until morning.

Howard Snyder, Louie Adrian and I had taken cover together. In keeping with his indifference to danger Snyder had picked us a *shallow* crater, even though there were deep ones nearby. When we sat up, our heads and shoulders were above its rim. This gave us a fine view of Mount Suribachi, but it also gave the volcano a pretty good view of us. And since there were said to be about two thousand Japanese manning its defenses I found myself feeling completely outstared.

The first thing we did after getting settled was clean our rifles. I also field-stripped the .45 caliber pistol I had found. After dusting it and putting it back together I slipped it into one of the socks from my pack, leaving only its handle exposed. Having this hard-hitting weapon thrust into my belt gave me a good feeling. I had always liked hand-guns, and I valued the .45 above my rifle.

During these moments Louie Adrian looked toward the volcano and saw a Japanese dart from a cleft at its base and enter a clump of brush. The Indian readied his BAR and watched the spot for a time, but the man didn't reappear.

Shortly afterward Chick Robeson and Phil Christman approached our crater, and Robeson said, "Wells wants four men from our squad to go back for barbed wire."

Snyder asked Adrian and me to join the pair for this task. We had to go back about a hundred yards to Easy Company headquarters, and we made the trip on the run. With the sand yielding under our feet running wasn't easy, but we weren't encumbered with gear. We carried only our weapons, having left even our cartridge belts behind. I myself carried only my trusty pistol.

At headquarters, which had been set up in the entrance section of a large isolated bunker, we found Captain Dave Severance, Lieutenant Harold Schrier, 1st Sergeant John A. Daskalakis and Gunnery Sergeant Philip F. Strout making their own preparations for the night. We saw also Pfc. Leonard J. Mooney, of Hackettstown, New Jersey, who had been with the 3rd Platoon through most of its training but was now handling the captain's communications equipment.

We were given two coils of wire. They weren't heavy, and since there were two of us for each we were able to run for most of the trip back. We took the wire to the very front, to the shell hole where Wells had his command post. Then we returned, once more on the run, to the welcome semi-security of our own craters. In spite of the fact that we had been within easy range of enemy guns for the whole of our mission, we had drawn no fire.

About fifteen minutes later the lieutenant called for another group from our squad to help stretch the wire and set up trip flares out in front of the line. I wasn't assigned to this detail but Adrian, Robeson and Christman were. They were joined by Ernest Thomas, Bob Lane, Clarence Hipp, Pfc. William J. McNulty and Wells himself. These men had to expose themselves starkly. They worked fast, talking as little as possible and in subdued tones, expecting momentarily to feel the impact of enemy bullets. None came, however, and they were soon finished and making a safe return to their craters.

Battlefield situations like this defy understanding. We men of the wire details must have been observed by many of the enemy, and we would have made easy targets. But not a weapon was raised against us.

Our platoon's position began to seem considerably less perilous than I had believed it would be. I wondered whether the Japanese were saving their ammunition for the close-quarters attack they knew we would launch in the morning.

Gaining a little spirit from this line of thinking I took a can of boned turkey from my pack, opened it with my combat knife and began to eat. When I bought this delicacy in Honolulu I had pictured myself eating it during a lull in the fighting, even as I was now doing. But I had imagined myself enjoying it. As it turned out, I might as well have been downing my least-liked type of K-ration, for the turkey, with the volcano watching me, was tasteless. It was merely an item of nourishment, something I knew my body needed to maintain its strength for the ordeals ahead.

Snyder and the Indian had their own rations, and they too began to eat. But we were shortly interrupted by the nearby crash of a mortar shell. It seemed as though the enemy had deliberately waited until this moment to open fire. The burst marked the beginning of an intensive shelling, the worse we had yet undergone. Up and down our lines the explosions walked, spewing steel and sand in all directions. Snyder, Adrian and I thrust aside our food and pressed ourselves as low as we could in our shallow crater.

The dread this shellfire caused our platoon was accompanied by a feeling of helplessness. There was nothing we could do but cower in our holes and take it. In the first place, the pits it was coming from were well concealed. And even if we had been able to pinpoint them we couldn't have done anything against them with our rifles.

When one of the shells burst very close to our own crater, Snyder exclaimed, "Damn! If I knew where they were firing from we'd sure go after them!"

And for the first time since we'd landed I myself felt a stirring of aggressiveness. Snyder's words should have struck me as fantastic. To go after the mortarmen we would have had to press across two hundred yards of open sand into the volcano's belt of defenses. But our plight seemed so critical that I had begun to feel, as Snyder must have felt, that we might as well get hit while trying to do something as while cringing in a hole waiting for our luck to run out.

Up in our platoon's forward line Hank Hansen and Robert Leader shared a crater. Hansen had the audacity to stick his head up and watch the shelling, and he noticed that it was being done by pattern. It would start on the left of our sector and jump a few yards along our lines with each explosion. When it reached our right flank it would start working its way back. Hansen once watched it move along his own line and approach his own position. Suddenly he pulled his head down and shouted to Leader, "Duck! The next one's coming close!" And it did— but it failed to explode. All the pair heard was the thump of a dud somewhere near them.

Several of the men around our lieutenant's command post tried to joke to cover their nervousness. After a close burst one hollered, "Knock, knock. Who's there?" Another asked Wells what he thought his girl friend was doing at that moment. "I don't rightly know," the lieutenant said. "But by God she'd better be thinking of me!"

During the pounding my two companions and I were missed three times by only a few feet. The third shell exploded on the rim of our crater and showered us with sand.

But there's a military saying that "no situation, however hot, stays hot very long." And about the time we decided we could take no more, the shelling let up.

Wells was afraid the Platoon had been torn apart, but the good luck we'd been enjoying was still holding. Only one man had been hit. Private Ogle T. Lemon had taken a blast of fine fragments on the chest. Lemon, a genial, mild-mannered Texan, was one of our older members and was well established as a family man. He was the father of two children.

In view of our light damage, it might seem that I have exaggerated this shelling. But men who have good cover and are well dispersed are not really easy targets for shellfire. The forty-three members of our platoon occupied about fifteen shell holes spread over an area of about 1,500 square yards. Even though our craters were quite broad, averaging perhaps twelve square yards at the rim, they took up only about 180 square yards in aggregate. By far the greater portion of our area was open sand.

Of course, this sort of reasoning isn't likely to be done by men being shelled. With the noise deafening and the ground trembling beneath them, all they can think about is that shells do sometimes land in holes where men are huddled. On Iwo, in fact, this was a fairly common occurrence. But for every shell that found a target there were many that exploded without effect.

After the shelling, we returned uneasily to our preparations for the night. Snyder, Adrian and I first finished eating. My turkey was now not only tasteless but almost impossible to swallow. 1 had to resort to washing it down with water as I had done with the fruit bar the day before.

About a half hour before dark a group of our company's machine gunners, walking in a well-spaced double file and conversing in surprisingly nonchalant tones, approached the front on our left. They had been assigned to the company's 2nd Platoon, whose leader was 2nd Lieutenant Edward S. Pennell, and they were being led up by Pennell's platoon sergeant, Joseph McGarvey.

McGarvey was from Philadelphia; he knew that I too was from eastern Pennsylvania, and as he and the group passed about twenty-five yards from me he called cheerfully, "Hiya, Wheeler! How do you think the Phillies will make out this year?"

The question came unexpectedly, and all I could think of hollering back was an insipid "Good, I hope!"

McGarvey's greeting was obvious bravado, but this sort of thing was excellent for morale. As long as men could pretend to be lighthearted the situation didn't seem entirely hopeless.

Both leaders of the 2nd Platoon would later perform feats of valor that would earn them decorations. Lieutenant Pennell would receive the Navy Cross and Sergeant McGarvey the Silver Star.

One man who didn't seem at all bothered by the nearness of Suribachi that evening was Chuck Lindberg, the sturdy ex-raider who led our assault squad and handled one of its flame throwers. He was a dedicated souvenir hunter, and as soon as he got his squad settled he went over to the platoon's right flank to investigate the diggings around an abandoned Japanese gun pit. When he returned, he came to the hole I was in to show me one of the objects he had found, a neatly cataloged Japanese stamp collection. He seated himself on the crater's rim, and I reluctantly drew myself up beside him. Then he calmly paged through the album for my benefit. I pretended interest but was much too conscious of our danger to really see the stamps. My chief thought about the paging was that it wasn't being done nearly fast enough. Lindberg seemed to give no consideration to the fact that we might be picked off at any second. When he finally left I slid back into the crater with a feeling of relief. It seemed incredible to me that anyone could be thinking about souvenirs at a time like this.

I admired our platoon's former raiders very much. They were uncommonly good men. But I had begun to wonder how they had managed to survive several bloody battles. I had about decided that I wouldn't survive this one if I kept trying to do as they did.

But now the act I had been maintaining paid off in the form of a commendation from my friend Snyder. He told me he liked my steadiness under fire and was glad to have me with him. This meant a lot to me, though honesty almost made me confess that most of those times when he thought me courageously steady I was probably closer to being petrified.

At dusk Ernest Thomas came to our crater to consult for a few minutes with Snyder. One of the first things he said was, "Did you hear about Sergeant Plumer? He was killed this afternoon. Imagine—a nice fellow like Plumer!" Thomas, who was seeing his first combat, was clearly having trouble accepting the fact that a man he liked had been killed. His attitude seemed odd. Sergeant Plumer, a member of another platoon of Easy Company, was indeed a nice fellow. But there seemed little doubt that a lot of nice fellows were going to be killed before the fight ended. As it would turn out, Fate had arranged for the list of dead to include likeable Ernest Thomas himself.

That evening, for the first time since coming ashore, I felt the need to move my bowels. Just before dark I crept out of the crater, scooped a hole in the sand and relieved myself. During our training days I had heard many joking remarks about a Marine's needing plenty of extra underwear on the battlefield. Fear was supposed to make for bowel looseness. I myself hadn't been affected this way. But perhaps there were men who had. One member of our platoon, as soon as we hit the beach, had taken his combat knife and put a slit in the seat of his trousers and his "skivvies." He explained that he did this so he would not only be completely ready for emergency bowel movements but could have them without exposing the white of his buttocks to enemy snipers.

With the coming of darkness the Navy once more began to send illuminating shells over the island. They didn't help us much to distinguish Japanese activity on the volcano, since their unsteadiness kept its rugged surface a mass of motion; but they enabled us to get a fairly constant view of the open stretch between our lines and the first defenses. The men in the forward squads spent much of the night anxiously scanning the strip of sand that held their barbed wire and trip flares. Since the Japanese hadn't counterattacked in force the first night, it was believed they might on the second.

Soon after dark our lieutenant got a call on his telephone from company headquarters. Captain Severance had some heavy demolitions, some flares and two cans of water for our platoon. Wells decided to go back for the stuff himself, taking Clarence Hipp with him. The pair made their way by following the telephone line, and they talked loudly the whole trip to keep from being shot by Marines with nervous trigger fingers.

Wells found himself strangely irritated by the sight of the company command post. "I guess it was jealousy," he said later, "but inside me I hated every man in that secure place."

Actually, the captain and his staff weren't as safe as they seemed. At this point, there still wasn't a safe place on the whole island.

To keep from becoming accustomed to being away from the front, Wells and Hipp quickly loaded up and left. Wells carried the two heavy water cans, and Hipp the demolitions and flares. Again following the phone line and talking loudly, they reached their starting point without incident.

The squad that Donald Ruhl, the lieutenant's runner, had joined for the night was located near the abandoned gun emplacement and diggings where Chuck Lindberg had found the stamp album. Ruhl boldly explored this area in the dark, knowing full well that some of the enemy might still be lurking in it. He discovered a pitch-black tunnel leading off from the gun pit, and he had the incredible nerve to push into it and investigate its entire length with the aid of lighted matches. He found a lot of enemy gear, including a number of woolen blankets. These he carried across the shadowy sand to Wells and the men around him for use in the cool night, an act that was much appreciated. Ruhl seemed intent on making us eat the critical words we had spoken about his independence and hard-headedness in training.

The shells sent against the volcano by the Navy, the 13th Marines and our company mortar units during the night burst vividly among its restless shadows, and many of the explosions gave rise to billowy white mushrooms.

Suribachi was also the background for another type of light. The Japanese sent forth white and amber pyrotechnic signals that called for shellfire from the north of the island. One variety of missile these flares brought down on us was a particularly frightful thing. It approached with a weird screeching noise and it burst with a tremendous concussion. We learned later that it was a monstrous rocket-powered bomb that was loaded with odds and ends of scrap metal.

With a lucky shell, the enemy eventually scored a direct hit on one of the ammunition dumps on the beach to our left rear. This set off a spectacular fireworks display. The series of explosions and red flashes

continued for perhaps an hour, sometimes diminishing for a few minutes but then bursting forth with renewed brilliance. During this time
the volcano and the reaches of sand around us took on a fluctuating
red glow. The effect was an eerie one. It was as though our evil little
island had suddenly been transported to hell.

Suribachi's defenders made one attempt to counterattack. They began
to mass and organize on a plateau that lay along the volcano's left flank.
But the *Henry A. Wiley*, a destroyer that was covering this area, spotted
the activity and quickly closed in to two hundred yards to contest it.
Switching on a powerful searchlight, the vessel opened up with all of its
bearing guns. We watched with fascination while a thunder-and-light-
ning concentration of shellbursts and ricocheting 20-millimeter tracers
raked the plateau for fifteen minutes. The organizing Japanese were
decimated, and the plan to counterattack was abandoned.

There was one infiltration attempt made in our platoon's sector. The
lone Japanese tried to come through on our right flank. He was dis-
patched by rifle fire.

Snyder, Adrian and I took turns at watches through the night. We used
my pistol as our watch weapon. This night, in spite of its perils, its noises
and its unearthly illuminations, was a better one for the three of us than
the first had been. This time we knew we were surrounded by Marines,
and we weren't cold. Snyder and I had our ponchos, and Adrian was
wearing the extra jacket I had been carrying in my pack. He also had a
cellophane cape from a gas mask pouch, and he used this to cover his
legs. All three of us managed to get snatches of sleep. Our naps, at best,
were troubled ones; but they helped in a small way to strengthen our
muscles and our minds for the awful test we now had to face.

Our second dawn on Iwo Jima wasn't as welcome a sight as the first
had been. As Mount Suribachi's hazy dome began to outline itself
against the sky we became fully aware of what we were up against. We
were now going to have to make a frontal assault, across a 200-yard

open stretch, into the volcano's maze of defenses. And there wasn't much doubt that we'd be fiercely resisted. The time had come when the Japanese had to repel us or die.

The day broke quietly enough. There was at first little firing from either side, a situation that contrasted sharply with the happenings of the night. But the stillness wasn't one that made for easy breathing, for a sinister tension hung over the sand. This was the calm before the storm. It was a time of last-minute prayers and melancholy thoughts. We'd reached a point where it seemed unlikely we'd ever again see the homes that lay thousands of miles across the restless water to our left. Though we'd all joined the Marines expecting tough assignments, the thing we were about to do seemed suicidal.

As soon as it was light enough to see, our lieutenant crawled out of his crater and squatted in front of it to study the enemy's lines. Visibility soon began to improve, and he suddenly spotted a squatting Japanese who appeared to be making a study of *our* lines. Wells had left his Thompson in his crater, so he pointed out the man to the squad nearest him. But the Japanese seemed to realize what was happening. He stood up, placed his hands boldly on his hips for a moment, then strode back into the brush before our men could shoot.

The stillness in our zone was soon broken by the crackle of rifle fire along our right front. One of our squads had spotted a bustling of enemy activity in a network of shallow trenches that lay in an area that was free of brush. There were dozens of men moving through the excavations. Most were hunched low and were running. One group went through with each man hanging onto the belt of the man in front of him. Our riflemen were unable to tell how many of these men they hit, but their fire soon caused the Japanese to drop out of sight, perhaps to continue their movements on their hands and knees.

About 7:30 Ernest Thomas paid another short visit to the crater my two friends and I occupied. He told us we would begin attacking at 8:25. There would be a pre-attack bombardment, he said, and we would have tank support when we jumped off.

Thomas asked me whether he could borrow my bayonet. He himself had none, since he was armed with a carbine. I turned mine over to him, wondering why he'd made the request. I'd learn later that he wanted to use it as a pointer while he helped Wells direct the assault.

As Thomas left, Snyder took his own bayonet from its sheath and fastened it to his rifle.

"You shouldn't have given yours away," he reproved. "You might need it."

"I hope not," I said, repelled by the thought. As long as I had a bullet left I didn't intend to do any bayonet fighting.

The pre-attack bombardment was dominated by the savage efforts of forty carrier-based planes. Many fired rockets that exploded with an ear-splitting sharpness and produced a concussion that seemed to shake the volcano as it might have been shaken by an earthquake. We pulled our heads down when clouds of shrapnel and debris came winging toward our lines.

As the planes made their last run and rumbled away across the water, we knew that our own turn to attack was at hand. And we began to look anxiously toward the rear for our tank support. But there were no tanks on the field. These important machines had again been delayed by refueling and rearming problems. The realization that we'd have to jump off without them made our situation seem even grimmer.

Snyder checked his watch. Then he began to observe our platoon's front line closely. And it wasn't long before Wells climbed out of his crater and signaled, with a sweep of his Thompson, for the rest of us to follow his example. He set off at a trot for Suribachi, and men started to issue from the sand all along our front.

"Okay, let's go," Snyder said quietly. And he, the Indian and I left our crater. The rest of our squad also moved out. We began to trot from hole to hole, pausing in each to catch our breath and scan Suribachi's green fringe for signs of activity. We saw our leading men drag aside the spirals of wire that lay across our path.

For a few moments the hulking fortress remained still. Then it began to react. First came the crack of rifles and the chatter of machine guns. This quickly grew to a heavy rattle, and bullets began to snap and whine about us. Then the mortars started coming, some being visible as they made their high arc, and shortly the area was being blanketed by roaring funnels of steel and sand. The noise and fury increased until our hearing was numbed and our thinking impaired. It was as though the volcano's ancient bowels had suddenly come to life and we were advancing into a full-scale eruption.

Chick Robeson said later of the shelling: "It was terrible, the very worst I can remember our taking. The Jap mortarmen seemed to be playing checkers and using us as their squares. I still can't understand how any of us got through it."

We were now part of a real hell-bent-for-leather attack, the kind the Marines are famous for. But there but nothing inspiring about it. None of our ex-raiders shouted "Gung Ho!"; none of our ex-paratroopers shouted "Geronimo!"; and none of our southerners let go the rebel yell. We felt only reluctance and enervating anxiety. There seemed nothing ahead but death. If we managed somehow to make it across the open area, we'd only become close-range targets for those concealed guns. I myself was seized by a sensation of utter hopelessness. I could feel the fear dragging at my jowls.

It is in situations like this that Marine Corps training proves its value. There probably wasn't a man among us who didn't wish to God he was moving in the opposite direction. But we had been ordered to attack, so we would attack. And our obedience involved more than just a resignation to discipline. Our training had imbued us with a fierce pride in our outfit, and this pride helped now to keep us from faltering. Few of us would have admitted that we were bound by the old-fashioned principle of "death before dishonor," but it was probably this, above all else, that kept us pressing forward.

Men were beginning to fall now, and the cry, "Corpsman! Corpsman!" became a part of the action's mixture of sounds. Raymond Strahm went down a few yards to my left, a piece of shrapnel having pierced his helmet just above his right ear. The helmet slowed the fragment and saved his life (so he could die in a postwar automobile accident). Pfc. Robert L. Blevins, of Galesburg, Illinois, next fell with a bullet in the leg. Then a mortar burst killed Corporal Edward J. Romero, Jr., our ex-paratrooper from Chicago.

And then it was my turn.

With shells starting to close in on us, five of us jumped into a huge crater that had probably been formed by a 500-pound bomb dropped by the 7th Air Force. Staying on our feet, we took positions on the forward slope that enabled us to look over the rim toward Suribachi. There was immediately a heavy crash just to our right, and then another a few yards behind us.

Someone said urgently, "Let's get out of here!"

"One place is as bad as another," I countered.

"Yeah," Howard Snyder agreed. "One place is as bad as another."

A moment later a shell exploded, with a fierce lashing of steel and sand and concussion, on our crater's left rim.

My rifle was torn from my hands and I reeled under a hard, ear-ringing blow to the left side of my face. I thought for an instant that I had taken only concussion, but when my hand leapt reflexively to the affected area, the tip of my thumb went through a hole at my jaw line. A fragment had broken my jaw, smashed through the roots of two molars and lodged in the muscles beneath my tongue.

Only one man besides me had been hit, and he received but a minor wound in the muscles of his lower back. Because of the way I'll have to discuss this man shortly, I'll give him the fictitious name "Smith."

My own wound started to bleed profusely, both externally and inside my mouth. While Snyder stuck up his head and shouted an urgent call for a corpsman, I took off my helmet, pack and cartridge belt and sat down against the crater's slope. Spitting out a stream of blood and the crown of a tooth, I wondered worriedly how my injury's two-way flow could be stanched. I was afraid my jugular vein had been hit.

Corpsman Clifford Langley was able to reach me almost at once. He quickly applied compresses, one inside my mouth and one outside, and the bleeding promptly decreased. The inside compress was held in place by my biting down on it, while the other was secured by a bandage that Langley wrapped vertically about my head.

Finishing with me, the corpsman moved across the crater to treat Smith's back.

Now that the emergency was over, Snyder asked whether he could have my pistol, and I was glad to give it to him. He also removed the two fragmentation grenades that were attached to the straps of the pack I'd discarded.

"We'll have to go now," he told me.

"Are we just going to leave him here?" the Indian asked.

"We've got to," Snyder answered. "We'll come back and check on him later."

I could talk, in spite of the bulky compress in my mouth, and I managed to say, "Go fight the war. I'll be okay." Then I added the standard statement for moments like this: "Get a couple for me."

The three unwounded men now climbed out of the crater and pushed on with the attack. Corpsman Langley remained with Smith and me to give us each an injection of morphine. Then he closed his first aid pouch and prepared to go. Deciding it might be wise that he arm himself, even though he was supposed to be a noncombatant, he picked up my rifle, the stock of which I noticed was shrapnel-scarred. He next climbed to the rim of the crater and peered toward Suribachi.

At that moment the crater rocked with another savage, ear-pounding explosion. We had taken a second direct mortar hit.

I let out a sharp involuntary cry as the blaze swept over me and tugged heavily at my left calf. My trouser leg, my canvas legging and a large area of skin and flesh had been torn away. The wound was an ugly sight. My calf's major muscle had been laid bare and sliced in two as though by a knife. One of these segments had been pushed slightly to the side, and my first reaction was to reach down and align it with the other.

With my jaw fractured, my blood supply diminished and my calf now severely torn, I felt for an instant that I was nearing death, and I said to myself, aloud, "Well, I guess this is the end." My tone was matter-of-fact. I felt no pain and no particular anguish. The worst had happened, but it really wasn't so terrible after all.

Corpsman Langley was at my side in a moment, and my death

vision faded. Langley himself had taken some shrapnel, though I wasn't aware of it at this time. He first sprinkled sulfa on my wound, which wasn't bleeding badly in spite of its seriousness. Then he covered it with an ankle-to-knee battle dressing that fastened along my shin with tie-ties.

As the corpsman finished with me I turned my eyes to Smith and found him to be a tragic sight. Lying on his stomach on the crater's floor, he was now mortally hurt. Both his legs had been horribly lacerated from heel to waist. On his right leg I couldn't see a particle of skin. To make a ghastly but accurate simile: the limb looked like a long pile of raw hamburger.

Smith was the man who had exclaimed apprehensively while we were on our way to the beach, "If only we get in okay!"

Still conscious, he was lying quietly with his head on his folded arms. His face was pale but calm. To make him think that something was being done for him Langley, placed a tourniquet, a white cord, around the leg that was most frightfully damaged. The cord contrasted signally with the red flesh it was compressing, and the limb's grisly appearance was heightened.

As the corpsman turned from this measure, he and I had another jarring experience. We heard a heavy thump, and we realized that a third mortar shell had hit the floor of our crater. But this one was a dud. It didn't explode; it merely buried itself. We watched, fearfully fascinated, as sand funneled in over the top of it. Had this shell exploded, we must certainly have been killed.

I now noticed that blood was seeping through the corpsman's clothes at several points, and I asked him whether he wanted me to take a look at his wounds. But he assured me that he wasn't badly hurt. He once more closed his pouch, picked up my rifle and climbed the crater's slope. After sizing up the situation ahead for a few moments, he slipped over the rim and was gone.

Death would soon come to my luckless friend while I sat near him in that evil crater. I would presently be found by stretcher bearers, at which time my brief career as a combat Marine would end. Though I wasn't to be a hero, I had lasted long enough to win an important personal battle. My courage had been put to an extreme test and had held up.

During those moments when Smith's life was slipping away, my own was having a new beginning. Life would seem much sweeter after this. In six months I would be recovered from my wounds, walking without a limp, bearing my scars with pride, enjoying a new confidence. There would seem little to fear after Iwo Jima. I'd know that I'd never be called upon to do anything harder than pit my flesh against Mount Suribachi, however long I lived.

Seeing my years accumulate would bring me more satisfaction than sadness. I'd view gray hairs and wrinkles as the medals that Nature awards to those of us who make it to maturity. As for Death, I had come face to face with that old ogre and had learned that he is mostly sham. I'd enjoy the truce he'd granted me, but would live with the feeling that when he finally renewed his fight in earnest I'd be able to make my surrender without begging for terms.

from We Were Each Other's Prisoners
by Lewis H. Carlson

The stress of combat meant that soldiers did not always treat prisoners according to war's highest conventions. Troops who managed to surrender— many were killed trying—could not count on humane treatment, as Oscar Schmoling learned at age 16. His story is from Lewis Carlson's collection of personal accounts by Americans and Germans who were taken as prisoners during the war.

I was born December 3, 1927, in Rastenburg, East Prussia, which is now part of Poland. I turned sixteen in December of 1943 and was drafted into the *Arbeitsdienst*, which during the war performed all kinds of jobs, from building barracks to transporting war materials. I was eventually put into an anti-aircraft unit and sent for six weeks of training to Linz, Austria. Then I was shipped to Normandy to work in an anti-aircraft unit. We were supposed to replace those members who had turned eighteen and were to be transferred into the regular army. We arrived outside of Cherbourg on June 4, just two days before the Normandy invasion. Our officers knew something was going on, so the older boys had to stay because we were not experienced enough to replace them. Initially, we just helped doing little things around the area, but after the Americans landed, we blew up our antiaircraft guns and fled into Cherbourg. By that time it didn't matter what kind of unit we came from—artillery, infantry, or *Arbeitsdienst*—we all became replacements for those who had been killed or wounded. The youngest of us were put to work carrying wounded soldiers to the rear and transporting ammunition to the front.

It's difficult to say what you feel as a sixteen-year-old boy. I didn't want to be a hero, but I wanted to be strong and do what the others before me had done. Sometimes I felt like a man, but there were also moments when I felt like a child. One of my brothers had already been killed in Italy. I had another brother in Russia and one in France. My dad had been in World War I, but he was also drafted into the Second World War and served in Poland and Russia. I wanted to be proud, but I could also still feel the child inside of me. I didn't know if I would ever see any of my family again and I even thought I might get killed. But then I would say to myself, "It doesn't matter what happens to us. Let's get them." Your attitude would change back and forth. If you had eaten and slept well, you felt more like fighting. But if you were tired, hungry, and thirsty, you thought, "I wish it was over."

I was captured on June 23, 1944. There were maybe 80 or 100 people around us. We had just delivered some ammunition to the front. When I came back, planes bombed and strafed us. Everybody was running around. Then their artillery opened up. We never knew exactly where the enemy was. Finally, machine guns and every other kind of weapon you can imagine started firing into our position. We expected the Americans to be in front of us, but they had already encircled us and were coming up from the rear. They pushed the German troops in front of them back into us. Our soldiers came in waving white flags and telling us to throw away our weapons. My first thought was, "The war is over. Maybe an armistice has been declared." There was total confusion. Then someone told us to put up our hands. So we threw away our weapons and raised our hands. It all happened so fast.

What happened next I have never told anybody, not even my parents. We were marched three or four miles back to the American rear lines with our hands up. Somehow we felt those guarding us were more frightened than we were. It was hot, and we hadn't had a bath for weeks. We were dirty, hungry, and tired. They put us in a big yard, and we were checked for weapons. Some of us lost our watches. I can remember one American was so proud that he had seven or eight of our watches on his arm. A rumor circulated that Germans had killed some civilians, and this American officer came up and picked out ten of us to be shot for revenge. I was one of the ten. He lined us up and told us to face this stone wall. A command was given, and we heard the ammunition being loaded. We knew they were lining up their machine guns. I could already feel the hot bullet searing my body. At that moment I remembered my religion and murmured a simple prayer: "Lord, I cannot better myself anymore; the end has come. I pray that my mother will be able to take the news, and I wish they would pull the trigger and get it over with."

To this day I don't know whether they were just trying to scare us or whether some higher-ranking officer ordered them not to kill us. I just don't know. But I do know I can't forget it.

Bond Rally

by E. B. White

E. B. White (1899–1985) is remembered for children's books and essays that blend folksiness, sophistication and writerly discipline. This Harper's article partakes of the boosterism that colored most wartime journalism. But White's sentiments ring true as he captures the homefront's mood at a 1942 war bond rally in rustic Maine.

D orothy Lamour left Portland, Maine, at 7:20 on the morning of September 17th, passed through Woodfords at 7:25, Cumberland Center 7:39, Yarmouth Junction 7:49, and two hours later arrived in Augusta, where she parted with one of her handkerchiefs to a gentleman who bought an unusually large war bond. She left Augusta at 1:38 p.m., passed through Waterville at 2:04, Burnham Junction 2:35, Pittsfield 2:49, Newport Junction 3:01, and arrived in Bangor at 3:40, at the top of the afternoon.

Like most river towns, Bangor is a metropolis loved by the heat, and it was hot there under the train shed that afternoon, where a few dozen rubbernecks like myself were waiting to see a screen star in the flesh. The Penobscot flowed white and glassy, past the wharves and warehouses. On a siding a locomotive sighed its great sultry sighs. The reception committee wiped its forehead nervously with its handkerchief and paced up and down at the side of the waiting Buick roadster—which the daily *News*, in an excess of emotion, described as "blood-red." The guard of honor—a handful of soldiers from the air field—lounged informally, and a sergeant with a flash camera arranged himself on top of a baggage truck. In the waiting room a family of three sat in some embarrassment on a bench.

"I feel so silly," said the woman.

"What d'you care?" replied her husband, obviously the ringleader in this strange daylight debauchery. "What d'you care? I like to come down here to the station and see how things act once in a while." The teen-age daughter agreed with her father and backed him to the hilt, against her mother's deep-seated suspicion of the male errant.

Miss Lamour's train pulled in cautiously, stopped, and she stepped out. There was no pool, no waterfall, no long dark hair falling across the incomparable shoulders, no shadow cast by the moon. Dorothy the saleswoman strode forward in red duvetyn, with a brown fuzzy bow in her upswept hair. She shook hands, posed for a picture, and drove off through the cheering crowd in the blood-red car, up Exchange Street, where that morning I had seen a motley little contingent of inductees shuffling off, almost unnoticed, to the blood-red war.

While Miss Lamour was receiving the press in her rooms at the Penobscot Exchange Hotel I went down to the men's room to get a shine

"See her?" I asked the porter.

"Yeah, I was standing right next to her at the curb." Then he added, studiously: "I'd say she was about thirty. A nice-looking woman."

"I suppose they're giving her the works, here at the hotel," I said.

"I'll say they are. Took the furniture right out of Cratty's room. Hell, she's got chairs in there that wide."

Having assured myself that Dorothy was being properly cared for, and having brightened my own appearance to some extent, I went out to the Fair Grounds at the other end of town, where a stamp rally was scheduled to take place. The grandstand alongside the race track was already bulging with children, each of whom had bought a dollar's worth of stamps for the privilege of seeing Lamour. The sale of stamps had been brisk during the week. A booth had been maintained in the square, and Madame Zelaine, the local seeress, had personally handed out stamps and taken in the money for the Treasury. And now the grandstand was a lively place, with much yelling and chewing and anticipation. The Boys' Band of the American Legion, on the platform in the infield, was flashy in blue and yellow silks. In the still air, under the hard sun, gleamed the flags and the banners and the drum majorette's knees. When the car bearing the beloved actress appeared at the infield gate and swept to the bandstand the children hollered and whooped in their delight and little boys threw things at one another in the pure pleasure of a bought-and-paid-for outing.

The meeting got down to business with an abruptness that almost caused it to founder. Miss Lamour was introduced, stepped up, shaded her eyes with an orchid, made a short appeal, and before the little girls in the audience had figured out whether her hair was brown or green, she asked everyone to step along to the booth and buy some stamps. This was an unlooked-for development. Presumably most pockets were empty. Nobody made a move and the silence was oppressive. I have an idea that Miss Lamour herself didn't know quite what she was getting into and perhaps hadn't been told, or hadn't taken it in, that the children were already paid-up supporters of the war and that their presence there, inside the gates, was evidence that they had shelled out. It was simply one of those situations—a situation in the hard, uncompromising sunlight.

Miss Lamour, obviously a sincere and diligent patriot, saw that she was in a spot, and the chairman was visibly embarrassed. He and she hurriedly went into a huddle, shameless in the glaring sun. Then she grasped the mike. "Don't tell me business is *this* slow," she said, rather desperately.

Two or three little millionaires, in sheer anguish at seeing a dream person in distress, got up and moved toward the booth. Miss Lamour seized the moment. "Listen," she said, "I've come a long way to see you—don't let me down." (The bothersome question arose in all minds, the question of who had come to see whom in this show.)

"Sing something!" hollered a youngster.

But there was undoubtedly something in her contract which prevented that. After another hurried conference the bandleader handed
over his baton.

"I've never done this before," said Dorothy, "but I'm willing to try
anything." She stepped up in front of the band, the leader got them
started, and then gave over. Miss Lamour beat her way doggedly
through a rather heavy number. In a long grueling bond-selling tour
this was obviously one of the low moments for her. Low for the children, too, some of whom, I am sure, had gone into hock up to their
ears. It was just poor showmanship. Disillusion in the afternoon. The
music ended and the star took a bow..

A couple of Fortresses flew overhead. This was a break. Miss Lamour
pointed up excitedly. "If you think it doesn't cost money to build those
things, look at them. That's what you're buying!"

"Sing something!" shouted the tiny heckler.

Some more customers filed awkwardly down to the booth and in a
few minutes the meeting was adjourned.

"I figured her hair was going to be down," said a little girl next me,
coming out of a trance. Miss Lamour left in the Buick, respectfully
encircled by the Army and the Navy, one man from each.

The big meeting was in the evening, after supper, in the Auditorium;
and if Bangor had muffed its afternoon show it made up for it by a
curiously happy night performance. It is no secret that enormous sums
of money have been raised in America through the generous efforts of
motion picture stars, and I was eager to be present at such an occasion.
This particular brand of rally is a rather odd American phenomenon—
that is, the spectacle of a people with homes and future at stake, their
own lives threatened and the lives of their sons hanging by a thread,
having to goad themselves to meet the challenge by indulging in a fit
of actor worship and the veneration of the Hollywood gods. Everywhere in the country people have shown a peculiar willingness to buy
bonds under the aegis of a star of the silver screen. Every race of people has of course its national and religious forms and ecstasies, its own
way of doing business, its own system of getting results. The Japanese

have their Emperor, an idol who is the same as God; the Germans have
the State, closely identified with the Führer. Americans warm to a more
diffuse allegiance—they have their Abe Lincoln and their Concord
Bridge and their Bill of Rights, but these are somewhat intellectual
appurtenances. For pure idolatry and the necessary hysteria which
must accompany the separation of the individual from his money, they
turn to Dorothy Lamour, or Beauty-at-a-Distance. At first glance this
might appear to be a rather shabby sort of patriotic expression, but
when you think about it, it improves. It may easily be a high form of
national ardor after all, since the Hollywood glamour ideal is an ideal
which each individual constructs for himself in the darkness and pri-
vacy of a motion picture house, after toil. The spell of Lamour, the
sarong, the jungle code, the water lily in the pool—these tell the frustration of the civilized male, who yearns in the midst of the vast tur-
moil and complexities of his amazing little life, with its details and its
fussiness, to chuck his desperate ways for a girl and an island moon—
a dream of amorous felicity and carelessness. To bring this dream into
line, for a national emergency, and adapt it to the exigencies of federal
finance is an American miracle of imposing and rather jovial proportions. Miss Lamour was introduced as the "Bond Bombshell"; the water
lily had become an orchid from a florist's shop, symbol of wealth and
extravagance.

The Bangor people, about twenty-five hundred of them, assembled
in the hall, which was a sort of overgrown grange hall. Admission was
by bond only, plus the Annie Oakleys. The big buyers were in the front
seats, the small fellows in the balcony. The notables and the Bombshell
and the Dow Field military band and WLBZ assembled on the platform,
a mixed group of civil and military servants, variously arrayed. Almost
the first thing that happened was the arrival of a contingent of Navy
recruits (about fifty of them) who were to submit to a public induction
under the combined sponsorship of Uncle Sam and the motion picture
industry. They filed down the center aisle and climbed sheepishly to the
platform, a rag-tag-and-bobtail company in their ready-to-shed citizens' clothes, sober as bridegrooms and terribly real. This was it, and

the people cheered. Miss Lamour, sensing the arrival of actors who could not fail to give an authentic performance and who would never get a retake, stepped deferentially into the wings. A Navy lieutenant lined up his charges and prepared to give the oath. On their faces, bothered by the sudden confusion of lights and the convergence of their personal fates, was a hang-dog look, a little tearful, a little frightened, a little resolved. They were just a bunch of gangling boys in a moderately uncomfortable public position, but they seemed like precious stones. The dust of glamour had shifted imperceptibly from Miss Lamour and settled on their heads. After they were sworn in she glided back on to the stage, shook hands, and gave each her blessing as he shuffled out to gather up his cap and his change of underwear and disappear into the theater of war.

The program continued. A Negro quartet sang. Two heroes were produced—a pint-sized radioman who had been wounded in the Coral Sea, a big lumbering Tiger who had flown for Chennault. They were the "had been" contingent. The radioman told, in masterly understatements, about Pearl Harbor on that Sunday morning. The Tiger, a laconic man in shirtsleeves, was interviewed by a small dapper announcer for WLBZ, and when he was asked how it felt to be an American on foreign shores, he choked up, the strength went out of him, and he couldn't answer. He just walked away. After the band had performed, a young Jewish soldier stepped forward and played a violin solo. For him there could be nothing obscure about war aims. It was a war for the right to continue living and the privilege of choosing his own composer when he played his fiddle. He played solidly and well, with a strength which the Army had given his hands and his spirit. The music seemed to advance boldly toward the enemy's lines.

Here, for a Nazi, was assembled in one hall all that was contemptible and stupid—a patriotic gathering without strict control from a central leader, a formless group negligently dressed (even Dottie had neglected to change into evening dress, thereby breaking the hearts of the women in the audience), a group shamelessly lured there by a pretty girl for bait, a Jew in an honored position as artist, Negroes singing through their rich non-Aryan throats, and the whole affair lacking the official seal of the Ministry of Propaganda—a sprawling, goofy American occasion, shapeless as an old hat.

It made me feel very glad to be there. And somewhere during the evening I picked up a strong conviction that our side was going to win. Anyway, the quota was heavily oversubscribed in this vicinity. I would have bargained for a handkerchief if Miss Lamour had had any to spare. It's the ape-man in me probably.

from With the Old Breed
at Peleliu and Okinawa
by E. B. Sledge

Eugene B. Sledge, 19 years old when he enlisted in the Marines in 1942, worried that the war would end before he had a chance to fight. It didn't: Sledge participated in two of the hardest-fought Pacific island battles. He loved his fellow Marines, but was appalled by the brutality of battle—the extent to which it quickly "made savages of us all." Paul Fussell calls With the Old Breed one of the finest memoirs to emerge from any war; it also is one of the most disturbing.

The 5th Marines now had the mission to secure the northern part of the island—that is, the upper part of the larger "lobster claw." Following that chore the regiment was to move south again on the eastern side of the Umurbrogol ridges to complete the isolation and encirclement. Most of us in the ranks never saw a map of Peleliu except during training on Pavuvu, and had never heard the ridge system referred to by its correct name, Umurbrogol Mountain. We usually referred to the whole ridge system as "Bloody Nose," "Bloody Nose Ridge," or simply "the ridges."

As we moved through the army lines, Japanese machine guns were raking the crest of the ridge on our right. The slugs and bluish white tracers pinned down the American troops on the ridge but passed high above us on the road. The terrain was flat and sparsely wooded. Tanks supported us, and we were fired on by small arms, artillery, and mortars from the high coral ridges to our right and from Ngesebus Island a few hundred yards north of Peleliu.

Our battalion turned right at the junction of West Road and East Road, headed south along the latter, and stopped at dusk. As usual, there wasn't much digging in as such, mostly finding some crater or depression and piling rocks around it for what protection we could get.

I was ordered to carry a five-gallon can of water over to the company CP. When I got there, Ack Ack was studying a map by the light of a tiny flashlight that his runner shielded with another folded map. The company's radioman was sitting with him, quietly tuning his radio and calling an artillery battery of the 11th Marines.

Putting the water can down, I sat on it and watched my skipper with admiration. Never before had I regretted so profoundly my lack of artistic talent and inability to draw the scene before me. The tiny flashlight faintly illuminated Captain Haldane's face as he studied the map. His big jaw, covered with a charcoal stubble of beard, jutted out. His heavy brow wrinkled with concentration just below the rim of his helmet.

The radioman handed the phone to Ack Ack. He requested a certain number of rounds of 75mm HE to be fired out to Company K's front. A Marine on the other end of the radio questioned the need for the request.

Haldane answered pleasantly and firmly, "Maybe so, but I want my boys to feel secure." Shortly the 75s came whining overhead and started bursting in the dark thick growth across the road.

Next day I told several men what Ack Ack had said. "That's the skipper for you, always thinking of the troops' feelings," was the way one man summed it up.

Several hours passed. It was my turn to be on watch in our hole. Snafu slept fitfully and ground his teeth audibly, which he usually did during sleep in combat. The white coral road shone brightly in the pale moonlight as I strained my eyes looking across into the wall of dark growth on the other side.

Suddenly two figures sprang up from a shallow ditch directly across the road from me. With arms waving wildly, yelling and babbling hoarsely in Japanese, they came. My heart skipped a beat, then began pounding like a drum as I flipped off the safety of my carbine. One enemy soldier angled to my right, raced down the road a short distance, crossed over, and disappeared into a foxhole in the line of the company on our right flank. I focused on the other. Swinging a bayonet over his head, he headed at me.

I dared not fire at him yet, because directly between us was a foxhole with two Marines in it. If I fired just as the Marine on watch rose up to meet the Japanese intruder, my bullet would surely hit a comrade in the back. The thought flashed through my mind, "Why doesn't Sam or Bill fire at him?"

With a wild yell the Japanese jumped into the hole with the two Marines. A frantic, desperate, hand-to-hand struggle ensued, accompanied by the most gruesome combination of curses, wild babbling, animalistic guttural noises, and grunts. Sounds of men hitting each other and thrashing around came from the foxhole.

I saw a figure pop out of the hole and run a few steps toward the CP. In the pale moonlight, I then saw a Marine nearest the running man jump up. Holding his rifle by the muzzle and swinging it like a baseball bat, he blasted the infiltrator with a smashing blow.

From our right, where the Japanese had gone into the company on our flank, came hideous, agonized, and prolonged screams that defied description. Those wild, primitive, brutish yellings unnerved me more than what was happening within my own field of vision.

Finally a rifle shot rang out from the foxhole in front of me, and I heard Sam say, "I got him."

The figure that had been clubbed by the rifle lay groaning on the deck about twenty feet to the left of my hole. The yelling over to our right ceased abruptly. By this time, of course, everyone was on the alert.

"How many Nips were there?" asked a sergeant near me.

"I saw two," I answered.

"There must'a been more," someone else put in.

"No," I insisted, "only two came across the road here. One of them ran to the right where all that yelling was, and the other jumped into the hole where Sam shot him."

"Well, then, if there were just those two Nips, what's all that groanin' over here then?" he asked, indicating the man felled by the rifle butt.

"I don't know, but I didn't see but two Nips, and I'm sure of it," I said adamantly—with an insistence that has given me peace of mind ever since.

A man in a nearby hole said, "I'll check it out." Everyone sat still as he crawled to the groaning man in the shadows. A .45 pistol shot rang out. The moaning stopped, and the Marine returned to his hole.

A few hours later as objects around me became faintly visible with the dawn, I noticed that the still form lying to my left didn't appear Japanese. It was either an enemy in Marine dungarees and leggings, or it was a Marine. I went over to find out which.

Before I got to the prone body, its identity was obvious to me. "My God!" I said in horror. Several men looked at me and asked what was the matter.

"It's Bill," I said.

An officer and an NCO came over from the CP.

"Did he get shot by one of those Japs?" asked the sergeant.

I didn't answer, just looked at him with a blank stare and felt sick. I looked at the man who had crawled past me to check on the groaning man in the dark. He had shot Bill through the temple, mistakenly assuming him to be a Japanese. Bill hadn't told any of us he was leaving his foxhole.

As the realization of his fatal mistake hit him, the man's face turned ashen, his jaw trembled, and he looked as though he were going to cry. Man that he was, though, he went straight over and reported to the CP. Ack Ack sent for and questioned several men who were dug in nearby, including myself, to ascertain exactly what had happened.

Ack Ack was seated off to himself. "At ease, Sledge," he said. "Do you know what happened last night?"

I told him I had a pretty good idea.

"Tell me exactly what you saw."

I told him, making clear I had seen two, and only two, Japanese and had said so at the time. I also told him where I saw those enemy soldiers go.

"Do you know who killed Bill?" the captain asked.

"Yes," I said.

Then he told me it had been a tragic mistake that anyone could have made under the circumstances and never to discuss it or mention the man's name. He dismissed me.

As far as the men were concerned, the villain in the tragedy was Sam. At the time of the incident Sam was supposed to be on watch while Bill was taking his turn at getting much-needed sleep. It was routine that at a preagreed time, the man on watch woke his buddy and, after reporting anything he had seen or heard, took his turn at sleep.

This standard procedure in combat on the front line was based on a fundamental creed of faith and trust. You could depend on your buddy; he could depend on you. It extended beyond your foxhole, too. We felt secure, knowing that one man in each hole was on watch through the night.

Sam had betrayed that basic trust and had committed an unforgivable breach of faith. He went to sleep on watch while on the line. As a result his buddy died and another man would bear the heavy burden of knowing that, accident though it was, he had pulled the trigger.

Sam admitted that he might have dozed off. The men were extremely hard on him for what had happened. He was visibly remorseful, but it made no difference to the others who openly blamed him. He whined and said he was too tired to stay awake on watch, but he only got sworn at by men who were equally tired yet reliable.

We all liked Bill a great deal. He was a nice young guy, probably in his teens. On the neatly typewritten muster roll for the 3d Battalion, 5th Marines on 25 September 1944, one reads these stark words: "———— William S., killed in action against the enemy (wound, gunshot, head)— remains interred in grave #3/M." So simply stated. Such an economy of words. But to someone who was there, they convey a tragic story. What a waste.

The Japanese who had come across the road in front of me were probably members of what the enemy called a "close-quarter combat unit." The enemy soldier shot by Sam was not dressed or equipped like their typical infantryman. Rather he wore only tropical khaki shorts, short-sleeved shirt, and *tabi* footwear (split-toed, rubber-soled canvas shoes). He carried only his bayonet. Why he entered our line where he did may have been pure accident, or he may have had an eye on our mortar. His comrade angled off toward the right near a machine gun on our flank. Mortars and machine guns were favorite targets for infiltrators on the front lines. To the rear, they went after heavy mortars, communications, and artillery.

Before Company K moved out, I went down the road to the next company to see what had happened during the night. I learned that those blood-chilling screams had come from the Japanese I had seen run to the right. He had jumped into a foxhole where he met an alert Marine. In the ensuing struggle each had lost his weapon. The desperate Marine had jammed his forefinger into his enemy's eye socket and killed him. Such was the physical horror and brutish reality of war for us.

Early the next morning our battalion made a successful assault on a small hill on the narrow neck of northern Peleliu. Because of its isolated position, it lacked the mutual support from surrounding caves that made most of the ridges on the island impregnable.

At this time the rest of the regiment was getting a lot of enemy fire from Ngesebus Island. The word was that several days earlier the Japanese had slipped reinforcements by barge down to Peleliu from the larger islands to the north; some of the barges had been shot up and sunk by the navy, but several hundred enemy troops got ashore. It was a real blow to our morale to hear this.*

"Sounds just like Guadalcanal," said a veteran. "About the time we think we got the bastards boxed in, the damn Nips bring in reinforcements, and it'll go on and on."

---

*On the night of 22–23 September about six hundred Japanese of the 2d Battalion, 15th Regiment came down from Babelthuap and got ashore on Peleliu as reinforcements.

"Yeah," said another, "and once them slant-eyed bastards get in these caves around here, it'll be hell to pay."

On 27 September army troops took over our positions. We moved northward.

"Our battalion is ordered to hit the beach on Ngesebus Island tomorrow," an officer told us.*

I shuddered as I recalled the beachhead we had made on 15 September. The battalion moved into an area near the northern peninsula and dug in for the night in a quiet area. It was sandy, open, and had some shattered, drooping palms. We didn't know what to expect on Ngesebus. I prayed the landing wouldn't be a repeat of the holocaust of D day.

Early in the morning of 28 September (D + 3) we squared away our gear and stood by to board the amtracs that would take us across the 500–700 yards of shallow reef to Ngesebus.

"We'll probably get another battle star for this beachhead," said a man enthusiastically.

"No we won't," answered another. "It's still just part of the Peleliu operation."

"The hell you say; it's still another beachhead," the first man responded.

"I don't make the regulation, ole buddy, but you check with the gunny, and I'll betcha I'm right." Several mumbled comments came out about how stingy the high command was in authorizing battle stars, which were little enough compensation for combat duty.

We boarded the tractors and tried to suppress our fear. Ships were firing on Ngesebus, and we saw Marine F4U Corsair fighter planes approaching from the Peleliu airfield to the south. "We gonna have lots of support for this one," an NCO said.

Our amtracs moved to the water's edge and waited for H hour as the

---

*Ngesebus had to be captured to silence the enemy fire coming into the 5th Marines' flank and to prevent its use as a landing place for Japanese reinforcements from the north. There was also an airfield on Ngesebus—a fighter strip—that was supposed to be useful for American planes.

thunderous prelanding naval gunfire bombardment covered the little island in smoke, flame, and dust. The Corsairs from Marine Fighter Squadron (VMF) 114 peeled off and began bombing and strafing the beach. Then engines of the beautiful blue gull-winged planes roared, whined, and strained as they dove and pulled out. They plastered the beach with machine guns, bombs, and rockets. The effect was awesome as dirt, sand, and debris spewed into the air.*

Our Marine pilots outdid themselves, and we cheered, yelled, waved, and raised our clenched fists to indicate our approval. Never during the war did I see fighter pilots take such risks by not pulling out of their dives until the very last instant. We were certain, more than once, that a pilot was pulling out too late and would crash. But, expert flyers that they were, they gave that beach a brutal pounding without mishap to plane or pilot. We talked about their spectacular flying even after the war ended.

Out to sea on our left, with a cruiser, destroyers, and other ships firing support, was a huge battleship. Someone said it was the USS *Mississippi*, but I never knew for sure. She ranked with the Corsairs in the mass of destruction she hurled at Ngesebus. The huge shells rumbled like freight cars—as the men always used to describe the sound of projectiles from fullsized battleships' 16-inch guns.

At H hour our tractor driver revved up his engine. We moved into the water and started the assault. My heart pounded in my throat. Would my luck hold out? "The Lord is my shepherd," I prayed quietly and squeezed my carbine stock.

To our relief we received no fire as we approached the island. When my amtrac lurched to a stop well up on the beach, the tailgate went down with a bump, and we scrambled out. With its usual din and thunder the bombardment moved inland ahead of us. Some Company K Marines on the beach were already firing into pillboxes and bunkers and dropping in grenades. With several other men, I headed inland a

---

*Ngesebus was one of the first American amphibious assaults where air support for the landing force came exclusively from Marine aircraft. In earlier landings, air support came from Navy and sometimes Army planes.

short distance. But as we got to the edge of the airstrip, we had to dive for cover. A Nambu (Japanese light machine gun) had cut loose on us.

A buddy and I huddled behind a coral rock as the machine-gun slugs zipped viciously overhead. He was on my right. Because the rock was small, we pressed shoulder to shoulder, hugging it for protection. Suddenly there was a sickening crack like someone snapping a large stick.

My friend screamed, "Oh God, I'm hit!" and lurched over onto his right side. He grabbed his left elbow with his right hand, groaning and grimacing with pain as he thrashed around kicking up dust.

A bypassed sniper had seen us behind the rock and shot him. The bullet hit him in the left arm, which was pressed tightly against my right arm as we sought cover from the machine gun out front. The Nambu was firing a bit high, but there was no doubt the sniper had his sights right on us. We were between a rock and a hard place. I dragged him around the rock out of sight of the sniper as the Nambu bullets whizzed overhead.

I yelled, "Corpsman!" and Ken (Doc) Caswell,* the mortar section corpsman, crawled over, opening his pouch to get at his first aid supplies as he came. Another man also came over to see if he could help. While I cut away the bloody dungaree sleeve from the injured arm with my kabar, Doc began to tend the wound. As he knelt over his patient, the other Marine placed his kabar under the injured man's pack strap and gave a violent upward jerk to cut away the shoulder pack. The razor-sharp blade sliced through the thick web pack strap as though it were a piece of string. But before the Marine could arrest its upward motion, the knife cut Doc in the face to the bone.

Doc recoiled in pain from the impact of the knife thrust. Blood flowed down his face from the nasty gash to the left of his nose. He regained his balance immediately and returned to his work on the smashed arm as though nothing had happened. The clumsy Marine cursed himself for his blunder as I asked Doc what I could do to help him. Despite considerable pain, Doc kept at his work. In a quiet, calm

*Habitually and affectionately, Marines call all U.S. Navy corpsmen who serve with them "Doc."

voice he told me to get a battle dressing out of his pouch and press it
firmly against his face to stop the bleeding while he finished work on
the wounded arm. Such was the selfless dedication of the navy hospital corpsmen who served in Marine infantry units. It was little wonder
that we held them in such high esteem. (Doc later got his face tended
and was back with the mortar section in a matter of a few hours.)

While I did as Doc directed, I yelled at two Marines coming our way
and pointed toward the sniper. They took off quickly toward the beach
and hailed a tank. By the time a stretcher team came up and took my
wounded friend, the two men trotted by, waved, and one said, "We got
the bastard; he ain't gonna shoot nobody else."

The Nambu had ceased firing, and an NCO signaled us forward.
Before moving out, I looked toward the beach and saw the walking
wounded wading back toward Peleliu.

After we moved farther inland, we received orders to set up the mortars on the inland side of a Japanese pillbox and prepare to fire on the
enemy to our company's front. We asked Company K's gunnery
sergeant, Gy. Sgt. W. R. Saunders, if he knew of any enemy troops in the
bunker. It appeared undamaged. He said some of the men had thrown
grenades through the ventilators, and he was sure there were no live
enemy inside.

Snafu and I began to set up our mortar about five feet from the
bunker. Number One mortar was about five yards to our left. Cpl. R. V.
Burgin was getting the sound-powered phone hooked up to receive fire
orders from Sgt. Johnny Marmet, who was observing.

I heard something behind me in the pillbox. Japanese were talking
in low, excited voices. Metal rattled against an iron grating. I grabbed
my carbine and yelled, "Burgin, there're Nips in that pillbox."

All the men readied their weapons as Burgin came over to have a
look, kidding me with, "Shucks, Sledgehammer, you're crackin' up."
He looked into the ventilator port directly behind me. It was rather
small, approximately six inches by eight inches, and covered with iron
bars about a half inch apart. What he saw brought forth a stream of
curses in his best Texas style against all Nippon. He stuck his carbine

muzzle through the bars, fired two quick shots, and yelled, "I got 'em right in the face."

The Japanese inside the pillbox began jabbering loudly. Burgin was gritting his teeth and calling the enemy SOBs while he fired more shots through the opening.

Every man in the mortar section was ready for trouble as soon as Burgin fired the first shot. It came in the form of a grenade tossed out of the end entrance to my left. It looked as big as a football to me. I yelled "Grenade!" and dove behind the sand breastwork protecting the entrance at the end of the pillbox. The sand bank was about four feet high and L-shaped to protect the entrance from fire from the front and flanks. The grenade exploded, but no one was hit.

The Japanese tossed out several more grenades without causing us injury, because we were hugging the deck. Most of the men crawled around to the front of the pillbox and crouched close to it between the firing ports, so the enemy inside couldn't fire at them. John Redifer and Vincent Santos jumped on top. Things got quiet.

I was nearest the door, and Burgin yelled to me, "Look in and see what's in there, Sledgehammer."

Being trained to take orders without question, I raised my head above the sand bank and peered into the door of the bunker. It nearly cost me my life. Not more than six feet from me crouched a Japanese machine gunner. His eyes were black dots in a tan, impassive face topped with the familiar mushroom helmet. The muzzle of his light machine gun stared at me like a gigantic third eye.

Fortunately for me, I reacted first. Not having time to get my carbine into firing position, I jerked my head down so fast my helmet almost flew off. A split second later he fired a burst of six or eight rounds. The bullets tore a furrow through the bank just above my head and showered sand on me. My ears rang from the muzzle blast and my heart seemed to be in my throat choking me. I knew damned well I had to be dead! He just couldn't have missed me at that range.

A million thoughts raced through my terrified mind: of how my folks had nearly lost their youngest, of what a stupid thing I had done to look directly into a pillbox full of Japanese without even having my carbine at the ready, and of just how much I hated the enemy anyway. Many a Marine veteran had already lost his life on Peleliu for making less of a mistake than I had just made.

Burgin yelled and asked if I were all right. A hoarse squawk was all the answer I could muster, but his voice brought me to my senses. I crawled around to the front, then up on top of the bunker before the enemy machine gunner could have another try at me.

Redifer yelled, "They've got an automatic weapon in there." Snafu disagreed, and a spirited argument ensued. Redifer pointed out that there surely was an automatic weapon in there and that I should know, because it came close to blowing off my head. But Snafu was adamant. Like much of what I experienced in combat, this exchange was unreal. Here we were: twelve Marines with a bull by the tail in the form of a well-built concrete pillbox containing an unknown number of Japanese with no friendly troops near us and Snafu and Redifer—veterans—in a violent argument.

Burgin shouted, "Knock it off," and they shut up.

Redifer and I lay prone on top of the bunker, just above the door. We knew we had to get the Japanese while they were bottled up, or they would come out at us with knives and bayonets, a thought none of us relished. Redifer and I were close enough to the door to place grenades down the opening and move back before they exploded. But the Japanese invariably tossed them back at us before the explosion. I had an irrepressible urge to do just that. Brief as our face-to-face meeting had been, I had quickly developed a feeling of strong personal hate for that machine gunner who had nearly blasted my head off my shoulders. My terror subsided into a cold, homicidal rage and a vengeful desire to get even.

Redifer and I gingerly peeped down over the door. The machine gunner wasn't visible, but we looked at three long Arisaka rifle barrels with bayonets fixed. Those bayonets seemed ten feet long to me. Their owners were jabbering excitedly, apparently planning to rush out. Redifer acted quickly. He held his carbine by the barrel and used the butt to knock down the rifles. The Japanese jerked their weapons back into the bunker with much chattering.

Behind us, Santos yelled that he had located a ventilator pipe without a cover. He began dropping grenades into it. Each one exploded in the pillbox beneath us with a muffled *bam*. When he had used all of his, Redifer and I handed him our grenades while we kept watch at the door.

After Santos had dropped in several, we stood up and began to discuss with Burgin and the others the possibility that anyone could still be alive inside. (We didn't know at the time that the inside was subdivided by concrete baffles for extra protection.) We got our answer when two grenades were tossed out. Luckily for the men with Burgin, the grenades were thrown out the back. Santos and I shouted a warning and hit the deck on the sand on top of the pillbox, but Redifer merely raised his arm over his face. He took several fragments in the forearm but wasn't wounded seriously.

Burgin yelled, "Let's get the hell outta here and get a tank to help us knock this damn thing out." He ordered us to pull back to some craters about forty yards from the pillbox. We sent a runner to the beach to bring up a flamethrower and an amtrac armed with a 75mm gun.

As we jumped into the crater, three Japanese soldiers ran out of the pillbox door past the sand bank and headed for a thicket. Each carried his bayoneted rifle in his right hand and held up his pants with his left hand. This action so amazed me that I stared in disbelief and didn't fire my carbine. I wasn't afraid, as I had been under shell fire, just filled with wild excitement. My buddies were more effective than I and cut down the enemy with a hail of bullets. They congratulated each other while I chided myself for being more concerned with strange Japanese customs than with being combat effective.

The amtrac rattling toward us by this time was certainly a welcome sight. As it pulled into position, several more Japanese raced from the pillbox in a tight group. Some held their bayoneted rifles in both hands, but some of them carried their rifles in one hand and held up their pants with the other. I had overcome my initial surprise and joined the others and the amtrac machine gun in firing away at them. They tumbled onto the hot coral in a forlorn tangle of bare legs, falling rifles, and rolling helmets. We felt no pity for them but exulted over their fate. We had been shot at and shelled too much and had lost too many friends to have compassion for the enemy when we had him cornered.

The amtrac took up a position on a line even with us. Its commander, a sergeant, consulted Burgin. Then the turret gunner fired three armor-piercing 75mm shells at the side of the pillbox. Each time our ears rang with the familiar *wham—bam* as the report of the gun was followed quickly by the explosion of the shell on a target at close range. The third shell tore a hole entirely through the pillbox. Fragments kicked up dust around our abandoned packs and mortars on the other side. On the side nearest us, the hole was about four feet in diameter. Burgin yelled to the tankers to cease firing lest our equipment be damaged.

Someone remarked that if fragments hadn't killed those inside, the concussion surely had. But even before the dust settled, I saw a Japanese soldier appear at the blasted opening. He was grim determination personified as he drew back his arm to throw a grenade at us.

My carbine was already up. When he appeared, I lined up my sights on his chest and began squeezing off shots. As the first bullet hit him, his face contorted in agony. His knees buckled. The grenade slipped from his grasp. All the men near me, including the amtrac machine gunner, had seen him and began firing. The soldier collapsed in the fusillade, and the grenade went off at his feet.

Even in the midst of these fast-moving events, I looked down at my carbine with sober reflection. I had just killed a man at close range. That I had seen clearly the pain on his face when my bullets hit him came as a jolt. It suddenly made the war a very personal affair. The expression on that man's face filled me with shame and then disgust for the war and all the misery it was causing.

My combat experience thus far made me realize that such sentiments for an enemy soldier were the maudlin meditations of a fool. Look at me, a member of the 5th Marine Regiment—one of the oldest, finest, and toughest regiments in the Marine Corps—feeling ashamed because I had shot a damned foe before he could throw a grenade at me! I felt like a fool and was thankful my buddies couldn't read my thoughts.

Burgin's order to us to continue firing into the opening interrupted my musings. We kept up a steady fire into the pillbox to keep the Japanese pinned down while the flamethrower came up, carried by Corporal Womack from Mississippi. He was a brave, good-natured guy and popular with the troops, but he was one of the fiercest looking Marines I ever saw. He was big and husky with a fiery red beard well powdered with white coral dust. He reminded me of some wild Viking. I was glad we were on the same side.

Stooped under the heavy tanks on his back, Womack approached the pillbox with his assistant just out of the line of our fire. When they got about fifteen yards from the target, we ceased firing. The assistant reached up and turned a valve on the flamethrower. Womack then aimed the nozzle at the opening made by the 75mm gun. He pressed the trigger. With a *whoooooooosh* the flame leaped at the opening. Some muffled screams, then all quiet.

Even the stoic Japanese couldn't suppress the agony of death by fire and suffocation. But they were no more likely to surrender to us than we would have been to them had we ever been confronted with the possibility of surrender. In fighting the Japanese, surrender was not one of our options.

Amid our shouts of appreciation, Womack and his buddy started back to battalion headquarters to await the summons to break another deadlock somewhere on the battlefield—or lose their lives trying. The job of flamethrower gunner was probably the least desirable of any open to a Marine infantryman. Carrying tanks with about seventy pounds of flammable jellied gasoline through enemy fire over rugged terrain in hot weather to squirt flames into the mouth of a cave or pillbox was an assignment that few survived but all carried out with magnificent courage.

We left the craters and approached the pillbox cautiously. Burgin ordered some of the men to cover it while the rest of us looked over the fallen Japanese to be sure none was still alive; wounded Japanese invariably exploded grenades when approached, if possible, killing their enemies along with themselves. All of them were dead. The pillbox was out of action thanks to the flamethrower and the amtrac. There were seven enemy dead inside and ten outside. Our packs and mortars were only slightly damaged by the fire from the amtrac's 75mm gun.

Of the twelve Marine mortarmen, our only casualties were Redifer and Leslie Porter, who had taken some grenade fragments. They weren't hurt seriously. Our luck in the whole affair had been incredible. If the enemy had surprised us and rushed us, we might have been in a bad fix.

During this lull the men stripped the packs and pockets of the enemy dead for souvenirs. This was a gruesome business, but Marines executed it in a most methodical manner. Helmet headbands were checked for flags, packs and pockets were emptied, and gold teeth were extracted. Sabers, pistols, and *hari-kari* knives were highly prized and carefully cared for until they could be sent to the folks back home or sold to some pilot or sailor for a fat price. Rifles and other larger weapons usually were rendered useless and thrown aside. They were too heavy to carry in addition to our own equipment. They would be picked up later as fine souvenirs by the rear-echelon troops. The men in the rifle companies had a lot of fun joking about the hair-raising stories these people, who had never seen a live Japanese or been shot at, would probably tell after the war.

The men gloated over, compared, and often swapped their prizes. It was a brutal, ghastly ritual the likes of which have occurred since ancient times on battlefields where the antagonists have possessed a profound mutual hatred. It was uncivilized, as is all war, and was carried out with that particular savagery that characterized the struggle between the Marines and the Japanese. It wasn't simply souvenir hunting or looting the enemy dead; it was more like Indian warriors taking scalps.

While I was removing a bayonet and scabbard from a dead Japanese, I noticed a Marine near me. He wasn't in our mortar section but had happened by and wanted to get in on the spoils. He came up to me dragging what I assumed to be a corpse. But the Japanese wasn't dead. He had been wounded severely in the back and couldn't move his arms; otherwise he would have resisted to his last breath.

The Japanese's mouth glowed with huge gold-crowned teeth, and his captor wanted them. He put the point of his kabar on the base of a tooth and hit the handle with the palm of his hand. Because the Japanese was kicking his feet and thrashing about, the knife point glanced off the tooth and sank deeply into the victim's mouth. The Marine cursed him and with a slash cut his cheeks open to each ear. He put his foot on the sufferer's lower jaw and tried again. Blood poured out of the soldier's mouth. He made a gurgling noise and thrashed wildly. I shouted, "Put the man out of his misery." All I got for an answer was a cussing out. Another Marine ran up, put a bullet in the enemy soldier's brain, and ended his agony. The scavenger grumbled and continued extracting his prizes undisturbed.

Such was the incredible cruelty that decent men could commit when reduced to a brutish existence in their fight for survival amid the violent death, terror, tension, fatigue, and filth that was the infantryman's war. Our code of conduct toward the enemy differed drastically from that prevailing back at the division CP.

The struggle for survival went on day after weary day, night after terrifying night. One remembers vividly the landings and the beachheads and the details of the first two or three days and nights of a campaign; after that, time lost all meaning. A lull of hours or days seemed but a fleeting instant of heaven-sent tranquility. Lying in a foxhole sweating out an enemy artillery or mortar barrage or waiting to dash across open ground under machine-gun or artillery fire defied any concept of time.

To the noncombatants and those on the periphery of action, the war meant only boredom or occasional excitement; but to those who entered the meat grinder itself, the war was a nether world of horror from which escape seemed less and less likely as casualties mounted and the fighting dragged on and on. Time had no meaning; life had no meaning. The fierce struggle for survival in the abyss of Peleliu eroded the veneer of civilization and made savages of us all. We existed in an environment totally incomprehensible to men behind the lines—service troops and civilians.

A trip inside the pillbox by Redifer and Burgin solved the mystery of how some of the occupants had survived the grenades and shell bursts. (Burgin shot a soldier inside who was feigning death.) Concrete walls partitioned the bunker into compartments connected by small openings. Three or four enemy soldiers occupied each compartment which had its own firing ports to the outside. Each would have had to be put out of action individually had we not had the help of Womack and his flamethrower.

When our gunny came by and saw the results of our encounter with the pillbox he had thought was empty, he looked sheepish. He gazed in amazement at the enemy dead scattered around. We really razzed him about it—or rather, we gave him the nearest thing approaching the razz that we Marine privates dared hand out to the austere personage of Gy. Sergeant Saunders. I have thought often that Burgin should have been decorated for the fine leadership he exhibited in coordinating and directing the knockout of the pillbox. I'm sure men have been decorated for less.

We set up our two mortars in a large crater near the now knocked-out pillbox and registered in the guns for the night. The ammo carriers dug into the softer coral around the edge of the crater. An amtrac brought up rations and a unit of fire for the company. The wind began to blow briskly, and it got cloudy and heavily overcast. As darkness settled, heavy clouds scudded across the sky. The scene reminded me of hurricane weather on the Gulf Coast back home.

Not far behind us, the heat of the fire burning in the pillbox exploded Japanese grenades and small-arms ammunition. All night occasional shifts of wind blew the nauseating smell of burning flesh our way. The rain fell in torrents, and the wind blew hard. Ships fired star shells to illuminate the battlefield for our battalion. But as soon as the parachute of a star shell opened, the wind swept it swiftly along like some invisible hand snatching away a candle. In the few hundred yards they still held at the northern end of the island, the enemy was fairly quiet.

The next morning, again with the help of tanks and amtracs, our battalion took most of the remainder of Ngesebus. Our casualties were remarkably low for the number of Japanese we killed.* In midafternoon we learned that an army unit would relieve us shortly and complete the job on the northern end of Ngesebus.

Our mortar section halted to await orders and dispersed among some open bushes. In our midst was the wreckage of a Japanese heavy machine gun and the remains of the squad that had been wiped out by Company K. The squad members had been killed in the exact positions to be occupied by such a squad "according to the book."

At first glance the dead gunner appeared about to fire his deadly weapon. He still sat bolt upright in the proper firing position behind the breech of his machine gun. Even in death his eyes stared widely along the gun sights. Despite the vacant look of his dilated pupils, I couldn't believe he was dead. Cold chills ran along my spine. Gooseflesh tickled my back. It seemed as though he was looking through me into all eternity, that at any instant he would raise his hands—which rested in a relaxed manner on his thighs—grip the handles on the breech, and press the thumb trigger. The bright shiny brass slugs in the strip clip appeared as ready as the gunner, anxious to speed out, to kill, and to maim more of the "American devils." But he would rot, and they would corrode. Neither he nor his ammo could do any more for the emperor.

The crown of the gunner's skull had been blasted off, probably by one of our automatic weapons. His riddled steel helmet lay on the deck like a punctured tin can. The assistant gunner lay beside the gun.

---

*Official accounts vary somewhat as to the actual casualty figures for the Ngesebus. However the Marines suffered about 15 killed and 33 wounded, while the Japanese lost 470 killed and captured. Company K suffered the largest portion of the casualties in 3/5 by losing 8 killed and 24 wounded. This undoubtedly resulted from the presence of a ridge and caves on Ngesebus in our sector.

Apparently, he had just opened a small green wooden chest filled with strip clips of machine-gun cartridges when he was killed. Several other Japanese soldiers, ammo carriers, lay strung out at intervals behind the gun.

A Company K rifleman who had been in the fight that knocked out the machine-gun crew sat on his helmet nearby and told us the story. The action had taken place the day before while the mortar section was fighting at the pillbox. The rifleman said, "The thing that I just couldn't believe was the way those Nip ammo carriers could chop chop around here on the double with those heavy boxes of ammo on their backs."

Each ammo box had two leather straps, and each ammo carrier had a heavy box on his back with the straps around his shoulders. I lifted one of the ammo chests. It weighed more than our mortar. What the Japanese lacked in height, they certainly compensated for in muscle.

"I'd sure hate to hafta lug that thing around, wouldn't you?" asked the Marine. "When they got hit," he continued, "they fell to the deck like a brick because of all that weight."

As we talked, I noticed a fellow mortarman sitting next to me. He held a handful of coral pebbles in his left hand. With his right hand he idly tossed them into the open skull of the Japanese machine gunner. Each time his pitch was true I heard a little splash of rainwater in the ghastly receptacle. My buddy tossed the coral chunks as casually as a boy casting pebbles into a puddle on some muddy road back home; there was nothing malicious in his action. The war had so brutalized us that it was beyond belief.

I noticed gold teeth glistening brightly between the lips of several of the dead Japanese lying around us. Harvesting gold teeth was one facet of stripping enemy dead that I hadn't practiced so far. But stopping beside a corpse with a particularly tempting number of shining crowns, I took out my kabar and bent over to make the extractions.

A hand grasped me by the shoulder, and I straightened up to see who it was. "What are you gonna do, Sledgehammer?" asked Doc Caswell. His expression was a mix of sadness and reproach as he looked intently at me.

"Just thought I'd collect some gold teeth," I replied.

"Don't do it."

"Why not, Doc?"

"You don't want to do that sort of thing. What would your folks think if they knew?"

"Well, my dad's a doctor, and I bet he'd think it was kinda interesting," I replied, bending down to resume my task.

"No! The germs, Sledgehammer! You might get germs from them."

I stopped and looked inquiringly at Doc and said, "Germs? Gosh, I never thought of that."

"Yeah, you got to be careful about germs around all these dead Nips, you know," he said vehemently.

"Well, then, I guess I'd better just cut off the insignia on his collar and leave his nasty teeth alone. You think that's safe, Doc?"

"I guess so," he replied with an approving nod.

Reflecting on the episode after the war, I realized that Doc Caswell didn't really have germs in mind. He was a good friend and a fine, genuine person whose sensitivity hadn't been crushed out by the war. He was merely trying to help me retain some of mine and not become completely callous and harsh.

There was little firing going on now because 3/5 was preparing to pull back as it was relieved by an army battalion. Our tanks, two of which had been parked near us, started toward the beach. As they rattled and clanked away, I hoped they weren't leaving prematurely.

Suddenly we were jolted by the terrific blast of a Japanese 75mm artillery piece slightly to our right. We flung ourselves flat on the deck. The shriek and explosion of the shell followed instantly. Fragments tore through the air. The gun fired again rapidly.

"Jesus, what's that?" gasped a man near me.

"It's a Nip 75, and God is he close," another said.

Each time the gun fired I felt the shock and pressure waves from the muzzle blast. I was terror stricken. We began to hear shouts of "Corpsman" on our right.

"For chrissake, get them tanks back up here," someone yelled. I looked toward the tanks just in time to see several wheel around and come speeding back to help the pinned-down infantrymen.

"Mortar section, stand by," someone yelled. We might be called to fire on the enemy gun, but as yet we didn't know its location.

The tanks went into action and almost immediately knocked out the weapon. Calls came from our right for corpsmen and stretcher bearers. Several of our ammo carriers went with the corpsmen to act as stretcher bearers. Word filtered along to us that quite a number of casualties had been caused by the terrible point-blank fire of the enemy cannon. Most of those hit were members of the company that was tied in with us on our right.

Our ammo carriers and corpsmen returned shortly with a distressing account of the men next to us caught directly in front of the Japanese gun when it opened fire from a camouflaged position. When I saw one of our men's face, I knew how bad it had been. He appeared absolutely stricken with horror. I often had seen him laugh and curse the Japanese when we were under heavy shelling or scrambling out of the way of machine gun or sniper fire. Never during the entire Peleliu campaign, or later during the bloody fighting on Okinawa, did I see such an expression on his face.

He grimaced as he described how he and the man with him put one of the casualties, someone we all knew, on a stretcher. "We knew he was hit bad, and he had passed out. I tried to lift the poor guy under his shoulders, and he [pointing to the other mortarman] lifted his knees. Just as we almost got him on the stretcher, the poor guy's body came apart. God! It was awful!"

He and the man with him looked away as everyone groaned and slowly shook their heads. We had been terrified by the enemy gun firing point-blank like that. It was an awful experience. It had been bad enough on us, but it was unbearable for those unfortunates who were in the direct line of fire.

Our company had been off to one side and had suffered no casualties during the ordeal, but it was one of the more shocking experiences I endured during the war. As I have said earlier, to be shelled was terrifying, and to be shelled in the open on your feet was horrible; but to be shelled point-blank was so shocking that it almost drove the most resilient and toughest among us to panic. Words can't convey the awesome sensation of actually feeling the muzzle blasts that accompanied the shrieks and concussions of those artillery shells fired from a gun so close by. We felt profound pity for our fellow Marines who had caught its full destructive force.

During mid-afternoon as we waited for the army infantry, we sat numbly looking at nothing with the "bulkhead stare." The shock, horror, fear, and fatigue of fifteen days of combat were wearing us down physically and emotionally. I could see it in the dirty, bearded faces of my remaining comrades: they had a hollow-eyed vacant look peculiar to men under extreme stress for days and nights on end.

"Short but rough. Three days, maybe four," the division CG had said before Peleliu. Now we had been at it fifteen terrible days with no end in sight.

I felt myself choking up. I slowly turned my back to the men facing me, as I sat on my helmet, and put my face in my hands to try to shut out reality. I began sobbing. The harder I tried to stop the worse it got. My body shuddered and shook. Tears flowed out of my scratchy eyes. I was sickened and revolted to see healthy young men get hurt and killed day after day. I felt I couldn't take any more. I was so terribly tired and so emotionally wrung out from being afraid for days on end that I seemed to have no reserve strength left.

The dead were safe. Those who had gotten a million-dollar wound were lucky. None of us left had any idea that we were just midway through what was to be a month-long ordeal for the 5th Marines and the 7th Marines.

I felt a hand on my shoulder and looked up at the tired, bloodshot eyes of Duke, our lieutenant. "What's the matter, Sledgehammer?" he asked in a sympathetic voice. After I told him how I felt, he said, "I know what you mean. I feel the same way. But take it easy. We've got to keep going. It'll be over soon, and we'll be back on Pavuvu." His understanding gave me the strength I needed, enough strength to endure fifteen more terrible days and nights.

When long files of soldiers accompanied by amtracs loaded with barbed wire and other supplies came by, we received orders to move out. We were glad to see those army men. As we shouldered our weapons and loads, a buddy said to me, "Sure wish we could dig in behind barbed wire at night. Makes a fella' feel more secure." I agreed as we walked wearily toward the beach.

After crossing back to northern Peleliu on 29 September, 3/5 bivouacked east of Umurbrogol Mountain in the Ngardololok area. We were familiar with this area from the first week of the campaign. It was fairly quiet and had been the bivouac area of the shattered 1st Marines for about a week after they came off the line and awaited ships to take them to Pavuvu.

We were able to rest, but we were uneasy. As usual we asked about the fate of friends in other units, more often than not with depressing results. Rumor had the 5th Marines slated to join the 7th Marines already fighting on those dreaded coral ridges that had been the near destruction of the 1st Marines. The men tried not to think about it as they sat around in the muggy shade, brewed hot coffee in their canteen cups, and swapped souvenirs and small talk. From the north came the constant rattle of machine guns and the rumble of shells.

Historian Stephen E. Ambrose, born in 1936, has spent much of his career interviewing World War II veterans. Those interviews have served as the raw material for books such as Band of Brothers (1992) and D-Day (1994). This passage from Citizen Soldiers (1997) suggests why Ambrose has chosen to record the veterans' stories.

A t the beginning of World War II my father, a small-town doctor in central Illinois, joined the Navy. My mother, brothers, and I followed him to the Great Lakes, then to Pensacola. When he shipped out to the Pacific in 1943, we moved to Whitewater, Wisconsin, to live with my grandmother. Consequently, I didn't see many GIs during the war. But in 1946, when Dad got out of the Navy and began to set up a practice in Whitewater, we had what amounted to a squad of ex-GIs for neighbors. They lived in a boarding house while attending the local college (today the University of Wisconsin–Whitewater) on the GI Bill.

Dad put up a basketball backboard and goal over our garage. The GIs taught me and my brothers to play the game. We were shirts and skins. I don't know that I ever knew their last names—they were Bill and Harry, Joe and Stan, Fred and Ducky—but I've never forgotten their scars. Stan had three, one on his arm, another on his shoulder, a third on his hand. Fred and Ducky had two, the others had one.

We didn't play all that often, because these guys were taking eighteen or twenty-one credits per semester. "Making up for lost time," they told us. Their chief recreation came in the fall, when they would drive up to northern Wisconsin for the opening weekend of deer season. Beginning in 1947, when I was twelve years old, I was allowed to go with them.

We slept in the living room of a small farmhouse, side by side in sleeping bags on the floor. There was some drinking, not much, as we would get up at 4 a.m. ("0400" to the ex-GIs, which mystified me), but enough to loosen their tongues. In addition, their rifles came from around the world—Czech, British, Russian, American, Japanese, French—and each man had a story about how he acquired his rifle. It was there that I heard my first war stories. I've been listening ever since. I thought then that these guys were giants. I still do.

Stan was the senior NCO in the bunch. He took charge. No one voted, there was no discussion, it was just taken for granted that he was our leader. In the morning, he got us organized. This was cultivated land, hilly, interspersed with woods of twenty or so acres each. Stan would study a wood with his binoculars, then bark out the assignments. Two men would go to the far end of the wood, two others would post up along the sides, two more would stand on the edge of the near end. The other six would march through the wood, shouting to drive the deer out so the posted men could get a clear shot. After they got their deer, they became the drivers and the others were put on post. We all got our deer.

They don't hunt that way in northern Wisconsin today. Hunters go out as individuals, most often building a platform in a tree for their stand (deer never look up for danger). A couple of weeks before opening day, they set out bait—apples or cabbages—around the tree. They too usually get their deer, but that kind of hunting has no appeal for me and I no longer participate.

By the time I went to Madison for my own college education, the ex-GIs had graduated and were off making their livings. Over the next four years I developed my fair share of academic snobbery, encouraged by my professors. They put me to reading such books as Sloan Wilson's *The Man in the Gray Flannel Suit* (1955), David Riesman's *The Lonely Crowd* (1951), and William Whyte's *The Organization Man* (1956). These books, like the professors, deplored the conformity of the 1950s. They charged that the young executives and corporate men of the 1950s marched in step, dressed alike, seldom questioned authority, did as they were told, worked always, were frighteningly materialistic, devoid of culture and individualism. By the time I became a graduate student, I was full of scorn for them and, I must confess, for their leader, President Eisenhower—the bland leading the bland.

But in fact these were the men who built modern America. They had learned to work together in the armed services in World War II. They had seen enough destruction; they wanted to construct. They built the Interstate Highway system, the St. Lawrence Seaway, the suburbs (so scorned by the sociologists, so successful with the people), and more. They had seen enough killing; they wanted to save lives. They licked polio and made other revolutionary advances in medicine. They had learned in the army the virtues of a solid organization and teamwork, and the value of individual initiative, inventiveness, and responsibility. They developed the modern corporation while inaugurating revolutionary advances in science and technology, education and public policy.

The ex-GIs had seen enough war; they wanted peace. But they had also seen the evil of dictatorship; they wanted freedom. They had learned in their youth that the way to prevent war was to deter through military strength, and to reject isolationism for full involvement in the world. So they supported NATO and the United Nations and the Department of Defense. They had stopped Hitler and Tojo; in the 1950s they stopped Stalin and Khrushchev.

In his inaugural address, President John F. Kennedy described the men and women of his generation: "The torch has been passed to a new generation of Americans—born in this century, tempered by war, disciplined by a hard and bitter peace, proud of our ancient heritage—and unwilling to witness or permit the slow undoing of those human rights to which this nation has always been committed."

The "we" generation of World War II (as in "We are all in this together") was a special breed of men and women who did great things for America and the world. When the GIs sailed for Europe, they were coming to the continent not as conquerors but liberators. In his Order of the Day on June 6, 1944, Eisenhower had told them their mission was: "The destruction of the German war machine, the elimination of Nazi tyranny over the oppressed peoples of Europe, and security for ourselves in a free world." They accomplished that mission.

In the process they liberated the Germans (or at least the Germans living west of the Elbe River). In Normandy, in July 1944, Wehrmacht Pvt. Walter Zittats was guarding some American prisoners. One of them spoke German. Zittats asked him, "'Why are you making war against us?' I'll always remember his exact words: We are fighting to free you from the fantastic idea that you are a master race.'" In June 1945 Eisenhower told his staff, "The success of this occupation can only be judged fifty years from now. If the Germans at that time have a stable, prosperous democracy, then we shall have succeeded." That mission, too, was accomplished.

In the fall semester of 1996 I was a visiting professor at the University of Wisconsin-Madison. I taught a course on World War II to some 350 students. They were dumbstruck by descriptions of what it was like to be on the front lines. They were even more amazed by the responsibilities carried by junior officers and NCOs who were as young as they. Like all of us who have never been in combat, they wondered if they could have done it—and even more, they wondered how anyone could have done it.

There is a vast literature on the latter question. In general, in assessing the motivation of the GIs, there is agreement that patriotism or any other form of idealism had little if anything to do with it. The GIs fought because they had to. What held them together was not country and flag, but unit cohesion. It has been my experience, through four decades of interviewing ex-GIs, that such generalizations are true enough.

And yet there is something more. Although the GIs were and are embarrassed to talk or write about the cause they fought for, in marked contrast to their great-grandfathers who fought in the Civil War, they were the children of democracy and they did more to help spread democracy around the world than any other generation in history.

At the core, the American citizen soldiers knew the difference between right and wrong, and they didn't want to live in a world in which wrong prevailed. So they fought, and won, and we all of us, living and yet to be born, must be forever profoundly grateful.

from Letters from the End of the
World: A Firsthand Account of
the Bombing of Hiroshima
by Toyofumi Ogura

On August 6, 1945, university teacher Toyofumi Ogura, 45, saw the sky "split open" over Hiroshima: The atomic bomb had fallen. Toyofumi, his wife, Fumiyo, 36, and their three children survived the blast—but Fumiyo died of radiation sickness two weeks later. In his grief Toyufumi wrote his dead wife a series of letters describing the family's experience of the bombing, including her own suffering and death. The letters were published in 1946.

Fumiyo,

I failed to realize how serious your condition was. While you were in the sickroom at the factory dormitory I was tremendously relieved to see that you had somehow emerged from the ordeal with only minor burns. And when you mentioned the onset of untimely menstruation, I handed you one of my spare loincloths and simply attributed it to the trauma you had experienced. When I returned briefly to Jigozen on August 15, I was told that you had a high fever and were suffering from diarrhea. But I still wasn't unduly worried. From what little knowledge I had of medicine, I assumed that, from sleeping on the cold ground on the night of the tenth, you had caught a cold that affected your bowels. I wasn't all that worried about your lack of appetite either. To ease your anxiety, I told you that I would be back soon, permanently, to take good care of you. That was my firm intent when I left you to go back to the factory.

But when I returned to Setsuko's at about four p.m. on the seventeenth, you were terribly exhausted and emaciated. Soon your nose started to bleed, but you had always been prone to such bleeding, and with your continuing high fever, some bleeding from the nose didn't seem all that unusual. However, the bleeding wouldn't stop: when I gently pinched your nostrils, blood oozed from your mouth. And squeezing the nape of your neck didn't help. Blood kept gushing out of your nose and mouth, into a basin we had readied. You couldn't speak because of the bleeding. Then you moved your bandaged hand toward your chin and repeatedly made a gesture of scratching at your throat.

"What's the matter?" I asked.

"Here! Here!" you said in a whisper.

"What's wrong?"

"There's a ball stuck in here," you said with great difficulty.

I couldn't understand that at all. I just sat there, perplexed. But those words turned out to be about the last you would speak while in complete possession of your senses.

In the evening, Setsuko brought a doctor to the house. He was an acquaintance of your sister and her husband's who lived nearby. He had been working continuously at the Teishin (Postal Service) Hospital, treating victims of the bombing. He had just arrived home for the first time in six days when Setsuko begged him to come over and treat you. I explained your symptoms to him as best I could, whereupon he forcibly stuffed some gauze into your nostrils.

"Will that stop the bleeding?" I asked.

"I hope so," he said without much conviction.

He inserted his fingers into your mouth and pulled out a lump of dark reddish matter about the size of a bantam's egg. Then, to my surprise, he pulled out another.

"These are blood clots," he explained.

I then realized what you'd meant when you said that there was a ball stuck in your throat. The blood you were vomiting had coagulated in your throat, making your breathing labored and causing you great distress. You seemed to breathe a little more easily once the clots were removed from your throat. The bleeding stopped too. But I could hardly bring myself to look squarely at your pale, emaciated face, with its protruding cheekbones.

I asked the doctor about giving you a blood transfusion, but he said he had tried that on a number of patients without success. He also said something about the blood type's actually being altered, and about a drastic reduction in victims' white blood cell count. He had only very recently treated hundreds of patients with the same symptoms that you had. He mentioned that common symptoms included irregular menstruation, vomiting, lack of appetite, bleeding, diarrhea, extreme fatigue and high fever. He took your temperature and the thermometer read forty-one degrees centigrade. He said that most victims' temperatures ranged betweeen forty and forty-two degrees. But there was no known treatment, and he offered no prognosis.

"Will she be all right?" I asked finally, but he didn't answer.

When he left, Setsuko actually ran out after him and repeated the question. She told me that his response was, "I don't think there's much hope." On hearing this, I almost passed out. All along, I had thought that you would eventually recover.

Your brother Tetsuji's family had already moved out of Setsuko's house and gone to live with relatives in the provinces. The back room they'd occupied in Setsuko's house was now your sickroom. I arranged Kinji's mattress next to yours and had him sleep beside you while I kept vigil by your bedside. There was nothing much I could do but apply a damp cloth to your forehead and chest, wringing it out periodically in a bucket of water brought from the kitchen. There was no ice whatsoever available. I felt your pulse by inserting my fingers under the bandage wrapped around your arm. Your heart was beating fast but there was nothing I could do about that. The only thing I could do was prevent mosquitoes from lighting on you or Kinji by chasing them away with a paper fan. Kinji was sound asleep, probably worn out from playing all day. His injuries had now healed completely. You also were fast asleep. After putting the children to bed, Setsuko joined me at your bedside. All was quiet. You didn't seem to be disturbed by the occasional steam or electric train that would rumble past the back of the house.

As there was nothing else to be done for the moment and you were resting calmly, I told Setsuko that she should get some sleep. The clock struck one. The electric trains had stopped running and the steam trains were now few and far between. It was completely quiet. I sat beside your bed, my mind numbed by the events of the day. Suddenly you opened your eyes and gazed up at me. You moved your lips, as if you were trying to say something. I bent over toward you but I couldn't hear anything. When I leaned back again, you raised your right hand and started to move it around in the air. Under the dim electric light, you moved your bandaged arm slowly up and down and from side to side. My stare alternated between your face and your moving hand.

You stopped and let your hand drop to your chest, as if you were tired. You seemed to be trying to say something with your eyes. I grew confused as you continued to stare.

"What's the matter?" I blurted out, almost reproachfully.

But you were quiet. After a while, you started moving your lips again, silently. You raised your right hand once more. Then I realized what you were trying to do.

You couldn't speak so you were forming characters in the air. I watched your hand carefully. It moved slowly, forming *katakana* characters with your hand! The movements were the same as before. At last, I was able to decipher the characters you were forming with your hand, "pencil and paper."

I nodded deeply in acknowledgment and said, "I understand. I understand."

You lowered your hand onto your breast and continued to gaze at me, your relief apparent.

I pulled out a notebook from my pocket, opened it to a blank page and put it into your left hand, the fingers of which were not bandaged. I inserted the pencil into a gap in the bandage covering your right hand. You brought both hands up onto your breast and paused for a moment. Then you began to write, shakily.

*There are cans of sugar and candy in the bottom drawer of the
second chest of drawers.*

You dropped your hands on your breast. After taking a few deep
breaths, you continued.

There is flour and some powdered milk in the rice container.

You lowered your hands and closed your eyes. Then you opened
them and gazed very pointedly at me. I was choking with emotion, but
I forced a smile. You had no way to know that our house had been
destroyed by fire, and you were concerned about the foodstuffs and
sweets you had painstakingly set aside for the children. Finally, you
raised your hands again and started writing again.

My love to Kazuko and Keiichi.

You let both hands drop onto your breast and closed your eyes. The
notebook had slipped from your left hand. You seemed to have gone
into a peaceful sleep. I took the notebook from you. Your awkward
writing looked a first-grader's. Tears dropped from my eyes onto the
notebook.

You seemed to be sleeping calmly now. Yet there had been something very unsettling about the intent gaze you had cast on me a while
ago. It had nothing to do with a foreboding of death. Rather your gaze
reminded me of the stare of a mentally unbalanced person. Visions of
the two extremely agitated women I'd seen in the ruins on August 6
came to mind. I wondered if the high fever had affected your brain.

So the next morning, on the eighteenth, I asked your youngest
brother Shiro, who was also there with us at Jigozen, to go and get
Kazuko and Keiichi from the villages out in the country where they had
gone with their classmates, and bring them back. We couldn't get a
doctor to come to the house that day, but I was sure now that the fever
had done something to your brain. You smiled inanely when you

opened your eyes, and uttered only incoherent phrases. You could speak now, which you had not been able to the night before, but this was a source of joy and sadness to me at the same time. Like a baby taking milk, you drank the fruit juice and sugared water that I fed you. I went to lie down for a while in the afternoon when Setsuko took over the vigil. When I woke up that evening, I found there had been no change in your condition. At about eight o'clock, Shiro came back with Kazuko and Keiichi.

Kazuko's diary of the last day she spent with you contains a detailed account of what happened from that point.

> *When we stepped onto the porch at Aunt Setsuko's house, Father was standing there waiting for us. His left arm was supported in a piece of white cloth slung around his neck. He said that Mother had gotten hurt when she was outside Fukuya's waiting for a train.*
>
> *The first time Father told her we were there she said, "What?" but the second time she said, "Oh, they are?" Her face was very thin.*
>
> *Kei-chan and I sat down on the floor side by side, right up near her head and greeted her.*
>
> *"Hello, Mother."*
>
> *She gazed at us for a while without saying anything. Father put his hand on my head and said, "Look, Kazuko is here."*
>
> *"You've gotten so big," she said. Then Father patted Kei-chan on the head and told Mother, "Keiichi too."*
>
> *"Oh yes, my little member of the 'smiling squad,'" Mother said. My teachers out in the country always made us smile a lot whenever they took group photographs to send our parents, so in her letters Mother always called my class the "smiling squad." She seemed to have gotten me and Kei-chan mixed up. I looked questioningly at Father. He lifted his hand to his forehead and told us that Mother's high fever had affected her head and that we should keep quiet. I suddenly felt very sad. Aunt Setsuko made dinner for us but I couldn't eat much.*

After dinner, Kei-chan and I went back to her room. Kei-chan fanned her face gently while I kept wetting down a hand towel and then squeezing it out and laying it on her forehead and chest. Father was sitting next to her. Kin-chan was grumpy because Kei-chan wouldn't play with him, but pretty soon he lay down beside Mother and fell asleep.

In the meantime Father, who had been checking Mother's pulse, noticed something strange. So he called Aunt Setsuko and Uncle Shiro, and everybody came into the room. Mother opened her eyes wide and said, "What are you doing here? What happened? What do you want?" I couldn't hold back my tears.

Then Father brought out a photo of baby Toshiko and showed it to Mother, asking, "Do you know who this is?"

"It's Toshiko," Mother said clearly.

Then I showed her a picture of Kenji Miyazawa.*

She looked at it and said "Kenji-chama," in a baby voice.

Tears started falling from my eyes again. Father's eyes were full of tears too.

Mother went on. "Let's go together into the blue sky. Let's hurry off to Hanamaki. Did you find out yet where Polan Plaza is? Let's hurry and ride on the Milky Way railroad!"

I thought she might be a little better now, because when she saw the photo of Kenji Miyazawa it reminded her of what we used to say about his stories.

But Father said, "She's really lightheaded."

This made me sad again and I tried hard to cool Mother's forehead and chest. Suddenly she opened her eyes and looked right at me, and said in a scolding tone, "It's late. Off to bed." When I realized Mother was worried about us even though she was so sick herself, I started to cry again. I went out in the kitchen to get a fresh bucket of water and then kept on cooling

---

* The author wrote several books of literary criticism on the humanist poet and children's writer Kenji Miyazawa (1896–1933), in the course of which both he and his family developed a close relationship with Miyazawa's family.

off Mother's forehead and chest. Soon she fell into a calm sleep.

"She seems to be a bit more stable now. Everybody please go and get some rest," Father said.

Aunt Setsuko and Uncle Shiro left and went off to bed. Then Father said to us, "You must be tired. Go to bed now." Kei-chan lay down beside Kin-chan and fell asleep. I stayed up a while longer, but since Father kept insisting, I finally lay down beside Kei-chan. But I couldn't get to sleep at first. I remember hearing the clock strike three.

Each time you opened your eyes that night, you muttered something senseless. One time, you gazed at the children sleeping and said, "Ye pathetic ones," almost as if it was Christ speaking. I wondered whether you were in your right mind.

Your condition was more or less the same on the nineteenth. Masako, from Kure, who had looked after you with Setsuko while I was off at the factory, came to visit. Your brother, Hideichi, came from Kanayacho and of course Setsuko and Shiro were with you constantly. I wonder how many of the tens of thousands of people who died as a result of the bombing were able to spend their last moments at home in their own bed, surrounded by family, as you were. In this sense you were blessed. You were delirious now, saying things like, "There's a mountain of sugar to the east. Let's bake a cake with lots of milk and flour." And when I called out "Fumiyo! Fumiyo!" to bring you to your senses, you'd frown and say, "Shh! So noisy!" Or you'd laugh and say to the children, "You're lucky to have such a funny papa." Your remarks had the unintended effect of brightening up the depressing atmosphere of the sickroom. In the meantime, you drank all the fruit juice and sugared water I gave you. In the afternoon, you passed a lot of blood in your stool and urine. You let me clean you up and I was reminded how emaciated you had become. Sometime in the late afternoon a big roundworm came out of your mouth. I had seen such worms crawling out of the mouths of some of the corpses I had come across in the days after the bombing. Apparently the worms could no longer exist in the decaying internal organs of the victims and were abandoning their hosts.

From about that time, your condition rapidly deteriorated, but all I could do was to keep on checking your pulse. Finally, at eight-thirty in the evening, your heart stopped beating. There was no doctor available even in your last moments.

Our three children and I cleansed your body in preparation for your funeral. We had no new bandages, so we left the old ones in place. On removing your clothing, I was astonished to see for the first time how badly your shoulders and waist had been bruised. You had never once complained about any pain from such bruises, though I did often feel that your movements were sluggish for someone whose burns were relatively minor and who was normally so strong-willed. The pain from the bruises must have been restricting your movements.

Forgive me, Fumiyo. I didn't realize how badly you were suffering. I don't deny that it was because of my own ignorance and inadequate attention to you. But I wasn't the only one who was ignorant. Even medical specialists didn't know the cause of the sickness afflicting so many survivors. The term "radiation sickness" was not part of the medical vocabulary of the time. So when I went to obtain a death certificate the next day, the doctor listed the cause of death as "heart failure." This was probably standard procedure then.

On the evening of August 19, I asked Setsuko to make the necessary arrangements for the wake. After I offered some Buddhist prayers, the children and I recited Kenji Miyazawa's best-known poem, "Standing Up to the Rain" all together, just like we used to do at home before the Buddhist altar when you were alive. We did the same thing the next day when people from the neighborhood gathered to pay their last respects. In fact, it would have been impossible to find a Buddhist priest to perform the funeral service, even if we had wanted to. As a result, your funeral was not conducted according to Christian, Shinto or Buddhist rites. Rather, it turned out to be based on a literary work by Kenji Miyazawa. I'm sure you were pleased with it.

On the night of the wake, I asked everyone to retire early and used the big mosquito net for the first time in three days. Then we all lay together, the five of us, side by side, as we often had when you were alive. You always used to say, especially in the last few years, that you didn't think you would be able to keep pace with me in life, and that you would like to die in my arms when the time came. So I held your rigid, cold body in my arms till morning.

Your funeral took place on August 20, which was also my birthday. The timing must have been one of those "strange quirks of fate" you often used to talk about. When I went to the Jigozen village office to notify them of your death and to get permission to have your remains cremated, there were lots of people lined up at the counter, almost as if they were waiting for food rations or cigarette quotas. Many who had been staying with relatives or friends in Jigozen or who had managed to make their way to the relief station set up at the local school were now dying of the same ailment as you had.

As a result, the crematorium was terribly congested. It was a small town, and the facility had only two furnaces. So holes had been dug in the ground around it, and corpses were being cremated in the open air. As coffins too were in short supply, they were being used over and over again. A corpse would be taken out of its coffin upon arrival at the crematorium and the same coffin would then be used to bring in another corpse. You were taken to the crematorium in this same way, but your departure was attended by your immediate family and your relatives and the people from the neighborhood. And you were cremated in one of the furnaces.

It was rare, at the time, for a cremation to be attended by so many people. There were usually only one or two relatives present, and cremations were often conducted by people who were complete strangers to the deceased. Therefore yours was truly a "grand" funeral. You were one of those rare people who are blessed in their final days. You deserved at least this much for having put up with such an intractable husband and for being such a good person all your life.

Considerable progress has since been made in research on radiation sickness, which was the cause of your death.

I think I wrote before that the symptoms are caused by radioactivity, which is emitted at the time of nuclear fission, and are the same as those seen in cases of overexposure to radium or X-rays. The most conspicuous symptoms are caused by drastic reductions in the number of red and white blood cells. The reduced number of white corpuscles, especially, retards the healing of wounds and burns. These consequently fester and suppurate, shrouding the living victim in the odor of a corpse. The odor of death that accompanied the mortally wounded victims I came across at rescue stations and other places was no doubt due to this condition. You were probably also in this state.

Bleeding from the gums and the mucous membranes throughout the mouth, nostrils and throat was a common symptom, which explained the blood that had come from your nose and mouth later. Radiation also interfered with the functioning of your internal organs and caused internal bleeding. Your untimely menstruation, vomiting and passing of blood, high fever, diarrhea, anemia, loss of appetite and fatigue were all symptoms. No doubt your white blood cell count was drastically low too.

By the way, I believe that the effective range of the radiation was not as great as that of the accompanying air blast or the thermal rays. Take the case of your sister, Aiko, for instance. Although she was hit by the blast and sustained burns from the heat rays, she wasn't apparently affected by radiation. Her burns were much more serious than yours, but they got better rapidly and she suffered no complications. According to investigations carried out by experts, the effective range of the radiation was generally less than that of the air blast or the heat rays, but that the relationship between distance and radiation dosage proved to be very inconsistent.

Some victims who were further away from the explosion suffered to a greater extent from radiation than people who were closer. Generally speaking, however, people who were near the hypocenter were exposed to radiation, while those who were more than about three kilometers away were not. Being indoors at the time afforded no protection, since radiation, unlike the blast or the heat rays, penetrates solid objects.

Actually, Setsuko's husband's aunt from Hirosecho is a good example. She managed to crawl out unhurt from the debris of her crushed house and went to an emergency site on the delta of the Tenma River. Then she got a lift and was able to make her way home. About the same time that you were ill in bed, she was running a high fever too, and suffering from severe diarrhea.

She was in bed for more than two months but finally made a full recovery. However, she had spots all over her body and had lost all her hair. The appearance of these spots and the loss of hair were very common symptoms at the time. I believe that the spots were caused by bleeding under the skin. Many people who showed these symptoms never recovered.

Lots of people who entered the city of Hiroshima after the day of the bombing also developed the same symptoms and eventually died. I believe this was because they walked through areas containing large amounts of residual radioactivity. According to one study, of the approximately 100,000 people who died, 75,000, or seventy-five percent, died on the sixth, and 15,000, or fifteen percent, died within two weeks, between August 7 and 20. These represent the victims of the first phase of radiation sickness. The remaining 10,000 people, or ten percent, died during the period August 21 to October 16, or between the third and eighth weeks. These were victims of the second phase of the disease; it's said that most people who survived this phase eventually recovered. You were one of victims who succumbed at the end of the first phase, while Setsuko's husband's aunt from Hirosecho survived the second phase and recovered.

Of the 100,000 dead, the 75,000 killed on the day of the bombing were not victims of the disease. Most were crushed when their houses collapsed. Of course, many were killed by the blast or were trapped under debris and incinerated in the fires that followed. Many who were rescued or managed to free themselves succumbed later to injuries and burns.

As I mentioned, almost none of these mortally wounded people were able to receive medical treatment that same day. So, it can generally be said that most people killed on August 6 were the victims of wounds and burns, while those who died later were victims of radiation sickness. In any case, whatever the direct or the indirect cause of death—external injuries were the result of the blast; burns were caused by heat rays; the disease that killed you was caused by radiation—all these were of course effects of the atomic bomb.

At the risk of repeating myself, I would like to summarize what I have observed about injuries and burns. As I mentioned, external wounds were caused mainly by the air blast accompanying the explosion: many people were killed or injured when buildings collapsed on them. Victims who were not killed at that time sustained injuries such as lacerations, bruises, sprains, broken bones or being showered with flying glass fragments. Such victims were generally inside at the time. Many people who were outdoors at locations near the hypocenter were flung to the ground and died instantly. The abdomens of some victims burst open, their intestines spilling out onto the ground. Some people's eyeballs popped out of their sockets. Your bruises, although they fell into this category of injury, were relatively light. There were many cases in which people more than four kilometers from the hypocenter still sustained injuries when they were knocked to the ground by the blast.

One member of the university staff was blown out through the door to his room, hurled into the room opposite and dashed against the wall on the far side of that room. But he suffered only minor injuries. Had he been smashed against the wall of his own room, he would probably have been killed instantly. Some of the most common and visually horrifying external injuries were caused by glass fragments. People with these injuries often bled heavily and had pieces of broken glass sticking out all over their bodies. Some were blinded; others had ears or noses severed. Many victims eventually recovered, with dozens of small glass fragments still embedded in their skin. Apparently not many died solely as a result of this type of injury.

The number of people burned by the heat rays was far greater among those who were outside than those who were inside, and the burns suffered outdoors were much more severe as well. Almost invariably, people who were burned by heat rays while indoors were near windows. On the other hand, people who were outside but had been shielded from the flash by some object, including clothing, were not burned. It appears that people who were within about three kilometers of the hypocenter sustained burns on any parts of their bodies that were exposed. As was the case with external injuries caused by the blast, the closer a victim was to the hypocenter, the greater the severity of the burns from the flash. Strangely, while black clothing was sometimes scorched and the skin beneath it burned, white clothing was usually not. I have heard stories too about the white background on the timetables posted up at railroad stations remaining untouched while the black lettering was scorched.

In the outskirts of Koi, I saw a rice paddy in which the crop had been seared white except for a small portion shielded by a house. This part, in the shape of the shadow formed by the house when the flash occurred, was as green as ever. Damage to plant life seemed to extend for a considerable distance from the hypocenter, but as most of the trees on the Hijiyama Hill and Mount Futaba began to sprout new leaves again soon afterward, apparently the effects were not long-term.

I heard a strange story about two passengers who were on a train waiting to depart from Hiroshima Station. As I might have mentioned when I was telling you about Aiko's burns, victims were usually unaware they had been burned until later, when the swelling and inflammation started. These two passengers were seated facing each other on the south side of the carriage. One closed the window on his side, while the other left his open. Just then they were assailed by the blast and the heat of the explosion. The passenger who had closed his window was wounded by shards of glass and soon covered in blood. The passenger who'd left his window open was not evidently injured. He immediately put the bleeding passenger on his back and hurried off with him to the East Parade Ground. But soon he was the one writhing in pain as his heat ray burns grew inflamed. Now it was the blood-soaked passenger's turn to look after him.

—June 20, 1946

from Flights of Passage
by Samuel Hynes

Samuel Hynes (born 1924) usually writes about literature, which he teaches at Princeton. His quietly precise and reflective memoir of a youthful career (he was 20 when the war ended) as a navy dive-bomber pilot is itself literature. There is no hint of melodrama, yet Flights of Passage *resonates with feeling: sadness for what Hynes and his fellow pilots lost, and a restrained pleasure at what they lived. This excerpt finds the pilots shifting residence between airfields on newly captured Okinawa.*

M oving from Kadena to Awase was like moving from the frontier to the suburbs. Kadena had been built in a hurry, while the war was being fought a mile or two away, and it had a hasty feeling, even after months of village life. The tents still had dirt floors, and every tent had its foxhole; the shower was still an oil drum, and officers and enlisted men still ate together in one mess tent. It was an agreeable kind of place, and I was happy there. But it was primitive—there was no denying that—and we moved to Awase with a sense of upward mobility.

Awase had been built like a real-estate development. Along the beach, at the edge of the eastern anchorage called Buckner Bay, ran the airstrip—new, hard-surfaced, and longer than we were used to. The Air Force had installed a P-51 squadron there, on the east side, by the water; we were to have the west side. Inland from the strip the land rose steeply in irregular, treeless hills. Roads had been built up into these hills, and the squadron quarters were scattered along the roads, like development houses. The roads even had development-sounding names—Roosevelt Road, Admiral Something Street, General Somebody Boulevard. They had been named, we were told, by the former congressman from Minnesota who commanded the base.

Our squadron area was high up, on a hilltop with a view of the field and the harbor. We had Quonset huts, tents with floors and screens, a mess hall with a separate officers' mess and an ice machine, electric lights, a hot-and-cold shower, even a laundry, staffed by flat-faced, gold-toothed, grinning native women. There were no foxholes, and we didn't dig any; it would have been like digging a foxhole in Edina, or Great Neck. It was summer 1945, the island was secure; it was a time and a place to be soft. We lay in the sun, drank in the evenings, and flew uneventful antisub patrols and mail runs, and occasionally an unnecessary strike to neutralize an already bombed-out island. It was like summer vacation, when we were kids—the sun always shining and hot on the skin, nothing much to do, the rhythm of life slowed.

For the moment our war had ended, and we lived a pleasant, suspended life while we waited for it to begin again somewhere else. The next assault, we knew, would be against the home islands of Japan; and we had heard from someone in group headquarters, who had it from someone in the wing, that our squadron would be the first bombing squadron to be based on Kyushu, as it had been the first one on Okinawa. When I thought about what that would be like, I felt doomed, with a Japanese fatalism. I imagined the desperate defense of the homeland, the suicide attacks, the fierce concentrations of AA fire. The whole population would fight against us. In my imagination farmers attacked with pitchforks, crying 'Banzai!' and geisha girls held grenades between their inscrutable thighs; every object was a booby-trap, and all the roads were mined. We would all be killed, I thought, by fanatics who had already lost their war. We would die a month or a week before it was all over; come all this way and die at the end of it, stupidly.

But now it was summer, and we lived a summer life. We wandered the hills above the camp, and found in the highest hill a tunnel, cut through the rock of the hill's core, that led to a chamber with gun ports overlooking the valley. Japanese defenders had crouched here with their weapons, scanning the valley, waiting for an attack that came another way. Looking through those slits in the rock was like looking through their eyes—you could imagine the expected battle, the machine-gun fire pouring down on troops as they toiled up the slope below. And you could imagine the lone despair of waiting, guarding those empty hillsides against an enemy who never came. Now the tunnel and the room at the end were empty too; only a sad dampness, the smell of cellars and funeral vaults, filled it. This one defensive post was the only sign around us that Japanese soldiers had lived here, that a war had been fought on this ground. All the other evidences had been erased, swallowed by the American suburb in which we lived and waited.

In our suburb the new mess hall with its officers' section and its ice machine was our country club; it was inevitable that we should have a Saturday night dance there. Women existed on the island; a few men had even seen them—nurses, mostly, in the hospitals that the war had filled. An invitation was sent, and on the Saturday night busloads of women appeared. They were of all sizes and shapes and ages, most of them rather plain-looking. I was surprised that after all these months away from women I still thought these plain; the myth of the Pacific war was that after a while even the natives turned white and became beautiful. A band began to play, drinks were poured, dancing began. I remember Sly engaged in an intricate bit of jitter-bugging with a stout nurse—and how comical her sensible nursing shoes seemed in those steps.

But most of us just stood around, watching. Nobody competed for the women—there were far fewer of them than of us, but we seemed to sense who wanted them most, and the rest of us drifted away after a while, up the hill to the Quonset hut, and started a card game. I could hear the dance music through the open door, like the sound of peacetime, the sound of our world before the war. I remembered Spring Lake Casino at Lake Minnetonka, and how when you walked with your girl along the beach the music followed across the water, all those songs that seemed so tender then—'Green Eyes,' 'I'll Never Smile Again,' 'Perfidia'? We sat there, in the hut, and down the hill the band played;

but we didn't go back to the dance. Nobody wanted to fight for a dance with a plain stranger; nobody wanted to make love to one.

We had been away from women then for nearly a year, yet felt no sexual need and neither, apparently, did anyone else. In all those months I could only remember two incidents that were explicitly sexual—the quiet man at Ulithi who wrote pornography, and the stud's guilty night with the Red Cross girl at Saipan. We were young men at the peak of our sexual powers, but those powers slept. The native Okinawan women— grinning, gold-toothed, perhaps obliging for all I know—were not looked upon as sexual partners at all (though there was a story around that some enlisted entrepreneur had established a makeshift brothel somewhere); and though the nurses had been at hand for months, no one had sought them out until the dance. Is it really true, then, that sex is a form of aggression like war, and that one form drives out the other? Were we living our sexual lives in the bombing and strafing? Or in the comradeship of the all-male, committed life of the squadron? I only know that for nearly a year we lived like monks—hard-drinking, obscene monks, but poor, obedient, and chaste.

Being Americans, with time on our hands, we set about to furnish and domesticate the camp, as we had done at Kadena, but this time in a more suburban way. The squadron's radar officer, our best scrounger, appeared one day with a truckload of plywood. He didn't particularly want plywood; nobody in the squadron wanted plywood; but if you were a good scrounger you scrounged first, and then found a use for whatever you turned up. We decided to build a sort of barroom at the end of our Quonset hut BOQ. The plywood made a dividing wall and covered the sides and the end. Somebody borrowed a blow torch and ran the flame over the plywood walls, giving, he claimed, a desirable decorator's effect of knotty pine (actually it looked more like burned plywood than anything else). A bar was built in one corner, and a poker table in another, covered with a green blanket that looked, to the casual eye, like green felt. We had everything we needed for a club except liquor.

The quartermaster solved that problem. He heard of an Air Force squadron based in the Philippines that was going home, and he bought the entire contents of their club bar.

'A bargain,' he assured us. 'You put up ten bucks, you get five bottles. If you don't want it, trade it for souvenirs.'

'Five bottles of what?' Rock asked suspiciously.

'How do I know? Whatever the Air Force drinks. Don't worry, it'll make you drunk.'

Eventually the stock arrived, and was delivered, rather ceremoniously, by the quartermaster and a couple of enlisted men. Box after box marked FRAGILE—GLASS was unloaded outside the Quonset, and as the stock grew we began to feel like millionaires, with all that booze. Then the divvying-up began. There was, we discovered, almost no whiskey; the Air Force types had drunk that before they left. What there was was rum, sauterne, sherry, crème de menthe, curaçao, crème de cacao. Rock got kümmel, in a bottle shaped like a sitting bear. Joe drew rock-and-rye, and stood holding the bottle up to the light, staring in a baffled way at the lumps of rock candy inside.

Some of these liquors we had never seen before, except maybe behind a bar, and we didn't know how you drank them. But they were all we had, and we settled down to find out. The party that night was memorable. There was a poker game that lasted until breakfast, and a fight in the course of which three cots were broken, and Joe invented two new choruses of 'Bless 'em All.' Even Billy Childers came, with his five bottles, and joined in the singing. When we sang one of our familiar songs, he would decorate the pauses between the choruses with traditional witticisms from his Mississippi country past. We'd be singing, say, a chorus of the endless limerick song, maybe the one about the man from Saint Paul, who went to a fancy-dress ball, and Billy would come in at the end, very drunk, with 'Do you wet yo'r hair in the morning, daughter?' 'No, mother, I pee through a straw,' or 'Don't cut no firewood tonight, mother—I'm comin' home with a load.' And then he'd look around, smiling, as though he'd said something original and funny. It seemed to be a part of the ritual of collective drunkenness, as practiced in Mississippi.

Next morning most of the new stock of booze was gone. Joe's rock-and-rye bottle had only some sticky lumps in the bottom, and the sitting bear, empty now, was on the Quonset hut roof. What was left was mainly things like green crème de menthe, liqueurs that even a drunk man could see weren't drinkable in large quantities. Later on, when there wasn't anything else to drink, we tried the crème de menthe poured over the shaved ice that we got from the mess hall ice machine—Billy called the drink a 'green frappie,' said it was like what he used to get in the drugstore back home—but nobody could bear to drink enough of it to do him any good.

We went on flying. Sometimes it seemed that we flew simply because we always had flown; that we were a machine that couldn't run down. We flew strikes against islands that now are only names—Gaga Shima, Kume Shima. We hunted Japanese radar installations on the little islands that ran north in a chain toward Kyushu, and attacked buildings and antenna towers with bombs and rockets. We went on flying the interminable antisub patrols, and never saw a sub, though Feeney found a small boat full of men, dropped a depth charge, the only bomb he had, and blew the boat in two. The men were wearing green hats and trousers, he said, but not shirts; but they must have been soldiers, trying to escape from the island, didn't we think so? He was very worried that they might have been civilians, just trying to get away from the Americans, or going fishing or something. We said they were almost certainly escaping Japs. The intelligence officer was pleased to have something new to report, and wrote in his log: 'Approx. seven (7) bodies were left lying motionless in the water.'

The impulse to do something spectacular, which had almost sent the squadron ship-hunting in the China Sea, was still strong in us. If not ships, well then, the Japanese mainland. Kyushu was barely within range of our planes, and we'd have to hit the extreme southern tip if we were to get back to Okinawa, but we could do it, and we'd have bombed Japan. A target was chosen—an airfield on the southern coast of the island—and a strike was launched. There was no particular reason to bomb that target. Surely the Navy and the Air Force's B-29's had been hitting it for months, and anyway the Japanese were virtually out of air-craft, and their fields were no serious threat to us. The strike wasn't really an attack; it was a sightseeing expedition, something to tell the grandchildren; it was as though we were getting ready, now that the war was near its end, to become boring old soldiers, full of interminable war stories and lies.

Everybody was excited by the plan, everybody wanted to go, and I was disappointed and angry when I wasn't chosen, and even felt a touch of satisfaction that the weather was going to be awful; with a little luck, I thought, they won't even find Kyushu. They did, but under a storm front that covered the island with low, solid cloud. They couldn't find their target, headed for another field, couldn't find that one either, and were about to head for home when someone saw an airfield through a hole in the clouds. Any target was better than lugging the bombs home again, and they straggled through the hole and dropped. They had bombed Japan, but nobody could be much more precise than that.

In mid-July the squadron tried another strike against Kyushu. This one was to be led by Jimmy, and all my friends—Rock, T, Joe—went, but once more I was left out. This time there would be an elaborate fighter cover, forty-eight Corsairs over the twelve TBM's; it was going to be a show, something to remember. The fighters took off first and circled in divisions of four, stacked up in the blue summer air above the field. Our planes were delayed, and by the time they were airborne the fighters didn't have enough fuel left to make it to Kyushu and back; and so the strike was diverted to the airstrip at Kikai. We had flown an eighteen-plane strike there the week before, and there couldn't be anything left that was worth bombing, only the patient gunners waiting for a sure shot. But once you have started such an elaborate operation you have to send it somewhere, if only to get rid of the bombs, and Kikai was handy.

I hung around on the hill, watching the squadron take off. It was hot and sunny, and after they had joined up and left I took off my shirt, and brought a chair out into the sun and tried to read. But I couldn't. It was too quiet on the hill—everyone else seemed to be on the strike—and I felt restless, up there alone, waiting for my friends to come back.

The ordinary air traffic moved around the field—a P-51 took off, sounding like an intent insect; a night-fighter landed. Down on the line a mechanic ran up an engine, up and up to a high scream like pain, and then suddenly back to a hoarse whisper. Then there was silence, only the hum of summer, and I waited in the sun.

I heard the flight before I saw it, a steady rumble out of the north, and then I could see them, first only a line, at eye level from where I stood on the hill, then separate planes, in tight formation, a column of three-plane V's, close, steady, and formal-looking. But in the last V there were only two planes, and the empty space seemed an enormous emptiness, like a catch in the breath, a skipped heartbeat. One plane was down somewhere—in the sea, or wheels-up on a beach, or crumpled in the rubble at Kikai field.

I waited. I could have gone down to the Operations tent and heard the story, but I stayed on the hill, and put off knowing. The pilots would land, they'd be debriefed by Intelligence, and then they'd come up to their quarters, and I'd hear then.

It was Joe who was missing, and he was dead. He had dived in his turn over the target, and had flown straight into the ground. Not even the beginning of a recovery, just straight in. He must have been killed in the air, Jimmy said, shot dead as he flew; otherwise he'd have got the plane somehow into level flight, and out to sea, as good a pilot as he was. There had been no explosion when he hit, and no fire—just the smash, like a car against a wall, or a tree falling.

In a month the war was over. The atom bombs were dropped, though we got only sketchy and confusing reports of what the bomb was exactly, and what it did to Hiroshima and Nagasaki. We were relieved; we told each other, drinking in our plywood bar, that we were relieved. But we were saddened, too, though we didn't talk about that. Our common enterprise had come to an end; the invasion of Kyushu, and our flaming deaths in combat, would not take place.

Our war ended officially on August 12th, and that afternoon we launched every plane that would fly in what my logbook calls Victory Flight, a sweep out over the fleet anchorage in a huge V-formation. The bay was crowded with ships, motionless at anchor; they looked very peaceful and tranquil in the August sun, as though they would never steam out to sea again, or fire a shell, or spray up tracers against attacking planes. It was a painting of a fleet that we flew over that hot, late-summer day; the fleet itself belonged to the past. We finished the sweep and turned, and the flight leader signaled us into a column. We dove back toward the ships below us, as though in an attack, and then, to my astonishment and alarm, the lead plane pulled suddenly up and heaved itself over into a portly barrel-roll—a sort of parody of a fighter pilot's Victory Roll. It was like seeing a fat lady somersault—it seemed impossible, it was certainly unwise, but she was doing it. The second plane followed, and the next, and it was my turn.

The TBM was not built for acrobatics: the wings would not bear negative stress, and if I faltered in the roll while the plane was upside down I would surely pull both wings off, and plunge into the bay. I told my crew to hang on, pulled the nose up sharply, and rolled. The plane seemed to resist at first, and then resignedly entered the roll. A year's accumulated rubbish flew up from under the floorboards, and I could hear loose gear rattling around in the tunnel behind me; I wondered how poor Edwards was surviving back there. Then we were rolling out, swooping up toward level flight, the horizon returned to its proper place, and I joined up on the plane ahead of me. So much for Victory.

It was a stupid thing to have done, but I understand why we did it— why it was, in a way, necessary. We were giving Death the chance that he'd missed at Kyushu. We had survived a war, and all the ways that airplanes can kill you, and we were going one step further, stretching our luck. Some of the sadness was in it, too; from now on our lives would never be daring and foolhardy again.

That night every gun—every AA gun, every machine gun, rifle, and pistol—seemed to be firing into the sky. Everyone was out in the company streets, outside tents and Quonset huts, firing into the air, drinking and yelling and firing the shells and bullets that they'd never need again. The air was full of noise and the red tracks of tracers, and falling shrapnel. It wasn't safe to be out there, and some prudent pilots crawled under the Quonset hut, regretting that they hadn't dug fox-holes. I was ashamed to be so chicken, but I lay inside on my cot, lis-tening to the spent bullets dropping on the tin roof, and thinking how ironic it would be to be killed tonight. Three or four men were killed before the night was over, most of them accidentally, but one—an unpopular Sergeant Major—almost certainly by intention, shot in the back in the uproar. It was an hysterical, frightening night, a purging of war's emotions.

The war was over, but the flying wasn't. The Navy's PBY's, which had flown the night-time antisub patrols, were sent to Japan to fly American prisoners out, and we took over their patrols. Some subs, we were told, were still at sea, hadn't heard that the war was over, might yet sink an American ship. The Seventh Air Force sent down ambigu-ous instructions—we were to continue to fly armed, but were not to attack unless fired upon, and were not to take shots at Japanese planes or attack ground targets. It was odd, like being halfway in and halfway out of war.

Night searching was a gloomy, fearful business. The weather had turned hot and stormy, the way it does sometimes in August, and every night there were squalls and thunderheads over the sea. The nights were black, without moon or stars or horizon line; even the lightning, which lit the piled clouds with a cold white light, didn't reach the dark-ness of the sea. My sector was a long triangle over the China Sea—west toward China, then north, then back to the island. As soon as the plane was airborne the lights of the island disappeared, and we entered the blackness. I reported on station, and the voice of the controller came back, but so broken by crashing static that though it was audibly human, it spoke in meaningless syllables: 'Hel . . . Four . . . ver. . . .'

I flew among the thunderheads as I would among mountains, watching ahead when the lightning flashed, altering course to avoid the mountains and fly the valleys. (A tall thunderhead is full of violent vertical currents; it will tear a plane apart, hurl the pieces up and down, and scatter them over the sea.) In the tunnel Edwards searched with his radar for submarines, but among such storms it was a useless exercise;

only the thunderheads appeared on his scope, as bright as battleships, and more dangerous. In that electric atmosphere the plane itself became charged, and balls of Saint Elmo's fire rolled up and down the wings, and whirled on the propeller. Lightning flashed, and for a time after each flash I could not read my instruments, and had to fly blindly, holding the plane on its course by feel until sight returned.

I was more afraid that night than I have ever been in the air. Fear is probably always there, subliminally, in an experienced pilot's mind; it is a source of that attentiveness that keeps you alive. But only rarely does it thrust itself into your consciousness. This never happened to me on a strike—I felt keyed up, tense, abnormally aware of the plane, but not exactly afraid—but it happened on those night patrols over the China Sea. I felt fear then; but I also felt something else—resentment, outrage that I was out there, with the war over, alone and half-blind with lightning and blackness, that I might die out there, on a pointless exercise in the dark.

I flew my last night patrol on my birthday, August 29th; and when I got back, toward midnight, we had a party—liquor had become a little easier to find by then—and I got pretty drunk. I was twenty-one, I kept telling everyone, and I was old enough to drink. I guess I must have used that line too often, or maybe it was something else, but at the end of the evening I found myself fighting with Rock. We struggled up and down the Quonset hut, over people's cots, and sometimes under them, wrestling (we couldn't really have hit each other), grunting, cursing, until at last he won, and sat straddling my chest the way a fight used to end in school. Then we got up and had a drink. If you have a fancy for symbolism, you could find some there; I had reached manhood and lost a fight on the same night; or, the war was over, and friends turned to fighting each other. Probably either reading would be a bit heavy, but I was sorry I had that fight. I don't think I cared about losing it, much.

Summer turned into fall. The trees on the hillsides above the strip turned brown and gold, and the nights were cooler, but the days were fine and clear, only with that metallic look that blue skies have in autumn. Our lives were aimless, without the momentum of war, and we spent our time mostly just waiting for the orders that would send us home. Flying was only another form of idleness—flying around and around the field testing an engine, or to another field on the island to deliver some mail, or for no reason at all, just to be doing something. Some pilots I knew flew to Japanese-held islands, and landed, and were received with formal courtesy; and there were several round trips to Kyushu, to the airfields we had never been able to find. But I didn't go on any of these tourist trips; I had had enough of islands.

In that fine autumn weather I might have taken a good look at the island on which I had lived for nearly six months. I could have walked over the ruins of Shuri Castle, or I might have driven north, into the steep, quiet valleys that the war had never reached. But I didn't; I stayed there in our tent at Awase, doing nothing, feeling emptied of all motives. A squadron of F7F's arrived—the first we had seen—and I went down to the line to look one over, but I didn't try to wangle a checkout flight. I went on flying Turkeys some, but there wasn't much fun in it anymore. The machine had run down at last.

The Navy announced the system by which we would be returned to the States. It involved an elaborate counting of points—so many for each month overseas, so many for each medal, so many for each dependent. The junior officers in the squadron had all come to the war together, so there was no competition there. And we all had the same medals, earned the same way—five strikes for an Air Medal, twenty for a Distinguished Flying Cross. It was embarrassing to get medals for such humdrum, unheroic actions; but each medal was worth five points in the system. The only variable among us was the number of dependents. Some of us were married and got points for that. A few, like T, had a child (a son, born to his wife in Birmingham in June), and that put them ahead of the rest. It seemed a good enough system, and nobody complained. We just calculated our scores, figured the order of departure, and waited.

Senior pilots began to leave; there were drinking parties in their tents, and then they were gone, and we became senior, and moved into the tents they had vacated. T and Rock and I moved together, and got a fine tent, with a wooden floor and sides, screens, and electricity—more like a cottage than a tent, with a view of the bay. I thought of the first tent we had shared at Kadena—the dirt floor, the wheat under the cots, the kerosene lantern. Now Bergie and Joe were dead, the war was over, and we had a wooden floor. We found a new partner, an amiable giant from Mississippi named Ed, and settled in to wait for orders.

In the meantime we made ourselves comfortable. That is, we began again the process of accumulating and homemaking, partly for comfort's sake, but partly to create a special place to exist in, a place that was marked by the persons who lived there, that wasn't simply something that had been issued. Rock appeared one day with a Seth Thomas clock; he had traded a fifth of whiskey for it, so it must have been important to him. Once it had decorated an Okinawan shop, or perhaps a government office. It had a loud, imperative tick, and was always right, though it never really looked at home hanging on a post in a tent. I found a phonograph, and I traveled the island's chaplains' offices begging phonograph records, 'to help the troops pass the time.' I accumulated quite a large selection, very random, since I followed the first rule of scrounging and never refused a record; but I remember only one song, Billie Holiday singing 'Travellin' Light.' We made a bookcase out of shell-cases, and filled it with books. Most of them were government-issue paperbacks, often very peculiar choices for the circumstances (what committee had decided that the troops would want to read Joseph Hergesheimer's *Three Black Pennys*?); but we had a few hardcover books, too, my *War and Peace* from Honolulu, a copy of *The Fountainhead* that Liz had sent me, and a New Testament with a steel cover (you carried it in your breast pocket, and Jesus stopped the bullets, but we kept it in the bookcase).

September passed. The days were sunny, and warm at noon, with a haze at the horizon—like good fall days at home. We took books out into the sun, and talked instead of reading, and watched the planes around the field. The P-51's still flew a lot—obviously it was more fun to play at dogfighting and acrobatics in a fighter than to lumber around in a TBM—and we watched them idly, out over the bay, twisting and diving, catching the autumn sun on their silver wings. Two began a dogfight, and we stopped talking to follow their maneuvers, crossing, turning steeply, and diving back toward each other, neither getting an advantage, weaving back and forth as in a formal dance. And then they hit. There was no noise, no explosion or any of the accompaniments of violence; they simply seemed to enter each other for a moment, and to emerge broken. One plane dropped gently into a shallow dive, and flew at that exact and careful angle into the sea; as it dove, a figure fell free, and a parachute whipped out behind it, but the chute did not open, and the figure dropped with the chute-lines streaming, into the shallows of the bay. The other plane broke apart; a wing, separated from the body, fell slowly and weightlessly, like a falling leaf, turning over and over; the rest of the plane began to spin, winding tighter and tighter, the engine winding, too, in a rising whine until it struck the mud flat at the edge of the strip. The water and the mud received the wreckage and the bodies, and in a minute there was nothing to show that two men had died there. Nobody said anything. We had thought the casual dying was over.

On one of those fall days I flew to Kikai to look for the wreckage of Joe's plane—and to say goodbye to him. It was an odd, uncomfortable feeling, to approach that hostile island, and to fly low and slow over the gun emplacements from which my enemies, the careful gunners, had looked up at my squadron's planes, and had killed my friend. The airstrip had not been repaired, it was still what it had been, a heap of useless, broken concrete; but the camouflaged guns had been uncovered, and I was struck by how many there were, a ring of them around the field. As I flew slowly across the field, a man came out of a shed and waved. I rocked my wings. Hell, the war was over.

I found the wreck just south of the field, not far from the beach. The engine was buried in the earth—he must have hit at a steep angle, and at high speed—and the tail stood up in the air, like a monument. The wings had crumpled with the impact, but I could read the number painted on the tail; it was Joe's plane, all right. I felt I should do something; but I didn't know how a man grieves. The reticence that made my father so inarticulate in his loving—I had it too; it was as much a part of my inheritance as my name. I waited for my body to instruct me—to burst into tears, or a howl or a moan of misery—but it did nothing but fly the plane. Down there, under that wreckage, was the disintegrated body of a friend I had loved, a part of my life before the war, and all through it. I felt that part as a vacancy, but I couldn't express how that vacancy felt. There was nothing that I, up there in the plane, could do for him, down there. I flew around the wreck once or twice, very carefully (Nick Nagoda had killed himself flying around the wreckage of his friend's plane), and then turned south and headed home.

Along the northern coast of Okinawa I flew in close to the shore; I would probably never see that part of the island again. It was just as I had first seen it, a bit of peaceful northern landscape—rather like Norway as I imagined it—that had not been touched by the war; its steep wooded hills and narrow valleys were too rugged and too small-scale to interest generals or contain armies. I turned up a narrow, wooded valley, and saw a small house by the stream, and two or three people working in a garden. They looked up, as though they had never seen a plane before, and stood with their hands shading their eyes and watched me out of sight. I went on to Awase and landed, making the squadron approach automatically, the dive to the strip, the steep, impossible-looking bank, wheels and flaps down in the turn, the sharp, last-minute rollout as the plane stalled to the strip. It was still pleasing to land in that extravagant way—if you could make a Turkey behave like a fighter, you could really fly. But there really wasn't any point, any more.

Later on we heard from a Navy unit that had landed on Kikai—maybe to accept the Commanding Officer's sword or something, I suppose somebody had to go round to all those little islands so that they could surrender—anyway, someone had been there, and had seen Joe's grave. The Japanese had removed the bodies from the wreck, had given them a decent burial, and had placed above the graves a marker that read: 'In Memory of the Brave American Fliers.' That seemed right.

◆ ◆ ◆

We woke one morning in late September to the sound of wind, the tent flapping, guy wires whistling. It was the typhoon season in the China Sea, and a storm was moving up from Formosa. Aerology said it would reach us in the early afternoon, but it never did, quite, though the edge of the storm that we got was violent, howling, and wet. It broke up some of our planes and beached some small boats; but we rode it out all right, our tent survived intact, and the squadron planes were repaired in a couple of days. Once the sky had cleared and we had dried out, we felt rather proud of ourselves, coming through a typhoon so easily—we were seasoned, Old China hands.

Three weeks later the real storm hit us. It began in the night, with a long, drenching rain; and then the wind began, driving the rain horizontally, with the force of buckshot. We closed and tied down the tent flaps and walked down to breakfast, leaning into the hard, punishing wind, hunched down in our foul-weather clothes. Afterward we sat in the tent, trying to think of what we could do, to be ready. This one was going to be a fierce one, and Aerology predicted that the eye of the storm would pass directly over the island. Already rain was driving in around the tent flaps. We went out into the gale and nailed the flaps to the frame. But still the rain came in, until the wooden floor was slick with mud and drops of water covered the blankets of our bunks like a fine dew. In the bookcase the books warped and swelled. The electric light flickered, brightened, and went out. Somebody stopped at the door to tell us that the anemometer on the control tower was reading one hundred knots and that the planes, which had been tied down facing into the wind, were actually airborne on the gale.

By mid-afternoon the tent was rocking on its pilings, like a small boat in a storm, and we were out in the storm again, putting up braces, ropes, and guy wires to hold the tent down. And still the wind rose— we couldn't tell exactly what velocity it reached, but someone said the anemometer had been registering a hundred and fifty knots when it blew away. The wind was strong enough by then to peel sheets of corrugated tin off the Quonset hut roofs and hurl them through the air like whirling machetes. It could snatch up a tent and whip it off into the storm, and then tear away the plywood flooring and send it spinning after.

Visibility was down to a few yards—our world was our own tent and the Executive Officer's tent next door. Then his went, opening in the air like a parachute and disappearing downwind. The Exec grabbed what he could save and started toward us, and as we watched his progress through the storm the entire plywood floor lifted behind him and struck him to the ground. The giant Ed plunged out into the wind, lifted the flooring, and carried the Exec into our tent. He lay for an hour on a bunk, unconscious, while the wind howled and the rain came in. There was no way of getting him to a doctor, or a doctor to him.

The force of the wind had separated the threads of the canvas in the tent roof without tearing it, and you could stand inside the tent and look up and see a dim light from the sky. Rain soaked in, everything was wet—our beds, our clothing, all the books—the very air inside the tent was a mist of rain. But the tent still stood. We would not have been much worse off without it, but it seemed important that we should win against the storm. The guy wires twanged, and the tent shifted on its pilings; but it stood. It was still a tent and not a scrap of blown canvas; it was the place we had made for ourselves.

When the weather cleared, ours was the only tent in sight. Where the others had stood there were only the pilings of the floors and a few tent pegs. The Quonset hut where we had built our bar had slid down the hill twenty or thirty feet, and lay there at an angle, like a ship aground. The squadron buildings—supply tents, repair facilities, ready room, Operations—were all gone. Of our twenty-four planes, only five were flyable, and some of the others were beyond repairing. The airstrip was littered with wrecked planes and rubbish. Along the edge of the bay, naval vessels and flying boats were beached, some of them wrecked. All communication lines were down; the east coast of the island could not reach the west coast, and we couldn't even speak to our flight line.

The island was once more like a battlefield, the scene of a battle fought against wind and rain. But there was an odd exhilaration in the experience; officers and men had moved together into the mess hall and were sleeping there on the tables and on the floor, and there was only food enough for two meals a day, but nobody complained. The violence of nature was somehow amiable compared to the violence of war, even though ten men had died in the storm. To survive a war, and then two typhoons—there was a kind of immortality in that.

My orders came a week later: 'When directed by the Commanding Officer, Marine Wing Service Squadron-2, you will stand detached from your present station and duties, and will proceed via first available government transportation—to the United States.' But there was no transportation—it was on the beach at Buckner Bay, or blown out to sea. We went on waiting—excited at first to be going home, then indifferent, bored, just waiting for the Navy to do something with us, as we had waited so many times before. When a transport ship at last appeared, and we were ordered aboard, the excitement was gone; it was just another move.

There were ten or twelve of us on the orders—married men with two DFC's, I suppose, and no children. We had a party, and the radar officer gave me his last bottle of whiskey as a farewell present, and I was surprised and touched. But it wasn't much of a party. We were ordered to report somewhere at five A.M.—it struck me as a nice Marine Corps touch that my last orders should involve such an unreasonable hour—and we sat up through the night, drinking a little, dozing, feeling bored, and depressed to be bored when we were going home. It was still dark when we drove away from the squadron camp, down Eisenhower Boulevard (or was it Admiral Spruance Drive?) to the coast road, and on south to the landing area.

The ship, we were told, was a converted United Fruit banana boat. The conversion consisted of stacking bunks nine-high in the hold for the enlisted men, so close together that a man had to get into a horizontal position first in order to get into bed, and three-high, nine to a cabin, in the officers' quarters. We mustered, marched aboard, and waited. And after some delays and confusion, and a lot of roll-calling, the ship sailed. I have no memory at all of the sailing, no nostalgic images of Okinawa receding in the distance, nor even any feelings about the occasion. We just left. But my island had already ceased to exist—it was the island at war, the strikes, the gunfire to the south, Joe Baird laughing and singing, the feeling of a good, working squadron. That was all gone now. I wasn't leaving anything.

The ship was headed east, but nobody knew our exact destination, though there were many rumors. We were going to Pearl Harbor, and would have shore leave there. We were headed directly for San Francisco. We would sail through the Panama Canal and dock in Norfolk. One day followed another, and the ship rolled and pitched in the long Pacific swells, lifting its screw from the water with every swell, so that the ship shuddered and rattled (troops were not as heavy as bananas, though they were packed in nearly as tightly). Everyone was seasick, which was just as well, since there wasn't enough food to satisfy appetites of all the men on board. Officers were all right; we sat down three times a day to well-cooked meals, served on tables with linen cloths and silver cutlery. But the enlisted men were limited to two meals a day, often eaten standing up, or sitting on the deck. Junior officers were assigned as 'Mess Control Officers' to see that the men didn't eat more than one serving per meal, or take an extra orange. I took my turn with the rest of the second lieutenants, but I couldn't do the job conscientiously. I just stood at the mess-hall door and tried to look severe as the men came and went, but I never stopped anyone, not even the ones with two oranges.

We were at sea for seventeen days. We didn't stop at Pearl, and we didn't go through the Canal. We went back into the port from which we had left—San Diego. Point Loma on the left, North Island on the right, the circling planes, the berthed carriers, and then the dock—it was all the same, the film run backwards. As the ship tied up, music on the dock below began to play. We surged to the starboard rail, and there below us was a uniformed band and a drum majorette. She marched and twirled and threw her baton in the air, while the band played 'From the Halls of Montezuma.' It was as though we had won the war all by ourselves. More and more of the troops on board crowded to the rail to see the show. The ship began to list. Over the ship's loudspeaker an official voice spoke:

'Now hear this. Now hear this. The starboard head is flooded. The starboard head is flooded.' We were moved back away from the rail, the band stopped playing, and the drum majorette moved off to her next docking. We were home. And the starboard head was flooded.

Once more we returned to Miramar. In many ways it was still the same. I roomed with another drunk, who might have been the intelligence officer who introduced me to French 75's, but wasn't. I drank in the bar and tried to put through telephone calls to Liz and to my father, but couldn't, and went on drinking, and went back into the booth from time to time to quarrel with the long-distance operator. The same San Diego tramps were there, in the same low-cut dresses, drinking and talking in low voices to strangers. But it was profoundly different, too. There was no excitement now, no one waiting for orders to the war, no eager young men hanging around some veteran while he told them how it had been at Rabaul. We had all been there, somewhere, and we were through with it. It was like a locker room after a game, a game that you've lost. Or like the morning after a party, when you wake up and realize what you did last night, and how much of it can't be undone, ever.

In a week or so new orders came, and Rock and I and some other pilots checked out and went up to Los Angeles for one last party. Everything was familiar and stale; it was like starting a big evening with a hangover; it was the end of something that had been good, perhaps like the breaking up of a marriage. The train we rode was the same one I had traveled on the year before, with my crutch and my fat ankle; it was just as crowded, with what seemed to be the same people. Sailors sat on their seabags in the aisles and drank from whiskey bottles, and passed them along; babies cried. In Los Angeles the hotel was the same—the Santa Rosa, next to the best in town. We went out to Hollywood, and the same bands were playing in the bars. We drank a lot, and told people that we had just come back from the war, and I tried to teach a bartender to sing 'The Fucking Great Wheel.' Then I was on the street somewhere, explaining to a Shore Patrol why I was not in the proper uniform, telling him about the two typhoons, and how my dress greens had blown away (a lie, but easier than the truth, when you're drunk). Later we were together in a hotel suite, but it wasn't ours at the Santa Rosa. Everyone was drinking, and there were some girls in the other room. The girls were unhappy, they had expected a party; they wanted to go home, and somebody was saying, in a tired voice, 'All right, then, go home. Fuck you.' And the girls were crying.

Then it was dawn, another drunk dawn—How many dawns had I been drunk in?—and I was walking alone down some anonymous Los Angeles street that seemed to go on forever. The streetlights were going out along the block, and now and then a car passed, but there weren't any taxis, and I went on walking in the cold November morning.

It was hard to get out of Los Angeles then. The commercial airlines were filled with high-priority bigshots, and every military airbase had a mob of returned troops waiting around for a seat on a cargo or a transport plane going anywhere east. I found another pilot who was headed east, and together we managed to get a two-berth compartment on a train for Chicago. We had no dress uniforms, only our unpressed khakis and flight jackets, and we looked and felt like aliens in that elegant train. But we had our wings, and some ribbons now; and we wore them all above our shirt pockets, as witnesses that we had been there, and were coming home. The working clothes seemed to us worthy. Apparently they impressed others, too; my compartment mate met a California congressman's wife in the compartment next door, and disappeared for the rest of the journey.

I rode out from Chicago on the El, over the slums and the flat empty lots through the gray afternoon, to my parents' factory-town suburb, and took a cab to their house. I hadn't told them I was coming. I imagined a scene of surprise and joy as I turned up unexpectedly, just in time for a home-cooked American supper. But they weren't at the house. It was empty, and their name was gone from the mailbox; they had moved the day before, nobody seemed to know where.

When at last I found the new house, dinner was over, and they were sitting together amid the disorder of packing, looking tired and disoriented. I had to climb over rolled-up rugs and around furniture to reach them. My stepmother kissed me, and my father gripped my hand and said, 'Well. Well, well. You're back.' Then my stepmother flustered into the kitchen, where everything was still in boxes, and produced my first home-cooked meal—fried Spam. I ate it among the boxes and the piled dishes, while my parents told me that I was looking well. Then we sat in the living room for a while. The furniture was the same stuff I had grown up with—I remembered the sofa, and the oak rocking chair, and the pictures leaning against the wall—but it had grown unfamiliar in this new place. After a while we put a bed together and found some bedding, and I left them sitting there and went to bed.

In the day or two I spent there, my father tried to tell me his feelings. 'Son—' he would begin, but then he'd stop. A lifetime of not talking about feelings was too strong a habit to overcome. But I showed him the medals, and he was pleased, almost as pleased, I think, as if he'd won them; and I got out some photographs, and they seemed to make the war more actual for him, and my life credible. Nothing got said, but he managed, just by putting his big hand on my shoulder and saying, 'Son—' to express love and pride. We never played the homecoming scene that I had imagined, but it was all right.

But the house wasn't my house, and the town wasn't my town. And I was married. I caught a train for Birmingham, for the other reunion.

Because Liz was waiting in Birmingham, I chose to be discharged from active duty at Pensacola, and we rode down from Birmingham together, on the same slow, dusty train, stopping, as you always did, at Flomaton, and on down to the Gulf. But it wasn't simply convenience that had brought me back to Pensacola. I wanted to return just once, just for a few days, to that place where I had learned the only skill I had, and where I had been happy in that timeless world of young men, before the dying began. Perhaps the impulse to return is a sign that one has grown up, an acknowledgment of the way the good times pass us. We go back in space because we can't go back in time.

Pensacola was peaceful-looking in the winter sunshine; everything was bright with sun—the white-painted buildings, the sandy earth, the palm trees, the quiet waters of the bay. In that mild stillness the sound of planes was as distant and peaceful as the buzzing of insects on a summer afternoon. It was as if the whole place knew that the war was over, that there was nothing urgent left to be done.

I was still on flight orders, and entitled to flight pay if I flew four hours in a month; so when I had reported in I went over to the Main Side hangar to look for a plane. There I found another Marine pilot on the same errand, and one plane—an N2S Yellow Peril, the kind I had learned to fly in, back at Memphis. One tank of gas would last, if we stretched it, for just about four hours. We didn't know each other; neither had any particular reason to trust the other's flying; we had nothing to do and barely enough gas to do it; but we took off together to fly somewhere, anywhere, for four hours.

My companion climbed carefully over the lagoon and took a cautious, level course north, over the piny woods. It was the same featureless landscape over which I had navigated two years before, and I felt the same withdrawal from the actual world. He flew on for an hour, made a cautious turn, and flew back toward the field. When it came in sight I took over the controls and headed back out over the pines again. Time passed with excruciating slowness; there was nothing to see but the lengthening shadows of the pines, and we could not communicate from one cockpit to the other, even if we had had anything to say. The plane seemed to move as slowly as the hands of my watch.

As the end of the four hours approached, I turned toward the field, checking my watch nervously against the fuel gauge. It looked as though we could make it, but without much gas to spare. I circled the field, using up the last few minutes. By then it was evening, and the hangar cast a long shadow across the landing mat, and the water of the lagoon was dark. I began an approach to landing, letting down out of the last late sun into the twilight, and landed in shadow, and taxied to the parking ramp and shut down the engine. We both got out and walked silently to the hangar, and separated with scarcely a word. I think we must have had the same feelings. It was all over now, we were at the end of the adventure; we had become men with families and responsibilities and futures. The end of flying had made us mortal.

acknowledgments

Many people made this anthology.

At Thunder's Mouth Press and Avalon Publishing Group:
Neil Ortenberg and Susan Reich offered vital support and expertise.
Dan O'Connor, Ghadah Alrawi and Jeri Smith also were indispensable.

At Balliett & Fitzgerald Inc.:
Designer Sue Canavan lavished her energy, talent and resourcefulness
on the book. Production editor Maria Fernandez not only found
some wonderful pictures, but took charge of the project and brought
it home under a very tight deadline. Thanks also to Kristen Couse
and Mike Walters. (And from f-stop Fitzgerald thanks to Pfc Peter
Minissali, Sgt. Richard Minissali, and airman Dominic Villanti.)

At the Writing Company:
Shawneric Hachey gathered books, permissions and facts. Mark
Klimek, Nate Hardcastle and Meghan Murphy cheerfully took up
slack on other projects while I read books for this one.

At the Thomas Memorial Library in Cape Elizabeth, Maine:
The librarians helped us to locate and borrow books from around the
country. Karla Sigel deserves special thanks.

At other institutions:

Frank Marie at the Caen Memorial in Normandy, France and
Elizabeth Ogata of Kodansha International were especially generous
and cooperative.

Among friends and family:

My father Charles Perry Willis told me war stories and let me read his
journals and other writings about his experiences during the Pacific War.
My old friend Andrew Stevens over the years has entertained and
instructed me with his conversation about war and its literature.
My mother-in-law Ellen Brodkey gave moral support and very gener-
ously helped expedite permissions for some crucial selections.
My wife Jennifer Schwamm Willis worked harder on this book than I
did: gathering materials, reading and helping to choose selections,
tracking rights, negotiating permissions, issuing contracts and doing
everything else that had to be done.
My friend Will Balliett made it happen and, as always, made it a
pleasure.

Finally, I am grateful to the writers whose work appears in this book.

b i b l i o g r a p h y

The excerpts used in this anthology were taken from the editions listed below. In some cases, other editions may be easier to find. Hard to find or out-of-print titles often can be acquired through inter-library loan services. Internet sources such as amazon.com and acses.com also may be able to locate these books.

Ambrose, Stephen E. *Citizen Soldiers: The U. S. Army from the Normandy Beaches to the Bulge to the Surrender of Germany, June 7, 1944-May 7, 1945*. New York: Simon & Schuster, 1997.

Carlson, Lewis H. *We Were Each Other's Prisoners: An Oral History of World War II American and German Prisoners of War*. New York: Basic Books, 1997.

Fahey, James J. *Pacific War Diary 1942-1945*. Boston: Houghton Mifflin Co., 1963.

Fussell, Paul. *Doing Battle: The Making of a Skeptic*. New York: Little, Brown and Company, 1996.

Hynes, Samuel. *Flights of Passage*. Annapolis, MD and New York: Naval Institute Press and Frederic C. Beil, 1988.

Jones, James.*The Thin Red Line*. New York: Charles Scribner's Sons, 1962.

New Yorker Magazine.*The New Yorker Book of War Pieces*. New York: Schocken Books, 1988. (For "Mollie" by A. J. Liebling and "The Escape of Mrs. Jeffries" by Janet Flanner).

Malthe-Bruun, Vibeke (editor). *Heroic Heart: The Diary and Letters of Kim-Malthe Bruun 1941- 1945*. New York: Random House, 1955.

Manchester, William. *Goodbye, Darkness: A Memoir of the Pacific War*. Boston: Little Brown and Company, 1980.

Ogura, Toyofumi. *Letters from the End of the World: A Firsthand Account of the Bombing of Hiroshima*. New York: Kodansha International, 1997.

Osmont, Marie-Louise. *The Normandy Diary of Marie-Louise Osmont: 1940-1944*. New York: Random House and Discovery Channel Press,1994.

Rawicz, Slavomir. *The Long Walk*. New York: Harper & Row, 1956.

Ryan, Cornelius. *The Longest Day*. New York: Simon and Schuster, 1959.

Sledge, E. B. *With the Old Breed at Peleliu and Okinawa*. Novato, CA: Presidio Press, 1981.

Webster, David Kenyon. *Parachute Infantry: An American Paratrooper's Memoir of D Day and the Fall of the Third Reich*. Baton Rouge, LA: Lousiana State University Press, 1994.

Wheeler, Richard. *The Bloody Battle for Suribachi*. Annapolis, MD: Naval Institute Press/Blue Jacket Books, 1994.

White, E. B. *One Man's Meat*. (For "Bond Rally") New York: Harper & Row, 1982.